Much has been written about the crusades, but very little about the crusaders. What moved them to go? What preparations did they need to make? How did they react to their experiences? This book comes up with detailed answers to these questions, and offers the first systematic reading of a large cache of contemporary source material.

Crusading drew upon the traditions of pilgrimage to Jerusalem and of pious violence. In 1095 these traditions were fused in Pope Urban II's radical conception of penitential war. The response of the armsbearers to his call was to be as important as the idea itself, since the proposal to liberate Jerusalem was dependent upon their cooperation. Some western family groups had become predisposed to respond positively, and the practical difficulties involved in fulfilling the vow – such as the raising of cash, the purchase of animals and equipment, and financial arrangements during the crusader's absence – anyway meant that the volunteer would be especially dependent upon his family, whose initial support was essential.

Clusters of crusaders can be identified in individual family groups, and the collective commitment of these clans manifested itself in support for the new settlements in the East. Indeed, crusading was so dependent upon the support and enthusiasm of family groups that the movement was open to domination by them: the example of the Montlhéry clan is cited, who tried to seize control of the crusading movement in the 1120s.

THE FIRST CRUSADERS,
1095–1131

An early twelfth-century crusader and his wife. Note the cross on the crusader's chest, and his pilgrim staff and purse. (Musée historique Lorrain, Nancy)

THE FIRST CRUSADERS,
1095–1131

JONATHAN RILEY-SMITH

University of Cambridge

CAMBRIDGE
UNIVERSITY PRESS

PUBLISHED BY THE PRESS SYNDICATE OF THE UNIVERSITY OF CAMBRIDGE
The Pitt Building, Trumpington Street, Cambridge, United Kingdom

CAMBRIDGE UNIVERSITY PRESS
The Edinburgh Building, Cambridge CB2 2RU, UK
40 West 20th Street, New York, NY 10011–4211, USA
477 Williamstown Road, Port Melbourne, VIC 3207, Australia
Ruiz de Alarcón 13, 28014 Madrid, Spain
Dock House, The Waterfront, Cape Town 8001, South Africa

http://www.cambridge.org

© Jonathan Riley-Smith 1997

First published 1997
First paperback edition published 1998
Third printing 2002

Typeset in Baskerville

A catalogue record for this book is available from the British Library

Library of Congress Cataloguing in Publication data
Riley-Smith, Jonathan Simon Christopher, 1938–
The first crusaders, 1095–1131 / Jonathan Riley-Smith.
p. cm.
Includes bibliographical references and index.
ISBN 0 521 59005 1
1. Crusades – first, 1096–1099. I. Title.
D161.2R485 1997
940.1′8–dc20 96–36669 CIP

ISBN 0 521 59005 1 hardback
ISBN 0 521 64603 0 paperback

Transferred to digital printing 2004

Forgo a fruitless search for absolutes.
Observe truth's manifold expressions
Revealed at every turn and vantage point.

   Allow our ancestors respect.
   Let their own voices speak to us
   In their particular tones, unmuffled by our certainties,
   Conveying to us their own convictions,
   Enlightening the past.

Contents

Acknowledgements   *page* x

Maps
    1 and 2 Recruitment for the First Crusade, 1095–1103
    3 and 4 Recruitment for crusades to the East, 1106–29
    5 The Latin East, 1128

Introduction   1

1   Crusading and crusaders, 1095-1131   7

2   Holy Sepulchre; holy war   23

3   Preaching and the crusaders   53

4   Recruitment, lordship and family   81

5   Preparing for crusades   106

6   Returning from crusades   144

7   Crusading and the Montlhérys   169

Conclusion and postscript   189

Appendix I   Preliminary list of crusaders   196

Appendix II Pedigrees
    A   Comital Burgundy
    B   The Montlhéry clan
    C   Some descendants of Almodis of La Marche   247

Bibliography   251
Index   275

Acknowledgements

Research and university teaching are in some ways different facets of the same activity and my first debt of gratitude is owed to my postgraduate and undergraduate students. I would also like to thank Drs F. G. Kingston, M. Bull, M. Brett and A. Prochaska for help in various ways. I do not think this book would ever have been written had I not had access to the collections of printed cartularies in the British Library and the Institute of Historical Research. The Institute was my research base for several years and like many other historians I owe it more than I can ever say.

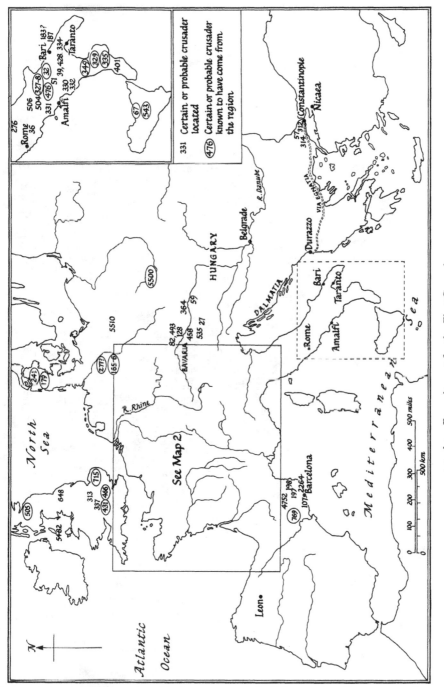

1 and 2 Recruitment for the First Crusade, 1095–1103

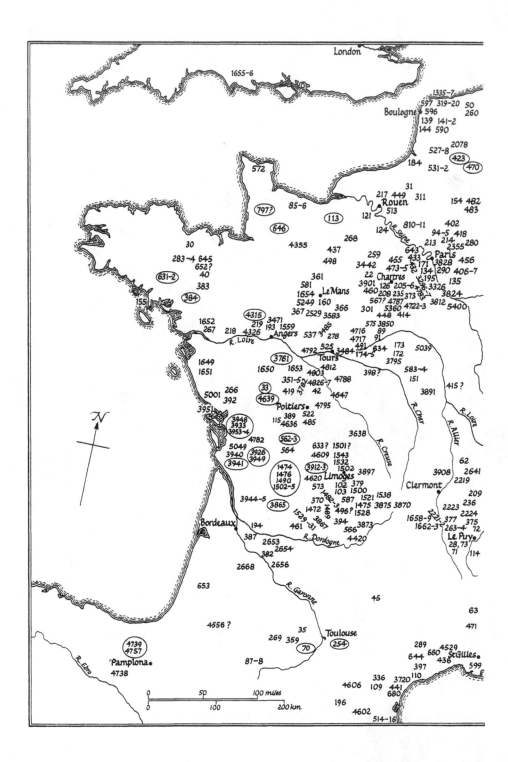

London

1655-6

1335-7

Boulogne 596   597 319-20 50
       139 141-2   260
       144 590

527-8 2078
531-2 184   (423)
              (470)

572

217 449 311   154 482
Rouen 513   483
    121   402
124 810-11 94-5 418
797? 85-6 (113)   213 214 2355 280
(646)   643 433 171 3828 456
        268   259 455 134 290 406-7
30   4355 437 34-42 473-5 195 3326 135
283-4 645 498 22 Chartres 3824
   652?   3901 126 205-6 3812
   40   361   460 208 235 373 5400
(631-2) 383 581 567? 4787
           1654 Le Mans 5360 4722-3
155   (384)   5249 160 301 448 414
        367 2529 3583 575 3850
   1652 (4315) 3471   537 278 4716 89
   267 218 4326 219 193 1559 4717 91
            R. Loire Angers 421 173
   1649   4792 525 3484 634 172 5039
   1651 (3761) Tours 4812 174-5 3795
        1650 1653 4803 398? 583-4
               351-5 4826-7 4788 151
   5001 266 (33) 419 4788 3891 415?
   392 (4639) Poitiers 4795
   3951   389 522
        3948 115 4636 485 3638
        3933   R. Creuse
        3953-4 4782 (562-3) 62
   5049 3926 564 633? 1501? 3908 2641
   3940 3949   4609 1543   2219
   3941   1474 (3912-3) 1532 Clermont 209
            1476 4620 Limoges 1502 3897 236
            1490   573 102 379 2223 2224
   3944-5   1502-5 103 1500 1658-9 377 375
        3865   370 587 1521 1538 1662-3 263-4 72
Bordeaux 194 461 1472 496? 1528 Le Puy 114
   387 2653 1529-3 3867 394 3873 28,73
   382 2654 R. Dordogne 566 4420 71
   2668 2656
        653 R. Garonne 45
   4556?   63
        35 Toulouse 471
   269 359 (70) (254) 289 4529
   (4739) 87-8 644 660 St Gilles
   (4757)   397 436 599
Pamplona 336 3720 110
   4738 4606 109 441
        196 680
        4602 514-16

50 miles
100 miles
100
200 km

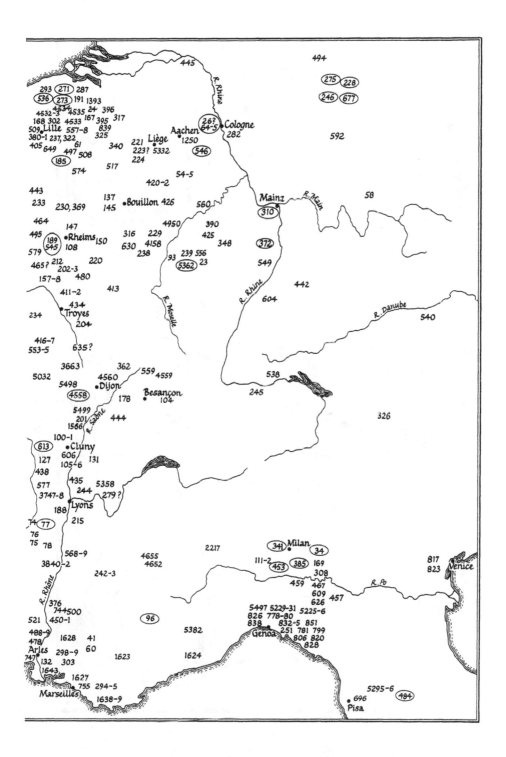

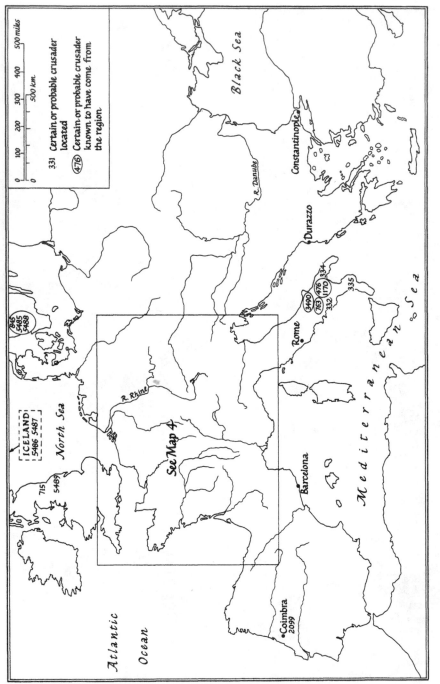

3 and 4   Recruitment for crusades to the East, 1106–29

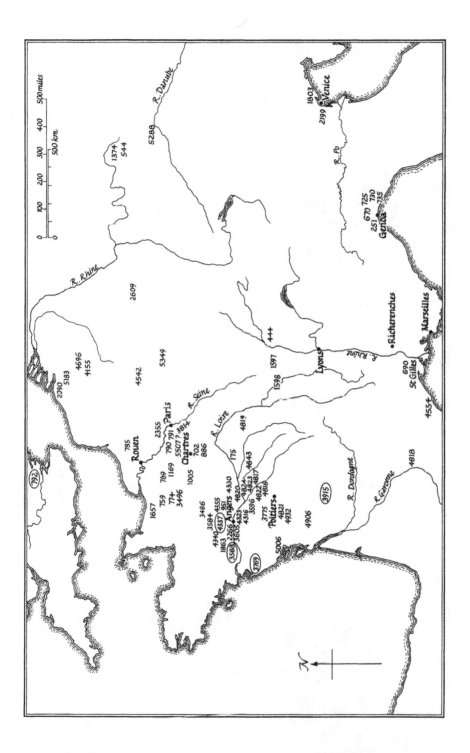

500 miles
500 km.
0 100 200 300 400

R. Danube

1374
544

5288

R. Rhine

2609

4696
5183
4155

2090

5349

4542

R. Seine

2355
Paris
790 791
5507? 3814
Chartres
702
886

Rouen
785

789
1169
1005

R. Loire

175

4819

1598

1597

Lyons

R. Rhône

690
St Gilles

4554

Marseilles

Richerenches

Venice
1803
2199

R. Po

725
730
735

670
251
Genoa

1657
759 4355
774 951
3496
3486
3584
4340
1863 2266
3583 3604 4323 4330
4316 4824
5306 4823 4817
3775 4816
4921
4932
4906
3915

4337 Angers
4820
4843

Poitiers

5006
3769

R. Dordogne

R. Garonne
4818

792

N

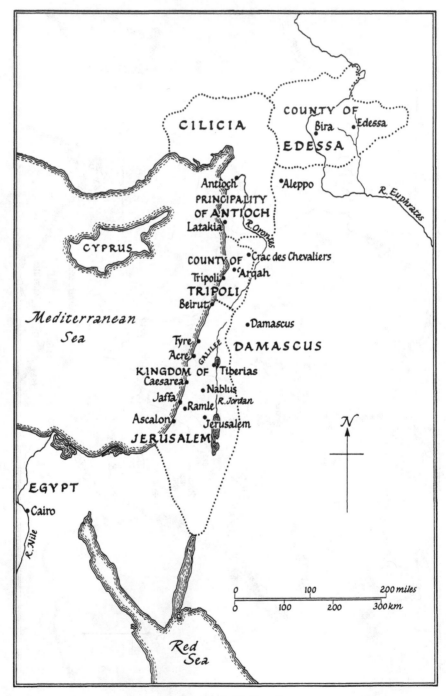

CILICIA

COUNTY OF
EDESSA
Bira •Edessa

•Aleppo

Antioch•
PRINCIPALITY
OF ANTIOCH
Latakia•
R. Orontes

CYPRUS

COUNTY OF   •Crac des Chevaliers
Tripoli•   •'Arqah
TRIPOLI
Beirut•

•Damascus

Mediterranean
Sea

Tyre•
Acre•
GALILEE
DAMASCUS

KINGDOM OF   Tiberias
Caesarea•
•Nablus
Jaffa•   R. Jordan
•Ramle
Ascalon•   •Jerusalem
JERUSALEM

N

EGYPT
•Cairo
R. Nile

Red
Sea

R. Euphrates

0   100   200 miles
0   100   200   300 km

5   The Latin East, 1128

Introduction

It often happens that research which is embarked on with a particular intention ends in a book about something else. I began by wanting to discover, if I could, some of the reasons why men and women took the cross during the first few decades of crusading, but in the course of my work I found myself being confronted by the sight of a few closely related families attaining a dominant position. Their ascent came into focus for me because I happened to have become interested in the circumstances which made it possible: the religious and social environment in which men committed themselves to a crusade and geared themselves up to take part in it, the experiences and attitudes of the survivors, and the ties between the settlers in the newly conquered Latin territories in the East and their homelands. The families concerned came from emergent nobility of moderate status. What was there in early crusading – in the ideology and the responses of nobles and knights to it, in the details of the preparations, and in the reactions of the survivors to their experiences – which made the movement susceptible to a take-over of this sort? I have tried to answer that question in this book.

The source material, particularly for the First Crusade, is rich. The triumph of the earliest crusaders was described over and over again by their successors, by later pilgrims and by theological commentators, but there are also four accounts of their experiences on the campaign that liberated Jerusalem written by participants[1] and a fifth which is so full of circumstantial detail that it deserves to be put beside them.[2] Two of these also provide a narrative of the early settlements and are supplemented by a famous chronicle, which was written in Jerusalem several decades later but drew on

---

[1] FC 153-322, 428-40; GF *passim*; PT *passim*; RA *passim*.   [2] AA 274-504, 559-93.

contemporary documents and the reminiscences of survivors.[3] Two versions of an epic poem at least partly composed by someone who took part in the First Crusade are known, although one of them was so heavily rewritten later that one cannot be certain what in it is by the first author, if there was a single one, and the original of the other survives only in fragments.[4] There are nine letters written by or for crusaders on the march.[5] There are contemporary accounts of the relics they brought home with them. There are hagiographical works and miracle stories. Above all there are charters. The documents associated with institutions in the Latin East have often been used, but the importance of those relating to churches and religious communities in the West as sources of information for crusade historians was barely recognized before Professor Giles Constable drew attention to them.[6] Quite a large number of them are buried in cartularies, collections of title-deeds and other documents made by churchmen for their own use, into which they were copied and recopied, organized and reorganized, sometimes long after the dates on which they were originally drawn up.[7] I cannot claim to have read everything, but I have seen enough, I think, to provide me with a reasonably sure grasp of what was going on.

Being on the whole legal documents describing transfers of property by endowment, sale or pledge, many of the charters record the benefactions and other financial arrangements made by the members of the property-owning classes who crusaded, wills drawn up on their behalf, and disputes in which their heirs and families were involved. Reading them, even in the garbled versions which are sometimes all that survive, greatly enlarges our knowledge of the preparations for, and even of experiences on and ideas about, crusading and provides us with the only evidence for many crusaders. The family of Arnold II of Ardres was maintaining a century later that he had taken part in the First Crusade and that his name was not to be found in the long lists of knights recorded in the epic, *La*

---

[3] See P. W. Edbury and J. G. Rowe, *William of Tyre* (Cambridge, 1988), *passim*.

[4] Ch d'A *passim*; Ch d'A Pr *passim* and GC 11-274 *passim*. See S. Duparc-Quioc in Ch d'A 2.171-205; R. F. Cook, '*Chanson d'Antioche*', *Chanson de Geste: le cycle de la croisade est-il épique?* (Amsterdam, 1980), *passim*.

[5] Kb 138-40, 141-2, 144-52, 153-5, 156-65, 167-74.

[6] G. Constable, 'The Second Crusade as Seen by Contemporaries', *Traditio* 9 (1953), 213-79; 'The Financing of the Crusades in the Twelfth Century', *Outremer*, ed. B. Z. Kedar, H. E. Mayer and R. C. Smail (Jerusalem, 1982), 64-88; and 'Medieval Charters as a Source for the History of the Crusades', *Crusade and Settlement*, ed. P. W. Edbury (Cardiff, 1985), 73-89.

[7] See M. G. Bull, *Knightly Piety and the Lay Response to the First Crusade* (Oxford, 1993), 15.

Chanson d'Antioche, because he had refused to bribe the author to include it.[8] The family was right, at least in believing that Arnold had been a crusader, because a charter shows him to have been in the entourage of Count Robert II of Flanders in the early stages of the march.[9]

It is no good pretending that the charters are easy to use. By the time they reach us many of them are shadows of their former selves, mutilated or corrupted. The paucity of evidence from such centres of pilgrimaging to Jerusalem in the eleventh century, and therefore presumably fertile grounds for recruitment, as Périgord, the Angoumois and Rouergue is probably to be explained by the fact that so much material from these regions has been lost. On the other hand, the scarcity of documents relating to crusaders in England and Germany may be a consequence of scribal conventions that favoured brief statements of legal fact, eschewing references to motives, as opposed to the more expansive and informative style employed in much of France, Lorraine and imperial Burgundy, even if not in all of it: a marked increase of grants around 1100 to the Cluniac house of Domène in Burgundy and to the cathedral of Grenoble may have been linked to the needs of the crusade, but the Domène cartulary contains few references to it and there is only one charter in that of Grenoble.[10] Pledge-agreements must have been very common, but the only ones recorded, unless they also included testamentary dispositions, were those describing loans which were not redeemed, since these were the ones which became title deeds.

Local factors probably affected charter evidence in other ways. The names of many more first crusaders from the Limousin survive than from most other regions of France. But a comparison of recruitment among the greater lords in the Limousin – the viscount of Turenne and the lords of Les Moulières, Lastours, Bré and Pierre-Bouffière – with that of other regions does not suggest that the nobles of the Limousin were much more enthusiastic than those elsewhere. Champagne also contributed a respectable body of nobles – the castellans of Bray and Châtillon-sur-Marne, and the lords of Chappes, Possesse, Méry and Broyes – and the reason we know the names of many more ordinary crusading knights from the Limousin may simply be that Champagne was a rich region, the lords of which could afford to subsidize their followers, whereas the knights of the

[8] LA 626-7.   [9] Flanders 67.
[10] Domène 91, 248; Grenoble 165-6. See Constable, 'The Financing of the Crusades', 75.

Limousin, living in a poor one, had to dispose of property to finance themselves, generating the charters which provide the evidence for their participation. The knight Raymond of Curemonte, for example, going in the viscount of Turenne's party, raised cash for the journey on his own account in a pledge authorized by the viscount himself, who promised to make sure that its terms were not infringed by Raymond's relations.[11] The absence of material from Normandy, from where we know a large force left for the East in 1096, may be because Duke Robert II, who had borrowed a huge sum of money from his brother King William II of England, could subsidize his followers.

It is often hard to date a document precisely or to be sure that we are faced by a crusader rather than a pilgrim, since in many charters the man or woman is referred to noncommittally as *Hierosolymam pergens* or *petens* or *tendens* or *proficiscens* or *iturus*.[12] I have had to decide on the status of the individual concerned in each case, assuming, for instance, that when the distinctly non-military verb *ambulare* is used of the journey to Jerusalem, or the motive is given as *orationis gratia*, the reference is probably to a pilgrim. In many charters the march is described by the neutral words *iter* or *via*, which had long histories in the language of pilgrimage; it is not often that the addition of a defining phrase clarifies the issue, as in a charter announcing how Quino son of Dodo planned to join the 'Jerusalem journey undertaken with force of arms'.[13] Faced by a record such as that of a gift by Astanove II of Fézensac in *c.* 1098 which was made 'on the day of his *peregrinatio* when he took the *iter* to Jerusalem',[14] and bereft of any other evidence, one can say only that Astanove was probably a crusader. And unless the scribe was good enough to let us know or a narrative account provides us with more material the identification of a crusader in a charter is no evidence that he joined a campaign, only that he intended to do so.

Most charters were drawn up by churchmen and the question arises whether the ideas expressed in them were fair reflections of the minds of the crusaders themselves. In fact they probably were. Benefactors, vendors and borrowers would certainly want to know what was being written in Latin in their names. For example, in 1101 Milo of Vignory, a pilgrim inspired by the liberation of Jerusalem two years before, received the scrip (purse) of pilgrimage from the

---

[11] Tulle 276-7,416-8.   [12] See also Constable, 'Medieval Charters' 75.
[13] St Mihiel 191.   [14] Auch 57.

prior of St Etienne de Vignory and then, after a meal with the monks, stood before the priory's altar and 'had his charter [of gift] read and explained in the vernacular'.[15] It has been pointed out recently that so close was the relationship between armsbearers and local religious houses, where kindred were often monks or nuns, that both sides were engaged in a sort of continuous dialogue, out of which a common approach to religion had been forged.[16]

If one feature of this book is my reliance on charter evidence, another is the use I have made of a computer. Since I had originally hoped to discover something of the influences on the recruitment of individuals, I decided that the best approach would be to build up a computerized directory of the men and women associated with crusading, pilgrimage (because of the close relationship between crusaders and pilgrims) and settlement in the Holy Land. I had a fairly good idea of the questions which initially needed asking, although I wanted a system flexible enough to take in new ones as they arose. The prosopographical system I used was developed for me by Dr F. G. Kingston from the relational database management package *Oracle* and consisted of eight tables, each with an associated data-entry form. A 'header record' table contained the name of each man or woman and other basic information about him or her. When a new entry was made the computer automatically assigned a serial number to the person, providing connections with the entries in the other tables and enabling one to produce family trees and to identify points of contact between groups of people. The remaining tables, each of which could contain many entries relating to the individual concerned, held information, including references to the evidence, about places of residence, family and feudal relationships, careers in the West and the East, all evidence of crusading, pilgrimages, settlement or membership of a military order, and persons and activities, such as fund-raising and endowments, associated with these.

The system was designed in 1987 and, given the speed of developments in computing, is now very old-fashioned, but at least it has proved its worth for me. Of course, unless they are particularly fortunate in their sources, medieval historians cannot use computers as modern historians do, because accurate statistical conclusions are

[15] St Bénigne de Dijon 2.172.   [16] Bull, *Knightly Piety*, 155-6.

unattainable. On the other hand, a computer can manipulate large quantities of material more securely than we can; and it can make us conscious of openings into potential fields of research which might otherwise lie hidden.

In Pope Urban II's call to bear arms as a penance in 1095 and in the answer of so many to what was as much a devotional as a military activity, Europe took an unexpected turning and the crusaders a step into the dark. They were not to know that they were founding a movement which was to last for seven centuries, involving vast numbers of people in many different theatres of war. Over time crusading was to become institutionalized and the original emphasis on fighting as a penance was to be diluted by the more conventional one of bearing arms in God's service, but in its early years the message conveyed to the faithful by the preachers was harsh and uncompromising. I have tried to see this through the eyes of the men and women from the armsbearing classes who took part, but I recognize that the task I have set myself is in many ways an impossible one. We are too distant from the personalities concerned to understand them fully, and anyway we have to reconcile their bleak, obsessed, savage and exceptionally religious world with ours and describe it in our own terms before we can comprehend them at all. They were drawn to a popularized version of a relatively sophisticated ideology which they saw to be relevant to their day-to-day religious concerns and which they affirmed, and seem genuinely to have believed in, even when they were being ruthlessly ambitious in the worldly sense. Their priorities often seem alien to us, and the movement in which they were engaged madness, because the basic religious elements common to Christians in any age were transformed in their case by adaptation to a society in which lordship, honour, family solidarity expressing itself at times in vendettas, reputation and commitment to extravagant social generosity played powerful parts. I do not suppose that I am alone in finding it very hard to stretch my mind to encompass the amalgam of piety and violence, of love and hate, which was characteristic of their response to the call to arms.

CHAPTER I

Crusading and crusaders, 1095–1131

Among the men who sailed with Count Fulk V of Anjou to Palestine in 1129 was his brother-in-law Hugh of Chaumont-sur-Loire, who was joining a crusade for a second time. Hugh had been born in c.1080 into a family which had risen to prominence in the service of the counts of Anjou. He had been the heir to one of the three towers of Amboise when he had first taken the cross in March 1096 at a ceremony at the abbey of Marmoutier presided over by the pope. He had experienced the sufferings and triumphs of a three-year campaign which had ended with the liberation of Jerusalem and during it he had gained a reputation for steadiness: he had been one of those deputed to guard the gates of Antioch against breakout as disintegration threatened the Christian army on the night of 10 June 1098, when crusaders, desperate to get away and on the road home, were escaping even through the latrine-drains in the city-walls.[1] Now elderly, hugely rich and in possession through marriage of the rest of the seigneurie of Amboise, he made it over to his eldest son. He obviously wanted to end his days in Jerusalem and it was there that he died two months after reaching Palestine. He was buried on the Mount of Olives, from where he would have first looked down on the city thirty years before.[2]

Although unusual in that he crusaded twice, Hugh of Chaumont-sur-Loire was typical in many ways of the middle-ranking nobles who were to dominate the early decades of crusading. By the time of his death members of a family of a similar standing to his own, or rather of a closely related group of them which shared descent from a castellan in the Ile-de-France called Guy of Montlhéry, were dominant in the settlements in the Levant established in the wake of the

---

[1] GAD 101-2; BB 65 note. For Hugh, see G. Duby, *The Knight, the Lady and the Priest* (London, 1984), 236-7, 245-9.
[2] GAD 115-16.

First Crusade and had a stranglehold on the movement. The king of Jerusalem was one of them. The semi-independent county of Edessa in northern Iraq and the two most important lordships in Palestine were in the hands of cousins. A fourth cousin was abbot of one of the most prestigious monasteries in Jerusalem, and a fifth was patriarch (although he proved to be a liability). Marriage-alliances had been made with the rulers of the two other settlements, the principality of Antioch and the county of Tripoli. Of the two crusades to the East of the 1120s, one was proclaimed in response to an appeal from the king by a pope who was his cousin and the preaching of the other seems to have been organized entirely by the king himself.

Few knights gained much in material terms from the crusades, but the Montlhérys benefited spectacularly, even if their ambitions were never entirely fulfilled: Fulk of Anjou, whose crusade culminated in his marriage to the king of Jerusalem's eldest daughter, had been invited by them out to Palestine to maintain the status quo, but he swept many of their policies away two years after Hugh of Chaumont-sur-Loire's death. They had had luck, of course, but there was more to their success than that. I believe that developments in the eleventh century had preconditioned the members of some western noble families to respond positively, if in their own way, to the early appeals to crusade; that the logistical and financial demands made upon them while they were preparing for the expeditions led to their relations being closely involved in a supporting rôle; and that this made the early crusading movement and the security of the new Latin settlements in the East particularly dependent on those kindred groups which showed commitment. It was on the foundations provided by this combination of ideology and blood-relationship that the Montlhérys' bid for glory rested.

Although a difficulty faced by all historians of crusading is that while it is usually clear when each crusade begins it is never easy to give a date for its ending, there seem to have been four separate crusades in the period covered by this book. The first and most successful, proclaimed on 27 November 1095 by Pope Urban II at Clermont in response to an appeal for assistance against the Turks from the Byzantine emperor Alexius I,[3] petered out towards the end of the first decade of the twelfth century. Elements of it had stayed to fight

---

[3] For the course of the First Crusade, see J. S. C. Riley-Smith, *The First Crusade and the Idea of Crusading* (London, 1986), *passim* and *The Crusades* (London, 1987), 1–36.

in an army in Lebanon scratched together by Raymond of St Gilles, who certainly considered himself to be still on crusade;[4] so did Raymond's son Bertrand and his Genoese allies, who in 1108 were completing the reduction of the Lebanese coast and had vowed to serve 'God and the Holy Sepulchre'.[5] Meanwhile Bohemond of Taranto, who had been one of the leaders between 1096 and 1098 and had become ruler of Antioch, began to recruit men in 1106 for another campaign, which would engineer a change of government in Constantinople on its way to the East. The army he attracted was large enough for the monastic historian Orderic Vitalis to write of it as the 'third expedition ... to Jerusalem';[6] presumably he thought of the forces of 1096 and 1100–1 as comprising the first and second. Bohemond's troops gathered in Apulia in the autumn of 1107 but, after landing on the Albanian coast and laying siege to Durazzo, they were surrounded by the Byzantine Greeks and forced to surrender in September 1108.[7] Some of them travelled on to the East. Most, without the means to continue, returned to western Europe,[8] although a fleet under the command of King Sigurd I of Norway, which turned up in Palestine in 1110 after spending three years on a voyage from Scandinavia, had perhaps also been recruited.[9]

A disaster for the Christians in northern Syria a decade later, the Battle of the Field of Blood in which the prince of Antioch was killed, led late in 1119 to the preaching by Pope Calixtus II of a new crusade, which took the important Palestinian port of Tyre in July 1124.[10] A few years later more crusaders were sought by the settlers in the Levant, when an embassy was sent from Jerusalem to offer the hand of King Baldwin II's daughter Melisende to Fulk of Anjou. The initiative for the new expedition seems to have been Baldwin's own.[11] A substantial number of fighters accompanied Fulk to Pales-

[4] St Victor de Marseille (Guérard) 2.151–3.
[5] AA 664-9, 671–2, 679; Caffaro, 'De liberatione civitatum orientis', 122–4; WT 507–9; Genoa (Church) 43.
[6] OV 3.182.
[7] See J. G. Rowe, 'Paschal II, Bohemund of Antioch and the Byzantine Empire', *Bulletin of the John Rylands Library* 49 (1966), 165–202; G. Rösch, 'Der "Kreuzzug" Bohemunds gegen Dyrrachion 1107–8 in der lateinischen Tradition des 12. Jahrhunderts', *Römische Historische Mitteilungen* 26 (1984), 181–90.
[8] HP 228–9.
[9] P. Riant, *Expéditions et pèlerinages des Scandinaves en Terre Sainte au temps des croisades* (Paris, 1865), 173–215; AA 675, 677–9; FC 543–8.
[10] J. S. C. Riley-Smith, 'The Venetian Crusade of 1122–1124', *I Comuni italiani nel regno crociato di Gerusalemme*, ed. G. Airaldi and B. Z. Kedar (Genoa, 1986), 339–50.
[11] See WT 620.

tine in 1129 and joined an army of settlers in an unsuccessful assault
upon Damascus.[12] After marrying Melisende Fulk stayed on to
succeed to the throne after Baldwin's death on 21 August 1131.

Compared to their thirteenth-century successors, over which the
authority of the popes was firmly established, the unregulated nature
of these early expeditions is apparent. When in 1103 the western
Emperor Henry IV committed himself to a penitential war in the
East without reference to the papacy and authorized the preaching
of it by the bishop of Würzburg,[13] it is arguable that he was trying to
reassert his traditional authority as defender of Christendom, an
authority which had been usurped by Pope Urban II when he had
summoned Christians to fight to recover Jerusalem. And at least one
other campaign which was clearly a crusade, that of 1129, seems to
have been launched without any authorization by Pope Honorius II,
who remained a bystander. The Church, which had invented
crusading, had very little control over it, partly because preaching,
recruitment and oversight demanded unprecedented responsibilities
of the clergy, who often were at sea when trying to cope with the
unfamiliar issues they had to face. It is understandable that one
historian has wondered recently whether we can speak of crusades at
all between the end of the First and the year 1187; he questions
whether contemporaries saw in crusading anything distinctive and he
suggests that they viewed it as one of several fairly traditional options
open to them as members of an exceptionally violent society.[14] It is
true that in the early twelfth century it is not always easy for us to
distinguish crusades from expeditions of pilgrims who had not taken
crusade vows but, presumably following the precedent created on the
First Crusade, were now armed.[15] When faced by contradictions in
evidence which is anyway sparse historians are often inclined to
suppose that contemporaries were as bewildered as they are, but the
material I will use in this book will, I hope, convince my readers that,
however inchoate crusading was in institutional terms, crusaders
were readily identifiable. Already in the early twelfth century the
sight of those who 'took the cross', the act which marked the making

---

[12] WT 618–22; Henry of Huntingdon, *Historia Anglorum* 250; Robert of Torigni, *Chronica* 113–15;
Ibn al-Athir, 'Sum of World History', 1.385–6; *The Anglo-Saxon Chronicle* 194–5.
[13] Ekk C 224–5; *Annales Hildesheimenses* 50–1; Otto of Freising, *Chronica* 318; H. E. Mayer, *The
Crusades*, 2nd edn (Oxford, 1988), 65.
[14] C. J. Tyerman, 'Were There any Crusades in the Twelfth Century?', *English Historical Review*
110 (1995), 553–77.
[15] See, for example, AA 596.

of the vow to crusade,[16] would have led everyone to know that an expedition was being planned or was in train.

The exact terms of the vows made by recruits in what must have been a very emotional environment are not known. For the eastern theatre of war they must have involved a promise to pilgrimage to Jerusalem combined with a pledge either to liberate it by force or to fight in its defence and in support of fellow-Christians living in Palestine and Syria. Volunteers were supposed to have the crosses which had been distributed to them sewn on to their clothes at once and they were expected to go on wearing these crosses until they came home with their vows fulfilled: in 1123 the bishops at the First Lateran Council decreed against those 'who had taken their crosses off' without departing on Pope Calixtus' crusade.[17] The language Pope Urban was reported using in 1095 suggests that he knew he was doing something new and that he intended the crosses to be distinctive,[18] and crusaders were certainly conspicuous, distinguishable from their contemporaries and perhaps even from other pilgrims, with whom crosses had never been regularly associated before the First Crusade.[19] The response in some places to the taking of the vow was hysterical, with individuals branding crosses on their bodies,[20] but it is easy to forget how visible the ordinary cloth ones must have been. An early twelfth-century sculpture, from the priory of Belval in Lorraine, shows a crusader wearing a cross made from two-inch strips of cloth on his chest; it looks as though it measured six by six inches.[21]

It was important that crusaders should be marked out in this way. The leaders of the early armies became convinced that there was a reservoir of additional manpower in the West which could be deployed if only the Church would force laggards to fulfil their vows.[22] Demands of this sort were made throughout the history of the movement and periodically attempts were made to establish just

[16] See RR 729–31; BB 15–16; Kb 142, 160, 165 (and see 175–6); OV 5.228–30; Brittany (Morice) I.490; HGL 5.757; 'The Council of Troyes, 23 May 1107' 93.

[17] *Conciliorum Oecumenicorum Decreta* 168.

[18] RR 729–30; BB 16.

[19] C. Erdmann, *The Origin of the Idea of Crusade* (Princeton, 1977), 345.

[20] Ekk H 19; Bernold of St Blasien, 'Chronicon', 464; GN Gesta 182–3, 250–1; BB 17; RA 102; FC 169–70; 'Historia de translatione sanctorum magni Nicolai ... ejusdem avunculi, alterius Nicolai, Theodorique ... de civitate Mirea in monasterium S. Nicolai de Littore Venetiarum' 255; OV 5.30.

[21] In the Musée historique lorrain in Nancy. See above p. iv.

[22] Kb 142, 160, 165; also 175–6.

how large the second force was. It was always a lot easier to rail
against 'false' crusaders than to make them do what they had
promised, but the pressure put on them and the publicity they
attracted underlined the seriousness of the commitment they had
made.

The First Crusade was a violent and brutal episode during which the
crusaders cut a swathe of suffering through Europe and western Asia.
But perceptions and motivation in the West were influenced more by
accounts of the trials undergone by the crusaders themselves,
ordeals, which, it is fairly clear, they had anticipated. The first
parties, made up largely of poor people but under noble command,
were already on the move in the spring of 1096, earlier than the pope
had wished and before they could enjoy the benefits of that year's
harvest. Most of them got no further than the Balkans, but before
leaving the West many of them took part in a ferocious persecution
of Jews, particularly in the Rhineland, but also in France, Bavaria
and Bohemia, in the course of which the important Jewish community at Mainz was almost wiped out. Two of the early armies reached
Constantinople relatively intact, but once they had crossed the
Bosphorus they were cut to pieces by the Turks. They were followed
from mid-August onwards by contingents with more effective military components, although their progress was also impeded by the
hordes of poor pilgrims who attached themselves to them. After long
and sometimes dangerous marches across Europe, the crusaders
were arriving outside Constantinople in late 1096 and early 1097.
They thought they were going to campaign under the command of
the Emperor Alexius, but they now had to face the realities of
Byzantine politics, for the Greeks felt threatened by forces which
were much larger than they had expected and used every means at
their disposal, from blandishment to ill-treatment, to persuade each
contingent to cross the Bosphorus into Asia independently as soon as
possible after its arrival. The various elements of the crusade only
came together before the walls of Nicaea, the first major city in
Turkish hands on the old imperial road to the East, which surrendered to the Greeks on 19 June 1097.
   A week later, realizing that they were not going to get the leadership and assistance from the Byzantine emperor they had expected,
the crusaders made the first of several exceptionally bold decisions.
They struck out on their own across Asia Minor, accompanied by a

token force of Greek soldiers and guides. In late October, after an exhausting and traumatic march which had been punctuated by victories over the Turks at Dorylaeum and Eregli, they reached Antioch, a city which, although a shadow of its former self, still controlled the easiest passes from Asia Minor into Syria. They invested it for seven and a half months, beating off two Muslim armies of relief. It fell to them on 3 June 1098, but almost at once they found themselves besieged in their turn by a new Muslim army, which would have caught them outside the walls had it not been held up for three weeks in a fruitless attempt to storm the town of Edessa, 160 miles to the north-east and already in crusader hands. On the night of 10 June morale was so low and panic levels so high in the western army that its leaders had to take steps to prevent a mass break-out, as we have seen, but this was followed by reports from visionaries of Christ appearing and promising victory and by the discovery of what was said to be the lance which had pierced his side when he was on the cross. It was generally believed that the whereabouts of this relic had been revealed to a Provençal servant called Peter Bartholomew by the apostle Andrew himself. Their morale restored, the crusaders sortied out of the city on 28 June and in a victory which was attributed by some of them to the appearance on their left flank of a heavenly army of angels, saints and the ghosts of their dead companions, routed the Muslims. Although the next move was not to be made for five months, this was the turning point of the campaign.

It was the poor who forced the leaders, who could not agree on the next step, to take the road again between 13 January and early February 1099. The crusaders seem to have planned the occupation of some of the major fortresses which lay in their path and could have cut their lifeline back to Antioch if held by the enemy, but after besieging 'Arqah in Lebanon in vain for three months they made another bold decision. Moving as they were from a region dominated by Turkish princes into one which had been recently recovered by the Fatimid rulers of Egypt, they resolved to ignore the strongpoints and hurry down the coast while the countryside was still in a state to feed them – it was harvest time – and before the Egyptians could raise an army to intercept them. They reached Jerusalem on 7 June and the city fell to assault on 15 July. On 12 August a large Egyptian counter-invasion was thrown back near Ascalon. Of the army of some 70,000 men and women, including about 7,000 knights, which had mustered at Nicaea two years before, only 12,000, of whom 1,200–1,300 were knights, besieged Jerusalem. Of course many crusaders had settled in Edessa and around Antioch and many others had deserted, but new arrivals had been joining the army all the time and the overall rate of loss must therefore have been running at around three to one.[23]

Most of the knights now decided to make for home, but in the spring of 1099, while they had still been in Lebanon, Pope Urban had commissioned the archbishop of Milan to preach the cross in Lombardy. Recruitment spread to France and Germany in 1100, and late that year and early in the next new armies, containing many fresh crusaders together with individuals who had not yet fulfilled their vows and deserters from Antioch and elsewhere, left the West. Instead of combining, however, these armies forced their way into Asia Minor separately and were picked off one by one by the Turks. Some of the survivors fought in an army which was defeated in Palestine by the Egyptians on 17 May 1102. These disasters paradoxically reinforced the belief in Europe that the liberation of the Holy Sepulchre in 1099 had been a miraculous event, for the defeats two years later 'proved' how powerful the forces were which had been brushed aside on the triumphant march on Jerusalem by men who had recognized how ill-provisioned, poorly equipped and mounted, and badly led they had been; only briefly had there been agreement on the election of a commander-in-chief, and the appointee, Stephen of Blois, had fled soon afterwards. The only feasible explanation for their success was that the hand of God had been helping them, and the failure of the epilogue in 1101 – in the long run a disaster for none but those taking part – simply demonstrated for contemporaries that the crusaders involved were not penitential and loving enough to be true instruments of the divine will.

On the other hand, no survivor of the army which had taken Jerusalem in 1099 can have been unscathed. His abiding memory would have been of a continual hunt for provisions. The chances were that within a year his horses and pack animals had died. So when he had fought, he had fought on foot, and when he had marched, he and his surviving servants had had to carry his arms and armour in sacks across their shoulders. Even before they left Europe

---

[23] J. France, *Victory in the East* (Cambridge, 1994), 122–42.

crusaders had begun to pass from reality into unreality, slipping into a dream world from which they did not escape until they returned home, a world in which for much of the time they were homesick, starving, diseased and exhausted, and in which they witnessed the deaths of those around them; a world in which acts of unspeakable cruelty were committed against the backdrop of a night sky glittering with comets, auroras and shooting stars, and in which Christ, Our Lady and the saints appeared to them in visions, and the ghosts of their dead returned to comfort and encourage them, and to assure them that death in such a holy war was martyrdom. Crusading was never to be a pleasant experience: the armies of 1101 were cut to pieces in Asia Minor; the crusade of 1107 ended in a disease-ridden army trapped just across the Adriatic; and although we know very little about conditions on the expeditions of the 1120s, which reached Palestine by sea, they cannot have been comfortable.

What drove so many men and women to take part in enterprises which were often as unpleasant for them as they were for their opponents and victims? The motives of crusaders have been a subject for debate since the movement began. In the early twelfth century, the chronicler Albert of Aachen portrayed a North Italian priest saying,

Men hold to different opinions about this journey. Some say that this desire to go has been aroused in all pilgrims by God and the Lord Jesus Christ; others that it was through lightheadedness that the Frankish magnates and the multitudes were moved, and that it was because of this that so many pilgrims encountered obstacles in Hungary and in other kingdoms, so that they could not fulfil their vows.[24]

Nine hundred years later, the most popular explanation, which takes various forms, is that the prospect of material gain attracted recruits. But although everyone agrees that material and ideological motivations are not mutually exclusive and it would be absurd to maintain that no one thought he could benefit in worldly terms, the generalizations about motivation for profit, which always rested on insufficient evidence, look less and less convincing the more we know of the circumstances in which the early crusaders took the cross.

There are still historians who believe that crusading was a colonial enterprise, the purpose of which was to gain land for settlement. In the age of positive imperialism around 1900 the crusades were

[24] AA 415–16.

supposed to be the opening act in the 'expansion of Europe', leading, in a phrase which appealed to French historians, to 'the first French empire'. This idea was picked up by the British, particularly at the time of Allenby's victories over the Turks and his entry into Jerusalem, and it was passed on to the first generation of Arab nationalists, who turned the rhetoric on its head, so that today crusading imperialism has a fixed place in Arab (and also Israeli) demonology. The evidence most commonly cited in support of it was provided by a German monk called Ekkehard, who described what appeared to be a passage of migration. He attributed the involvement of the poor in the First Crusade to disorder, to an epidemic of ergotism which was sweeping western Europe and to economic distress.

The western Franks could easily be persuaded to leave their farms. For the Gauls had been severely afflicted for some years by civil sedition, hunger and death. Finally that plague, which burst out at Nivelles ... terrified men to the despair of their lives ... [He went on to describe ergotism] ... Some of the ordinary people and other persons in those nations to which the pope had not directly appealed acknowledged themselves to be summoned to the Promised Land by certain prophets newly arisen among them, by signs in the heavens and by revelations, while others recognized that they had been impelled to take such vows [to crusade] by all kinds of inconveniences; certainly very many of them travelled weighed down by wives, children and all their domestic goods.[25]

The economic distress in France at the time was also referred to in an account, written ten years after the event, of the sermon at Clermont in which Pope Urban first called for crusaders.[26] Several years of drought had certainly led to poor harvests and shortages, and hence to the ergotism, a terrifying condition which could lead to insanity and death and was brought on by eating bread made from rye which had not had ergot removed from it. The poor were very numerous in all the armies of the First Crusade, although there were few if any of them on the other crusades before 1131: the cost of buying passage when contingents were being transported by sea must have been prohibitive. It is possible that between 1096 and 1101 many of them took advantage of the chance to seek a new life for themselves, but we actually know very little about them, let alone their ideas and aspirations. They appear often enough in the narrative accounts, but usually only as an amorphous mass causing

[25] Ekk H 17.   [26] RR 728.

problems for the leaders, particularly when it came to feeding them. Their needs were built into the penitential calendar of the First Crusade; alms, often linked to fasts and processions, were provided before important engagements and large foraging parties were organized for their benefit.[27] They must have suffered a very high death rate and it is hard to envisage the survivors having the means or energy to return home once the campaign was over. Some certainly remained in northern Syria when the armies marched south; others must have stayed on in Palestine when the crusaders who could afford it left for home.

Another group brought into the argument are the sailors and merchants of the Italian maritime cities, which were already climbing to prominence in the revival of Mediterranean trade and were quickly involved: Genoa in 1098, Pisa in 1099 and Venice in 1100. It has often been pointed out that the First Crusade provided Genoa and Pisa with the opportunity to join Venice on the profitable eastern trade routes. The three cities soon established factories on the Levantine coast and were granted commercial privileges in return for their assistance in taking the ports.[28] But Genoa and Pisa certainly, and Venice possibly, had not taken any initiative; they had responded to direct appeals from the pope for help in provisioning the armies and their own accounts described their participation in ideological terms.[29] The Levantine ports were to become sources of great profit for them, but in the 1090s they were not in the same league as the Egyptian ones. It was to be the changes in the Asiatic trade routes seventy years later which made the larger ports of Palestine and Syria the terminuses of the main spice roads from the Far East.

The evidence for the armsbearers being knowingly engaged from the first in a colonial venture is even weaker than that for the poor or the merchants. There is a hostile contemporary reference to Bohemond of Taranto in the *Gesta* of Geoffrey Malaterra, a Norman monk settled in southern Italy and a partisan of Bohemond's uncle and political opponent, Roger I of Sicily. Geoffrey stated bluntly that Bohemond took the cross only because he wanted to carve a territory for himself out of the Byzantine empire.

Bohemond, who already shortly before this had invaded the Byzantine

[27] Riley-Smith, *The First Crusade*, 68.
[28] M.-L. Favreau-Lilie *Die Italiener im Heiligen Land* (Amsterdam, 1989), *passim*.
[29] See for example Caffaro, 'De liberatione', *passim*; 'Historia de translatione', *passim*.

empire with [Robert] Guiscard his father and always wanted to subjugate it to himself, seeing a large number [of crusaders] hurrying [to Greece] through Apulia, but without a head, wanted to become their leader by binding them to him. He placed the symbol of that expedition, a cross, on his clothes.[30]

Bohemond was a disappointed man, whose father had left him his conquests from the Greeks on the eastern shore of the Adriatic, which were soon lost, while his younger half-brother had inherited the duchy of Apulia. He had created a large and possibly independent principality for himself in the far south of Italy, including the cities of Bari and Taranto, but he did not have the status he must have craved;[31] an admirer wrote of him that he was 'always seeking the impossible'.[32] Another man who may have been after a principality elsewhere was Baldwin of Boulogne, whose elder brothers were count of Boulogne and duke of Lower Lorraine. He had also been disappointed at home because as someone originally destined for the Church he had not shared in the partition of the family lands.[33] But otherwise there is little to go on. Even the Montlhéry clan, which was to exploit the movement in such an extraordinary way, seems at first to have been drawn to crusading primarily by its spiritual benefits.

It should be remembered that although the First Crusade began the process by which western Europeans conquered and settled many of the coastal territories of the eastern Mediterranean, it is very unlikely that this was planned from the start. I have already pointed out that the pope and the military leaders must have thought that once the armies reached Constantinople they would be elements in a much larger force under the command of the Byzantine emperor, to whose empire Jerusalem had once belonged, and that from then on the campaign would be one which, if successful, would restore Greek rule to the Levant. It was only when the westerners discovered that the emperor was not interested in leading them and was not prepared to send with them anything more than a comparatively small force of Greeks that they made the decision to strike out on their own: they were still hoping that he and his army would join

---

[30] Geoffrey Malaterra, 'De rebus gestis Rogerii Calabriae et Siciliae comitis et Roberti Guiscardi ducis fratris eius', 102.
[31] D. Matthew, *The Norman Kingdom of Sicily* (Cambridge, 1992), 18–19.
[32] Romoald of Salerno, 'Annales', 415.
[33] H. E. Mayer, *Mélanges sur l'histoire du royaume latin de Jérusalem* (*Mémoires de l'académie des inscriptions et belles-lettres* NS 5, Paris, 1984), 13–31.

them when they were at Antioch over a year later. Most crusaders returned to Europe once the campaign was over; according to one account 20,000 of them (obviously an exaggeration) were assembling in the autumn of 1099 at Latakia in Syria on their way home.[34] By the summer of 1100 it was reported that there were only 300 western knights and the same number of foot in those parts of southern Palestine under Christian control. Of course there had also been settlement in Syria and northern Iraq, and settlers were moving into Galilee, while 300 knights would comprise 25 per cent of the 1,200 who were reported besieging Jerusalem a year before. But there had been reinforcements over the intervening winter and spring. More to the point, an analysis of the individuals about whom something is known suggests that most crusaders left as soon as they could.

I have identified 549 men and women who definitely took the cross for the First Crusade, and a further 110 who probably, and 132 who possibly, did so. Of these 791 individuals, 104 at most are known to have settled in the East. Fifteen stayed for only a few years before returning to the West; some of them may have been contributing to the new settlements' defence as a religious duty. Of the eighty nine who appear to have settled more permanently, eleven belonged to the households of great magnates who for one reason or another decided to remain and twenty-one were churchmen. It looks as though at least some of the remaining fifty-seven regarded settlement in the East as an ideologically motivated 'exile' for the faith, and others, for instance Raymond of St Gilles and perhaps Ralph of Aalst, were elderly and may have been attracted to Jerusalem as a place in which to die. Of course there was also colonization, but most settlers were not crusaders. Of 697 settlers in Palestine and Syria (from before 1131) known to me, only 122 – a figure which includes the 104 first crusaders – had taken the cross. In other words we have evidence of only eighteen additional crusaders settling in the East between 1102 and 1131.

A second modern explanation of motive is that the early crusades were little more than large-scale plundering expeditions, with which western knights were already familiar from their forays into Spain and elsewhere.[35] The bishops at the council of Clermont had certainly been concerned that men might join the crusade 'for money'[36] and there can be no doubt that it attracted violent

[34] AA 503.   [35] France, *Victory in the East*, 11–16.   [36] *Decreta Claromontensia* 74.

individuals. There were no means available for screening recruits for suitability, other than the decisions of magnates on the composition of their households; indeed there could not have been, because as pilgrimages crusades had to be open to all, even psychopaths. The appetites of the violent may well have been sharpened by disorientation, fear and stress as they sackaged their way to the East. The vicious persecution of Jews in France and Germany, which opened the march of some of the armies, was motivated largely by a desire for vengeance, but it was all the same marked by looting and extortion,[37] and the passage of the crusaders through the Balkans was punctuated by outbreaks of pillaging. Eyewitness accounts often contain descriptions of the knights' desire for booty, as in a message passed down the lines on 1 July 1097 before the first major battle beyond Nicaea: 'Today, if God pleases, you will all become rich men.'[38] Jerusalem itself was comprehensively sacked two years later and, according to a contemporary, 'many poor men were made rich', although he was referring to the occupation of houses in the city.[39] The victory over the Egyptian counter-invasion force a month later was reported to have been rewarded with large quantities of spoil.[40] How much an army coming up from Egypt really could have carried with it, how much of this loot would have been dissipated on the return journey and how a man could anyway have found the physical means to carry his share home to Europe with him are other questions. I will show later how few of the crusaders who returned to the West seem to have brought treasure or valuables back with them. It was reported that many in the exodus from Palestine in the autumn of 1099 were impoverished by the time they reached northern Syria.[41]

The reality was that, because the earliest crusaders had no proper system of provisioning, foraging was essential for their survival. While in Christian territory they were dependent on hand-outs from local rulers; once in the devastated no-man's land that Asia Minor was becoming they were far from any worthwhile rendezvous-point with European shipping until they reached Antioch; and then they were near one which brought them only limited supplies, although they were now in touch with Cyprus, which seems to have been quite a generous provider. All the leaders, from great to small, had to live

---

[37] Riley-Smith, *The First Crusade*, 52–3.   [38] GF 19-20.   [39] FC 304.
[40] See Riley-Smith, *The First Crusade*, 122.
[41] OV 5.270-6. For the payments they were making for provisions, see AA 499–500, 503–4.

with the fact that their followers expected from them at the very least a subsistence level of provisioning. This alone would have accounted for an obsession with plunder.

A third popular twentieth-century explanation of the attraction of crusading is that families, growing larger and worried about the pressure on their lands, adopted strategies which encouraged or forced unwanted male members to seek their fortunes elsewhere and that crusading provided these supernumeraries with an outlet.[42] I shall demonstrate that far from being an economic safety-valve crusading cost the families of volunteers a lot in financial terms. The only strategy for which there is evidence is one in which the kindred cooperated in damage-limitation once a relation had taken the cross.

A feature common to all these explanations of motives is that in them the popularity of crusading is exaggerated. Although it was an activity which appealed to people living in many different parts of western Europe and to intellectuals at the same time as to the general public, inspiring men and women with a wide range of perceptions, cerebral and emotional, there was always a majority which was not prepared to engage in something so inconvenient, dangerous and expensive. We do not, in other words, have to find explanations for motivation which would cover all western society or some lowest common denominator. Crusaders were members of a group defined by its commitment to a demanding and unpleasant activity and many of those who answered the popes' summonses must have regretted the vows they had made on the spur of the moment in fevered public gatherings fired by the preaching of churchmen, who were employing all the razzmatazz needed to create religious hysteria. But a collective ethos, conditioned by internal traditions and conventions, can lie behind even spontaneous decisions. I shall point out how many early crusaders are clustered into certain kindred groups. The most likely reason for this seems to be that some families were predisposed in various ways to respond favourably to the call to take the cross. Once it had been taken, the dynamics of the collective would anyway come into play, because each decision could not be divorced from the group, or often interlocking groups, to which a crusader belonged. There are many examples of them rallying round to provide support. Crusading relied to a peculiar degree on a combination of individual sponta-

---

[42] G. Duby, *The Chivalrous Society* (London, 1977), 120.

neity and collective collaboration. Following where the material leads me I hope to demonstrate how essential was the part played by kindreds, how reliant the Church was on them, and how in all of this there were opportunities for them to exploit the movement to their advantage. But first it will be necessary to explain how in the eleventh century the armsbearing classes in general, and these cousinhoods in particular, were being prepared subconsciously to be receptive to the call to crusade.

CHAPTER 2

Holy Sepulchre; holy war

JERUSALEM

On 15 July 1149, the fiftieth anniversary of the liberation of Jerusalem and twenty years after Hugh of Chaumont-sur-Loire had been buried on the Mount of Olives, the church of the Holy Sepulchre, which was nearing completion, was consecrated. The event should have been an occasion for rejoicing, but the king of Jerusalem may have been already hurrying north to Syria, where another prince of Antioch had just fallen in battle with the Muslims, and the king of France, the last of the leaders of a recent crusade to leave, had embarked for home. That crusade, eloquently preached by Bernard of Clairvaux and planned to be fought on a stupendous scale in three separate theatres-of-war, had been a fiasco and Catholic Christianity was demoralized and in crisis.[1]

Nevertheless, the church is a confident and profound theological statement in stone. Before the crusaders took Jerusalem a compound had enclosed several separate shrines, the most venerated of which was Christ's tomb, or what remained of it, detached in the fourth century by the Emperor Constantine's engineers from the rest of the quarry wall out of which it had been hollowed, and encased in an aedicule, a small free-standing chapel which now stood under a rotunda built in the mid-eleventh century. Nearby was the site of the crucifixion, the chapel of Calvary on top of the rock column to which the hill of Golgotha had been reduced, and, somewhat apart, the ruins of Constantine's basilica, built over the spot where his mother had reputedly discovered the wood of the True Cross in 320. Now, with Jerusalem under Latin rule, the locations of Christ's death and resurrection were physically related to each other for the first time under a single roof in one enormous, sumptuously decorated build-

---

[1] S. Runciman, *A History of the Crusades* (Cambridge, 1951–4), 2.247–88. For the church, see V. C. Corbo, *Il Santo Sepolcro a Gerusalemme* (Jerusalem, 1981–2), part 1 *passim*.

ing, the apotheosis of shrine churches. An outside stair led directly
up to the Calvary chapel. After venerating the site of the crucifixion
there, pilgrims descended and entered the body of the church, past a
crack in the living rock which was said to have split open at the
moment of Christ's death and was considered to be still spattered
with the dried remnants of his blood. They walked round a long
ambulatory out of which opened chapels, two of which contained
reliquaries of the True Cross, one fragment being that found soon
after the crusaders had liberated Jerusalem. They went down a flight
of steps leading to the site of the original discovery of the cross and
then, returning to ground level and passing the spot where Christ's
corpse was supposed to have been anointed before burial, they
reached the aedicule of the Sepulchre itself.

One cannot go through the mouth of the cave except by bending one's
knees. But on entering one finds the hoped-for treasure, the Sepulchre in
which our most kind Lord Jesus Christ rested for three days. It is
marvellously decorated with Parian marble, gold and precious stones. In its
side there are three round holes through which the pilgrims can offer the
stones on which the Lord lay the kisses they have longed to give.[2]

It was here that there took place each year on Holy Saturday the
miracle of the Holy Fire, the auto-lighting of one of the seven lamps
in the aedicule during the liturgy of the sacred fire which, throughout
the rest of Christendom, depends on the striking of flint. This, a
wonder to Muslims as well as to Christians for centuries, was
preceded on Good Friday by the extinguishing of the lamps in the
aedicule, which was locked and would not be opened again until the
miracle had taken place, although it had little windows through
which the flickering light of one of the wicks could be seen once it
had been kindled. In the early twelfth century the Easter Vigil would
begin in a crowded rotunda at nine o'clock on Holy Saturday
morning. Although the timing of the arrival of the fire could be quite
erratic and it was even known to flare up at one of the other holy
places in the city such as the Temple or the church of St John,[3] it
usually came to the Sepulchre in the afternoon. At about three
o'clock, after the appointed readings, sung alternately in Greek and
Latin, and their associated psalms and prayers, a Greek cantor
standing in one part of the rotunda would start to chant the triple
appeal *Kyrie eleison* with its response, which heralded the fire's

---

[2] Theoderic, *Libellus de locis sanctis*, 12–13.   [3] Theoderic 22.

appearance. At the same time the patriarch would approach the aedicule, carrying a candle and preceded by the True Cross. Once the miracle had taken place he would enter and light his candle from the lamp, before passing the light on to the candles of all those present and then processing with it across Jerusalem to the Temple.[4]

This marvellous church, the centre of the world, the focus of God's intervention in history, a stone reliquary encasing the tomb where Christ's body had been transmogrified and the hill of Calvary stained with his blood, was also a memorial to the First Crusade and those who had taken part in it. Without the first crusaders the new church of the Holy Sepulchre would never have been built, just as without the Sepulchre they would never have fought their way to Jerusalem.

In 1009, one hundred and forty years before the consecration of the great new church, the Sepulchre had been vandalized on the orders of the Fatimid caliph Hakim, who had set upon Christians in a persecution which only ended in 1017 after he had become convinced that he himself was God incarnate and had turned on the Muslims as well. The cave-tomb had been levelled almost to the ground, so that only the floor and the lower part of its walls survived. As the news of its destruction reached the West it gave rise to an extraordinary rumour. It was said that Hakim was reacting to false information sent by western Jews – in one account the community in Orléans – who had bribed a pilgrim to carry messages hidden in a hollow staff warning him that a western army was being raised to conquer the Levant. Although it is not entirely clear what then transpired, a wave of persecution broke on parts of France, with Jews being driven from the cities and treated so savagely that some of them committed suicide. There were also attempts to convert them and some bishops forbade any Christian to have dealings with them unless they were baptized. Bishop Hilduin of Limoges, who had been on pilgrimage to Jerusalem with his brother the viscount some years before, gave the Jews in his city the choice of conversion or expulsion and subjected them to a month of disputations with doctors of theology. Only three or four were baptized, although the number of converts may have been higher elsewhere. At any rate some Jewish commu-

---

[4] J. S. C. Riley-Smith, 'The Latin Clergy and the Settlement in Palestine and Syria, 1098–1100', *Catholic Historical Review* 74 (1988), 551–4. See also B. Hamilton, 'The Impact of Crusader Jerusalem on Western Christendom', *Catholic Historical Review* 80 (1994), 709–10.

nities in France appear to have been decimated; that in Orléans
almost ceased to exist.[5] An outburst of ferocious anti-Judaism, again
associated with concern for the Holy Sepulchre, was to feature
eighty-six years later, in the early stages of the First Crusade.

The destruction of the Holy Sepulchre and the persecution of the
Christians in Palestine interrupted a flow of pilgrims to Jerusalem
which seems to have been on the way to becoming a flood in the last
decade or so of the tenth century and the first of the eleventh. The
increased traffic probably reflected anxiety that the Last Days were
near as the Millennium approached, for it was to be in Jerusalem
that the final acts in this dimension – the appearance of Anti-Christ,
the return of the Saviour, the earliest splitting of tombs and
reassembling of bones and dust in the General Resurrection – would
take place. Pilgrims had of course been visiting Jerusalem for
centuries and centres of its cult had already been established in
western Europe, but contemporary piety encouraged the almost
feverish obsession with the holy places which was to be one of the
marks of the eleventh and twelfth centuries. Men and women were
acutely conscious that a feature of their society was a predisposition
to sin, not only because it was violent and because standards and
paths to preferment were conditioned by a martial class, but also
because the Church, increasingly under the influence of monks and
engaged in a programme of evangelizing the secular world, was
asking of them impossibly high standards of behaviour. In a developing economy churchmen had the resources, as well as the structures, to engage in an effective mission and they had evolved the
techniques they needed to touch the minds of many lay men and
women, who were becoming profoundly anxious about a sinfulness
from which they could never escape unless they withdrew from the
world into the religious life. On the other hand, the pastoral
measures needed to calm the consciences of those who had been
aroused had not yet been developed. One of the achievements of the
twelfth century was the provision of palliatives: the mature indulgence; more regular recourse to confession; the growing use of the
Mass as a comparatively inexpensive but efficacious means of inter-
ceding for sin; a refined view of purgatory, now clearly identified and

---

[5] Ralph Glaber, *Historiarum Libri Quinque*, 132–6; Adhémar of Chabannes, *Chronicon*, 169–71.
    See D. F. Callahan, 'Ademar of Chabannes, Millennial Fears and the Development of
    Western Anti-Judaism', *Journal of Ecclesiastical History* 46 (1995), 23–34. For Hilduin's
    pilgrimage, see Adhémar of Chabannes 162.

geographically located; the emergence of 'layness' as a vocation in itself and the consequential increase in the number of lay religious associations and of specifically lay devotions. But in the eleventh century there was a gap between the demands of the Church and the means available to lay men and women to help them meet those demands.

A society in which there was no privacy, little literacy and no cheap books found it hard to cope with regular private devotions; piety expressed itself publicly, through attendance at Mass and participation in pilgrimages, which were for most people the natural ways of showing religious feeling and sorrow for sin. There was a constant traffic between the local cult-centres which dotted every region of western Europe, but many pilgrims travelled further afield to shrines of international importance, although they might begin these journeys by visiting local ones, often with some associated significance, as Duke Robert I of Normandy did when he went to Fécamp, a centre for the veneration of Christ's blood, at the start of his pilgrimage to Jerusalem in 1035.[6] Pilgrimages were stimulated by, and they reinforced, the relations of the laity with their local religious communities, which were often the guardians of shrines and to which they were anyway growing increasingly close. If they were planning to travel long distances on pilgrimage, they would ask if they might benefit from the monks' prayers or borrow money from them. They might also make endowments as acts of gratitude for their safe return.[7]

What drew them to the cult centres were not only the devotional and penitential aspects of a temporary and often demanding exile on the road, but also the relics held at them and the miracles performed by the saints they represented, such as Faith at Conques, Benedict at Fleury and Cuthbert at Durham, which ranged from idiosyncratic, sometimes capricious and even vengeful acts of protection to cures.[8] On the other hand, while miracles sometimes occurred at or near the greatest long-distance shrines, Compostela, Rome and Jerusalem, it was usual to go to Rome or Jerusalem not for miraculous assistance but out of devotion and for forgiveness. Count Fulk III, who ruled Anjou for fifty-three years with energetic

[6] St Saveur-le-Vicomte 12.
[7] Bull, *Knightly Piety*, 205–49; and M. G. Bull, 'Origins', *The Oxford Illustrated History of the Crusades* (Oxford, 1995), 13–33.
[8] B. Ward, *Miracles and the Medieval Mind* (London, 1982), 33–66.

violence, combined ferocity with exceptional piety, so that during his life acts of bestial cruelty regularly alternated with extravagant expressions of devotion.[9] The motive for his first pilgrimage to the Holy Sepulchre six or seven years before its destruction by Hakim was fear of Hell resulting from all the blood he had shed.[10] The vandalizing of the Sepulchre did not lessen the attraction it had for him in the least or the obligation he felt under to do penance there. He made three more journeys to Jerusalem and it was said that on his last, when he was an old man approaching the end of his life, he stripped himself naked and had himself led to the Sepulchre by a halter looped round his neck, while a servant scourged his back and he called on Christ to accept his penance.[11] Count Thierry of Trier, who had killed his archbishop in 1059, made the journey,[12] as did a citizen of Cologne in c.1080 who had disposed of his brother; his sentence was a multiple pilgrimage to all the great shrines with the weapons he had used chained to his body.[13] In c.1030 a Norman clerk wanted 'to lament my sins, weeping at the most holy places'.[14] In 1039 Guy I of Laval set out 'not despairing of the Lord's mercy but desiring to obtain remission of punishment' and his charter confirmed a renunciation of a right unjustly claimed.[15] In 1064 Archbishop Siegfried of Mainz was going 'to cure me of my sins'; he wanted 'to venerate and kiss the sacred Sepulchre'.[16] In c.1080 Bishop Raymond Ebo of Lectoure wished to go to Jerusalem 'on account of my sins'[17] and in 1087 Herbert of Sennecé stood 'silently bewailing the enormity of his sins' before the altar of the church of Beaujeu before leaving for the East.[18]

Pilgrims to Jerusalem were, broadly speaking, of three types. The first, represented by Fulk of Anjou, Thierry of Trier and the townsman of Cologne, were those performing a penance imposed on them by a confessor. By the thirteenth century this category had been defined and further subdivided into three, depending on the

---

[9] Anjou (Halphen) 126–32.

[10] Ralph Glaber 60. Bull (*Knightly Piety*, 207) suggests that this might have been a formal penance.

[11] WMGR 2.292–3.

[12] *Annales Hildesheimenses* 47; Berthold, 'Annales', 275–6; Bernold of St Blasien 429–30; Sigebert of Gembloux, 'Chronica', 361–2.

[13] WMGP 425–6. It was supposed by some that Robert of Normandy had gone in 1035 to fulfil a penance imposed for the murder of his brother. CGCA 50. See D. C. Douglas, *William the Conqueror* (London, 1964), 32.

[14] Normandy 241.   [15] Le Mans Cart 1.2.   [16] *Mainzer Urkundenbuch* 1.190.

[17] St Sernin de Toulouse 98 (for the date, see p. clx).   [18] Beaujeu 17.

nature of the sin and the status of the confessor. The second, often hard to distinguish from the first because there was a penitential element in their journeys as well, were those engaged in what was called a *peregrinatio religiosa*, an act of devotion undertaken voluntarily and perhaps vowed, but not enjoined by a confessor. The third were those who were going to Jerusalem to live there until they died; the special position of the city in the geography of providence meant that it was a place in which devout Christians wanted to be buried.[19] To this day one can visit the charnel pits, still filled with the bones of the pious, in the crypt of the twelfth-century Hospitaller church outside Jerusalem at the site the pilgrims identified as Acheldamach. So when fear of the Last Days welled up it was Jerusalem that people sought. The contemporary chronicler Ralph Glaber wrote that people believed in the 1030s that the large numbers now visiting Jerusalem were evidence that Anti-Christ would soon appear; the scholar and chronicler Adhémar of Chabannes seems to have been moved to go himself for this reason.[20] The great pilgrimage of 1064 was triggered by the conviction that Easter Day 1065 was going to fall on exactly the same date as it had in AD 33 and that this presaged the end of the world.[21]

After the low point in eleventh-century pilgrimaging which followed Hakim's destruction of the Sepulchre,[22] the stream was bound to swell again, and in the mid-1020s there is evidence for many pilgrims on the move.[23] They included men and women from Autun,[24] Tours,[25] Limoges[26] and possibly Poitou.[27] In 1026 there was a pilgrimage of 700 persons, financed by the duke of Normandy and led by Richard, the abbot of St Vanne of Verdun,

[19] C. Vogel, 'Le pèlerinage pénitentiel', *Pellegrinaggi e culto dei santi in Europa fino all Ia crociata* (Todi, 1963), 37–94. For Jerusalem as a shrine in which to die, see also Ward, *Miracles*, 124–5.

[20] Ralph Glaber 204; Callahan, 'Ademar of Chabannes' 21–2, 25.

[21] 'Vita Altmanni episcopi Pataviensis' 230. In a descriptive phrase prefiguring the crusaders, they 'crucem baiolantes Christum secuti sunt'.

[22] The following evidence survives for pilgrims between 1009 and 1024: Carcassonne 1.80; 'Passio S. Cholomanni' 675–6; Ramsey Cart 3.173; Ramsey Chron 124, 340; St Florent-lès-Saumur Hist 267–8; St Julien de Tours 15–17; Monte Cassino 229–30. See M. A. F. de Gaujul, *Etudes historiques sur le Rouergue* (Paris, 1858), 2.38. Halphen (Anjou (Halphen) 214–15 n.3) thought that no one pilgrimaged in the aftermath of the Sepulchre's destruction and so may have dismissed too easily a dating of Fulk III of Anjou's second pilgrimage to 1014–15. The pilgrimage of St Haimerad (Ekkebert, 'Vita sancti Haimeradi presbiteri', 600) should probably be dated before 1009.

[23] See Ralph Glaber 198–200; Le Ronceray d'Angers 22; Hugh of Flavigny, 'Chronicon', 393.

[24] Hugh of Flavigny 393; Ralph Glaber 200.   [25] St Julien de Tours 16.

[26] Adhémar of Chabannes 194; Aumônerie de St Martial de Limoges 15.

[27] Adhémar of Chabannes 194.

and his bishop.[28] Perhaps because of Richard's reputation for sanctity, this journey seems to have been a particularly other-worldly experience.[29] He was joined on the road by pilgrims from northern France[30] and by a large party, mostly from Angoulême and led by Count William IV Taillefer but also including the great lord Eudes of Déols from near Paris.[31] At Antioch the pilgrims befriended a Sicilian Greek monk from Mt Sinai called Symeon, who was planning to go to Normandy to collect the alms which the duke regularly sent to his monastery. Symeon joined them on their way back and travelled to the West with them. He settled at Trier, and one of the leaders of the First Crusade, Godfrey of Bouillon, apparently carried some of his bones with him back to the East.[32]

Although from the 1020s onwards there is hardly a year when we do not have evidence for pilgrims, there were certain periods when enthusiasm was reaching fever pitch. The year 1033 was believed to be the thousandth anniversary of Christ's crucifixion and throughout the decade pilgrims from many parts of the West were converging on Jerusalem: from Metz,[33] Paderborn,[34] Orléans,[35] Auvergne,[36] Limoges,[37] Normandy,[38] Anjou,[39] Maine,[40] Burgundy,[41] Flanders[42] and Verdun.[43] The next major wave appears to have surged East in the 1050s,[44] by which time the shrines in Jerusalem had been partially restored by the Byzantine emperor. Pilgrims can be identified from Rouergue,[45] Lorraine,[46] Cambrai,[47] Bavaria and Normandy,[48]

[28] Adhémar of Chabannes 189–90; Hugh of Flavigny 393–7; Hariulf, *Chronicon Centulense*, 210–11.
[29] Hugh of Flavigny 393–7.
[30] Hariulf 210–11; Hugh of Flavigny 393–4.
[31] Adhemar of Chabannes 189–90, 192, 194; St Cybard d'Angouléme 206.
[32] Hugh of Flavigny 394, 397; Eberwin, 'Ex miraculis sancti Symeonis', 209–11; Riley-Smith, *The First Crusade*, 93.
[33] 'Notitiae fundationis monasterii Bosonis-Villae' 977–8.
[34] *Vita Meinwerci episcopi Patherbrunnensis* 128–9; Busdorf in Paderborn 1.7.
[35] 'Un pèlerinage à Jérusalem dans la première moitié du XIe siècle' 204–6.
[36] *Gallia Christiana* 2, Instrumenta, 105.
[37] See Callahan, 'Ademar of Chabannes', 22.
[38] Jumièges 1.99; St Saveur-le-Vicomte 12; Ralph Glaber 202–4; William of Jumièges 111–14; OV 2.10,116; Normandy 231, 235, 333, 439. See St Martin de Pontoise 1.
[39] Third pilgrimage of Fulk III: CGCA 50–1. Fourth pilgrimage of Fulk III: St Maur-sur-Loire 356; Ralph Glaber 212–14; WMGR 2.292–3.
[40] APC 359, 370; Château-du-Loir 7; Le Mans Cart 1.1–3; Le Mans Liber 24, 97.
[41] Paray-le-Monial 59; Cluny 4.123.   [42] St Pierre-au-Mont-Blandin 110.
[43] 'Gesta episcoporum Virdunensium' 49.   [44] 'Vita Theoderici abbatis Andaginensis' 44.
[45] Villeneuve d'Aveyron 538–9.   [46] 'Vita Theoderici' 44.   [47] *Acta SS Junii* 4.595–9.
[48] OV 2.68–72, 254.

England[49] and northern France.[50] Then in 1064 there was a large pilgrimage, recruited in France and Germany; the German contingent, led by the bishop of Bamberg, accompanied by the archbishop of Mainz, the bishops of Utrecht and Regensburg, and the empress's chaplain, was estimated – probably grossly overestimated – to contain between 7,000 and 12,000 persons.[51]

In the 1070s passage across Asia Minor, now being overrun by nomadic Turks, must have become much more difficult, but the traffic does not seem to have lessened and it certainly increased again in the 1080s and early 1090s, when many pilgrims were making the journey from Robert I of Flanders's pilgrimage in 1085 onwards.[52] They were setting out from Toul,[53] Cambrai[54], Luxembourg,[55] Münster,[56] Mainz,[57] Swabia,[58] Navarre,[59] southern Italy,[60] Velay,[61] the Lyonnais,[62] Nevers,[63] Poitou,[64] the Saintonge,[65] the Limousin,[66] Languedoc,[67] Burgundy[68] and possibly Normandy.[69] The departure of the First Crusade in 1096 was, therefore, the last of the waves of pilgrims which had regularly surged to the East for seventy years.

Enthusiasm in Europe was fuelled by the arrival of relics from Jerusalem.[70] On one of his pilgrimages Fulk III of Anjou brought back 'a large piece' of the Sepulchre, which he must have picked out of the rubble, and a relic of the Manger at Bethlehem,[71] and he returned from another with a fragment of the True Cross.[72] In the later 1020s Bishop Ulric of Orléans gave his church one of the Sepulchre's lamps which had been lit by the Holy Fire, together with its oil.[73] In 1027 Richard of St Vanne brought back relics, among

[49] *The Anglo-Saxon Chronicle* 124,134; Florence of Worcester 1.217.
[50] *Acta SS Junii* 4.599; Noyon 155.
[51] *Annales Altahenses maiores* 66–71; Lampert of Hersfeld 92–100; Marianus Scottus, 'Chronicon', 558–9; Sigebert of Gembloux, 'Chronica', 361; 'Vita Altmanni' 230; *Mainzer Urkundenbuch* 1.199–200; OV 2.90.
[52] Kb 187–90; 'Genealogiae comitum Flandriae' 323.
[53] 'Gesta episcoporum Tullensium' 647; Bar 1.16; St Mihiel 165.
[54] 'Chronicon S. Andreac castri Cameracesii' 543.
[55] Marcigny 27; 'Gesta episcoporum Tullensium' 647.
[56] 'Annalista Saxo' 727; Cosmas of Prague, 'Chronica Boemorum', 100.
[57] *Mainzer Urkundenbuch* 1.297.   [58] Bernold of St Blasien 455.   [59] Leire 210.
[60] OV 4.66.   [61] St Chaffre du Monastier 13–4.   [62] Beaujeu 13, 17.
[63] La Charité-sur-Loire 96–7.   [64] Noyers 279; Maillezais 236–7.
[65] St Jean d'Angély 30.231; St Florent-lès-Saumur (Saintongeaises) 22, 41.
[66] Aureil 174; Tulle 60, 83, 255, 266; GV 12.425.   [67] Auch 9,44.
[68] St Marcel-lès-Chalon-sur-Saône 90–1; St Philibert de Tournus (Chifflet), Preuves, 329–30.
[69] OV 4.306–8.
[70] See A. H. Bredero, *Christendom and Christianity in the Middle Ages* (Grand Rapids, 1994), 91–5.
[71] Toussaint d'Angers 147.   [72] CGCA 51.
[73] Ralph Glaber 202.

which was a piece of the True Cross, concealed in a bag hanging round his neck.[74] In the early 1030s Hervey, archdeacon of Orléans, founded the priory of Notre-Dame de la Ferté-Avrain to house the relics he had acquired in Jerusalem.[75] While Adalbert of Metz was making the pilgrimage shortly before 1033 'on account of his love of the Holy Sepulchre', his wife Judith remained at home and founded a community at Bouzonville (Busendorf) dedicated to the cross. During his stay in Jerusalem Adalbert was given a piece of the True Cross by the patriarch and this was the start of a family devotion to it – members were often buried at the abbey – which was perhaps to influence those of his descendants who crusaded in the twelfth century.[76] The abbey of Moissac in Languedoc must have been typical of many in the impressive collection of relics of Jerusalem it had assembled by 1100. It had pieces of the True Cross, the Manger at Bethlehem, the Crown of Thorns, Christ's clothes and a palm he had held, and stones from the Column of the Flagellation, the Sepulchre and Calvary.[77]

The growing interest in the Sepulchre was marked by the many benefactions made to it. Duke Richard II of Normandy sent 100 pounds of gold, perhaps at the time he financed Richard of St Vanne's pilgrimage in 1026,[78] and Bishop Aldred of Worcester presented a gold chalice worth 5 marks when he went to Jerusalem in 1058.[79] In 1053 a priory in Rouergue was founded as a proprietary church of the Sepulchre itself, to which it was expected to pay an annual *census* of a gold besant; its priors were to be subject to the Greek patriarch of Jerusalem.[80] The patriarch had more possessions in western Europe than is generally realized: Moissac managed one of his properties for him and expected to transfer the rent from it to his envoy each year.[81] In 1079 Pope Gregory VII confirmed the subjection to Jerusalem of another proprietary church of the Sepulchre, in the county of La Marche, although he himself seems to

[74] Hugh of Flavigny 396.   [75] 'Un pèlerinage à Jérusalem' 205–6.
[76] 'Notitiae fundationis monasterii Bosonis-Villae' 977–80. Another fragment of the cross, presented to him on the way home by the Byzantine emperor, was brought back by Pibo of Toul in 1086. 'Gesta episcoporum Tullensium' 647.
[77] A. Gieysztor, 'The Genesis of the Crusades: the Encyclical of Sergius IV', *Mediaevalia et Humanistica* 6 (1950), 24 and note 97.
[78] Ralph Glaber 36. Fulk III of Anjou was generous to the churches in Jerusalem on his visit in 1039. Ralph Glaber 214.
[79] *The Anglo-Saxon Chronicle* 134.
[80] Villeneuve d'Aveyron 538–9.
[81] Gieysztor, 'The Genesis of the Crusades', 6.25–6.

have provided its prior.[82] A third proprietary church may have been established at Commisago; it was granted by the Latin patriarch of Jerusalem to the abbey of San Benigno di Fruttuaria in 1112.[83] These churches were among many dedicated to the Sepulchre and often founded by pilgrims: the monastery beside his castle built by Gerard of Fontvannes and his wife and given to the abbey of Bèze in 1027–8;[84] the church at Jaligny founded in 1036 by a pilgrim called Hictor;[85] the abbey of Beaulieu and the priory of Langeais established by Fulk III of Anjou;[86] the monastery founded in 1055 by Bishop Lietbert of Cambrai and two of his lay companions;[87] and the priory close to the castle at Beaugency built in the 1070s by Lancelin of Beaugency, among whose descendants were several first crusaders[88] – his son Ralph was to endow it on his return from the First Crusade.[89] The measurements of the Sepulchre, paced out by Abbot Wyno of Helmarshausen on the 1033 pilgrimage, were used to build the Jerusalem church at Busdorf near Paderborn; Wyno had been commissioned by Bishop Meinwerk of Paderborn to get them.[90] Interest also manifested itself from around 1060 in the appearance of 'Jerusalem' as a female name. Three geographically isolated cases, from Blois,[91] the Saintonge[92] and the Dauphiné,[93] are known; the son, grandson and daughter-in-law of one of these women made the pilgrimage in the early 1090s.[94]

In their preparations pilgrims employed measures which were to be put to use on a larger scale in the months before the First Crusade. Arrangements had to be made for the management of their lands while they were away: in 1090 Peter Carbonel left his brother, a knight called Boniface, in charge of his property.[95] The journey must have been expensive, but I know of only four pledge-charters, all involving *vifgages*, in which the lenders occupied the properties

[82] Greg Reg 457–8.   [83] *Bibliotheca Sebusiana* 378–9.   [84] Bèze Liber 551–2.
[85] *Gallia Christiana* 2, Instrumenta, 105. For the date, see Bourbonnais 109–10.
[86] Toussaint d'Angers 147–8; CGCA 51.   [87] *Acta SS Junii* 4.600.
[88] La Trinité de Vendôme Cart 2.3–6. By the 1050s a church dedicated to the Holy Sepulchre had also been built at Calahorra. Rioja 2.44.
[89] La Trinité de Vendôme Cart 2.108–9.
[90] Busdorf in Paderborn 1.1–2, 7, 10 and see 13; *Vita Meinwerci* 128–9. For another set of measurements, see GF 103.
[91] Marmoutier (Blésois) 76; Marmoutier (Dunois) 147–8.
[92] La Trinité de Vendôme (Saintongeais) 36, 50; Notre-Dame de Saintes 98, and see pp. 95–7.
[93] Les Ecouges 83.   [94] Maillezais 236–7.
[95] St Marcel-lès-Chalon-sur-Saône 90.

themselves and profited from them until the loans were redeemed;[96] two borrowers, in an arrangement which was to be familiar in crusade agreements, willed the property concerned to the lenders after their deaths, even if it had been redeemed in the meantime.[97] One charter included a clause, which must have already been a standard formula, covering the eventuality that the pilgrim might settle in the Holy Land.[98]

It was to become common for recruits to the early crusades to renounce disputes with churches over rights to which they had doubtful claims. I know of only four renunciations of this type made by pilgrims before 1095, all but one apparently dating from the decade before the First Crusade, evidence perhaps of the growing influence of churchmen as the eleventh-century reform movement gained ground and doubts spread whether laymen could legitimately possess churches and tithes.[99] Only one of the renunciations seems to have been made in exchange for money,[100] the others being motivated by the natural desire of pilgrims to leave with clear consciences.[101] Renunciations in exchange for cash were to be a feature of preparations for the First Crusade. The sole case known before 1095 and the small number of surviving pledge-charters suggest that, unlike a crusade, a peaceful pilgrimage to Jerusalem was just within the financial capabilities of most land-owners.

On the other hand, as a penitential exercise pilgrimage to Jerusalem was likely to be severe, even dangerous, and pilgrims were anyway concerned to make sure that it would be spiritually profitable. Their state of mind on departure, and the way monks resorted to age-old techniques to exploit it, are illustrated by events at the start of the fourth pilgrimage of Fulk of Anjou in the late 1030s. Accompanied by his wife, who was going with him, and the bishop of Angers, he spent the first night of the journey at the abbey of St Maur-sur-Loire. His party was honourably received and given a

---

[96] Carcassonne 1.80; Vigeois 4; Cluny 4.123-4; St Marcel-lès-Chalon-sur-Saône 90-1. One also included a sale. Carcassonne 1.80.

[97] Vigeois 4; St Marcel-lès-Chalon-sur-Saône 90-1.

[98] St Marcel-lès-Chalon-sur-Saône 90; J. Richard, 'Départs de pèlerins et de croisés bourguignons au XIe s.: à propos d'une charte de Cluny', *Annales de Bourgogne* 60 (1988), 139-43. For this clause in crusaders' charters, see Cluny 5.52; St Pierre de la Réole 141; St Jean d'Angély 30.384; Göttweig 194; perhaps St Victor de Marseille (Rolland) 26.

[99] By Guy I of Laval: Le Mans Cart 1.2-3; Le Mans Liber 24; by William Seguin: St Vincent de Lucq 19; by Peter of Vic: Auch 8-10; and by Gerald of Vouhé: St Jean d'Angély 30.231.

[100] St Vincent de Lucq 19.   [101] See Le Mans Cart 1.2; Le Mans Liber 24.

magnificent meal, during which one of the monks read from the Life of St Maur. After the meal the bishop entertained the company with stories about the saint and so fired Fulk that he was persuaded then and there to finance the rebuilding of the abbey church.[102] Endowments to churches or wills in favour of them before leaving[103] and on return[104] were common, and these sometimes made reference to a desire for prayers. In the decade or so before 1095 William Fredelann of Blaye and Helias of Didonne and his family were received into the societies of prayer of the abbeys of La Sauve-Majeure and Maillezais respectively.[105] In *c.*1090 Peter of Vic put one of his sons into the chapter of Auch as an oblate and provided a substantial entry gift; this was a common way of ensuring that one benefited from a community's prayers.[106] At about the same time Pons of Cuiseaux was promised an obit by the monks of St Philibert de Tournus.[107] Pilgrimage could lead directly to interior conversion. In the 1030s or 1040s Bernard of Merzé had on his return begun 'to think about the salvation of my soul[108] and in the late 1090s the Norman knight Odard, who seems to have come back from his pilgrimage after the First Crusade had been launched, entered the abbey of Jumièges.[109] Two endowments and one will were made while the pilgrims concerned were actually in Jerusalem. In 1053 Odilus of Morlhon founded and endowed the priory of Villeneuve d'Aveyron[110] and in *c.*1090 Garderade Barbotin the Old of Pons gave land to the priory of St Martin de Pons in gratitude for having reached his goal; he wrote that he intended to stay there for a while.[111] A year or two

---

[102] St Maur-sur-Loire 356. Fulk's widow, Hildegarde, was to go again in 1046, with the intention of dying in Jerusalem. Le Ronceray d'Angers 10, 27, 40, 46.

[103] Endowments: Aureil 36; St Pierre-au-Mont-Blandin 110; St Maur-sur-Loire 356; Le Ronceray d'Angers 10, 27; St Victor de Marseille (Guérard) 1.287; Tulle 60, 83, 97, 255; Oulx 41; La Sauve-Majeure fol. 253 (information provided by Dr Bull); Beaujeu 13–14, 17; La Charité-sur-Loire 96–7; Leire 210; Maillezais 236–7; Noyon 155; Normandy 231; *Mainzer Urkundenbuch* 1.297; St Philibert de Tournus (Chifflet), Preuves, 329–30; and see Uzerche 338. Wills: Carcassonne 1.80; Le Ronceray d'Angers 56; Tulle 46–7, 82; Beaujeu 17; La Charité-sur-Loire 96–7; Auch 10; Leire 210; Conques 166, 236; and see also Auch 44.

[104] Endowments: St Julien de Tours 15–16; Cluny 4.64–5, 123–4; *Gallia Christiana* 2, Instrumenta, 105; Jumièges 1.122–3; 'Un pèlerinage à Jérusalem' 205–6.

[105] La Sauve-Majeure fol. 253 (information provided by Dr Bull); Maillezais 237.

[106] Auch 9–10.

[107] St Philibert de Tournus (Chifflet), Preuves, 329–30. On coming home in 1025 Walter of Tours wanted the monks of St Loup to pray not only for himself and his family but also for the Church in general. St Julien de Tours 15–16.

[108] Cluny 4.64.   [109] Jumièges 1.122.   [110] Villeneuve d'Aveyron 538–9.

[111] St Florent-lès-Saumur (Saintongeaises) 22, 41.

later Boso I of Turenne willed two *mansi* to the abbey of Tulle as he lay dying in the holy city.[112]

If in *c.*1015 the party led by Ralph of Tosny, which travelled through Rome to southern Italy and began the Norman conquest of the region, really were pilgrims to Jerusalem, they were presumably intending to cross the Adriatic from Bari and take the old imperial road, the via Egnatia, to Constantinople.[113] This route was popular throughout the eleventh century, but the conversion of Hungary had made the land passage through central Europe much more secure; it was pointed out that pilgrims no longer had to go by sea.[114] In 1026 William IV of Angoulême 'took the Bavarian road', travelling by way of Bavaria and Hungary to Constantinople,[115] where he must have met up with Richard of St Vanne, who had made his way by a third route: through Dalmatia and along the via Egnatia.[116] In 1057 Thierry of Mathonville, abbot of St Evroul, and his party[117] and in the following year Lampert of Hersfeld[118] and Bishop Aldred of Worcester[119] went the same way as had William of Angoulême; so did Gunther of Bamberg in 1064.[120] In 1054 Lietbert of Cambrai and his companions travelled through Dalmatia.[121] These three roads to Constantinople – down Italy to Bari and across to Greece; by way of Hungary and Bulgaria; and through Dalmatia – were to be used by the armies of the First Crusade. From Constantinople everyone seems to have taken the old imperial highway to the East: Fulk of Anjou and Robert of Normandy set off together along it in 1035.[122] It ran to Antioch, from where the pilgrims travelled south down the Syrian and Palestinian coasts, but that final stretch – by way of Latakia, Tripoli, Caesarea and Ramle to Jerusalem[123] – was considered to be a dangerous one and in 1057 Norman pilgrims, who had reached Antioch, debated whether to avoid it by taking a ship.[124] After all the troubles which will be described below, Gunther of Bamberg took a merchant ship from Jaffa back to Latakia.[125] Richard of St Vanne returned to Antioch by land and then travelled

---

[112] Tulle 266. His wife Gerberga was professed on her deathbed as a nun attached to Tulle. Tulle 271.
[113] CSPVS 112.   [114] Ralph Glaber 96.   [115] Adhémar of Chabannes 189–90.
[116] Hugh of Flavigny 393–4.   [117] OV 2.68.   [118] Lampert of Hersfeld 74.
[119] Florence of Worcester 1.217.   [120] *Annales Altahenses maiores* 66–7.
[121] *Acta SS Junii* 4.597.   [122] CGCA 50.
[123] *Annales Altahenses maiores* 67–70; Lampert of Hersfeld 94–8.
[124] OV 2.70. In *c.*1040 Mainfred of Magdeburg and his companions were delayed from sailing by contrary winds at Latakia. Ekkebert 606.
[125] See *Annales Altahenses maiores* 70; Lampert of Hersfeld 98–9; Marianus Scottus 559.

by way of Belgrade to the Dalmatian coast, from where he crossed the Adriatic to visit Rome.[126]

The journey to the Holy Land could be made surprisingly quickly. In 1026 William Taillefer left Angoulême on 1 October and reached Jerusalem just over five months later, in the first week of the following March.[127] Lampert of Hersfeld departed from Aschaffenburg in late September 1058 and was back almost a year later.[128] Gunther of Bamberg left Jerusalem for home on 25 April 1065 and had reached Hungary by the time of his death on 23 July.[129] But there were aggravations and worse. The Greeks, whose exactions caused regular complaints – they had probably begun the practice, which was to be so familiar to crusaders, of freeing or shutting their markets as a method of control[130] – closed the route through the Byzantine empire for three years after 1017 as a protest about the Norman assistance to the rebellion against them in southern Italy.[131] In 1064 Bishop Gunther of Bamberg, who was very young, ran into trouble in Constantinople, because he was suspected by Greek officials of being the western emperor-elect in disguise![132] He was warned in Latakia that there were Muslim bandits ahead and his large party was ambushed near Caesarea and severely mauled; it was reported later that two-thirds of his following did not return to the West.[133] In 1022 Gerald of Thouars, the abbot of St Florent-lès-Saumur, was taken prisoner and, it was believed, martyred by Muslims before he reached Jerusalem.[134] Four years later Richard of St Vanne was stoned when he said Mass openly in Islamic territory.[135] In 1053 Abbot Thierry of St Hubert-en-Ardenne, who had planned to travel by way of Hungary, was turned back because of the 'incursions of barbarians' – presumably Pechenegs – ahead. He changed course with great difficulty, redirecting his journey through Italy with the intention of crossing the Adriatic, although he got no further than Rome.[136]

---

[126] Hugh of Flavigny 397; Eberwin 209–10. Bishop Raimbert of Verdun died at Belgrade on his pilgrimage in 1038. Hugh of Flavigny 402.
[127] Adhémar of Chabannes 189–90.   [128] Lampert of Hersfeld 74–5.
[129] *Annales Altahenses maiores* 70; Lampert of Hersfeld 99.
[130] William of Jumièges 113 (an interpolation). See J. Sumption *Pilgrimage* (London, 1975), 183–4.
[131] Adhémar of Chabannes 178.   [132] *Annales Altahenses maiores* 67.
[133] *Annales Altahenses maiores* 67–70; Lampert of Hersfeld 94–8; Marianus Scottus 559; Sigebert of Gembloux, 'Chronica', 361.
[134] St Florent-lès-Saumur Hist 267–8.   [135] Hugh of Flavigny 396–7.
[136] 'Vita Theoderici' 44–5.

Visits to Jerusalem itself could be irritating, as when the door-keepers to the Sepulchre compound made difficulties,[137] and also dangerous: an English hermit, who was persuaded by his bishop not to make the pilgrimage, had envisaged his death at the hands of the Muslims.[138] The atmosphere in the city seems to have been tense in 1027. Stones were thrown by Muslims into the Sepulchre compound during Holy Week and the pilgrims were worried by the number of armed men in the streets at the time of the miracle of the Holy Fire.[139] In *c*.1040 Ulrich of Breisgau, whose pilgrimage was eccentric – he took with him one servant and one horse, which he never rode until he had recited the whole psalter – was stoned by a hostile crowd near the river Jordan.[140] In 1055 the authorities expelled the Christians from the Sepulchre compound and closed the pilgrim roads: Lietbert of Cambrai and his companions were held up for three months at Latakia and for a further two in Cyprus; they never reached their destination.[141] After 1071 conditions must have deteriorated as Asia Minor was swept by marauding Turks and Palestine was disputed by Seljuks and Fatimids. Perhaps more people were travelling by sea again.

William Taillefer of Angoulême spent nearly four months in Jerusalem, from the first week of March to the third week of June 1027.[142] This length of stay, covering the feasts of Easter[143] and Pentecost, must have been common, although Gunther of Bamberg, delayed by the assault on his party, missed Easter in Jerusalem and spent only thirteen days there.[144] On his return home William Taillefer was received in splendour by the abbeys of St Martial de Limoges and St Cybard d'Angoulême.

When the rumour of his approach reached Angoulême, all the magnates, not only from Angoulême but also from Périgord and the Saintonge, and of every age and sex, rushed joyfully to meet him, wanting to see him. The monastic clergy of St Cybard, in white vestments and ecclesiastical panoply, processed rejoicing with a large crowd of people to meet him a mile outside the city, singing praises and antiphons. And they led him in, singing the *Te Deum* loudly, as is customary.[145]

In the accounts of eleventh-century pilgrimages one can see traditions already well established in the arrangements for the manage-

---

[137] CGCA 50–1.   [138] WMGP 286.   [139] Hugh of Flavigny 394–7.
[140] 'Vita sancti Udalrici prioris Cellensis' 252, 255–6.   [141] *Acta SS Junii* 4.597–9.
[142] Adhémar of Chabannes 190. See Hugh of Flavigny 395–6.
[143] See Hugh of Flavigny 395–6; Ralph Glaber 202.
[144] *Annales Altahenses maiores* 70.   [145] Adhémar of Chabannes 190.

ment of estates, pledges, renunciations, wills and endowments on departure, requests for prayer, the routes taken and ceremonial home-comings. In many ways the armsbearing classes to which the nobles and knights who were to take the cross belonged had got thoroughly used to the patterns of behaviour so many of them had experienced in the seventy years before the First Crusade, which was, after all, much the largest of the mass pilgrimages of the eleventh century. It differed from the others, however, in one important respect. It was at the same time a war. Rich magnates had sometimes pilgrimaged in splendour and with panache. Robert of Normandy had travelled in great magnificence, scattering alms as he went, and there was a later tradition in Normandy that, approaching Constantinople, he had had his mule shod with gold so that the Greeks should not think him mean – apparently the Franks had a reputation for avariciousness among them – although it is noteworthy that he was thought to have been riding a mule rather than a horse.[146] But the intentions of eleventh-century pilgrims from the armsbearing classes were generally pacific. Pilgrims performing enjoined penances were certainly forbidden to carry weapons, although Pope Gregory VII was to exempt those who took up arms 'in the preservation of their rights, or those of their lord, their friend [relation], or the poor or in defence of the churches' from the rule that no one in serious sin should fight,[147] which must have been a precedent for crusaders. It is not clear whether the same ban applied to all of those engaged in *peregrinationes religiosae* – they were also penitents, of course, if of a less formal kind – but when in 1064 Bishop Gunther of Bamberg brought trouble from Palestinian robbers on himself by the ostentatious richness of his train and his followers were attacked they agonized whether they could resist their assailants at all, although in the end some fought back with whatever they could get their hands on.[148] The crusaders, on the other hand, intended war to be an integral part of their penitential exercise. A new and revolutionary element had entered the tradition of journeying to the Holy Land and a major question is why.

---

[146] William of Jumièges 112–13. See E.-R. Labande, 'Recherches sur les pèlerins dans l'Europe des XIe–XIIe siècles', *Cahiers de civilisation médiévale* 1 (1958), 339.

[147] Greg Reg 471–2.

[148] Lampert of Hersfeld 94–8; *Annales Altahenses maiores* 68–70; Marianus Scottus 559.

PIOUS VIOLENCE

For a time in the late 1020s Alan Caignart, the count of Cornouaille in Brittany, was gravely ill. In his delirium he believed he saw a golden cross falling from heaven into his mouth and so convinced did he become that his recovery was associated with this vision that he sent his wife and his brother, the local bishop, to Rome to ask Pope John XIX for advice. John suggested that he build a monastery in honour of the cross and on 14 September 1029, the feast commemorating the discovery of the True Cross in Jerusalem, Alan founded the abbey of Ste Croix de Quimperlé.[149] In the following year, before he threw back an invasion of Cornouaille by Alan III of Brittany in the Battle of Gueth-Ronan, Alan Caignart 'invoked the strength of the glorious cross of the Lord and begged for the aid of St. Ronan'. Then he fought, 'protected by the sign of the healing cross'.[150] He looks like a precocious crusader, but he was only expressing the conventional belief that the religious symbol or saint to which an individual was particularly devoted could protect him in a difficult or dangerous situation. The common association of violence with a shrine to which the perpetrator was strongly attached was theatrically demonstrated in Gascony by Arnald Sancho, who had granted property to the monks of Sorde so that 'God might give him the traitor', a man called William Malfara who had killed his brother. Arnald overpowered William, mutilated his body, and castrated him – 'In this way his prestige, his capacity to fight, and his dynastic prospects were all irreparably damaged' – before solemnly presenting his blood-stained armour to the abbey.[151]

Apprehension when faced by the prospect of engagement in violence has always triggered acts of piety, as a group of charters recording dispositions made by men sailing in 1066 with Duke William of Normandy to conquer England illustrate. Before embarkation Roger II of Montgomery renounced in the duke's presence claims on property he had been making against the community of Ste Trinité-du-Mont de Rouen and Roger son of Turold endowed the monks there 'for the health of his soul'.[152] During the crossing there was some rough weather and Osmund of Boudeville, falling ill and presumably fearful of death, gave the

---

[149] Ste Croix de Quimperlé 36, 93–4; Brittany (ducs) 22–7.
[150] Ste Croix de Quimperlé 101.   [151] Bull, 'Origins', 15; Bull, *Knightly Piety*, 159.
[152] Ste Trinité-du-Mont de Rouen 442, 453–4.

monks tithes.[153] But in the eleventh and twelfth centuries violence perpetrated under the patronage of saints, even, in the collections of miracle stories, engaged in by the saints themselves, was a feature of a culture in which self-help predominated because arbitration was so often ineffective. The endemic insecurity must have contributed to the flourishing of extended families. There has been argument about how extended families actually were, but the early crusading movement provides evidence for the importance to people of even quite distant ties of kinship. Family relationships loomed large, because they provided men and women with 'natural friends' in times of insecurity and perhaps also because the church was trying to enforce marriage-rules of consanguinity which had very wide definitions and involved the acknowledgement of even remote cousins.[154] Many of the noble kindreds which were to play significant parts in early crusading have the appearance of being relatively recently established. This is another difficult subject, given the fact that we now know that many of the 'new men' of the tenth and eleventh centuries were not new at all and that some of the castellan families which rose to prominence in the seventy years before the First Crusade were descended from junior branches of older noble lines, but the fact remains that many of them had only risen through the use of naked force.

Extended families carving places for themselves in an unstable society created the ideal conditions for vendettas and in an age dominated by them it was natural for the blood feud to enter religion as an expression of caring. In the popular poem *La Venjance Nostre Seigneur*, Christ was portrayed prophesying that his crucifixion would be avenged by the destruction of Jerusalem in AD 70. This was adapted to the events of July 1099 in the greatest of the crusade epics, *La Chanson d'Antioche*, which opens with a scene of Christ on the cross assuring the thieves on either side of him that he will be avenged by the crusaders.[155] As soon as the crusade was preached the blood-feud surfaced in the pogroms against the Jews, in which the crusaders' motives appear to have stemmed less from avarice than from a conviction that they were engaged in a vendetta against those who had disparaged the honour of Christ, their father and lord. They

---

[153] Ste Trinité-du-Mont de Rouen 451–2; and see 446, 450–1.

[154] C. B. Bouchard, 'Consanguinity and Noble Marriages in the Tenth and Eleventh Centuries', *Speculum* 56 (1981), 268–87.

[155] Ch d'A 1.25–8.

found it impossible to distinguish the Jews, who by demanding his crucifixion in AD 33 had broken his body, from the Muslims who had stolen his patrimony in 638 when they had entered Jerusalem.[156] However abhorrent it is to us, violence – even ethnic violence – was not an antithesis of piety, but could be an expression of it.

It was, in fact, perfectly possible for members of these families, whether risen or well-established, to be both rough and pious, as the case of Fulk III of Anjou has already demonstrated. Other examples are to be found in successive generations of the families of Montlhéry and Le Puiset in the Ile-de-France, the second of which was to be lashed by the pen of Abbot Suger of St Denis for its savagery,[157] and of Lusignan in Poitou. The future crusader Hugh VI of Lusignan was devout, but he was in more or less continuous conflict with the abbey of St Maixent, his lord for some of his lands: the abbey's chronicler referred to him as 'the Devil'.[158] His dispute with the monks must have begun almost as soon as he had succeeded his father in 1060 and it reached a climax towards the end of his life – he was to die in 1110 – occasioning interventions from the duke of Aquitaine, the bishops of Poitiers and Saintes, and the pope himself.[159] One of Hugh's legacies may have been a savage little war between his son and the duke of Aquitaine which broke out on his death.[160]

Churchmen condemned the use of force to secure material ends, but they tolerated, even encouraged, certain expressions of pious violence, partly because they had been bred in the same world as laymen and took them for granted, and partly because most of them were convinced that the use of force was justifiable when the fighter was performing a service to God such as assuring peace or protecting the Church. Although there were differences of emphasis among the eleventh-century theorists and a concern about the state of soldiers' souls after battle – sometimes, but not always, leading to advice to combatants to do penance – there was general agreement that provided it fulfilled certain criteria warfare could be a positive activity and could be waged on God's direct authority. The eleventh-century wars in Sicily and in Spain, where the frontier with the

[156] Riley-Smith, *The First Crusade* 52–7.
[157] Suger of St Denis, *Vita Ludovici Grossi regis*, 128–30.
[158] St Maixent Chron 134.
[159] St Maixent Chartes 16.155–6, 240–3 , 256–61; 18.482.
[160] St Maixent Chartes 16.266, 273, 276. Cf. S. Painter, 'The Lords of Lusignan in the Eleventh and Twelfth Centuries', *Speculum* 32 (1957), 38.

Moors was still dangerously close to the Pyrenees, are not treated nowadays as 'precrusades'[161] and the exigencies of life on the Iberian frontier might have made those who engaged in them behave inconsistently at times, but it is undeniable that contemporaries believed that the Christian warriors had God's support. And although the knights who streamed across the mountains from the north usually came either to help out relations or to take part in what were little more than looting expeditions, at least one campaign seems to have had a deeper significance for them.

On 23 October 1086 the army of King Alfonso VI of Leon-Castile, who had caused a sensation the year before by occupying Toledo, was destroyed in the battle of Sagrajas by the North African Almoravids, in alliance with the Muslim *taifa* kings who had invited them into the peninsula. Alfonso, although severely wounded, escaped, but carts filled with the heads of the Christian dead trundled round Spain and North Africa to demonstrate to the Muslim faithful that the Christians need not be feared. Although the Spanish casualties may not have been as numerous as is sometimes supposed, shock-waves spread north to Poitou[162] and beyond. King Philip of France called on his subjects to lend support and French contingents marched into Spain in 1087, although they were diverted to the siege of Tudela in the Ebro valley and eventually withdrew with little accomplished.[163] A number of those who were to be prominent in the First Crusade six years later were involved, including Hugh of Lusignan,[164] William the Carpenter of Melun,[165] Duke Eudes I of Burgundy[166] and possibly Raymond of St Gilles.[167] A charter, issued in Leon and recording an admission by Eudes that he had unjustly withheld property belonging to the abbey of St Philibert de Tournus, allows us to see into the minds of the French contingent. St Philibert had been patronized by Constance of Burgundy, Eudes's exceptionally pious aunt, who was married to

[161] For Spain see Bull, *Knightly Piety*, 70–114; R. A. Fletcher, 'Reconquest and Crusade in Spain c.1050–1150', *Transactions of the Royal Historical Society* 5th series, 37 (1987), 31–47.

[162] Nouaillé 252.

[163] St Maixent Chron 148; CSPVS 136; 'Chronicon Trenorciense' 112–13; 'Historiae Francicae Fragmentum' 2; Nouaillé 249–52; B. F. Reilly, *The Kingdom of Leon-Castilla under King Alfonso VI 1065–1109* (Princeton, 1988), 180–94.

[164] Nouaillé 249–50.

[165] St Maixent Chron 148. For the later references to William's cowardice during the First Crusade, see Bull, *Knightly Piety*, 84–5.

[166] 'Chronicon Trenorciense' 113; St Philibert de Tournus (Juënin) 134–5.

[167] J. H. and L. L. Hill, *Raymond IV de Saint-Gilles* (Toulouse, 1959), 20–1.

Alfonso of Leon-Castile.[168] Eudes, who had come to Leon after the siege of Tudela, probably to arrange the marriage of his cousin Raymond of Burgundy to Alfonso's sister Urraca, had to give way to pressure from Constance and withdraw his refusal to recognize a gift she had made to St Philibert several years before. His recantation was witnessed by his brother, Bishop Robert of Langres, and by other Burgundians, including Savary of Vergy who was later to help finance the crusade of his nephew Geoffrey II of Donzy. Eudes demonstrated his conviction that he had come to Spain in obedience to a divine mandate when he stated that he had answered Alfonso's summons 'with that great army in which nearly all the nobles of the kingdom of France came to Spain at the orders of God'.[169]

Senior churchmen felt increasingly in need of the support righteous violence could give them as a radical programme of reform embarked on by the papacy encountered resistance and in a febrile atmosphere bred disorder and civil war in Germany and northern Italy. They encouraged the development of a movement in support of the papal policies, which expressed itself in commitment to service to St Peter, providing an example of the way the religious instincts of nobles and knights and their family relationships manifested themselves in pious violence. Pope Alexander II seems to have begun the practice of persuading some armsbearers to take oaths to help defend the papacy[170] and by 1080 a disparate assortment of individuals, ranging from great magnates to knights, had been recruited. They did not all make the same commitment: some took solemn vows; some recognized themselves as papal vassals; some expressed their support informally. Some undertook to apply the reforms in their territories; others did not. Pope Gregory VII (1073–85) referred to them in various ways, but most commonly as *fideles beati Petri*.[171]

Many *fideles* were closely associated through the way they tended to choose, or to have chosen, each other's families when it came to marriage: it is not clear whether shared partisanship led to marriage alliances or whether existing alliances encouraged the sharing of commitment, although there was probably a bit of both. The *fidelis* William Tête-Hardi of (imperial) Burgundy's daughters were

[168] See C. B. Bouchard, *Sword, Miter, and Cloister* (Ithaca, 1987), 143–5.
[169] St Philibert de Tournus (Juénin) 134–5; reflected in the description of the army as 'gens dominica' in GN Gesta 175. See also 'Chronicon Trenorciense' 112–13.
[170] See Greg Reg 35–6, 70-1.
[171] Erdmann, *The Origin*, 206–8; I. S. Robinson, *Authority and Resistance in the Investiture Contest* (Manchester, 1978), 20.

married to Humbert II of Savoy, Robert II of Flanders, Thierry II of Montbéliard, and Eudes I of (French) Burgundy, all being from the families of *fideles* or at least supporters of Pope Gregory.[172] Robert of Flanders's sister was married to Welf IV of Bavaria, another *fidelis*. The *fidelis* Ebles of Roucy was married to the *fidelis* Robert Guiscard's daughter.

A network of supporters of reform can be identified in Languedoc, where it included Raymond of St Gilles, his brother-in-law Peter II of Melgueil, William IX of Aquitaine who was married to Raymond's niece, Bernard II of Besalù, Gaston IV of Béarn, Centule II of Bigorre and Bertrand of Provence.[173] Also associated with this circle was Hugh of Lusignan, although he was geographically isolated from most of the other members since he lived far to the north. When, towards the end of his life, Hugh was engaged, as usual, in conflict with the abbey of St Maixent, he was threatened with excommunication by Pope Paschal II. The pope opened his letter, which must have been written in 1110 or shortly before, by stating that 'We love Hugh of Lusignan especially, because we know him to be a *fidelis beati Petri.*'[174] The title of *fidelis* was not, as used to be thought, abandoned with the preaching of the First Crusade, because William VI of Montpellier was addressed as a *beati Petri miles* as late as 1132,[175] but it is likely that Hugh, who was very old by 1110, had been recognized as a *fidelis* by Pope Gregory VII.

How had he come to be involved? The answer may lie partly with his mother, Almodis of La Marche, who was married in turn to Hugh V of Lusignan, known as 'the Pious', Pons of Toulouse and Raymond Berengar I of Barcelona.[176] She bore Hugh V of Lusignan two sons, of whom Hugh VI was the elder, Pons of Toulouse three sons, of whom Raymond of St Gilles was the second, and a daughter, and Raymond Berengar of Barcelona two sons.[177] A century later she had a reputation for having been a bolter,[178] but in fact it may have been that her husbands found it hard to cope with her personality, which was probably overbearing. She encouraged Raymond Berengar to challenge his grandmother's possession of his

---

[172] J. S. C. Riley-Smith, 'Family Traditions and Participation in the Second Crusade', *The Second Crusade and the Cistercians*, ed. M. Gervers (New York, 1992), 102–3.
[173] Erdmann, *The Origin*, 221–2, 224.   [174] St Maixent Chartes 16.260.
[175] Montpellier 1.37.   [176] St Maixent Chron 132.
[177] St Maixent Chron 132; HGL 3.338, 387–9.   [178] WMGR 2.455–6.

county and was excommunicated by Pope Victor II for this.[179] She was eventually murdered by one of her step-sons.[180]

Hugh V of Lusignan repudiated her on the grounds of consanguinity in the late 1030s. He then seems to have arranged her marriage to Pons of Toulouse[181] and some kind of lasting relationship between the families resulted: it has been suggested that Hugh's revolt against William VIII of Aquitaine in 1060, in which he lost his life, was in support of his ex-wife's son William IV of Toulouse.[182] For her part Almodis did not lose touch with the children of her previous marriages: in 1066–7 she travelled to Toulouse to be present at the wedding of her daughter.[183] Hugh VI of Lusignan's part in the military expedition to Spain in 1087 may have been motivated by knowledge of the danger his Catalan half-brothers were facing in the aftermath of Sagrajas.[184] His relationship to his half-brother Raymond of St Gilles was well-known at the time of the First Crusade.[185]

At any rate Almodis had moved into a network of Occitan families within which the *fideles* were going to be prominent and a feature of her offspring from three husbands is how many of them were committed supporters both of papal reform and the crusade. Hugh of Lusignan and Raymond of St Gilles were *fideles*, and Hugh, Raymond and probably their half-brother Berengar Raymond II of Barcelona took the cross for the First Crusade, as did the husbands of their nieces Philippa of Toulouse and Ermessens of Melgueil.

The interests and intellectual capacity of the *fideles* must have varied widely, but they had what would nowadays be called a think-tank, comprising a brilliant group of scholars – Anselm of Lucca, John of Mantua and Bonizo of Sutri – gathered round the *fidelis* Mathilda of Tuscany, one of the most committed and influential supporters of radical reform,[186] who put an army at the papacy's disposal and attracted such epithets as 'catholic knight'[187] and 'most wise general and most faithful knight of St Peter'.[188] Ideas, perhaps

[179] HGL 3.328.
[180] *Gesta comitum Barcinonensium* 7, 32–3; B. F. Reilly, *The Contest of Christian and Muslim Spain 1031–1159* (Cambridge, Mass. and Oxford, 1992), 119.
[181] St Maixent Chron 132.   [182] Painter, 'The Lords of Lusignan', 33.
[183] HGL 3.351.   [184] See Bull, *Knightly Piety*, 87–8.
[185] FC 438.   [186] See Robinson, *Authority and Resistance*, 100–3.
[187] John of Mantua, 'Tractatus in Cantica Canticorum', 65; and see also 38, 51–2.
[188] Bernold of St Blasien 443.

in simplified forms, must have been seeping down through a network of relationships from the intellectuals to the rest. It is probable, for example, that the Fulcher of Chartres referred to as 'our *fidelis*' in a letter from Pope Gregory VII in September 1074 was Fulcher fitz-Gerard, a canon of Notre-Dame de Chartres and himself the father of sons who were to be leading first crusaders.[189] His eldest son was married to the heiress of the family of the vidames of Chartres and he was therefore probably related by marriage to the Le Puisets, the viscounts of the city. In 1073 Everard II of Breteuil, the head of the Le Puiset family, underwent a particularly intense conversion. He disposed of all his property, giving most of his lands to his kin and his gold and silver to the poor, and went abroad on pilgrimage 'naked and poor', before entering the abbey of Marmoutier.[190] His brothers Hugh I, who succeeded him as viscount and established a priory of Marmoutier at Le Puiset, and Waleran I of Breteuil followed up this dramatic event with gifts to the abbey. In his charter Waleran referred to himself as 'devoted to the lay rôle of Christian knighthood by the grace of faith', a phrase which strikes one as being in line with the ideas of advanced reformers on Christian knights. We do not know why it came to be included in Waleran's charter, but it cannot have been written without his permission and it may be that reform ideas were reaching him through Fulcher.[191]

One subject engaging the attention of the Mathildine scholars, not surprisingly, was the theory of holy war. They concentrated on reviving, anthologizing and developing the ideas of St Augustine of Hippo (354–430), the most authoritative theoretician of Christian violence, who in a long career had evolved an intellectually satisfying theory of positive force and a justification for serving God in arms.[192] They elaborated Augustine's thesis in two ways. First, the Church, and particularly the papacy, was for them an authority which could legitimately summon knights to fight in its defence. John of Mantua maintained, basing his argument on the incident in the Garden of Gethsemane when St Peter had drawn a sword and had cut off the ear of the high priest's servant, that although as a priest Peter had

[189] Greg Reg 133. Fulcher's sons were Bartholomew Boel and Fulcher of Chartres.
[190] Marmoutier (Dunois) 38–40.
[191] Marmoutier (Dunois) 36.
[192] For Anselm of Lucca's *Collectio canonum* (1081–3), see J. Flori, *L'Essor de la Chevalerie XIe–XIIe siècles* (Geneva, 1986), 182–4. See also John of Mantua *passim*; Bonizo of Sutri, 'Liber ad amicum', *passim*.

not been permitted to wield the sword himself, he and his successors
the popes had authority over it, since Christ had told him to put it
back into its scabbard rather than throw it away.[193] Secondly,
Bonizo of Sutri took up the idea of martyrdom in battle, which had
been expounded by the papacy at times from the ninth century,
when two popes had averred that soldiers who died in the right
frame of mind in combat against infidels or pagans would gain
eternal life. One of them had reinforced this by promising absolution
to the dead,[194] a precedent which seems to have persuaded the great
canonist Ivo of Chartres, when composing his canon law collections
shortly before the First Crusade, that death in engagements against
the enemies of the faith could be rewarded.[195] Meanwhile, the title
of martyr had been extended by Pope Leo IX to those who fell
simply in defence of justice, when he referred to the 'martyrdom' of
those who had fallen in the defeat of his forces by the Normans in the
battle of Civitate in 1053.[196]

The Mathildine scholars do not seem to have attached merit to the
act of war itself, as opposed to death in it. With respect to knights
who survived, there is no evidence that they had gone more than a
few steps beyond St Augustine, who had had little sense of merit and
had simply maintained that soldiers engaged in a holy war would
incur no blame, since they were only doing their duty.[197] Striking as
the arguments in their writings were, therefore, they had not
provided more than part of the theoretical foundations crusading was
going to need. A crusade was to be much more than the service to
God in arms envisaged by them, because it was going to be preached
as a penance and this, as the conservative opponent of reform
Sigebert of Gembloux pointed out, was a departure from previous
Christian teaching on violence.[198] It is no exaggeration to say that
the idea of penitential warfare was to be a revolutionary one, because
it put the act of fighting on the same meritorious plane as prayer,

---

[193] John of Mantua 52. See I. S. Robinson, 'Gregory VII and the Soldiers of Christ', *History* 58
      (1973), 185–6.
[194] *Epistolae Karolini Aevi* 3.601; 5.126–7. See J. A. Brundage, *Medieval Canon Law and the Crusader*
      (Madison, 1969), 22–3.
[195] See also Thomas Aquinas, *Quaestiones quodlibetales*, Quodl.2, q.8, a.2; Quodl.5, q.7, a.2
      (pp. 36–8, 106).
[196] Bruno of Segni, 'Vita S. Leonis', 1117–18. See Anonymus Haserensis, 'De Episcopis
      Eichstetensibus', 265; 'Historia mortis et miraculorum S. Leonis IX' 527; also Wibert, 'Vita
      S. Leonis', 500.
[197] J. S. C. Riley-Smith, 'Crusading as an Act of Love', *History* 65 (1980), 187.
[198] Sigebert of Gembloux, 'Leodicensium epistola adversus Paschalem Papam', 464.

works of mercy and fasting, presumably ranking it in merit above many attitudes and actions – generosity, kindness, long-suffering and so forth – which would hardly have been considered satisfactorily penitential by contemporaries. But if the Mathildine scholars were relatively conservative on paper, it is fairly clear that the concept of penitential war did eventually emerge out of a dialogue between them and Pope Gregory and that one of them, Anselm of Lucca, was quick to seize on it once it had been presented to him.

Penitential warfare requires the premise that fighting itself can be meritorious, whatever the fate of the fighter. Even into the twelfth century a spectrum of opinions on this issue ranged from doubts whether sin could be avoided in any act of war to the conviction that altruistic violence could be virtuous.[199] Pope Leo IX had promised absolution of their sins to those rulers who would assist him militarily[200] and before the battle of Civitate he had come before 'all his knights to absolve them of their sins',[201] but these seem to have been in the nature of general absolutions, assurances to soldiers that they would be entering battle, and perhaps meeting their maker, in as good a state as possible; they involved no judgement on the merit or otherwise of the act of violence in which the men were to be engaged. And although in the preliminaries to Civitate the pope apparently took a more radical step when he 'remitted the penance they [his knights] ought to have performed for their sins',[202] it is clear from one account that this remission was not considered by him to be a consequence of taking part in battle, as the crusade remission would be;[203] perhaps he saw it as some kind of dispensation.

It used to be thought that the first evidence of new ideas in papal circles was an indulgence granted by Alexander II in 1063–4 to Christian soldiers going to besiege the Muslim stronghold of Barbastro in Spain. It has recently been shown, however, that there is no reason to suppose that the pope's letter was addressed to fighters at all – it was probably written for pilgrims[204] – and one can conclude that Gregory VII was the first to state categorically that taking part in war of a certain kind could be an act of charity to which merit was attached and to assert in the end that such an action

---

[199] J. Gilchrist, 'The Erdmann Thesis and the Canon Law, 1083–1141', *Crusade and Settlement*, ed. P. W. Edbury (Cardiff, 1985), 37–45.

[200] Aimé of Monte Cassino, *Storia de'Normanni*, 138–9.

[201] Aimé of Monte Cassino 154.   [202] Aimé of Monte Cassino 154.

[203] 'Vita et Obitus S. Leonis Noni Pape' 320.

[204] Bull, *Knightly Piety*, 73–8.

could indeed be penitential; this is certainly what Sigebert of Gembloux thought when he wrote that the idea had been Gregory's own.[205]

Gregory's advice to warriors was generally couched in conventionally pastoral terms,[206] but early in his pontificate he came up with a scheme to lend military assistance to the Byzantine empire. As the plan evolved it became more and more heady. He hoped to lead himself an army of 50,000 men, which after helping the Greeks against the Turks would march on to the Holy Sepulchre. Several of his leading supporters became involved: the Empress Agnes and her brother William VIII of Aquitaine, Mathilda of Tuscany and her mother Beatrice, Amadeus II of Savoy, Raymond of St Gilles, Richard I of Capua, Sancho IV Ramirez of Aragon and William Tête-Hardi of Burgundy. Gregory portrayed his expedition as one in defence of the Christian faith and on behalf of the heavenly king; if it was a beautiful thing to die for one's country, it was still better to die for Christ. He stressed, in terms which created the necessary conditions for meritorious violence and were to be used constantly by crusade apologists, that aid to the Christians in the East – which he compared to laying down one's life for one's brother – was an expression of compassion and love of neighbour. It followed from this, of course, that to take part in the campaign would be an act of merit which would be recompensed, whether one died or not: 'for the work of a moment you can gain heavenly reward'.[207]

The scheme to send a force to Asia Minor was later believed in the Roman curia to have foreshadowed the First Crusade,[208] but it evaporated, overtaken by growing tension between Gregory and those hostile to radical reform. The pope, whose emotions were pushing him into taking more extreme measures, now called on his supporters to use force to resist those who opposed his programme and he repeated that such an act of merit on their part would be rewarded. Although they could 'attain the crown', he does not seem to have considered that only death brought reward. They were engaged, he wrote, 'in defending righteousness for the name of Christ and in order to win eternal recompense in a holy war so

---

[205] Sigebert of Gembloux, 'Leodicensium epistola', 464.
[206] See Greg Reg 190, 276–7, 524.
[207] Greg Reg 70–1, 75–6, 128, 166, 173; Greg Ep Vag 10–12. See also H. E. J. Cowdrey, 'Pope Gregory VII's "Crusading" Plans of 1074', *Outremer*, ed. B. Z. Kedar, H. E. Mayer and R. C. Smail (Jerusalem, 1982), 27–40.
[208] *Liber pontificalis*: 'Vita Urbani II' 2.293. See also *Studia Gratiana* 22 (1978), 699.

pleasing to God'.[209] He called on the faithful to help Christ and the Roman Church, 'your father and mother, if through them you desire absolution of all your sins and blessing and grace in this world and the next'.[210]

He had a close spiritual relationship with Mathilda of Tuscany and there is evidence that ideas were being exchanged between his circle and hers. In 1079 he wrote in threatening terms to a noble called Wezelin, who had rebelled against the romanizing King Demetrius Zwonomir of Dalmatia, that if he did not mend his ways, 'know that we will unsheath the sword of St Peter against your presumption'.[211] This looks like a reference to the right of a pope to authorize the use of force which was to be justified a year or two later by John of Mantua.

It was in the course of this dialogue that the concept of penitential war appeared, leading the opponent of reform Wenrich of Trier to accuse Gregory of 'inciting to bloodshed ... secular men seeking release from their sins'.[212] Sigebert of Gembloux was later to write that Gregory had first put forward the idea that warfare could be penitential when he 'had ordered the Marchioness Mathilda to fight the Emperor Henry for the remission of her sins'.[213] The phrase *remissio peccatorum*, echoing the Nicene Creed's definition of baptism, could hardly have had a more potent sound to it. Gregory's reasoning is revealed in a life of Anselm of Lucca, in which one of Anselm's priests described how he transmitted a blessing from Anselm to Mathilda's army in 1085.

We were to impose on the soldiers the danger of the coming battle for the remission of all their sins.[214]

Anselm had obviously been persuaded of the validity of penitential war and was justifying it with the argument that the act of fighting in a just cause was a penance because it was dangerous.

This created a new category of warfare. For a time crusading was to be only one manifestation of it, although the most important: a Pisan attack on Mahdia in North Africa in 1087 was believed to be an engagement 'for the remission of sins';[215] and in the euphoria that

---

[209] Greg Ep Vag 54. [210] Greg Ep Vag 134.
[211] Greg Reg 463–4. See also Erdmann, *The Origin*, 203–4.
[212] Wenrich of Trier, 'Epistola sub Theoderici episcopi Virdunensis nomine composita', 296.
[213] Sigebert of Gembloux, 'Leodicensium epistola', 464.
[214] Bardo, 'Vita Anselmi episcopi Lucensis', 20.
[215] Monte Cassino 453. For further details, see H. E. J. Cowdrey, 'The Mahdia Campaign of 1087', *English Historical Review* 92 (1977), 1–29.

followed the liberation of Jerusalem Pope Paschal II appealed to
Robert of Flanders, who had just got back home, to fight another
penitential war against the opponents of reform.[216] In the decade
before the First Crusade the concept must have been permeating
through the networks of *fideles* and other supporters of the reform
papacy, spreading through their families and also from sympathetic
monastic communities into the countryside around. But like so much
of the radical thought bubbling up during the Investiture Contest, it
would have been hard to defend on theological grounds. It would
never have been easy to justify the inflicting of pain and loss of life,
with the consequential distortion of the perpetrator's internal dispositions, as a penance simply because the penitent was exposing himself
to danger, however unpleasant the experience might have been for
him. It was to be Pope Urban II's achievement to give the idea a
context in which it could be presented more convincingly, because
he associated it with the most charismatic of all traditional penances,
the pilgrimage to Jerusalem.

[216] See N. J. Housley, 'Crusades against Christians: Their Origins and Early Development,
    *c.*1000–1216', *Crusade and Settlement*, ed. P. W. Edbury (Cardiff, 1985), 20.

CHAPTER 3

Preaching and the crusaders

During a dry hot summer, which must have been that of 1095, the last of several years of drought, 'the fiery heat of the sun was burning up the land of Aulnay and all that was in it, castles, villages, houses, cornfields and vineyards, and meadows and all green places, and men could not find rest anywhere from the sun's excessive heat'. The viscount, Chalo VII, and his subjects sought divine intervention by processing barefoot to the abbey of St Jean d'Angély, carrying a feretory (a portable reliquary) in which were the bones of St Just. On the way they stopped at the chapel of the priory of St Julien, a dependency of the nunnery of Notre-Dame de Saintes, and placed the feretory on the altar. After spending some time in prayer they wanted to set off again, but they were astonished to find the feretory so firmly attached to the altar that it could not be lifted and it remained unmovable even after they had been reduced to scourging themselves in penance for their sins. At this point the prioress and her chaplain complained that Chalo had been oppressing St Julien's tenants – there had obviously been some dispute about their obligations to him – and they predicted that the feretory would remain fixed until he renounced his pretensions. Chalo and his leading subjects caved in at once and agreed to abandon all the rights he had claimed from St Julien's tenants, whereupon 'we lifted the feretory, which had become so light that we could scarcely feel its weight, and we proceeded to St Jean with the greatest joy'. Some time later Chalo volunteered to join the First Crusade and solemnly confirmed his renunciation of rights before the altar of Notre-Dame de Saintes.[1]

A historian has drawn attention to the part played by the prioress in this episode as an example of the self-confidence and standing of

---

[1] Notre-Dame de Saintes 139–40.

the heads of female religious houses at the time.[2] As to what actually happened at St Julien on that hot summer's day, one should never discount the paranormal effects of auto-suggestion, induced by exhaustion, the solemnity of the procession in the heat and the repetition of mantras, on pilgrims who had been conditioned to expect physical manifestations in this world of divine pleasure or displeasure. But why was Chalo moved to become a crusader? What was the link between a local act of peaceful devotion and his decision to pilgrimage abroad to war? It must be significant that between the traumatic events at St Julien and Chalo's taking of the cross there had occurred Pope Urban's cavalcade through the region.[3]

The pope had entered Provence, far to the south-east, in the late summer of 1095, visiting Valence and Romans before proceeding to Le Puy and La Chaise-Dieu. He had then turned south by way of Chirac and Millau to Nîmes, St Gilles and Tarascon, before travelling up the Rhône valley through Avignon to Lyons. He was at Mâcon on 17 October, at Cluny from the 18th to the 25th and at Autun at the end of the month. He reached Clermont on 14 November and stayed there until 2 December. The council he had summoned sat from 18 to 28 November; on the 27th he preached his famous sermon proclaiming the crusade.

It has often been said that at the front of his mind during his year-long journey through France was the reform of the French Church. He certainly spent a significant amount of time grappling with local and national ecclesiastical issues, but it is possible that he had been considering calling for military assistance for the Byzantine empire since 1089 and a charter-writer in Le Mans stated explicitly that he had 'come to these parts to preach the journey to Jerusalem',[4] which suggests that it was thought in some quarters that the crusade had priority. No man was better qualified than he for the task he had set himself. He was French, from a family of knights in Champagne. He had been educated at, and had been a canon and archdeacon of, Rheims, before entering Cluny, the most prestigious abbey of the time, where he had reached the office of prior, second-in-command to the abbot, and had been exposed to a pastoral approach which encouraged lay men and women to seek salvation through serving

---

[2] P. D. Johnson, *Equal in Monastic Profession: Religious Women in Medieval France* (Chicago, 1991), 237–9.

[3] For the details of Urban's journey, see A. Becker, *Papst Urban II* (Stuttgart, 1964–88), 2.435–57.

[4] St Pierre-de-la-Cour du Mans 4.15.

the Church in the world. He had then been called to the Roman curia, where he had been a cardinal and diplomatist involved in the whirlwind politics of reform and where he must have come across recent developments in the theology of violence. He could have had little notion how great the response to his summons would be: even after the council of Clermont, in December 1095, he was calling upon the Flemings to join the rest of the crusade at Le Puy, which suggests that he was expecting a relatively small army to gather there.[5] But the outline of his plans must have been reasonably well thought-out before he reached French-speaking territory, because the essential elements in his message – the idea of a war on Christ's behalf as a penitential devotion with Jerusalem as its goal, the introduction of a vow to be made and a cross to be worn by the knights taking part, some explanation of the secular benefits they would enjoy and a preliminary choice of leaders for the expedition – emerge as a package.

Waves of rumour must have been sweeping ahead of his progress, generating interest in advance of his arrival at Clermont. The summoning of an expedition to march to the East had been aired at a council he had chaired at Piacenza in the spring, to which a Byzantine embassy had come to ask for help. Soon after he had entered French territory he must have discussed the matter with Adhémar of Monteil, the bishop of Le Puy who was to be his representative on the crusade, with Raymond of St Gilles, the count of Toulouse, whom he already wanted to be leader, and with Bishop Gerald of Cahors, who was probably involved early in the planning.[6] It is most unlikely that these meetings were confidential and it could be that a tradition in Burgundy that 'the first vows to go on the Jerusalem journey' were made at a council of thirty-six bishops which had met at Autun earlier in the year was well founded.[7]

At the very least there must have been a lot of talk in advance of the formal proclamation of war. The chronicler Albert of Aachen, the author (or adapter) of the *Chanson d'Antioche*, and the Byzantine princess Anna Comnena believed that the wandering evangelist Peter the Hermit was already proposing something similar to the crusade before November 1095 and had put the idea into the pope's

---

[5] Kb 137.
[6] WMGR 2.456–7. See Becker, *Papst Urban*, 1.20; R. Somerville, 'The Council of Clermont (1095) and Latin Christian Society', *Archivum Historiae Pontificiae* 12 (1974), 69 note 76.
[7] 'Annales Besuenses' 250; 'Annales S. Benigni Divionensis' 43.

head. Peter must have been preaching some kind of religious expedition to Jerusalem before the council of Clermont, because, engaged as he was in frenzied activity, he would hardly have had the time to muster the force which was already on the march under his leadership by the spring of 1096 if he had only begun to recruit followers in December 1095.[8] But I have come across no mention of him in the charters of departing crusaders, whereas references to Urban's initiative are regularly to be found. A charter-writer for Robert of Flanders stated that in taking the cross Robert had been 'responding to a divine command published by the authority of the apostolic see' and in 1098 Gerald of Cahors referred to the fact that Raymond of St Gilles had gone on crusade 'at the orders of and in obedience to Urban, the Roman pontiff, and many archbishops and other bishops'.[9] Robert and Raymond were to be among the leaders of the army in Syria, who addressed the pope in September 1098 as the 'begetter of the holy journey' – 'you who originated this journey and by your speeches made us all leave our lands and whatever was in them' – and asked him to 'fulfil what you have encouraged us to do', and to complete 'the journey of Jesus Christ begun by us and preached by you' and 'the war which is your own'.[10] Peter the Hermit seems to have been a congenital boaster and the story of his pilgrimage to Jerusalem, the appeal made to him by the Greek patriarch, the vision he experienced of Christ and the interview he had with the pope in Italy at which he persuaded Urban to summon men to Jerusalem's aid seems to have originated in Lorraine, not far from the abbey of Neumoustier where he lived out his last years; he became known there as the crusade's 'preacher and originator'.[11]

After leaving Clermont Urban crossed France by way of Sauxillanges, Brioude, St Flour, Aurillac and Uzerche to Limoges, where he spent Christmas. He took the road again at the end of the first week of January 1096 and reached Angers on 6 February. After a stay of a week he travelled north through Sablé to Le Mans and Vendôme, where he was on the 26th. He then reversed direction,

---

[8] AA 272–4; Ch d'A 1.30–5; Anna Comnena, *Alexiade*, 2.207; E. O. Blake and C. Morris, 'A Hermit Goes to War: Peter and the Origins of the First Crusade', *Studies in Church History* 22 (1984), 79–107; J. Flori, 'Faut-il réhabiliter Pierre l'Ermite?', *Cahiers de civilisation medievale* 38 (1995), 35–54.

[9] Flanders 63; HGL 5.753. For other references to papal authority, see Marmoutier (Dunois) 80; St Aubin d'Angers Cart 1.407; St Vincent du Mans 190.

[10] Kb 164.

[11] Neumoustier 815; Giles of Orval, 'Gesta episcoporum Leodiensium', 93.

reaching Tours on 3 March. He remained there for three weeks, before journeying by way of Poitiers, St Maixent, St Jean d'Angély and Saintes, Chalo of Aulnay's local centre, to Bordeaux. In May he continued by way of Nérac and Moissac, and he spent late May and early June in Toulouse, before proceeding through Carcassonne, Maguelonne and Montpellier to Nîmes. He returned to Italy in early September by way of Avignon, Arles, Apt, Forcalquier and Gap. He was about sixty years old and the journey must have been exhausting for him,[12] but for the residents of country towns, who had never in living memory seen a king, let alone anyone of such international importance, the excitement of his progress must have been intense.

He had brought an impressive entourage with him from Italy, including several of the senior officials of his curia. He entered Limoges on 23 December 1095 with a following that included two cardinals, the archbishop of Pisa who was to be sent out to the East as papal legate and was to become the first canonical Latin patriarch of Jerusalem, and a flock of French prelates: the archbishops of Lyons, Bourges and Bordeaux, and the bishops of Poitiers, Périgueux, Saintes and Rodez, together, of course, with the bishop of Limoges himself.[13] If one allows for the riding households accompanying these personages, the pope's train must have been enormous.

That would have been dramatic enough, but the theatricality displayed by Urban wherever he went must have heightened the sense of occasion. This was not self-indulgence on his part; he was deliberately playing to the taste of his audiences. He wrote later that he had been 'stimulating the minds of knights to go on this expedition'[14] and no one knew better than him, since he insisted on crusaders making a vow which, like all vows, had in Church law to be voluntarily entered into, that the success of his summons depended on the spontaneous response to it of individuals from the armsbearing classes. Coming, like most of the bishops and abbots who accompanied him, from their milieu he often focused his message directly on the French-speaking magnates, castellans and knights, wrapping it up in compliments; in the Limousin, for example, he referred to them as 'disciplined in arms and war'.[15] As well as the set-piece occasions he must have been targeting certain

---

[12] Becker, *Papst Urban*, 1.31.
[13] 'Notitiae duae Lemovicenses de praedicatione crucis in Aquitania' 352–3.
[14] 'Papsturkunden in Florenz' 313.   [15] 'Notitiae duae Lemovicenses' 352.

nobles face to face; one would dearly like to know what he said to them.

Everywhere he went he dedicated cathedrals, churches and altars, giving his imprimatur in the most solemn way to a massive building programme which had been undertaken in recent years by the French Church.[16] He presided over councils at Clermont (November 1095), Tours (March 1096) and Nîmes (July 1096), at which his already impressive following was greatly augmented. He preached his first public sermon on the crusade in the open air, in a field outside the town of Clermont. This, it should be remembered, was at the onset of winter. Although it was risky to attempt anything like this so late in the year, the occasion seems to have been carefully stage-managed, from Adhémar of Monteil's melodramatic response to Urban's sermon – he came forward at once to take the cross – to the acclamations of at least some of the crowd, which must have been rehearsed. Urban seems to have instructed bishops to bring with them to the council the leading nobles in their dioceses, but not many important laymen had turned up and the theatre must have fallen a little flat.[17] He also preached in the open air at Tours on the banks of the Loire; that was in March.[18] He made a detour to celebrate the feast of the Assumption at the great Marian shrine of Le Puy and he kept the feasts of St Giles and St Hilary at their respective cult-centres, St Gilles and Poitiers.[19] At Limoges he celebrated two Christmas Masses, at the abbeys of Notre-Dame de la Règle and St Martial. He was 'triumphantly crowned', presumably with his tiara, at this time a conical white cap with one circlet of gold and gems around the base,[20] and he processed, wearing his tiara, to the cathedral of St Stephen, where he presided over the rest of the day's office. He dedicated the cathedral church on 29 December and on the following day the basilica of St Martial; he celebrated Mass there and then preached the cross.[21] Geoffrey, the founder of the

---

[16] R. Crozet, 'Le voyage d'Urbain II en France (1095–6) et son importance au point de vue archéologique', *Annales du Midi* 49 (1937), 42–69.

[17] Lambert of Arras, 'De primatu sedis Atrebatensis', 645; Somerville, 'The Council of Clermont (1095) and Latin Christian Society', 57–8, 78–9.

[18] Becker, *Papst Urban*, 2.446.

[19] Becker, *Papst Urban*, 2.436–7, 444.

[20] F. Cabrol, H. Leclercq *et al.*, *Dictionnaire d'archéologie chrétienne et de liturgie* 15,2 (Paris, 1953), 2294.

[21] 'Notitiae duae Lemovicenses' 350–3; Geoffrey of Le Chalard, 'Dictamen de primordiis ecclesiae Castaliensis', 348.

priory of Le Chalard, who himself wanted to crusade but was prevented from going by his community, wrote:

At Limoges we saw [the pope] with our own eyes and we were in the crowds of the faithful at his consecrations ... In a good sermon he encouraged the people standing there to take the road to Jerusalem. Thanks be to you, Oh Christ; for you watered the swelling corn which grew from the seed sown by him, not only in our region, but also throughout the world.[22]

On the pope's arrival at Angers we catch a glimpse of his progress through the eyes of one of the nobles, Count Fulk IV of Anjou.

At the approach of Lent the Roman pope Urban came to Angers and encouraged our people to go to Jerusalem to drive out the heathen, who had occupied that city and all Christian territory as far as Constantinople. Then on Septuagesima Sunday [10 February 1096] the church of St Nicolas was dedicated by the pope and the body of my uncle Geoffrey was translated into the same church ... Then he left and went to Le Mans and from thence to Tours. There ... in the middle of Lent he was crowned and was led in solemn procession from the church of St Maurice to the church of St Martin, where he gave me the golden flower he carried in his hand. In loving memory of this I have ordered the flower to be borne on Palm Sunday by me and by my successors.

Fulk did not join the crusade himself, but the events he thought worth recording are significant: the preaching of the cross at Angers; the dedication of the abbey church of St Nicolas d'Angers, a monastery founded by his family, and the transference into the body of the church of the corpse of his uncle, who had ended his days as a member of the community; Urban in procession at Tours, wearing his tiara, and his gift to Fulk of the golden rose publicly carried by popes on the Fourth Sunday in Lent.[23] This is an early example of the practice by twelfth-century popes of presenting the rose to those they wished to honour. The marks of favour to the count are usually explained as Urban's reaction to a scandal that was sweeping France at the time, for the king had made off with the count's wife. But were they unique? This is the only eyewitness account dictated by a magnate; we cannot tell whether Urban made equally extravagant gestures to nobles who, unlike Fulk, actually took the cross, such as Raymond of St Gilles, Helias of La Flèche, or Hugh the Great of Vermandois, the last of

---

[22] Geoffrey of Le Chalard 348. See G. Tenant de la Tour, *L'Homme et la Terre de Charlemagne à Saint Louis* (Paris, 1943), 357–60.

[23] Fulk IV of Anjou, 'Gesta Andegavensium peregrinorum', 345–6.

whom was to be carrying a *vexillum sancti Petri* – a banner given him by
the pope – when he entered the Byzantine empire.[24]

The purpose of the theatre was, of course, to focus minds on Urban's
message. A lot of effort has gone into trying to establish what his
thoughts and words were, but the evidence which survives is not
much to go on. We have six of his letters which refer to the
expedition,[25] three purportedly verbatim accounts by eyewitnesses of
his proclamation of war at Clermont[26] – although all were written
several years later, after the crusade had triumphed, and they differ
in significant ways – and one passing reference to it by another
eyewitness,[27] some brief reports of other sermons delivered in
France,[28] and the texts of two crusade decrees of the council of
Clermont and the description of another.[29] The unsatisfactory
nature of the material has given rise to endless debate, but no one
has ventured to analyse the perceptions of Urban's audience,
although the crusade was a product as much of the reactions of the
men and women who were inspired to join it as of the pope's
intentions. In one striking respect his message was distorted by some
of them when they embarked on their savage vendetta against the
western Jewish communities.[30] But an examination of their charters,
the most revealing evidence for their feelings, leads one to the
conclusion that this was not a typical reaction. While on the whole
they did not run away with Urban's message down paths of their
own choosing – if anything they were more conventional than he was
– they did take from it those elements that matched their preconcep-
tions and aspirations.

The aim of the crusade was described in one of the surviving
decrees of the council of Clermont as 'the liberation of the Church of
God [in Jerusalem]'.[31] Urban referred to it in a letter sent to
Flanders a month later as 'the liberation of the eastern churches'[32]
and in another, written to the abbey of Vallombrosa, as 'the

[24] Anna Comnena 2.213–14.
[25] Kb 136-8; 'Papsturkunden in Florenz' 313–14; *Papsturkunden in Spanien 1. Katalonien* 2.287–8;
    Urban II, 'Epistolae et Privilegia', 504; *HGL* 5.744–6.
[26] FC 132–8; RR 727–30; BB 12–16.
[27] Geoffrey of Vendôme, 'Epistolae', 162.
[28] See H. E. J. Cowdrey, 'Pope Urban II's Preaching of the First Crusade', *History* 55 (1970), 181.
[29] *Decreta Claromontensia* 74, 150; HP 169–70; HGL 5.748. See R. Somerville, 'The Council of
    Clermont and the First Crusade', *Studia Gratiana* 20 (1976), 325–37.
[30] See Riley-Smith, *The First Crusade*, 52–7.
[31] *Decreta Claromontensia* 74.   [32] Kb 136.

liberation of Christianity'.[33] In the letter to Flanders he justified his summons to war as a response to Muslim aggression.

The barbarians in their frenzy have invaded and ravaged the churches of God in the eastern regions. Worse still, they have seized the Holy City of Christ, embellished by his passion and resurrection, and – it is blasphemy to say it – they have sold her and her churches into abominable slavery.[34]

He explained to the monks of Vallombrosa that he had been summoning knights 'to restrain by their arms the Muslims' savagery and restore the Christians to their former freedom'[35] and he informed some nobles in Catalonia that the crusaders had decided 'with one mind to go to the aid of the Asian Church and to liberate their brothers from the tyranny of the Muslims'.[36]

He was calling, therefore, on men to vow to fight on Christ's behalf a war of liberation from Muslim tyranny, which related to people – the 'Church of God', 'the eastern churches', 'Christianity', 'their brothers' – as much as to a place: the Holy Sepulchre in Jerusalem.[37] It was suggested sixty years ago, and it is still argued by some, that a distinction in his letters between the eastern churches in general and Jerusalem in particular reveals a contradiction between his immediate intention, which was to lend assistance to the Byzantine empire, and his use of the goal of Jerusalem as a weapon of propaganda; a march to Jerusalem would necessarily involve assisting the 'eastern churches' of Constantinople and perhaps Antioch.[38] But no mention is made anywhere in the crusaders' charters of helping Constantinople, whereas references to Jerusalem are to be found everywhere. This is not surprising when one considers that the Byzantine emperor Alexius may have been floating the idea of the liberation of Jerusalem himself in letters written to western nobles in advance of the pope's journey through France.[39] Although it is possible that Urban's audience simply took him literally, so that even while he was still engaged in preaching in France the desire to liberate Jerusalem had taken centre stage, it is more likely that the charters reflect the fact that the goal of Jerusalem was a reality. Some of them, indeed, are so resonant with expressions which we know for certain the pope used or approved that the composers must have had before them something of his in writing. Robert of Flanders was

---

[33] 'Papsturkunden in Florenz' 313. [34] Kb 136.
[35] 'Papsturkunden in Florenz' 313. [36] *Papsturkunden in. . .Katalonien* 2.287.
[37] Riley-Smith, *The First Crusade*, 18. [38] Erdmann, *The Origin*, 355–71.
[39] Gislebert of Mons, *Chronicon Hanoniense*, 40.

'going to Jerusalem to liberate the Church of God' – here almost the same words are used as in the Clermont decree – 'which has been trodden under foot by barbaric nations for a long time'.[40] Bishop Gerald of Cahors in Languedoc reported that Raymond of St Gilles had gone 'on pilgrimage to wage war on foreign peoples and defeat barbaric nations, lest the Holy City of Jerusalem be held captive and the Holy Sepulchre of the Lord Jesus be contaminated any longer'.[41] A charter written for the castellan Nivelo of Fréteval in Touraine made reference to 'Jerusalem which has been hitherto enslaved with her children'.[42]

Other aspects of the pope's message were echoed, or are clarified for us, in the responses to it. Although the belief expressed by the bishop of Cahors that Muslim rule had contaminated the Holy Sepulchre is not to be found in any surviving letter from Urban, it is included in the accounts of his sermon at Clermont written by the eyewitnesses Robert of Rheims and Baldric of Bourgueil.[43] That they must have been remembering something that was actually said is confirmed by another charter reference to it. The Gascon lord Amanieu of Loubens was reported feeling inspired to 'fight and kill those opposed to the Christian religion, nay rather to cleanse the place in which the Lord Jesus Christ deigned to undergo death for the restoration of the human race'.[44] Introducing the cross as a distinctive symbol of the vow of commitment, Urban was reported by those who had heard him at Clermont associating the taking and wearing of it in a highly charged way with Christ's precept, 'If any man will come after me, let him deny himself and take up his cross and follow me' (Matthew 16:24 or Luke 14:27).[45] The assertion by the crusade leaders in Syria, when writing to him in 1098, that 'you ordered us to follow Christ carrying our crosses',[46] is evidence that he had spoken in this way and I have found three charter references to the imagery of bearing the cross, two in endowments made by the crusaders Wolfker of Kuffern and Henry II of Regensburg to the community of Göttweig in Upper Austria.[47] Presumably someone from the region had been to Clermont and had been particularly struck by the pope's words: one eyewitness reported the presence of

---

[40] Flanders 63. See also his wife Clemency's charter. Kb 142.   [41] HGL 5.753.
[42] St Père de Chartres 2.428.   [43] RR 727–8; BB 13.
[44] St Pierre de la Réole 140.   [45] RR 730; BB 16.   [46] Kb 164.
[47] Göttweig 194, 197. In 1118 Count Fulk V of Anjou applied this scriptural reference to the pilgrimages in the early eleventh century of Count Fulk III. Toussaint d'Angers 147.

German bishops at the council.[48] The third reference is in a charter issued by Bishop Peter of Limoges, who in 1101 was managing the diocese of Périgueux in the absence of its bishop, Rainald of Thiviers. He described Rainald as 'carrying Christ's cross to Jerusalem'.[49] Peter had only recently succeeded to his bishopric, but Rainald of Thiviers had been at Clermont[50] and, as we have seen, Urban had preached in Limoges during Christmastide 1095.

The emphasis given in the accounts of the pope's sermon at Clermont to his conviction that he was speaking on God's behalf is also reflected in the documents. The Burgundian castellan Achard of Montmerle believed he was going to fight for God;[51] so did Godfrey of Bouillon and his brother Baldwin of Boulogne, who, according to a charter issued for their mother, were 'preparing to fight for God in Jerusalem'.[52] Crusaders in their letters written on campaign referred to themselves as 'fighting for Christ'[53] and to the crusade as 'the army of God', 'the army of the Lord', and 'the army of Christ'.[54] Urban had written that those who took the cross were inspired by God[55] and this idea certainly struck home. Robert of Flanders's heart was 'inflamed with the grace of the holy spirit',[56] and he and Baldwin of Mons were inspired by divine grace.[57] Eudes of Burgundy was 'fired with divine zeal and love of Christianity' and 'inspired by divine clemency'.[58]

The pope also stressed the old notion of the knight serving God in arms,[59] although it took second place in his message to the idea of the knight as a penitent. The Provençal lord Guy of Roumoulès 'desired to go to the Lord's Sepulchre in the service of Our Lord Jesus Christ'[60] and the north French castellan Anselm II of Ribemont wrote from Syria of 'those who sweat here in the service of God'.[61] According to the crusader Raymond of Aguilers, Raymond of St Gilles refused to pay homage to the Byzantine emperor in Constantinople, saying that 'he had not come to make another man his lord or to fight for another save him on whose account he had left his

[48] RR 727. See the lists of bishops in Somerville, 'The Council of Clermont (1095) and Latin Christian Society', 62–82.

[49] Limoges 18.

[50] Somerville, 'The Council of Clermont (1095) and Latin Christian Society', 72.

[51] Cluny 5.51.   [52] 'Document inédit pour servir à l'histoire des croisades' 99.

[53] Kb 162.   [54] Kb 138, 139, 144, 149, 150, 157, 160.   [55] Kb 137.

[56] Kb 142.   [57] Robert: Flanders 66. Baldwin: St Lambert de Liège 1.47.

[58] Molesme 2.18; St Bénigne de Dijon 2.174. For other examples, see Afflighem 19; Forez 1.1; St Mihiel 191.

[59] FC 136–7; BB 14–15.   [60] Lérins 289.   [61] Kb 144.

country and its goods'.[62] In the long run, as chivalry began to permeate crusading, the concept of service for Christ was to threaten to outweigh that of personal penitence. A second theme in later crusading thought, fighting for the name of Christ, was expressed by a charter-writer for Robert of Flanders when he claimed that the crusade might be a means 'by which the holy honour of God's name may be spread'.[63] Shortly after Robert's return the bishop of Tournai referred to the way he had 'fought faithfully and manfully against the pagans to the praise and glory of Christ's name'.[64] Perhaps this was another echo of an element in Urban's original message, because Robert and the other leaders wrote to him from Syria that 'you impressed upon us the need to exalt the Christian name'.[65]

The pope was reported drawing attention at Clermont to the exploits of the Franks under their Carolingian rulers.[66] One might assume that this would have been a natural thing for him to do, since he was a Frank himself. If educated clergy could be struck by the fact that this was an appeal to the Franks like those made by the popes in the days of the Carolingians[67] – it would, in fact, have been the first since then and Urban's solemn crown-wearing in procession through the streets carried echoes of the forged historical document, the *Donation of Constantine*, with its implications of papal imperium, which had justified the conquests of the eighth-century Franks in Italy – then surely the symbolism would not have been lost on the armsbearers, brought up on legends of Carolingian greatness, whom the pope was summoning to reconquer lands that had once belonged to the Roman empire.[68] But it is unlikely that Urban would have dwelt consistently on this theme, at any rate when recruiting in Provence, Upper Burgundy and Languedoc, regions peopled not by 'Franks' but by 'Burgundians' and 'Goths' or Aquitanians, who would not have taken kindly to it,[69] and although the idea of the Franks as a chosen people, expressed in the theme *Gesta Dei per Francos*, was to be dominant in the narrative accounts of the crusade, I have seen no charter written on behalf of a first crusader containing the word 'Frank'. In fact it was very rarely used in the crusaders' own correspondence: once by Stephen of Blois and once by Anselm of

---

[62] RA 41.   [63] Flanders 63.   [64] Afflighem 19.   [65] Kb 164.
[66] RR 728.   [67] See GN Gesta 135–6.
[68] See Ibn al-Athir 1.193; also GF 66; PT 108; Kb 160.
[69] For tension between the different peoples on the First Crusade, see Riley-Smith, *The First Crusade*, 86.

Ribemont.[70] In his letter to Flanders the pope had written simply that 'we visited the Gauls [the whole of Roman Gaul which had encompassed much more than did Francia] and urged most fervently the lords and subjects of that land . . .'[71] An echo of this is to be found in a charter from Auvergne in which reference was made to the response of the people of the Gauls,[72] but most, even those written in Frankish regions, alluded to recruitment among Christians or Christianity in general. When writers wanted to be more specific they used the term 'westerners',[73] although one also mentioned 'northerners'.[74] Some, indeed, were keen to demonstrate how universal the reaction to the pope's appeal had been. A charter writer from Angers referred to the time 'when Pope Urban first incited all the world to go to Jerusalem'; and in Auvergne Peter and Pons II of Fay wished 'to journey to Jerusalem, just as was being done by all Christian people'.[75]

The earliest reference to the crusade as an army of the Franks was made not by a westerner but by the Emperor Alexius once it had struck out into Asia Minor on its own, although he may well have been repeating a phrase in a letter written to him by the abbot of Monte Cassino.[76] As we have seen, the crusaders had probably set out believing that they would be joining a Byzantine army in Constantinople and would be serving under the command of Alexius himself. It was only after they had discovered that they would have to operate on their own and as the greatness of their achievement began to dawn on them that the uniqueness of a 'Frankish' contribution became worth stressing, at least by those of them who were Franks themselves. The Frankishness of the enterprise, in other words, should be added to the list of ideas which grew out of their experiences on the march.[77]

So far we have seen the charters confirming or amplifying Urban's rhetoric. But their language sometimes differs from that found in the pope's letters or in the eyewitness reports of his sermons. For example, Urban assured his audiences that the enterprise would be a demonstration of Christian charity, because the

[70] Kb 150, 160.
[71] Kb 136. [72] Sauxillanges 884.
[73] Le Ronceray d'Angers 93; St Julien de Tours 72; Afflighem 13.
[74] St Julien de Tours 72. See also Kb 141.
[75] St Aubin d'Angers Cart 1.407; HGL 5.751. See also Cluny 5.51; St Père de Chartres 2.628; Cormery 104.
[76] Kb 153.
[77] For other ideas developing during the crusade, see Riley-Smith, *The First Crusade*, 91–119.

crusaders were going to risk their lives out of love of God and their neighbour.[78] The notion of charity was in theological terms an essential prerequisite for any justification of penitential violence, because fighting could then be treated as an act of mercy. But although recruits expressed their love of God – Amanieu of Loubens had been 'incited by love of' and Gerald of Landerron 'fired by the ardour of' the holy spirit,[79] and Peter Jordan of Châtillon had been 'fired with love of Christ'[80] – I have found no direct reference in the charters to the crusade as an exercise of fraternal love. This idea, so important to the theoreticians, cannot have had any appeal for the armsbearers, whose interest was in the seizure of a place, the tomb of Christ; in this respect they were treating the venture as a kind of *furtum sacrum*, the sanctified theft of a relic which, in the words of a Monte Cassino chronicler, they had set out to 'snatch'.[81]

It is obviously important to discover how they understood the central element in Urban's message, his preaching of a type of the penitential war first proposed by Pope Gregory VII. When in 1089 Urban had tried to persuade Catalans to contribute to the 'restoration' of the church of Tarragona in no-man's land between Christian and Moorish Spain – essentially its occupation, settlement and defence against the Moors – he had described this as a penitential activity for the remission of sins and, wanting to persuade those who intended to pilgrimage to Jerusalem to redirect in Tarragona's direction their energies and the cash they would have spent, he had promised them the same reward they would have gained by visiting the Holy Sepulchre. In other words, he had treated an act of war for the remission of sins as equal in merit to a pilgrimage to Jerusalem.[82] He followed this in 1095 by taking the logical step of associating the physical liberation of the Sepulchre directly with pilgrimages to it. This had a theoretical advantage over Gregory's formulation, which seems to have been justified merely by the danger involved, because violence was now associated with an act which was indubitably penitential and the council of Clermont was careful to attach the penance involved to the pilgrimage itself,[83] as was the abbot of

---

[78] Kb 137; *Papsturkunden in . . . Katalonien* 2.287–8. See 'Notitiae duae Lemovicenses' 352.
[79] St Pierre de la Réole 140, 141.   [80] Cormery 104.
[81] Monte Cassino 475. For *furta sacra*, see P. J. Geary, *Furta Sacra: Thefts of Relics in the Central Middle Ages* (Princeton, 1978), *passim*.
[82] Urban II 303.   [83] *Decreta Claromontensia* 74.

Lérins six months later when he enjoined the Jerusalem journey on Fulk Doon of Châteaurenard.[84] The danger and physical hardships of the coming expedition still had significance of course, but they no longer provided the main justification for treating war as a penance; instead they gave added value to a penance which was primarily justified through its association with pilgrimage.[85]

At any rate, while on the one hand the pope used of the coming crusade the language of pilgrimage – *iter, via, labor*[86] – on the other he employed the military term 'Jerusalem expedition' (*Jherosolimitana expeditio*).[87] The pilgrim terms *peregrinatio, via, iter, iter beatum, iter Domini* and *sanctum iter*[88] were used in letters written on the march and in these the crusaders occasionally referred to themselves as 'pilgrims', but they also wrote of the 'army' (*exercitus*) in which they were serving. A similar marriage of pilgrimage and military terminology is to be found in the charters. In one written for Achard of Montmerle the crusade was not only referred to as 'the Jerusalem pilgrimage', but also as 'such a ... great ... expedition (*expeditio*) of the Christian people contending to go to Jerusalem to fight for God against the pagans and the Muslims'.[89] Another Burgundian charter, issued for two men called Bernard and Eudes, repeated that the crusade was both a pilgrimage (*peregrinatio*) and an expedition (*expeditio*);[90] and twenty years later one written in Anjou on behalf of Geoffrey Fulcard of Loudun showed how interchangeable these words had become in this context by referring to the crusade of 1120 as a 'pilgrimage or expedition (*peregrinationem sive expeditionem*)'.[91]

Other charters written at the time of the First Crusade reveal how Urban's audience understood and responded to the concept of a war-pilgrimage. Aimery Brun in the Limousin both wanted 'to go with the Christian people to fight against the Muslims and wished to visit the Sepulchre of the Lord which is in Jerusalem'.[92] In Provence the brothers Guy and Geoffrey of Signes took the cross 'on the one hand for the grace of the pilgrimage and on the other, under the protection of God, to wipe out the defilement of the pagans and the

[84] Lérins 312.   [85] See OV 5.16–18.
[86] Kb 136, 138; 'Papsturkunden in Florenz' 313.
[87] HGL 5.745; 'Papsturkunden in Florenz' 313. Urban also used the word *expeditio* of the plans in Catalonia to reoccupy and hold Tarragona. *Papsturkunden in Spanien* 2.287.
[88] Kb 138, 139, 150, 160, 165, 177.   [89] Cluny 5.51–2.
[90] Cluny 5.59. For other references to *expeditio*, see Aureil 161; Cluny 5.59; St Chaffre du Monastier 89, 140; St Vincent de Mâcon 315.
[91] Le Ronceray d'Angers 186; for the date, see 354.
[92] St Martial de Limoges 347.

immoderate madness through which innumerable Christians have already been oppressed, made captive and killed with barbaric fury'.[93] 'The grace of the pilgrimage' was, of course, the merit gained through the performance of penances. The Council of Clermont had decreed that whoever joined the crusade 'for devotion alone, not to gain honour or money ... can substitute this journey for all penance'.[94] Urban himself promised the crusaders that

if any men among you go there not because they desire earthly profit but only for the salvation of their souls and the liberation of the Church, we, acting as much on our own authority as on that of all the archbishops and bishops in the Gauls, through the mercy of almighty God and the prayers of the Catholic Church, relieve them of all penance imposed for their sins, of which they have made a genuine and full confession.[95]

He also enjoined the crusade on the recruits 'for the remission of all their sins'.[96] Some historians have drawn attention to what they believe to be another contradiction here – between on the one hand dispensing crusaders from the performance of penances imposed in the confessional and on the other relieving them from the punitive consequences of past sins in this world or the next – and it has been suggested that a confusion in Urban's thinking was resolved only because those who preached on his behalf and those who answered his call took what he said to mean relief rather than dispensation.[97] But in the context of contemporary penitential theology there can have been no contradiction, because the terms Urban used came to the same thing. Urban's crusade 'indulgence' was not really an indulgence at all. It was the categorization of the crusade as a penitential war of the type established by Pope Gregory VII and it was an authoritative pastoral statement that the penance the crusaders were taking on themselves was going to be so severe that it would be fully 'satisfactory', in the sense that God would be repaid not only the debts of punishment owed on account of their recent sins, for which penances had not yet been performed, but also any residue left over from earlier penances which had not been satisfactory enough. Urban, therefore, was not granting a spiritual privilege, which was what the developed indulgence would be in that it presupposed that God would treat a meritorious act as if it was 'satisfactory' even though it was not; he was proclaiming a war in

---

[93] St Victor de Marseille (Guérard) 1.167.   [94] *Decreta Claromontensia* 74.
[95] Kb 137.   [96] Kb 136.   [97] See Mayer, *The Crusades*, 30–1.

which the fighters would be imposing condign punishment on themselves by their own efforts.

In this the pope was, in effect, creating a new type of pilgrimage, like the *peregrinatio religiosa* in that it was volunteered out of devotion, but also like the penitential one in that its performance constituted a formal penance and was set by him in the context of the confessional;[98] in fact a century later a distinction was being made between a crusade enjoined by a confessor and one volunteered out of devotion. The writer of the Monte Cassino Chronicle, probably a curial official who came to know Urban's mind, believed that he had set the crusade in motion to provide a means of satisfying 'the penitence of the princes ... because they could not do penance at home for their innumerable crimes and as laymen were very embarrassed to be seen keeping company without weapons'. The nobles, he continued, 'vowed on the authority and with the advice of Pope Urban to take the road overseas to snatch the Sepulchre of the Lord from the Muslims in penitence and for the remission of their sins'.[99] In other words, the summons to crusade was at one level a pastoral move, giving armsbearers the chance of contributing to their own salvation by undertaking a severe penance which did not entail the abandonment of their profession of arms and the humiliating loss of status involved in pilgrimaging abroad as normal penitents without weapons, equipment and horses. And a commentary on the crusade as something deliberately created so that nobles and knights could function as soldiers not just for the Church's benefit but also for their own is to be found in the contemporary historian Guibert of Nogent's famous statement.

God has instituted in our time holy wars, so that the order of knights and the crowd running in their wake ... might find a new way of gaining salvation. And so they are not forced to abandon secular affairs completely by choosing the monastic life or any religious profession, as used to be the custom, but can attain in some measure God's grace while pursuing their own careers, with the liberty and in the dress to which they are accustomed.[100]

There can be no doubt that the crusaders understood that they were performing a penance and that the exercise they were embarking on could contribute to their future salvation. On 22 May 1096 Fulk Doon of Châteaurenard in Provence came to the abbey of Lérins, where the abbot handed him the symbols of pilgrimage and

---

[98] See Kb 137.   [99] Monte Cassino 475.   [100] GN Gesta 124.

'enjoined the journey to Jerusalem on him as a penance'.[101] While Miles of Bray from Champagne was absent in the East he was reported 'doing penance for his guilt'.[102] Ulric Bucel, who was going in 1101 in the company of Count Geoffrey I Jordan of Vendôme, 'made ... his brother his heir and took the road to Jerusalem so that he might gain Christ, caring more for the salvation of his soul than the honour of an earthly inheritance'.[103] In 1096 Godfrey of Bouillon and Baldwin of Boulogne were 'seized with the hope of an eternal inheritance and with love'.[104]

A consequence, to which Guibert of Nogent drew attention, was that crusading could be considered a valid alternative to profession into the religious life, which had been popularly thought to be the only trustworthy route to salvation available to the repentant sinner. In the Limousin, Brunet of Treuil had intended to enter the priory of Aureil, but now he changed his mind; he must have seen in the crusade a way of satisfying his desire for a more positive life while remaining in the world. He persuaded the priory to use the rent from his entry-gift to buy him equipment – possibly armour – and a young man, probably a relation, was found to take his place in the community.[105] A similar case may have been that of Eudes Betevin from near Châteaudun, who had been involved in a dispute with Marmoutier over property he was claiming as part of his patrimony. Eudes fell ill and informed the local prior that he wanted to enter the abbey and that he would renounce his claims as his entry gift. But when the prior returned from a visit to Marmoutier he found that Eudes had recovered and was now saying that he preferred to go to Jerusalem than become a monk.[106] In southern Italy, the mind of the future crusade leader Tancred Marchisus had been troubled by the contradictions for a Christian in the life he led.

But after the judgement of Pope Urban granted remission of all their sins to all Christians going out to fight the gentiles, then at last, as if previously asleep, his vigour was aroused, his powers grew, his eyes opened, his courage was born. For before ... his mind was divided, uncertain whether to follow in the footsteps of the Gospel or the world. But after the call to arms in the service of Christ, the two-fold reason for fighting inflamed him beyond belief.[107]

---

[101] Lérins 312.   [102] Longpont 184. See also St Bénigne de Dijon 2.174.
[103] La Trinité de Vendôme Cart 2.158. See also Cluny 5.108; St Pierre de la Réole 141.
[104] 'Document inédit' 99.   [105] Aureil 29.
[106] Marmoutier (Dunois) 123.   [107] RC 605–6.

One element in Urban's 'indulgence' does seem to have constituted a spiritual privilege, at least in embryo. Two of the eyewitnesses at Clermont reported that he assured his audience that any remission of sins for those who died after taking the cross but before reaching Jerusalem would be granted immediately rather than being dependent on the completion of the penitential act: 'God distributes his own penny, at the first and the eleventh hour.'[108] This, one of them quoted him saying, was 'a gift from God'.[109] He seems to have returned to this subject in the letter to the Catalan nobles, in which he tried, unsuccessfully as it turned out, since at least two of the four counts addressed paid no attention,[110] to persuade them not to join the crusade but to remain at home instead, to resist 'the tyranny and oppression of the Muslims' on their own frontier and to restore the city of Tarragona. He assured them that the war in Catalonia was one 'for the remission of sins' and that 'no one must doubt that if he dies on this expedition for the love of God and his brothers his sins will surely be forgiven and he will gain a share of eternal life through the most compassionate mercy of our God'.[111] There were certainly elements here which pointed forward to the mature indulgence, even if this 'gift' was simply a ruling that death while performing a penitential exercise was such a sacrifice that God would consider the penance to have been completed in its entirety.

But there are no echoes of this in the charters. Phrases are occasionally to be found which in their assumption that merit can be stored point forward to the concept of the Treasury of Merits which was to underpin the developed indulgence – the Lorrainer Quino son of Dodo, who surrendered property to the abbey of St Mihiel, went so far as to hope that this would benefit him by 'an augmentation of merit'[112] and Robert of Flanders believed God 'would restore to me the largesse of the unfailing penny'[113] – but I have yet to come across any notion of divine privilege. On the contrary, the burden of obligation is placed firmly on the backs of the crusaders and running through many charters is a pessimistic piety, expressing itself in a horror of sin and a fear of its consequences. Responding to Urban's emphasis on the necessity for contrition, the crusaders openly craved forgiveness. They joined the expedition, as one of Nivelo of

[108] BB 15.   [109] FC 135.
[110] Geoffrey III of Roussillon and William Jordan of Cerdagne.
[111] *Papsturkunden in ... Katalonien* 2.287–8.
[112] St Mihiel 191.   [113] Flanders 63.

Fréteval's charters put it, 'in order to obtain the pardon that God can give me for my crimes'.[114] The same sentiments were put more elaborately on behalf of the Burgundian Stephen I of Neublans.

Considering how many are my sins and the love, clemency and mercy of Our Lord Jesus Christ, because when he was rich he became poor for our sake, I have determined to repay him in some measure for everything he has given me freely, although I am unworthy. And so I have decided to go to Jerusalem, where God was seen as man and spoke with men and to adore in the place where his feet trod.[115]

A related question, which has generated some debate,[116] is how far those who died on the crusade were regarded from the first as martyrs. The idea of the martyrdom of soldiers is obviously a much more positive one than that of the remission of their sins and it has had a longer history; we have seen that since the ninth century some churchmen, including popes, had been occasionally assuring those going into battle in a just cause that they would be martyrs if they died and that this assurance was being made more firmly as the eleventh century progressed. Images of crusading martyrdom were to be exploited by propagandists in the future, but although it was relatively easy for churchmen to refer to this in general terms in their rhetoric, it was more difficult for them to apply it in specific cases, because no one could pretend to fathom the internal disposition of an individual cut down in the heat of battle. The crusade remission may have been more radical, because those who fought, and not simply those who died fighting, were assured of it, but it was an easier concept for churchmen to handle because, being dependent on the dead crusader having made an adequate confession – something known only to God and the crusader himself – it was not necessary for the church to make a public judgement on the whereabouts of his soul. There is an explicit reference to the prospect of martyrdom on the coming crusade in one account of Urban's sermon at Clermont, written by someone who was almost certainly not present,[117] and an implicit one, in another account written by

---

[114] St Père de Chartres 2.428.

[115] Cluny 5.87–8. See also Cluny 5.59; St Martial de Limoges 347; St Bénigne de Dijon 2.174.

[116] Riley-Smith, *The First Crusade*, 114–19; H. E. J. Cowdrey, 'Martyrdom and the First Crusade', *Crusade and Settlement*, ed. P. W. Edbury (Cardiff, 1985), 46–56; J. Flori, 'Guerre sainte et rétributions spirituelles dans la 2e moitié du XIe siècle', *Revue d'histoire ecclésiastique* 85 (1990), 617–49 and 'Mort et martyre des guerriers vers 1100. L'exemple de la prèmiere croisade', *Cahiers de civilisation médiévale* 34 (1991), 121–39.

[117] GN Gesta 138.

someone who was.[118] And as the crusaders who broke into Syria and marched on Jerusalem became convinced that their astounding success could be attributed only to divine intervention, some of them certainly came to believe that their dead were martyrs.[119]

It might be thought that the prospect of fathers, sons, brothers and husbands as martyrs would have appealed to their grieving families, but I have found no references to martyrdom in the charters of their heirs or other relations which mention their deaths. Nor did there develop anything like the *cultus* of an early crusader in the West, with perhaps one exception, the veneration in southern Italy of Rainald Porchet, who had been paraded on the walls of Antioch by the Muslims and killed in the sight of his co-religionists when he had refused to cooperate with his captors.[120] It was, of course, hard for cults to develop without bones or other relics, and the bodies of the crusading dead were very far away. It is worth noting that miracles were to be reported occurring when the corpses were more available, as at the tombs of two crusaders killed during the siege of Lisbon in 1147.[121]

If the dead had been regarded as martyrs they should have had no need for prayers, as a story circulating forty years before the crusade illustrates. After the defeat of his army by the Normans in the Battle of Civitate Pope Leo IX was said to have had a vision in which an angel persuaded him that there was no point in him saying Mass for the souls of his dead soldiers because they were saints whose death had been precious in the sight of God.[122] In the aftermath of the crusade, however, Archbishop Manasses of Rheims provided evidence for the confusion reigning on this issue when he called on one of his suffragans – perhaps all of them – to pray for the dead, stating at the same time that they were 'crowned with glorious martyrdom'.[123] In their own charters crusaders asked for prayers for themselves when envisaging the prospect that they might be killed[124] and made endowments for the safety of their souls on their deathbeds during the campaign.[125] In their letters home their companions asked for prayers for the army's dead[126] and at least one heir of a man who did not come back, Hugh II of Burgundy,

---

[118] BB 15.   [119] Riley-Smith, *The First Crusade*, 114–15.
[120] HP 194. For his death, see PT 79–81; Ch d'A 1.205, 212–33.
[121] 'Annales Sancti Disibodi' 28.   [122] Anonymus Haserensis 265.   [123] Kb 176.
[124] Aureil 192; Longpont 190; Lézat 17.189; St Georges de Rennes 270.
[125] Aureil 113–14, 126, 179; Vigeois 67–9.   [126] Kb 145, 160.

showered the churches in his duchy with gifts in return for intercessory prayer on behalf of the soul of his father Eudes, who had died in Asia Minor in 1101.[127] There was, of course, a legal reason why requests for prayers should be inserted in the eleemosynary grants made by crusaders and their families, because only then would their gifts qualify as free alms and be exempted from the jurisdiction of secular courts, but intercession could have been sought for parents and other relations rather than for the crusaders themselves. The charters suggest that the faithful could not be sure that the dead were really martyrs. Or they wondered whether adequate remission of sins had been gained by them: writing from Syria, Anselm of Ribemont may have wanted to flatter the archbishop of Rheims, but he went so far as to assure him that 'we are very dependent on your prayers and we put whatever we gain down not to our merits but to your prayers'.[128] Or, perhaps most likely, men and women doubted whether remission was certain for those who had died before reaching Jerusalem. The pope's assurances on this matter do not seem to have convinced his flock; as late as the middle of the thirteenth century St Thomas Aquinas was still dealing with anxieties on this score.[129]

Most of the sentiments revealed in the charters, therefore, were conventional, sometimes more conventional than those of the pope and his entourage. The armsbearing public and its charter-writers, faced by a new penitential exercise which certainly attracted them, could not find an equivalently novel way of putting it into words, but had recourse to the ways of thought and forms of expression with which they were already familiar. Crusaders knew that they had been summoned by the pope to fight a war-pilgrimage on God's behalf – indeed they claimed their decisions to take the cross had been made under divine inspiration – and the liberation of Jerusalem was their goal from the start, but they were far more interested in freeing the place than in the sufferings of the eastern Christians. They saw themselves as penitents performing a severe penance, but they seem to have had little notion of what a full remission of sins meant – I know of only one charter, relating to the abbey of Cluny,

---

[127] St Etienne de Dijon 11; Burgundy (Plancher) 1, Preuves, xxxiv–xxxv; Burgundy (Pérard) 82–4; Chalon-sur-Saône, Preuves, 47–8. See also the endowment of Roger Mandeville, whose father Stephen died on the crusade of 1147. Montacute 140, 184–5.

[128] Kb 160.

[129] Thomas Aquinas, *Quaestiones Quodlibetales*, Quodl.2, q.8, a.2; Quodl.5, q.7, a.2 (pp. 36–8, 106).

which contains the phrase 'pro peccatorum ... remissione'[130] – and they worried about dying on campaign with their vows unfulfilled. Nevertheless, there can be no doubt that the essence of Urban's message had been understood by them. They believed that their military service, at any rate if completed, would profit their souls. The crusade was for them as individuals only secondarily about benefiting the Church or Christianity; it was primarily about bene- fiting themselves. It was an act of self-sanctification and, as such, provided an answer to a question which had been troubling them and their families for a century. How could they make their peace with God except by abandoning the world for a monastic community and thereby turning their backs on their obligations and responsibil- ities? The pope had presented them with an alternative solution.

Enthusiasm can be traced along the path of Urban's journey through France – a high proportion of the first crusaders known to me came from localities within a day or two's ride of it – but he was anxious to spread the word further, although the evidence for what went on in his name in those regions he could not visit is fragmentary. Among his surviving letters there are two exhortatory ones, to Flanders and Bologna, but there must have been others. He encouraged bishops to preach the cross in their dioceses[131] and several did so,[132] although the only names we know for certain are those of Anselm of Buis, the reforming archbishop of Milan,[133] and the Venetian prelates Peter Badoaro, the patriarch of Grado, and Henry Contarini, the bishop of Castello.[134] Hugh, the archbishop of Lyons and an energetic promoter of reform, must have preached as well; his influence accounted for the recruitment in 1096 of Galdemar Carpenel of Dargoire, who acknowledged his debt to him,[135] and probably of Count William III of Forez, Hugh II of Usson-en-Forez and Durand Cheuvre, together with three others who left in 1101, including Count William VI of Auvergne. In 1100 Hugh, who asked permission of Pope Paschal to go himself, presided over a synod at Anse, attended by four other archbishops and nine bishops, at which the crusade and the enforcement of crusade vows were debated, and Paschal despatched two legates to France, but although these men held councils at Valence and at Poitiers, where there was an

---

[130] Cluny 5.59.   [131] FC 134–5; BB 15; NF 356.   [132] BB 16.
[133] Landulf the Younger, 'Historia Mediolanensis', 22.
[134] 'Historia de translatione' 255–6.   [135] RA Cont 307.

impressive assembly of eighty bishops and abbots, there are no descriptions of them preaching the cross.[136]

Monks also acted as recruiting agents. Robert of Normandy was apparently persuaded to crusade by 'certain religious'[137] and it is clear that some communities, which will be described in a later chapter, were active centres of recruitment, although the only monks known by name to have preached the First Crusade were Abbot Peter of Maillezais[138] and perhaps Abbot Hugh of Cluny.[139] Outside the ranks of established churchmen in 1095–6, we know only of Peter the Hermit, who was active in Berry, northern France and Germany.[140] Berry and the Orléannais were not on Pope Urban's itinerary and although men and women from those regions could have travelled to Tours, Angers or Le Mans to hear him it may be that the response in them, which included men such as Geoffrey lord of Issoudon, of the dominant family of Déols,[141] the lords of Châtillon and Aigurande, and probably Arnold II, the castellan of Vierzon,[142] was due to Peter's efforts. There was a further striking case of commitment in 1100, when Eudes Arpin, the viscount of Bourges, sold his viscounty and his lordship of Dun to the king before leaving for the East.[143]

Pope Urban's rhetoric, enveloped in theatre, was an appeal to the guts rather than to the head, the earliest in a line of similar displays, which stretched at least as far as the prodigious efforts of St John of Capistrano in the middle of the fifteenth century. It is hard to avoid the conclusion that the old pope's itinerary was a clever propaganda exercise in which he deliberately played on the senses of an audience he knew well, packaging his message in terms that people would find appealing. The same emphasis on the dramatic characterized the preaching campaigns in France and Germany of Peter the Hermit, who carried with him a letter he claimed had been sent him from heaven, ordering all Christians to march to the liberation of

---

[136] Hugh of Flavigny 487–8, 491–4; St Maixent Chron 172.
[137] OV 5.26.   [138] BB 5.
[139] Sauxillanges 966–7. This document is very corrupt and looks like a forgery. See also Cluny 5.89. Robert of Arbrissel is sometimes referred to as a crusade preacher, but there is no good evidence for this; he seems to have been commissioned by Urban to preach a general Christian message.
[140] GN Gesta 142–3; AA 272, 274; OV 5.28.
[141] See G. Devailly, Le Berry du Xe siècle au milieu du XIIIe Siècle (Paris, 1973), 375.
[142] See the table in Devailly, Le Berry, 357.   [143] See Devailly, Le Berry, 382–4.

Jerusalem,[144] and in Lombardy of Anselm of Buis, who made use of a popular song, *Ultreia, ultreia,* to get his message across.[145]

Theatrical Urban may have been, but nothing should be allowed to obscure the revolutionary nature of his proclamation of a penitential war-pilgrimage. His references to holy war were, as far as one can tell, as hyperbolic as were many of the more extreme statements of the Gregorian reformers, but his association of it and pilgrimage was emphatic and unprecedented. It is amazing that no protests from senior churchmen are recorded, even though figures like Ivo of Chartres and Anselm of Canterbury, who was at Hugh of Lyons's synod at Anse, may well have had doubts. If the First Crusade had failed, there would surely have been criticism of so radical an initiative and the association of war with pilgrimage could have been dropped. But the enterprise was a triumph and those who took part were convinced that the only explanation for the victorious progress of an army so short of supplies and material, so badly led and so weighed down by non-combatants, was that God had intervened to help it physically. The liberation of Jerusalem confirmed for those at home as well that the crusade had really been a manifestation of God's will: 'The Lord has certainly revived his miracles of old', wrote Pope Paschal.[146]

So potential criticism was bound to falter. It is notable that Sigebert of Gembloux did not mention the crusade at all when he wrote attacking the summons to penitential war against the opponents of reform made by Pope Paschal in a letter to Robert of Flanders, in which there was a reference to Robert's return from Jerusalem.[147] The eyewitness reporters of the crusade used of it phrases which until then had been customarily applied only to monks and the monastic profession – the knighthood of Christ, the way of the cross, the heavenly Jerusalem, spiritual warfare[148] – and most of these were taken up and refined by better educated commentators, who stressed the miraculous nature of the crusade and the unique way its course had demonstrated divine approval: 'Apart from the mystery of the healing cross, what more marvellous deed has there been since the creation of the world than that which was achieved in

---

[144] 'Annalista Saxo' 728; Helmold of Bosau, 'Chronica Slavorum', 33–4.
[145] Landulf the Younger 22.   [146] Kb 178.
[147] Sigebert of Gembloux, 'Leodicensium epistola', 451–64.
[148] Riley-Smith, *The First Crusade*, 91–119.

modern times in this journey of *Jerosolimitani*?'[149] These learned men, all monks, dwelt on the crusade's penitential and loving nature and seized on the idea that it paralleled monasticism. The crusaders, moved by love of God and their neighbour, renouncing wives, children and earthly possessions, and adopting temporary poverty and chastity, had gone into voluntary exile as brothers professed into a great military abbey on the move, following the way of the cross: one writer compared the liberation of Jerusalem to Joseph of Arimathea taking Christ down from the cross.[150] In the monastic commentaries of the first decade of the twelfth century the association of war and penance proposed by the papacy and confirmed in the experiences of the crusaders was given coherence and intellectual weight.[151]

Of Urban's successors, Paschal II and Calixtus II authorized crusades to the East, but there are no surviving references to them preaching. Of their legates, Bruno of Segni, who had been with Urban on his journey through France, did preach when he returned there with Bohemond of Taranto in 1106. According to Suger of St Denis, who heard him at Poitiers, he called on men to defend the Holy Sepulchre,[152] but we have no more details than that and he was anyway overshadowed by his companion. Since leaving southern Italy in 1096 Bohemond had enhanced his reputation as the best general among the crusade leaders and as the first Latin ruler of Antioch; and he had spent nearly three years as a prisoner of the Turks. He opened his visit to France in a melodramatic fashion with an ostentatious pilgrimage to the shrine of St Léonard-de-Noblat, where he gave thanks for his deliverance from gaol; his experiences as a prisoner of the Muslims quickly became incorporated in St Leonard's *Miracula*.[153] He then embarked on a triumphal journey, lecturing about his adventures to large audiences. Many French nobles wanted him to be godfather to their children[154] and it was said that Henry I of England discouraged him from visiting his kingdom because he was worried that he might tempt away his best knights to the East.[155] His progress, in the company for some of the

[149] RR 723.		[150] BB 101.
[151] Riley-Smith, *The First Crusade*, 135–52.
[152] Suger of St Denis, *Vita*, 48. See also St Maixent Chron 178; HP 228.
[153] *Acta SS Novembris* 3.160–8, 177–82; WMGR 2.454.
[154] Riley-Smith, *The First Crusade*, 137.		[155] OV 6.68.

time of a pretender to the Byzantine throne, was marked by gifts of relics and silks to churches; he had stripped the treasury of Antioch on his departure.[156] There is an account of him speaking on a dais before the Lady altar in the cathedral of Chartres on the day of his marriage to the king of France's daughter. He began by telling the story of his adventures and in calling for a crusade to Jerusalem he also proposed an invasion of the Byzantine empire, promising rich pickings to those who would go with him.[157] Speeches of this sort were supplemented by the despatching of agents to regions he could not visit himself; although the king had prevented him from coming to England, his chaplain crossed the Channel on his behalf.[158] He may also have made use of the written word. A version of the anonymous account of the First Crusade, the *Gesta Francorum*, which had been written by someone in his contingent, may have been circulating France[159] and it is possible that a forged letter purporting to be from the Emperor Alexius to Count Robert I of Flanders, which suggested that the Greeks had become so desperate that they had been prepared to envisage Latin rule in Constantinople, was being publicized at the same time.[160]

Bohemond's crusade ended disastrously and there was talk of ambition, greed and deceit.[161] There was more censure after the recruiting drive of 1128 in England and Scotland of another unlikely crusade preacher, the lay brother and Templar master, Hugh of Payns: 'He said that a great war was afoot between Christians and the heathens. Then when they arrived there [in Palestine] it was nothing but lies – thus miserably were all the people afflicted.'[162] But occasional criticism could not blight a general concern for the Christian custody of the Sepulchre and some preachers exploited the image of Jerusalem to lend its authority to other enterprises. In 1124, introducing an idea which was to become a theme in Reconquest

---

[156] RC 713–14.   [157] OV 6.70.   [158] *Quadripartitus* 161.

[159] But see R. Hill, introduction to GF, x note 3.

[160] Kb 130–6. Two scholars (E. Joranson, 'The Problem of the Spurious Letter of Emperor Alexius to the Count of Flanders', *American Historical Review* 55 (1949–50), 811–32; and M. de Waha, 'La lettre d'Alexis Comnène à Robert I le Frison', *Byzantion* 47 (1977), 113–25) have argued that the letter is a genuine one which has been retouched, rather than a total forgery. For a forged papal bull circulating at the time of the First Crusade, see Gieysztor, 'The Genesis of the Crusades', *passim*.

[161] OV 6.68–72, 100–4; Suger of St Denis, *Vita*, 44–50; WMGR 2.454; 'Chronicon Vindocinense seu de Aquaria' 171–2; 'Zur Geschichte des Investiturstreites (Englische Analekten II)' 280–2; HP 228–9; BN 538.

[162] *The Anglo-Saxon Chronicle* 194–5. See also 'Annales de Waverleia' 221; Robert of Torigni 113.

propaganda, Archbishop Diego Gelmirez of Compostela justified crusading in Spain on the grounds that the recovery of the peninsula was the key to a better route to the Sepulchre.

Just as the knights of Christ, the faithful sons of Holy Church, opened the way to Jerusalem with much labour and spilling of blood, so we should become knights of Christ and, after defeating his wicked enemies the Muslims, open the way to the same Sepulchre of the Lord through Spain, which is shorter and much less laborious.[163]

The interest in the Sepulchre also manifested itself in the stream of pilgrims going to and returning from Jerusalem each year and it was reinforced by contacts within those family circles which had kin on both sides of the sea, by the official relations between the popes and the members of the new Latin hierarchies in the East and by the little extensions of Jerusalem which were establishing themselves everywhere in the European countryside, as estates were granted to religious institutions in Palestine and these set up dependencies in them, sometimes erecting round churches which echoed the shape of the Sepulchre rotunda. The Hospitallers of St John, who may have inherited some properties which had already been donated before the First Crusade to the hospital in Jerusalem, were joined by the canons of the church of the Holy Sepulchre, the monks of St Mary of the Latins and St Mary of the Valley of Jehoshaphat, and the Templars. The presence in the West of these representatives of the guardians of the holy places probably had an effect on recruitment, although it is hard to be precise. But far more important, influencing not only decisions to take part but also the resources which would be at a crusader's disposal, were the attitudes to be found within the nexuses of relationships created by lordship and above all by blood and marriage.

[163] *Historia Compostellana* 379.

CHAPTER 4

Recruitment, lordship and family

Although one could take the cross semi-privately,[1] the norm was to assume it at a large, noisy, hysterical assembly. The earliest of the public cross-takings, in the field outside Clermont on 27 November 1095, immediately followed Pope Urban's proclamation of war,[2] and during his preaching tour there were others presided over by him: perhaps at Le Mans[3] and certainly at Tours,[4] where yet another was to be held in June 1128.[5] Many obviously had to take place without him: at Rouen, the archbishop of which had been on pilgrimage to Jerusalem thirty-eight years before – it was followed by a riot[6] – and at Etampes,[7] possibly at Verdun,[8] and at the siege of Amalfi, where Bohemond of Taranto, 'moved by the Holy Spirit, ordered the most valuable cloak he had with him to be completely cut up and made into crosses at once, and most of the knights who were at the siege began enthusiastically to join him'.[9]

In none of the early descriptions of cross-taking, or in other references to them, are the pilgrimage symbols, the purse and staff, mentioned,[10] just as crosses are never mentioned when the reception of the symbols is recorded, at least until 1146 when the Breton crusader Bardoul Le Large may have taken cross, purse and staff together.[11] As late as 1248 John of Joinville received the symbols of pilgrimage, and apparently them alone, from the abbot of Cheminon.[12] Crosses and

---

[1] See Reginald of Durham, *Libellus de Vita et Miraculis S. Godrici*, 33; Cluny 5.89.
[2] RR 729-31; BB 15-16 See also Kb 164-5; GF 2; FC 140-1.
[3] See OV 5.228-30.
[4] GAD 101, although note here the closeness of the language to that of BB 16.
[5] CGCA 161; Cart Temp 9.
[6] GM Vita 246. For the archbishop's pilgrimage, see OV 2.68-72 , 254.   [7] Morigny 40.
[8] In 1100. Laurence of Liège, 'Gesta episcoporum Virdunensium' 497.   [9] GF 7.
[10] For example see, for the crusade of 1107, 'The Council of Troyes', 93; and for that of 1120, St Hilaire-le-Grand de Poitiers (1847) 128; St Julien de Tours 87.
[11] 'suscepta cruce et habita'. St Sulpice-la-Forêt 35.350.
[12] John of Joinville, *La vie de Saint Louis*, 108.

symbols, therefore, were received separately and the usual course of events was probably that described by a monk of St Denis, Eudes of Deuil, in his account of the preparations of King Louis VII of France for the crusade of 1147. Eudes wrote of two distinct ceremonies for the taking of the cross and the granting of the purse and staff, separated in time and space. The king took the cross on 31 March 1146 at Vézelay. It looks as though there was a semi-private cross-taking for him and the greater nobles, followed immediately by a public assembly, the success of which was assured by the sight of the king wearing his cloth cross, which had been sent by the pope, when he joined the preacher, Bernard of Clairvaux, on a platform. So great was the enthusiasm at the public meeting that a stock of made-up crosses ran out and Bernard had to tear his habit into strips to provide additional ones; perhaps he had heard the story of Bohemond at Amalfi fifty years before and was deliberately imitating him for effect. Over a year later, on 11 June 1147 at St Denis, Louis received from the pope in person a pilgrim's purse and the oriflamme, the sacred battle-standard of the French crown which was presumably presented to him in place of a staff.[13] It cannot have been the case, therefore, that the rite for the taking of the cross developed out of the ceremony for blessing the purse and staff, the symbols of pilgrimage, or that there was at first little distinction made between pilgrims and crusaders and their vows.[14] It should be remembered that many eleventh-century pilgrims would not have made vows at all; those, for instance, who were performing formal penances would have had these imposed on them by their confessors. We have been misled by the fact that the ceremonies had been conflated by the time they are to be found in the pontificals and manuals, which survive only from the third quarter of the twelfth century onwards.

It seems that after nobles and knights had taken the cross, they would make private arrangements to receive the purse and staff, and perhaps also the blessing which appears in the later rites,[15] from a local bishop, abbot or prior: Herbert II of Thouars wished to receive the 'dress of pilgrimage' from the bishop of Poitiers in 1101.[16] It was

[13] Eudes of Deuil, *De profectione Ludovici VII in Orientem*, 8–10, 16–18. For later pilgrim/crusader rites, in which the reception of the purse and staff was accompanied by blessings, see J. A. Brundage, '*Cruce Signari*: the Rite for Taking the Cross in England', *Traditio* 22 (1966), 297–310.

[14] Brundage, '*Cruce Signari*', 289–310 *passim*; J. A. Brundage, *Medieval Canon Law*, 119–20.

[15] Brundage, '*Cruce Signari*', 297–310; C. Vogel and R. Elze, *Le pontifical romano-germanique du dixième siècle* (Vatican City, 1963–72), 2.227–9, 362.

[16] Chaise-le-Vicomte 6.

perhaps at this time that the recruits made confession and had the penance they had already voluntarily agreed to undergo formally imposed on them; the abbot of Lerins 'enjoined the Jerusalem journey on him as a penance' when he gave Fulk Doon of Château-renard a napkin and staff in May 1096.[17] The reception of purse and staff was sometimes associated with a financial arrangement with, or an endowment for, the religious community concerned. In this the crusaders were probably following ancient custom – in 1036 a pilgrim to Rome had received his scrip from the abbot of Bèze at the same time as he had renounced claims he had made against the abbey[18] – as well as complying in their own way with an instruction issued by Urban that those who had taken the cross should seek a blessing from their parish priests.[19]

The reasons for volunteering to crusade must have been many: the desire of a repentant sinner, terrified of the prospect of hell, for an adequate penitential exercise – Berengar Raymond II of Barcelona had murdered his brother[20] and Lagman of Man had put his brother's eyes out;[21] or concern for a father who had died and, probably suffering purgatorial torments, needed intercession – this seems to have motivated Herbert of Thouars in 1101;[22] or fear of a portent in nature, like the lunar eclipse which drove the future King Conrad III of Germany into taking the cross in 1124;[23] or rage, like that probably felt by Arnulf of Hesdin in 1096, who had been unjustly accused of treason against King William II of England;[24] or a private reaction to tragedy, as with Hugh of Ste Maure-de-Touraine, who seems to have been at least partly driven by grief following the murder of two of his sons 'in secret and by treachery'. Hugh had accepted an offer from the monks of Noyers to have them buried in their churchyard. He endowed the community with the church at Ste Maure and when the papal legate, the bishop of Angoulême, visited Noyers he prevailed upon him to pray over his sons' tombs and to absolve them from their sins on papal authority. It was shortly after this that he decided 'to go to Jerusalem', probably on the crusade of 1120.[25] But the geography and genealogy of recruitment suggest that two factors, lordship and family, which were

---

[17] Lérins 312.   [18] Bèze Liber 562.
[19] Archbishop Hugh of Lyons sought permission from Pope Paschal II. Hugh of Flavigny 487.
[20] *Gesta comitum Barcinonensium* 7, 37.   [21] *Chronicle of the Kings of Man and the Isles* 8, 62.
[22] Chaise-le-Vicomte 6.   [23] Ekk C 262.
[24] 'Chronica monasterii de Hida juxta Wintoniam' 301–2.   [25] Noyers 329–32.

linked to one another and dominated society around 1100, especially preconditioned men and women to respond positively to the preaching of the cross.

Crusading shared with marriage and monastic profession the feature that promises freely entered into were asked of those involved. In theory the Church was bound to maintain the voluntary nature of such vows, although it was hard to expect society to respect an independence of thought and action from its members which was alien to them. In an anarchic and insecure world, men and women, grouped in the nexuses provided by lordship and kinship, could not act effectively without mutual dependence, internal discipline (however undisciplined they might be when facing others) and cooperation. It was, for example, unusual for an individual to resist a collective decision by the kindred on marriage and when a woman like Christina of Markyate did so she would be faced with incomprehension or worse; it is arguable that in Christina's case she only got support from some churchmen because she wanted to become a solitary contemplative, perhaps the one area of life in which individualism was generally admired.[26] It was easier to make relatively free choices in religion than in marriage. Progressive churchmen disapproved of the practice of handing over children as oblates to religious houses and there are many examples of adults freely deciding to embark on particular forms of monasticism; indeed their phenomenal growth in the period was founded partly on the ability of masters of the religious life to attract disciples. Even so, few child-oblates could stand up to a family decision to put them into a religious community, although there is evidence from the Limousin for one independently-minded boy making things so difficult for the monks that he nearly succeeded in doing so.[27]

Crusading, like monasticism, was characterized by both free and forced commitments. While some dependants, even very distinguished ones, were forbidden to join because they were needed at home, others must have been pressurized into taking the cross, although it is certain that many accompanied their lord willingly. Some years before the First Crusade a man called Stabelo, the chamberlain of Godfrey of Bouillon and later a companion of Godfrey's on crusade, dreamt that he saw his lord climbing a golden stairway which stretched from earth to heaven, accompanied by

---

[26] Christina of Markyate, *Life, passim.*   [27] Tulle 65.

another member of his household called Ruthard, who was carrying a lamp. The lamp went out and Ruthard scampered down in terror, leaving Godfrey alone. Stabelo seized the lamp, relit it, and joined Godfrey on the stairs. Together they reached a hall of heaven where a delicious meal was laid for them. In the past Godfrey had often confided to his familiars his longing to make a pilgrimage to the Holy Sepulchre and Stabelo's dream came to be interpreted as a prediction of the course of the crusade and of Godfrey's election as ruler of Jerusalem. Its effect on Stabelo would have been to reinforce the sense of loyalty he was conditioned to feel anyway.[28]

Of course there must have been many spontaneous decisions to join crusades which came as unpleasant surprises to the lords and kindred concerned, but the concentrations I have found in regions where a leading magnate was committed and in certain families suggests that there was in these a prevailing ethos which helped to trigger the original decision of the volunteer and then a collective agreement to help him in his preparations. The fact is that without the support of the groups at home with which crusaders were associated few promises to undertake something so demanding and expensive could have been fulfilled.

LORDSHIP

In the autumn of 1096 Count Robert of Flanders, on an early stage of his march to the East, reached the abbey of St Thierry, north-west of Rheims, to be greeted by a procession of monks. He must have lodged there, with his army pavilioned around. In an agreement he made with the abbey he renounced his claims to property given to the monks by his sister and in exchange was promised a share in the merits of the community's prayers and alms-giving. His charter was witnessed by Ebles of Roucy, the head of the most important local family, a *fidelis beati Petri* who had fought in Spain and must have been there to see him off, and by some of his companions on the march: his seneschal, his butler, two of his chaplains, one of the two castellans of Lille who were crusading, and the lords of Aalst and Ardres.[29] When Robert I Burgundio of Sablé reached Marmoutier a year later he was accompanied by a chaplain and nine other men,

---

[28] AA 481–2.
[29] Flanders 66–7. For Ebles of Roucy, see M. Bur, *La formation du comté de Champagne v.950–v.1150* (Nancy, 1977), 253–7; Bull, *Knightly Piety*, 81–2.

most of whom seem to have been knights; one of them, Ardouin of Vione, was definitely going with him to the East.[30] The companions of a lord would have been selected after thought and discussion, because an important consideration for him, whether he was a magnate or a petty landowner, was the choice of his household for what was certain to be a long campaign. Established household conventions, or those governing clientage or vassalage, could prevail even in the chaos of the crusade; when Gerard of Buc, one of the castellans of Lille, died in Syria, Robert of Flanders behaved in exactly the way he would have done at home by demanding, and getting, his possessions.[31] Traditions of loyalty could lead to extraordinary demonstrations of it from subordinates. In January 1103 Raymond of St Gilles, now the 'head and prince' of what he called 'a tiny Christian force' at Tripoli in Lebanon, issued a charter which was witnessed by a bevy of men from his home domains, including three, his chaplain Herbert of Chaise-Dieu, William Hugh of Monteil and William Peyre of Cunlhat, who had been close to him since he had left western Europe seven years before.[32]

The decisions of a lord on this matter were important for the crusade as a whole, since only he could screen out psychopaths and other undisciplined individuals, but the make-up of his following was something over which he could lose control. In the anarchic conditions of a crusade knights could desert him for another patron, who could provide the necessities for them better than he could, or his entourage could be swollen by men whose service he was able to subsidize. During the siege of Jerusalem Hugh II of St Pol was employing knights for pay;[33] these men could have attached themselves to him at any time during the course of the expedition. Allegiances were to shift so much during a campaign of this sort that it is usually impossible to establish the composition of households at the time of departure and anyway we have only fragments of information about them. Like Robert of Flanders, Alan Fergent of Brittany and Godfrey of Bouillon were accompanied by their seneschals,[34] and Godfrey had at least one other member from his ducal household in Lorraine with him.[35] Even minor lords seem to have taken chaplains along, and the magnates had several: Robert of

---

[30] Marmoutier (Manceau) 89; and see 91.
[31] 'Narratio quomodo relliquiae martyris Georgii ad nos Aquicinenses pervenerunt' 251.
[32] St Victor de Marseille (Guérard) 2.151–3.   [33] AA 463.
[34] Mainfinit and Baldric.   [35] Stabelo.

Flanders had at least three;[36] Stephen of Blois had at least two;[37] and so perhaps had Robert of Normandy.[38] These priests, like most clerics willing to serve in the households of the great, were not generally of a high calibre.[39] Senior churchmen, who often travelled in the companies of the more important lords, also had their own chaplains: Adhémar of Monteil appears to have had two[40] and Gerard, the abbot of Schaffhausen, possibly had one.[41]

Since some of the lords had their hunting birds and dogs with them,[42] they must have taken their huntsmen. A huntsman called Everard Venator was on the First Crusade, while a William Venator, a subject of Juhel of Mayenne, took the cross for the crusade of 1120. The practice of taking hunting animals was condemned by Pope Eugenius III when he proclaimed the crusade of 1147,[43] but there was some sense in a practice which could provide supplementary rations. Two servants taking part in the First Crusade – Mala-Corona and Peter Bartholomew, who were employed by Bohemond of Taranto and William Peyre of Cunhlat respectively – are named in the sources. There must also have been farriers, grooms, squires and armourers; weapons would only remain effective if they were properly oiled and stored when not in use and one story current after the First Crusade, of the Muslims' scorn at a Christian peasant's rusty weapons,[44] carries with it the implication that the knights' arms were being kept rust-free and serviceable. There were doctors in the army in Asia Minor in 1097 and in Palestine in 1102,[45] although it is not clear whether these were freelance or were attached to households. If they had been trained in the fashionable Salernitan method, which stressed the importance to recovery of quiet, warmth, cleanliness and a wholesome diet, they would have found conditions impossible in an army which had often to keep moving come what may and in which there were endemic food-shortages.

A crusading lord's estimate of his needs could well have led him to order some of his subordinates to take the cross as his companions-in-arms and servants, but it is obvious that the relationship between

---

[36] Sannardus, Cono and Rainer.   [37] Alexander and Fulcher of Chartres.
[38] Arnulf of Chocques and perhaps Robert of Rouen. It was said that Rigaud IV of Tournemire had been accompanied by an almoner. St Flour ccvii.
[39] Riley-Smith, *The First Crusade*, 79–86.
[40] Bernard of Valence and perhaps Bertrand of Bas, who was a canon of Le Puy.
[41] Zaizolfus.   [42] See AA 340–1.
[43] Eugenius III, 'Quantum praedecessores', 304.
[44] GN Gesta 191.   [45] AA 342; Chaise-le-Vicomte 8.

the greatest magnates and their subjects could affect recruitment whether the magnates concerned were going or not. Rainald III of Château-Gontier sought permission from Count Fulk IV of Anjou before he crusaded in 1097 and was granted it;[46] conversely Archbishop Gerard of York was prevented by King Henry I of England from joining the crusade of 1107.[47] The zeal of a great lord could encourage the richer of his subjects to join him, with knock-on effects down the social scale, especially were he and they to follow Pope Urban's injunction to subsidize the less well-off. In the Chartrain in 1096, where the count, Stephen of Blois, was an enthusiast, the entire ruling class of Chartres took the cross[48] – the vidame and his brother, and the viscount – together with the provost and perhaps two canons of the cathedral, the castellans of Mondoubleau, Fréteval, Gallardon and Beaugency, and the prévot of Blois, another of Stephen's cities. In 1120 Count Fulk V of Anjou led a force to the East which included the bishop of Angers, the lords of Mayenne and Le Plessis-Macé, and probably the castellan of Ste Maure-de-Touraine.[49] Great lords did not have to go themselves to foster recruitment. Count Fulk IV of Anjou did not commit himself, but he must have encouraged his vassals to do so. When he followed the pope to Tours in the spring of 1096 he was accompanied by some of them, including Hugh of Chaumont-sur-Loire, the co-heir of Amboise, and Aimery of Courron, a member of his household who was married to Hugh's cousin and co-heiress. Hugh and Aimery took the cross at the ceremony at Marmoutier presided over by the pope himself.[50] The Angevin crusaders, who left in several different contingents, also included the castellan of Matheflon and the lords of Segré (Rainald of Château-Gontier, whom we have already seen had Fulk's 'licence'), Sablé and probably Clervaux.

An example of the positive effect even a non-participating lord could have is provided by the number of recruits to the First Crusade from the region around Paris. They included the king's brother, Hugh the Great of Vermandois, the constable and the seneschal, Walo II of Chaumont-en-Vexin and Gilbert Payen of Garlande, the viscount of Melun and the lords of Montlhéry and Boissy-sans-Avoir.

[46] CGCA 'Additamenta' 149.   [47] *Quadripartitus* 161–2.
[48] For the nobles in the region, see A. Chédeville, *Chartres et ses campagnes (XIe–XIIIe s.)* (Paris, 1973), 251–330.
[49] Noyers 329–32. For the castellans in the region, see Anjou (Guillot) 1.299–352, 456–68.
[50] GAD 100–1.

Hugh deserted the crusade, but, like Stephen of Blois, he went again in 1101, accompanied by the bishop of Paris, the count of Rochefort, and probably the lord of Trie-Château and the vicar of Pontoise. Peter the Hermit must have passed through the district on his preaching tour – Walter Sansavoir, who led one of the early armies, came from there – but towns such as Le Mans and Vendôme which had been on Pope Urban's itinerary were not too distant and men could have ridden over to hear the pope in person.

On the other hand, the influence of the king himself should not be underestimated. It is true that Philip never took the cross, that he was to benefit through the purchase of important honours from Everard III of Le Puiset and Eudes Arpin of Bourges[51] and that he was in trouble with the pope. In 1092 he had repudiated his wife, Bertha of Frisia, and had run off with Bertrada of Montfort-l'Amaury, Fulk of Anjou's wife. The couple had been bigamously married by the bishop of Senlis in the presence of all the bishops of the royal demesne and apparently with the approval of the arch-bishop of Rheims and the papal legate. But Bishop Ivo of Chartres, the influential reformer and canonist, had openly opposed the wedding which he had refused to attend, had withheld service from the king and had fled to the pope. After Bertha of Frisia's death, Philip had summoned to Rheims as many bishops as he could to confirm his second marriage, but a council in Autun in 1094 under the chairmanship of another papal legate, Hugh of Lyons, had quashed the proceedings at Rheims and had excommunicated the king, a judgement which was confirmed by the Council of Clermont.[52] Philip met Hugh of Lyons, Adhémar of Monteil and Eudes of Burgundy at Mozac, just north of Clermont, shortly before the council was convened[53] and negotiations were taking place throughout Pope Urban's journey through France. While Urban was presiding over the Council of Nîmes in July 1096 he was told that Philip had repented and would give Bertrada up. Meanwhile Hugh the Great of Vermandois had decided to lead a contingent to the East within weeks of the council of Clermont, if not even before it, since a council-of-war, at which the king himself was present, was held in Paris as early as 11 February 1096.[54] The adhesion of Hugh

---

[51] Morigny 11; OV 5.324.   [52] Duby, *The Knight*, 4–18.
[53] A. Fliche 'Urbain II et la croisade', *Revue d'histoire de l'église de France* 13 (1927), 300.
[54] GN Gesta 149.

the Great and the interest of the king must have been partly responsible for the large number of recruits from the region

Conversely, men and women could be driven into taking the cross through fear of their lord or because they wanted to secure their futures through close association with another one. In 1096 King William II of England was not openly hostile to the First Crusade, but, although he raised an enormous sum of money to hold the duchy of his brother in pledge, he does not seem to have been sympathetic. There was some enthusiasm in England, giving rise to a worried letter from Archbishop Anselm of Canterbury, expressing concern about Abbot Hamo of Cerne, who had encouraged his monks to join the enterprise, had sent one young man abroad and had bought a ship to carry him and his companions. Anselm asked the bishop of Salisbury to take steps to prevent monks in his diocese going and he wanted him to transmit these instructions to the bishops of Exeter, Bath and Worcester as well.[55] There were men from England in a large army which marched into the Rhineland in the spring of 1096 and took part in the persecution of the Jews there,[56] but most of the crusaders whose names are known left later in the year in the following of established leaders and were nearly all Anglo-French. Some had got on reasonably well with the king. They included Ivo of Grandmesnil, who had supported an uprising of Robert of Normandy's against William I in the late 1070s but had probably succeeded to his father's sheriffdom of Leicester,[57] Payen Peverel, whose brother was a magnate, and probably William of Percy, who became lord of a stretch of the Jabal Sumaq in Syria before dying near Jerusalem. There was also Edgar Atheling, the 'heir' to the Anglo-Saxon throne, who had lived an extraordinarily unsettled life since 1066: in Scotland, where his sister was queen; in England and Normandy; and in Apulia, for which he had left in 1086 with 200 knights, although he had soon returned. He had had a changeable, but at times good, relationship with the king. In 1095 he had probably been in the army with which William had crushed the rebellion of Robert of Mowbray in Northumberland. In 1097 he commanded another army recruited in England, which defeated King Donald of Scotland and established his nephew on the Scottish

[55] Anselin of Canterbury, 'Epistolae', 4.85–6.
[56] AA 291. See *The Anglo-Saxon Chronicle* 173–4.
[57] F. Barlow, *William Rufus* (London, 1983), 34, 188, 279, 361. He was to be exiled by Henry I in 1102. *Ibid.* 366 note.

throne as an English vassal.[58] After this he took the cross and was the leading figure in a fleet which brought a large force of English and northern European crusaders directly to Syria in 1098.[59] The name survives of one member of his household, a knight called Robert son of Godwin, who held lands in Lothian, accompanied Edgar to the East and died there in 1101. Presumably he was a tenant in an honour granted to Edgar by his brother-in-law or by his nephew.[60]

But there was also a significant contribution to the Norman contingent in 1096 by individuals who were in trouble with the king of England. The man behind a rebellion engineered by Robert of Normandy against William in 1088 had been their uncle, Bishop Eudes (Odo) of Bayeux. The king had never forgiven him and he went on crusade with Robert because, according to one contemporary, he preferred not to stay in Normandy with the prospect of William taking it over. He was to die in Sicily.[61] One might add that associated with Robert in the rebellion of 1088 had been Eustace III of Boulogne, who had inherited vast English possessions, the Honour of Boulogne, concentrated particularly in Essex and Hertfordshire. Eustace, who had independent command on the crusade, had probably been dispossessed of his English honour, which does not seem to have been returned to him until 1101.[62]

Also crusading in Robert of Normandy's contingent was a Breton lord, Ralph I of Gaël, his wife Emma of Hereford and one of their sons called Alan. In *c.*1069 Ralph had inherited the earldom of Norfolk from his father, who had served as Staller at the court of Edward the Confessor and had given his allegiance to William the Conqueror. In 1075 Ralph had rebelled in association with Earl Roger of Hereford, whose sister Emma he married: the revolt had been planned at their wedding feast at Exning, near Newmarket. It had been crushed – Emma herself had unsuccessfully defended the castle of Norwich – but Ralph, who may have been one of those engineering a Scandinavian invasion of England at that time, got away. His earldom had been forfeited and in 1076 William I had entered Brittany to seize him but had been forced to retire when the king of France intervened.[63] More recent exiles were Philip the

---

[58] Barlow, *William Rufus*, 264–6, 348, 353, 371.
[59] WMGR 2.310; OV 5.270–2. See Runciman, *A History*, 1.227, 255.
[60] See R. L. G. Ritchie, *The Normans in Scotland* (Edinburgh, 1954), 95, 97–8.
[61] OV 4.118; 5.34, 208–10. See GN Gesta 232–3.
[62] Barlow, *William Rufus*, 90–1; Mayer, *Mélanges*, 16–17.
[63] Douglas, *William the Conqueror*, 231–4.

Grammarian of Montgomery, Arnulf of Hesdin and Stephen of Aumale. Philip was the son of Roger II of Montgomery, the earl of Shrewsbury, and Mabel of Bellême. He had been implicated in Robert of Mowbray's rebellion of 1095, as had been Arnulf, who was a major landowner and land improver, a tenant-in-chief in ten counties, and a man of marked piety.[64] Philip was sentenced to imprisonment but fled.[65] Arnulf's vassal won a judicial duel on his behalf, but he nevertheless left, to die, like Philip, on the crusade.[66] Stephen of Aumale had been involved, perhaps passively, in the plot – one idea of the conspirators had been to place him on the throne – but he avoided sentence.[67]

The attachment to Robert of Normandy of men exiled from England or in one way or another at odds with the king is understandable. Since Robert had pledged his duchy to William, it would have been safer for them to travel with him far away, as Eudes of Bayeux recognized. And they probably looked to him for patronage and protection in the future as a result of a shared commitment and common experiences. Similar thoughts may have moved another group of Anglo-French, who normally lived on the continent but had close relations in England: Alan, the seneschal of the archbishopric of Dol and the brother of Flaald, the progenitor of the house of Stewart;[68] Ilger Bigod, who must have been related to Roger Bigod, the sheriff of Norfolk who himself wanted to pilgrimage to Jerusalem eight years later;[69] William of Bayeux, the great-nephew of Hugh of Avranches, earl of Chester; William of Ferrières, the son of Henry of Ferrières, castellan of Tutbury and sheriff of Derbyshire; and probably Ralph of Montpinçon, the son of Ralph I of Montpinçon, the steward of England.[70] Perhaps their families were anxious to keep feet in both camps and this was a defensible way of doing so.

Among the Anglo-French ties of blood were strong. Stephen of Aumale was Robert of Normandy's first cousin. Ivo of Grandmesnil's sister was the wife of Ralph of Montpinçon's brother; and Ivo's brother Robert III was married to William of Bayeux's sister. Alan

---

[64] R. Lennard, *Rural England 1086–1135* (Oxford, 1959), 49–50, 56n, 57, 64, 67, 69–70, 72, 85, 210–12.
[65] Florence of Worcester 2.39; Barlow, *William Rufus*, 347, 358, 366.
[66] 'Chronica monasterii de Hida' 301–2; Barlow, *William Rufus*, 347, 358.
[67] Barlow, *William Rufus*, 347–8, 358.
[68] J. H. Round, *Studies in Peerage and Family History* (London, 1901), 120–9.
[69] Geoffrey, 'Historia coenobii Thetfordensis', 151.   [70] See OV 3.164–6.

the seneschal of Dol's nephew had married (or was yet to marry) Arnulf of Hesdin's daughter.[71] Eustace of Boulogne's brother Baldwin, admittedly in another contingent, crusaded in the company of his wife Godehilde of Tosny, a first cousin of Emma of Hereford. These family ties are only to be expected in a close-knit and relatively small aristocracy, but they are parallelled everywhere and they had an influence on motivation even more potent than that of lordship; indeed the commitment of many magnates was itself founded on family predispositions.

FAMILY

A feature of recruitment to the First Crusade – and to crusading in general until at least the middle of the twelfth century – was the way many of those who took the cross were clustered into certain families. There has been debate how far late eleventh- and twelfth-century families were extended and it has been pointed out that, as far as property was concerned, rights and obligations tended to involve the closely related, even if the group of individuals recognized as kindred could assume many different forms, expanding and contracting according to circumstances.[72] In the context of crusading, it seems to have been expanded, but even taking a narrow view of family relationships, confined to brothers, fathers and sons, the concentrations of crusading relations are striking. In the Limousin they are to be found in castellan and knightly families, many already, or soon to be, related: three from Bernard of Bré[73] and probably from Durnais,[74] and two each from Le Breuil,[75] La Chèze,[76] Las Gaydias,[77] Les Murs[78] and probably from La Rivière,[79] Lastours[80] and La Vue.[81] Among those from elsewhere in the kingdom of France, Count Baldwin I of Guines in Flanders crusaded with his four sons.[82] So did five members of the family of Poissy in the Ile-de-France[83] and three

---

[71] Round, *Studies*, 128.
[72] S. D. White, *Custom, Kinship and Gifts to Saints: The Laudatio Parentum in Western France* (Chapel Hill and London, 1988), 124–9.
[73] Aimery Bernard, and Bernard II and Guy of Bré.
[74] Aimery I, Aimery II and Bernard Durnais.
[75] Jordan and William of Le Breuil.   [76] Boso and Rainald of La Chèze.
[77] Adhémar and G. of Las Gaydias.   [78] Josbert and William of Les Murs.
[79] Bego and probably Itier of La Rivière.   [80] Gouffier and probably Guy III of Lastours.
[81] Probably Peter and Itier of La Vue.
[82] Fulk, Guy, Hugh and Manasses Robert of Guines.
[83] Robert of Paris, and Simon, Walter II, Walter Sansavoir and William of Poissy.

each of those of the counts of Roussillon[84] and the lords of Toucy in Burgundy,[85] Gaël in Brittany,[86] Grandmesnil in Normandy (and England)[87] and Tudebode in Poitou.[88] From the empire came Cono of Montaigu with two sons,[89] three members of the family of the counts of Burgundy[90] and three of the family of the viscounts of Marseilles.[91] I have records of over forty other families in each of which at least two members took the cross for the First Crusade.

The fact that crusading interested only a minority among those armsbearers qualified to go gives these clusters even more significance and suggests that certain families were collectively predisposed to respond favourably to the summons to take the cross. Some of them are known to have customarily venerated particular religious images or saints and I have already drawn attention to the traditions of devotion to the cross in the families of the counts of Cornouaille and Metz, both of which bred early recruits. The Polignacs, who provided three first crusaders,[92] had a long-standing devotion to the Greek military saint and patron of early crusaders, George, whom they had confused with another George, a local missionary who had been originally venerated in their district.[93] The family of Thouars, which sent two crusaders,[94] had a devotion to St Nicholas, another saint associated with the East, to whom their foundation of Chaise-le-Vicomte was dedicated.

Other traditions which might incline a family to crusading – such as those of pilgrimage to Jerusalem, benefactions to Cluny and support for the reform papacy – can be traced in the comital house of Burgundy. Of Count William Tête-Hardi's six sons, Rainald II, Stephen I and Hugh were on the First Crusade, and Guy, as Pope Calixtus II, proclaimed the crusade of 1120–4. Of William's four daughters, three were married before 1095 to men who were to become first crusaders: Clemency to Robert of Flanders, Gisela to

---

[84] Ermengald, Geoffrey III and Gerard of Roussillon.
[85] Hugh, Itier I and Norgeot I of Toucy.
[86] Ralph I of Gaël, his wife Emma of Hereford and Alan of Gaël.
[87] Aubrey, Ivo and William of Grandmesnil.
[88] Arnald, Arvedus and Peter Tudebode.
[89] Gozelo and Lambert of Montaigu.
[90] Rainald II, Stephen I and Hugh of Burgundy.
[91] Achard and Bertrand of Marseilles, and Fulk of Solliès.
[92] Heraclius I of Polignac, and Peter and Pons II of Fay.
[93] Polignac 1.1–20. See also C. Lauranson-Rosaz, *L'Auvergne et ses marges (Velay, Gévaudan) du VIIIe au XIe siècle* (Le Puy-en-Velay, 1987), 232, 267.
[94] Geoffrey III and Herbert II of Thouars.

Humbert II of Savoy (although he did not take part in the end) and Sibyl to Eudes of Burgundy. The fourth daughter, Ermintrude, was the mother of a first crusader, Louis of Mousson, as indeed was Sibyl, whose daughter Florina accompanied her husband Sven of Denmark to the East. So the contribution of the family to the First Crusade was immense. William Tête-Hardi's mother was Adelaide of Normandy, whose brother Duke Robert I had made the ostentatious pilgrimage to Jerusalem in 1035. William's grandfather, Count Eudes William, had been a benefactor of Cluny and had established a tradition within the family of support for Cluniac monasticism, with William's cousin Guy entering the community. William himself had been a *fidelis beati Petri*.[95]

Another family, this time in the Limousin, demonstrates the importance of some of these connections. The Bernards of Bré, as we have seen, sent three men on the First Crusade. At least one of the kin, Aimoin Bernard, had been on pilgrimage to Jerusalem before-hand[96] and it has been shown that the family had been instrumental in the reform of the abbey of Vigeois, of which they had probably been lay abbots. After a disastrous fire, which had weakened the abbey's resistance to despoilers, it was put in the charge of the Cluniac community of St Martial de Limoges in 1082. The Bernards remained active supporters and Vigeois was to figure prominently in the will of Guy of Bré, drawn up while he lay dying in Syria.[97]

The customary veneration of certain saints, earlier pilgrimaging to Jerusalem, a history of benefactions to the abbey of Cluny and its daughters, and support for the papal programme of reform could each have played a part in creating a family ethos which would be responsive, but they did not necessarily do so. Many families with a marked devotional outlook did not generate early crusaders. While an ancestor or relation in the paternal line who had pilgrimaged to Jerusalem could also have been recalled by first crusaders from the families of Born,[98] Chalon-sur-Saône,[99] Fézensac,[100] Flanders,[101] Limoges,[102] Luxembourg,[103] Malemort,[104] Normandy,[105]

---

[95] Riley-Smith, 'Family Traditions', 102–3.   [96] He went in 1088. Aureil 174; Tulle 255.
[97] Bull, *Knightly Piety*, 274–80.   [98] William of Born 1084 × 91.
[99] Hugh I of Chalon-sur-Saône 1036.   [100] Aimery II Forton of Fezensac 1090.
[101] Robert I of Flanders 1085.
[102] Hilduin and Guy I of Limoges 1000; Adhémar II of Limoges *c.*1090.
[103] Conrad of Luxembourg 1086.   [104] Josbert of Malemort 1010.
[105] Robert I of Normandy 1035; Nicholas of Normandy 1091. Duke Richard II had been a benefactor of the Holy Sepulchre and backer of pilgrimages.

Turenne,[106] and possibly Beaugency[107] and Le Puiset,[108] and in the maternal line by crusaders from the families of Aalst[109] and Boulogne,[110] many descendants of eleventh-century pilgrims did not take the cross. Crusaders with ancestors who had founded satellites of Cluny are to be found in the royal house of France[111] and in the families of Béziers,[112] Chalon-sur-Saône,[113] Montlhéry,[114] Mortagne[115] and Poitou-Aquitaine,[116] but Cluniac monasticism was so fashionable that it is surprising that there are not more examples. Most of the *fideles beati Petri*, those committed supporters of reform who have been already described, would have been hard put to explain the finer points of papal policy, but one cannot avoid the conclusion that at some, probably unconscious, level their commitment was intellectual preparation for the summons to crusade in 1095, because five of them were to take the cross,[117] as did the children of eleven,[118] the close relations of three[119] and the sons-in-law of two.[120] But some, like Ebles of Roucy, did not respond in 1096 (although Ebles came to Rheims to see the Flemish contingent off and his daughter went in 1107) and one also finds those who were indifferent or hostile to reform playing prominent rôles in early crusading. Godfrey of Bouillon and his brothers were lukewarm about the new forces in the Church, and Godfrey, who had been engaged in a long struggle with Mathilda of Tuscany over his possessions, to which she as his uncle's widow had claims, had served the emperor Henry IV loyally in his wars against the forces of radical reform in Italy.[121] The most

[106] Boso I of Turenne 1091.
[107] Lancelin of Beaugency's establishment of a church of the Holy Sepulchre at Beaugency suggests that he had made the pilgrimage.
[108] Everard II 1073.   [109] Conrad of Luxembourg 1086.
[110] Frederick II of Upper Lorraine c.1000.
[111] The priory of St Martin des Champs de Paris.
[112] The abbey of Lézat.   [113] The priory of St Marcel-lès-Chalon-sur-Saône.
[114] The priory of Longpont-sous-Montlhéry.   [115] The abbey of Nogent-le-Rotrou.
[116] The abbey of Montierneuf de Poitiers, the priory of Sauxillanges and, of course, the abbey of Cluny itself.
[117] Bernard II of Besalù, Hugh VI of Lusignan, Raymond IV of St Gilles, Welf IV of Bavaria and William IX of Aquitaine. Perhaps Eudes I of Burgundy should be included as a sixth.
[118] The eleven were Alfonso VI of Castile, Centule IV of Béam, Ebles of Roucy, Fulcher of Chartres, Robert Guiscard of Apulia, Robert I of Flanders, Sancho IV Ramirez of Aragon, Sven II of Denmark, Thibaut I of Blois, William Tête-Hardi of Burgundy and William VIII of Aquitaine.
[119] The three were Amadeus II of Savoy, Frederick of Montbéliard and Hugh I of Burgundy.
[120] Bertrand II of Provence and Peter of Melgueil.
[121] Mayer, *Mélanges*, 22–31; Runciman, *A History*, 1.145–6.

distinguished member of the family of the viscounts of Marseilles, Achard, had been accused of simony, deposed from the archbishopric of Arles and excommunicated when he had refused to give up his control of the cathedral, but he had hung on – and his successor had been frightened off by threats from Achard's family – up to the time when he took the cross, together with relations and local supporters.[122] Since another recruit to the expedition of 1100–1 was Albert of Parma, the brother of the anti-pope Wibert of Ravenna, it has been suggested that the distinguished opponents of Gregorianism recruited for the First Crusade signified a triumph of Pope Urban over his rival.[123]

But there are exceptions to everything and in this case they are overshadowed by the circumstantial evidence that the traditions I have referred to helped build up an ethos which conditioned some kindred groups to respond positively to the appeals to crusade. And another feature, already apparent in the family of the counts of Burgundy and among the descendants of Almodis of La Marche, comes into view when one raises one's eyes from nuclear to extended families. It looks as though women had a positive influence on the responses of men to crusade appeals.

The early twelfth-century sculpture of a man and his wife, which once stood in the cloister of the priory of Belval in Lorraine, has already been mentioned. The man is not in armour. He wears simple travelling garments, but his staff and purse, and the cross sewn on the front of his cloak show him to have been a crusader, dressed as all crusaders would have been for most of the time, as a pilgrim. The woman, in a gesture of great tenderness, even anguish, has her arms around him and her face pressed close to his. The crusader stands quite still, staring forwards and a little upwards. Is he leaving, with his eyes fixed already on a first sight of Jerusalem, or has he just come back, his mind still filled with the horrors he has witnessed? Is his wife determined not to let him go or is she passionately welcoming him home? Whatever scene the figures were supposed to be depicting, it was popular: a similar one, carved in oak by the master of Salzburg and depicting Louis IX of France, who is, significantly, in armour, and his wife, dates from a century and a half later. It recalls one of the most clear and straightforward messages of

---

[122] J. P. Poly *La Provence et la société féodale (879–1166)* (Paris, 1976), 262–4, 268.
[123] P. Riant, 'Un dernier triomphe d'Urbain II', *Revue des questions historiques* 34 (1883), 247–55.

the sources for crusading: that women were inhibitors. With one exception, the story of Adela of England persuading her husband Stephen of Blois to take the road to Jerusalem again after his flight from Antioch,[124] commentaries, histories, treatises, sermons, papal injunctions and popular songs over and over again reported the distress of women at crusaders' departures, sometimes even their attempts to prevent their men from taking the cross, and the sadness of the men themselves at leaving their loved ones.

The message of the sources is not in the least surprising, given the experiences of women left behind for several years to manage estates and bring up families, surrounded by rapacious neighbours and litigious relations. As late as the thirteenth century, when the crown was involved in the protection of families and properties, English legal records contain a depressing inventory of the injury of every sort to which crusaders' wives were exposed – bigamy, murder, theft, legal chicanery – and although we know only of the bad cases, because it was those which reached the courts,[125] there can be no doubt that women left behind had an anxious and precarious time, apart from the temptations to which they would have been exposed and the chance that they would be widowed and their children orphaned. The consequences for family and tenants of a landowner's absence could be so grave that the image drawn in the material of the woman as an inhibitor makes sense, but the genealogical evidence I have examined suggests that it is misleading. Women probably played the same positive rôle in the transmission of support for crusading from one family to another as they did with respect to monastic reform.[126] They seem to have been exercising an influence on crusading which no one wished to acknowledge, not even the women themselves, who must have appreciated as much as men the portrayal in songs of females weeping at the gate. No one seems to have been prepared to admit that in some cases, perhaps in many, they had been instrumental in providing recruits.

The genealogical tables reveal their influence at work, because in them a woman is often to be found at the junction between her own family, which produces many crusaders, and the one she has married into, in which the only recruits are associated with her in one way or

---

[124] OV 5.324.
[125] C. J. Tyerman, *England and the Crusades 1095–1588* (Chicago and London, 1988), 209–15.
[126] Clemency and Ermintrude of Burgundy, for example, were responsible for the spread of Cluniac influence and attachments. Bouchard, *Sword, Miter, and Cloister*, 146.

another. Outstanding among the mothers and wives from lineages predisposed to crusade were the four Montlhéry sisters, whose wider influence on the crusading movement will be described in detail below. But there are plenty of other examples. The head of the family of Aalst, Baldwin of Ghent, went on the First Crusade with his brother and his uncle; so did the husbands of both his sisters.[127] Ralph of Beaugency, who took the cross with his brother Eudes, was married to the crusade leader Hugh the Great of Vermandois's daughter Mathilda; Eudes of Beaugency was Hugh's standard bearer or seneschal.[128] Ralph's sister Agnes of Beaugency was the mother of the brothers William II and Robert who began the participation of the Nevers family in the movement, although in that case she may have been reinforcing a predisposition that was already present because their great-uncle was the crusader Robert I Burgundio of Sablé. Thomas of Marle was married to Ida of Hainault, the daughter of the crusader Baldwin of Mons and the cousin of the crusade leader Robert of Flanders. The wife of Duke Welf IV of Bavaria, who led a large force in 1101, was Robert's aunt. Hugh II of Le Puiset may well have joined Bohemond of Taranto's crusade of 1107 because he was married to Bohemond's niece, although Hugh himself belonged to a family of enthusiasts.

Faced by such a hidden area of life one cannot now establish how the women did it. The period was one in which mothers could take a real interest in their children, but it may be that the influence of women on recruitment was more indirect, perhaps by the way they brought about changes to the ethos of a household by introducing chaplains of a particular kind. It may be that the traffic between families through women could pass more quickly one way than the other. A family which was not predisposed to crusade would not necessarily be fired simply by becoming associated with zealots through the marriage into them of one of their daughters. An example is perhaps the Le Riches of Maule, who, incidentally, demonstrate that religious devotion and support of reform did not inevitably lead to immediate recruitment. In the later eleventh century their lordship west of Paris was a centre of evangelical piety under Peter and Ansold, the second of whom had served in the Norman army under Robert Guiscard which had invaded the

[127] Arnold II of Ardres and Engilbert of Cysoing.
[128] RR 831; Gilo, 'Historia de via Hierosolymitana', 775; Ch d'A 1.426–7, 442 (called Eudes of Beauvais).

Byzantine empire in 1081. The knights of Maule had a close and
warm relationship with their local priory and used to visit it regularly
to discuss 'practical as well as speculative matters' with the monks.[129]
So here was a secular lordship under the influence of reform, some of
the knights of which were interested in theology. The Maule family
also had marriage ties with a group of enthusiastic crusaders, for
Ansold's sister Odeline was married to Walter II of Poissy, who took
the cross in 1096 together with no less than four other members of his
family, one of whom was Peter the Hermit's collaborator, Walter
Sansavoir. The Maule family looks like one which ought to have
responded positively to crusade preaching, but the first known
commitment was made not by a close relation but by a knight on the
estate called Grimoald. The first member of the family to take the
cross appears to have been Robert, Ansold's nephew (through
another sister), who joined Bohemond of Taranto's crusade of 1107
with his cousin Hugh Sansavoir of Poissy.

News of the crusade appeal must have spread as fast down the
networks of kin relationships as it did through preaching, if not faster.
Members of the same family can be found crusading in each other's
company; indeed whole contingents and even small crusades could be
dominated by cousinhood. The crusade of 1129, which will be
described later, was an example of this. Another was Bohemond of
Taranto's army from southern Italy in 1096. According to the author
of the *Gesta Francorum*, who marched with it, recruitment started in
June 1096 at Bohemond's initiative.[130] Although it is hard to believe
that Bohemond had heard nothing until nearly seven months after
the council of Clermont, he was apparently surprised by the arrival of
crusaders in southern Italy, probably a force of Catalans, because a
contingent under Count Geoffrey III of Roussillon was to leave with
him.[131] The following he recruited does not look particularly impressive, perhaps because those who knew him had doubts about his
motives,[132] although it also included a substantial figure from central
France, the vidame of Chartres Bartholomew Boel. It is worth noting
that only two Normans from the island of Sicily, Robert of Sourdeval

---

[129] OV 3.206, and see 180.
[130] GF 7. For the date, see E. Jamison, 'Some Notes on the *Anonymi Gesta Francorum*, with
Special Reference to the Norman Contingent from South Italy and Sicily in the First
Crusade', *Studies in French Language and Mediaeval Literature presented to Professor Mildred K. Pope*
(Manchester, 1939), 191.
[131] GF 8.   [132] See Geoffrey Malaterra 102.

and Roger of Barneville, both quite substantial landowners, are known to have joined the crusade; and Roger, who may have been leading a body of Sicilians, does not seem to have served with Bohemond. Although one contemporary numbered those in Bohemond's company at over 500 knights,[133] an analysis of the individuals known to have followed him provides us with representatives of only four leading families besides his own: Richard and Rainald of the Principate (Salerno), Geoffrey of Montescaglioso, Robert of Buonalbergo and Robert of Molise. Richard, Rainald and Geoffrey were his relations anyway, as were others in his company: his half-brother Guy, Richard of Caiazzo and Alife, Hermann of Canne, Tancred Marchisus, and Tancred's brothers William and Robert. Of Bohemond's fifteen 'captains',[134] eight were fairly closely related to him and a ninth, Ralph the Red of Pont-Echanfray, had been his father's knight.[135] Another relation and a close associate were enrolled by Bohemond as the crusade passed through Constantinople. They were William of Grandmesnil, who was married to Bohemond's sister Mabel and had taken refuge in the Byzantine empire in 1093 after an unsuccessful rebellion in Apulia,[136] and Peter of Alifa, who had been one of Robert Guiscard's vassals and was now a mercenary serving with the Byzantine forces.[137]

In some families a tradition of crusading seems to have been quickly established. I will describe the contribution of the Montlhéry clan below. Another epicentre of continuing zeal may be located among leading castellan families in the district immediately to the north of Angers. Among those Angevins who had taken part in 1096 had been Fulk I of Matheflon, Rainald III of Château-Gontier and Segré, and Robert I Burgundio of Sablé. Robert was one of the greatest, and certainly the best born, of the count of Anjou's subjects, being the son of Count Rainald I of Nevers and Adela, the daughter of King Robert II of France and Constance of Arles. He had migrated to Anjou in the middle years of the eleventh century. He probably took the cross with other Angevins at Tours in the presence of Pope Urban II; his son Rainald was certainly there.[138]

---

[133] Lupus Protospatharius, 'Annales Barenses', 52. See also J. Shepard, 'When Greek meets Greek: Alexius Comnenus and Bohemond in 1097–8', *Byzantine and Modern Greek Studies* 12 (1988), 244.
[134] Monte Cassino 476–7.
[135] Hermann of Canne was both a cousin and a vassal. Jamison, 'Some notes', 198–9.
[136] AA 414–15; Jamison, 'Some notes', 199.   [137] OV 4.34 note.
[138] Anjou (Guillot) 2.242.

He set out in the autumn of 1097, accompanied by Rainald of Château-Gontier, who was related by marriage.[139] Descendants of these Angevin castellans seem to have been engaged in the early twelfth-century crusades. Of Fulk of Matheflon's sons, it may be that Robert took part in the crusade of 1107 and Hugh joined that of 1129. Of Robert Burgundio's grandsons, one, Robert, had travelled East to serve in Palestine before 1127 and became a Templar, and another, Henry, probably joined the crusade of 1129.[140] But in other families the establishment of traditions had to wait until later. The Bernards of Bré in the Limousin, who sent three men in 1096 and four in 1147,[141] provided no recruits in the interim and the descendants of Count William Tête-Hardi of Burgundy, who had been so active at the time of the First Crusade and were to contribute no less than ten crusaders in 1147,[142] seem to have provided only one between 1102 and 1146,[143] although it was William's son, Pope Calixtus II, who proclaimed the crusade of 1120-4. In these kin groups, as in fact in most, it looks as though the zeal of 1096 was only rekindled in 1146.

Nevertheless, it is clear that by the 1140s the crusading experiences of previous generations, and pride in them, had been locked deeply into the collective memory of some cousinhoods. It was this pride which was to be exploited by Pope Eugenius III and Bernard of Clairvaux in their preaching of the crusade of 1147, when they called on armsbearers to emulate the achievements of their ancestors.

It will be seen as a great token of nobility and uprightness if those things acquired by the efforts of your fathers are vigorously defended by you, their good sons. But if, God forbid, it comes to pass differently, then the bravery of the fathers will have proved to be diminished in the sons.[144]

---

[139] It has been suggested by H. E. Mayer ('Angevins *versus* Normans': The New Men of King Fulk of Jerusalem', *Proceedings of the American Philosophical Society* 133 (1989), 10) that the first crusader Geoffrey Parented, the father of two settlers, Anselm and Godfrey Parented, who were resident in Jerusalem from at least 1108 and 1125 respectively, came from Segré. If so Geoffrey must have been in Rainald's company; perhaps Anselm and Godfrey were as well.

[140] The kindred must have built up the grand myth of crusading which is reflected in the *Chronique de Parcé* 12.

[141] In 1147 Bernard IV, Guy, Peter III Aimery and William Eudes of Bré.

[142] William IV of Mâcon, Alfonso VII of Leon-Castile, Louis VII of France and his brother Robert I of Dreux, Amadeus III of Savoy, William the Old of Montferrat, Rainald I and Stephen of Bar-le-Duc, and Guy II and William of Ponthieu. Among William Tête-Hardi's female descendants there were women married to a further four men who took the cross for the Second Crusade: Archimbaud VII of Bourbon, Humbert III of Beaujeu, Alfonso I of Portugal and William III of Warenne.

[143] Rainald I of Bar-le-Duc in 1129.   [144] Eugenius III 303.

The success of this propaganda can be measured not only by the response to it – the crusade of 1147 was much the largest since the First – but also by the number of those taking the cross who came from families which had provided recruits to earlier expeditions. I have identified 262 men and women taking the cross for the 1147 campaign in the East. Of these, thirty-six are known to have been the direct descendants of earlier crusaders to the East or of men who had joined the embryonic military orders: twenty-two of fathers,[145] thirteen of grandfathers[146] and one of a great-grand-father.[147] Thirteen, who were not directly descended from earlier participants, had uncles,[148] and one a great-uncle,[149] who had already fought. One had a brother[150] and five had other relations.[151]

This suggests that by the middle of the twelfth century there was a pool of potential crusaders, drawn especially from those committed kindred-groups in which recruitment had been concentrated at the time of the First Crusade. At this stage the crusading movement was developing as much in the collective consciousness of certain noble and knightly families as in action and in the thinking of the theoreticians. Ideas were taking root below the surface, formulating themselves all the while out of sight in family environments, leaving few traces in historical records.

[145] Alfonso Jordan of Toulouse, Baldwin of Ardres, Bartholomew of Vendôme, Bernard IV of Bré, Drogo II of Mouchy-le-Châtel, Engelrand II of Coucy, Guy of Bré, Hugh Tirel I of Poix, Hugh VII of Lusignan, Itier II of Toucy, Rainald of Tonnerre, Raymond Trencavel, Robert of Boves, Roger I of Béziers, Sibylla of Anjou, Simon of Vermandois, Thibald of Payns, William Aiguillon II of Trie, William II Peverel, William III of Nevers, William IV of Mâcon and William VII of Auvergne.

[146] Adhémar IV of Limoges, Eleanor of Aquitaine, Gaucher of Montjay-la-Tour, Guy II of Ponthieu, Henry I of Champagne, Henry I of Toul, Humbert III of Beaujeu, Louis VII of France, Robert I of Dreux, Roger of Mowbray, Waleran of Meulan, Welf VI of Bavaria and William III of Warenne.

[147] William of Ponthieu.

[148] Amadeus III of Savoy, Bertrand of St Jean, Conrad III of Germany, Everard III of Breteuil, Frederick I of Germany, Guy IV of Lastours, Henry of Alsace, Otto of Freising, Rainald I of Bar-le-Duc, Stephen of Bar-le-Duc, Thierry I of Flanders, William the Old of Montferrat and William of Courtenay.

[149] Philip of Gloucester.

[150] William Peverel of Dover.

[151] Bernard of Le Dognon, Fulcher of Le Dognon, Norgeot of Cruz, Peter III Aimery of Brè and William Eudes of Bré. At least another three crusaders from families which had not so far taken part, Archimbaud VII of Bourbon, Hugh I of Vaudemont and Ivo II of Nesle (who may also have been related to earlier crusaders himself), were married to the daughters of earlier crusaders.

Any map of recruitment, misleading as it is bound to be, would show
that while no part of western Europe was immune from enthusiasm,
the influences on men and women of the ties of lordship and blood
were reflected in the geography of response. Lordship tended to
operate at a regional level and it stamps itself on the map in the
concentrations of recruits in the seigneuries of great magnates, whose
own reactions may have been conditioned by a predisposition in
their families. The local ties which bound men together must have
been an important factor in preserving morale during a campaign,
because little companies from localities can be seen keeping their
cohesion during its rigours. Snapshots of neighbours huddled together in the East are to be found in some of the wills drawn up on
behalf of sick or dying crusaders; naturally, since final dispositions
needed witnesses who would be known locally and could transmit
them by word of mouth when they returned home. When Bertrand
of Bas, a canon of Le Puy, fell ill at sea, presumably on the way home
in 1099, and renounced tithes he had held unlawfully at a place
called Bauzac, his deed was witnessed by six companions, all of them
neighbours from Velay and on board ship with him.[152] When Guy of
Bré from the Limousin lay dying in Latakia in Syria in 1102 he made
several wills, leaving property to local religious communities, which
were witnessed by seven men, all from the Limousin and including
another lord, Peter II of Pierre-Buffière, who was a relation by
marriage.[153] When Herbert of Thouars, deeply upset at what turned
out to be the false news of his brother's death, had a stroke or heart
attack at Jaffa on 28 May 1102, his last words concerned the family
foundation at Chaise-le-Vicomte, which he wished to enlarge
through endowment, and they were witnessed by five men, of whom
one was a member of his household, two were local Poitevin knights,
a fourth was a knight whose home was not very distant and the fifth
was a doctor from Nantes who must have been treating him.[154]

Family influence, on the other hand, is revealed more in chains of
recruits linked to one another over great distances. Rotrou of Perche
was related to the Anglo-Norman nobility and travelled East on the
First Crusade with Robert of Normandy; his sister was the wife of the
Limousin crusader Raymond of Turenne, who went with Raymond
of St Gilles. And Rotrou's maternal aunt had married into the ruling

[152] Chamalières 54.   [153] Aureil 179; Solignac fol. 23v; Vigeois 67–9.
[154] Chaise-le-Vicomte 7–8; and see 25, 347. See also Bèze Liber 614.

house of Aragon, which explains why he spent so much of the early twelfth century campaigning in Spain.

Although many different factors must have played a part in the response of each individual, the decision to crusade usually took place within the contexts provided by lordship and especially kindred. Other associations, including the relationship so many of the armsbearers had with local religious communities, also came into play. It was in their preparations for their crusades that the links crusaders had with local churchmen come to our notice, because they are revealed in the charters which recorded the arrangements by which donations were made in exchange for prayer or money was raised for the journey. Indeed, pre-eminent among the practical questions facing any potential crusader and his family must have been the question of costs. The venture was obviously going to be a very expensive one. How were the bills to be paid? And it was here, and in all the practicalities of preparation, that a crusader's family could demonstrate its value.

CHAPTER 5

Preparing for crusades

STRATEGY

The pope and his advisers seem to have been originally thinking of raising one army, but even that could not have been assembled for a long campaign without planning and some of the details must have been discussed before the council of Clermont, because the decisions announced there cannot have been made on the spot. It seems to have been during the council that the date of 15 August 1096 for the army's departure was fixed.[1] A decree, which defined the crusade as a fully satisfactory penance for those who joined 'not for honour or money',[2] suggests that someone had raised the behaviour of French knights who for a century had been looting in Spain,[3] a part of the world which had been anyway on Urban's mind. Others laid down that the property of crusaders should be protected,[4] that donations (perhaps a euphemism for arrangements that involved counter-gifts) and pledges made by them should be guaranteed by the church,[5] and that they should wear crosses.[6] Regulations were issued in a vain attempt to limit the crusade to those who were qualified to fight - the old and infirm ought not to go;[7] women and priests were to take part only in special circumstances and with official permission,[8] monks not at all[9] - and to establish some method of control by encouraging laymen to seek the blessing of their parish priests before they left.[10] Adhémar of Monteil, the bishop of Le Puy whom Urban must have wanted to be his representative, came forward immediately after the pope's sermon to take the cross.[11] Raymond of St Gilles had been apparently chosen to be the military commander, at least as far as

---

[1] Kb 137. [2] *Decreta Claromontensia* 74. [3] Bull, *Knightly Piety*, 78–86.
[4] HP 169–70.
[5] 'donationes et laxas'. HGL 5.748. For the use of the word 'laxa' for pledge, see Tulle 418.
[6] HP 170; RR 729–30. [7] RR 729. [8] RR 729.
[9] Geoffrey of Vendôme 162; 'Papsturkunden in Florenz' 313. [10] RR 729.
[11] BB 15–16; FC 138–9. See RR 731.

Constantinople after which it was probably assumed that the Byzantine emperor would take command. A delegation from Raymond which must have been pre-arranged arrived at Clermont to pledge his service only a few days after the pope's sermon.[12]

But as usual the drawing board was one thing, the realities of a stressful and ambitious enterprise another. Adhémar enjoyed great authority, partly because of the strength of his personality, but he died two-thirds of the way through the campaign. Raymond was never recognized as generalissimo and Stephen of Blois, the only crusader who briefly held the position of commander-in-chief, ran away. The Greeks would not take part and their emperor would not take charge, being content to follow the crusade at a safe distance; he hurried back to Constantinople when his own troops seemed to be threatened. The western army looted with a will; it had to if it was to survive. The Church was not yet in the position to give adequate protection to the crusaders' dependants and was anyway confused about its rôle. It had become clear by April 1096, when a charter drawn up at Cluny contained a reference to 'such a populous and great arousal or expedition of Christian people',[13] that recruitment was going to be on a much larger scale than originally envisaged and there turned out to be not one, but many contingents, some of which left well before 15 August and others long afterwards. There was no way the pope could have limited a pilgrimage, particularly one to a shrine like Jerusalem where the elderly went to die, to young healthy male warriors and it is striking how old many of the leading crusaders were. Rainald of Château-Gontier,[14] Robert Burgundio of Sablé,[15] Ralph of Gaël[16] and Hugh of Lusignan[17] must have been past the fighting age or nearly so. Large numbers of the 'unsuitable' joined, or tried to, including monks[18] (although those employed as chaplains by the magnates had presumably got permission to go) and many women, among whom were seven wives travelling with husbands,[19] a nun from Trier who was taken by the Muslims in the catastrophe that befell Peter the Hermit's force and then, when she was liberated

---

[12] BB 16.   [13] Cluny 5.51.
[14] See CGCA 'Additamenta' 149.   [15] See Marmoutier (Manceau) 457.
[16] Born before 1040. *Complete Peerage of England, Scotland, Ireland, Great Britain and the United Kingdom*, ed. G. E. Cokayne *et al.*, 2nd edn. (London, 1910–40), 9.572.
[17] He must have been born in the mid 1030s at the latest, which would have made him well over sixty in 1101. See St Maixent Chartes 16.242–3.
[18] See 'Papsturkunden in Florenz' 313; Anselm of Canterbury 4.85.
[19] Elvira of Leon-Castile, Emeline, Emma of Hereford, Florina of Burgundy, Godehilde of Tosny, Hadvide of Chiny and Humberge of Le Puiset.

in the summer of 1097, eloped with her erstwhile Turkish captor,[20] and the religious leader of a sect which believed her goose was filled with the Holy Spirit, at least until the bird died.[21] There is one surviving example of a woman following the pope's instructions and asking for permission to go. Emerias of Altejas went to her bishop for his blessing and was persuaded to commute her vow to the foundation of a hospice for the poor.[22]

There were more discussions at Nîmes in July 1096, because immediately after the church council there had ended the bishops of Grenoble and Orange were despatched to Genoa to seek assistance.[23] The arrival of a Genoese fleet sixteen months later at Suwaidiyah, the port of Antioch, suggests that in this respect there had been quite sophisticated forward planning. Urban kept in touch with, and reacted to, events during the crusade as far as he was able, although he was to die before the news of the liberation of Jerusalem reached him. In 1098 he sent a delegation to call on Pisa to join the enterprise.[24] He appointed Daimbert of Pisa to replace Adhémar of Monteil as legate when he heard of the latter's death.[25] He sought reinforcements, presiding over a council in Rome in April 1099 which decreed that the penance for an arsonist should be 'that he should remain in the service of God in Jerusalem or Spain for one year'[26] and at about the same time commissioning the archbishop of Milan to preach the cross in Lombardy.[27]

But there were limits to what he and the higher clergy could do and the practical details had generally to be decided by those laymen who had taken the cross and were on the spot. The commentator Guibert of Nogent referred to a 'time when the organization of this expedition was engaging the leaders of the kingdom [of France] and was the subject of a discussion held by them with Hugh the Great in the presence of King Philip in Paris on 11 February [1096]'.[28] In spite of the scale of the operation and the fact that departure dates were staggered to suit the times of harvest in different parts of Europe,[29] there seems to have been some coordination of the march of the contingents, because they proceeded by different, although conventional, routes and arrived at intervals at Constantinople between

---

[20] AA 327–8.   [21] GN Gesta 251; AA 295.   [22] HGL 5.757.
[23] *Italia pontificia* 6,2.323; P. Riant 'Inventaire critique des lettres historiques des croisades', *AOL* 1 (1881), 119–20.
[24] *Italia pontificia* 3.359.   [25] See Runciman, *A History*, 1.299.
[26] *Acta pontificum Romanorum inedita* 2.168.   [27] *Italia pontificia* 6,1.54.   [28] GN Gesta 149.
[29] FC 154.

November 1096 and May 1097. When Robert Burgundio of Sablé left with Rainald of Château-Gontier later in 1097 he was said to be 'in secunda profectione',[30] which must have been a premeditated army of reinforcements: the crusaders ahead of him at Antioch were expecting one.[31] Most of the knights in this new force presumably withdrew from central Asia Minor with the Emperor Alexius in the summer of 1098, although Rainald got to Jerusalem eventually, because he died there.[32] Similar forward planning must have been in train in 1100 and 1101. A charter issued on behalf of Eudes of Burgundy referred to him, Hugh the Great of Vermandois and Stephen of Blois leaving 'in prima profectione', presumably the first army of the third wave of the crusade to leave France.[33]

INDIVIDUAL PLANNING

As we have seen, a crusader usually took the cross at some large and turbulent assembly at which the enthusiasm of the audience was whipped up by a preacher, but he would then have had to face the first of many questions posed by the situation in which he now found himself. How was he going to pay for his crusade? Warfare has always been a costly business and the First Crusade was war of a type never experienced before and on a scale not known for six centuries. Its soldiers were not conscripts or vassals performing feudal service, but were volunteers, at least theoretically, and those who could not attract the support, or were not in the household, of a great noble had to finance themselves. Any knight would need to take with him a number of servants, as we have seen. These were indispensible and a recent historian is surely right when he suggests that to get some idea of the effectives, as opposed to the non-combatants, in a crusade force one has to add the servants to the number of knights.[34] If one assumes that the most recent estimate of about 7,000 nobles and knights on the expedition of 1096–9 is correct,[35] by taking account of squires, grooms, and others in supporting rôles one reaches a figure of 21,000–28,000 effectives in the army in Asia Minor in the summer of 1097. Each of these men had to be horsed, equipped and fed, a prospect which many knights must have viewed with feelings of despair.

[30] Marmoutier (Manceau) 90; also Marmoutier (Anjou) 39.   [31] RA 47.
[32] CGCA 'Additamenta' 149.   [33] Molesme 2.13.
[34] France, *Victory in the East*, 126.   [35] France, *Victory in the East*, 142.

The various armies of the First Crusade were to march overland, although a surprisingly large amount of shipping was also involved.[36] The crusade of 1107 assembled in southern Italy and was transported across the Adriatic; after the débâcle before Durazzo those who went on to Palestine presumably travelled from the south Italian ports. Elements of the crusade of 1120–4 made the sea-crossing to the Holy Land, some of them from Venice in 1122,[37] and the crusade of 1129 also went to Palestine by sea.[38] Maritime transportation created its own problems, of course, and we do not know how the crusaders of 1107 and the 1120s coped with them, but these expeditions, which were anyway smaller, cannot have caused the headaches the volunteers in 1096–7 or 1100–1 had as they prepared for a march of 2,000 miles, much of it in hostile territory where there would be no system of provisioning. Although they could carry supplies for the early part of the march,[39] they must have known that for most of the time they would have to forage to survive. They had to make sure that they had adequate equipment and they would have recognized that they would have to carry large quantities of *matériel* with them, including ordinary clothing, leather (tack and saddlery), saddlebags – there are descriptions of the knights taking the saddle-bags off their horses before a battle[40] – and tenting, which were perishable, armour and weapons, horse-shoes, sacks, barrels and cash, or items which could be exchanged for it.

Large quantities of money or precious metal are bulky and heavy and their use by the crusaders is a problematical subject. The treasury of Peter the Hermit's army in the Balkans was a waggon filled with gold and silver, although it is not clear how much of this was spoil looted on the way.[41] The army in Syria and Palestine in 1097–9 had a common fund, to which Stephen of Blois was apparently referring when he wrote to his wife that now he was commander-in-chief he had doubled the amount of 'gold and silver and many other riches' he had brought with him when he left home.[42] The early crusaders carried large quantities of European money with them: one eyewitness referred to an exchange rate in use and listed coinage of Poitiers, Chartres, Le Mans, Lucca, Valence, Melgueil and Le Puy; other coin types were in use as well.[43] An army this size would have

---

[36] See J. S. C. Riley-Smith (ed.) *The Atlas of the Crusades* (London, 1991), 30–1.
[37] FC 657. horses were reported being transported.   [38] WT 618.
[39] See FC 154.   [40] See FC 192.   [41] AA 281.   [42] Kb 149.
[43] D. M. Metcalf, *Coinage of the Crusades and the Latin East in the Ashmolean Museum Oxford*, 2nd edn.

had its own internal market, but nevertheless the practical difficulties involved in transporting coins, particularly billon ones which cannot have had much external value, can barely be imagined. Coin was also used on the expedition of 1101; the abbey of Lérins was storing cash collected for it and Pope Paschal II ordered part of the horde to be given to Fulk the Lombard of Grasse.[44] Even the crusaders of 1107 and the 1120s, who were making for a region now occupied by westerners, must have found it hard to pay their way. It is not surprising that the armsbearers had a penchant for precious cloths, which could be folded up, were a great deal lighter to carry, and could have been easily exchanged.[45]

Carriage and mounts were priorities, especially since everyone must have assumed that the death rate among the army's animals was going to be high. Besides horses and mules, the first crusaders made use of asses, oxen and camels,[46] but all the references to these are to be found once they were well into the march, when they were seizing what they could. It is clear, however, that at the planning stage they knew well that they would need many pack-animals and the charters are peppered with references to mules. Very often the cost of an animal was expressed, a particularly expensive one, worth 10 pounds, being acquired by Guy of Thiers, the count of Chalon-sur-Saône.[47] In 1101 Berald Silvain had already pledged some mills to the abbey of St Jean d'Angély for sixty *solidi*. He now wished to sell them.

When Berald wanted to go to Jerusalem he asked the lord abbot to give him, over and above the forty and twenty *solidi* he owed, twelve silver marks and a mule and fox pelts ... This the lord abbot did. For he gave him twelve silver marks, each of which was then worth fifty *solidi*, and a mule worth 200 *solidi*, and pelts costing forty-five *solidi*.[48]

Even allowing for the different values in provincial money in western Europe, the cost of the mules available to religious communities seems to have been rather higher than that of horses, which is an indication of how valuable pack-animals were. There are fewer references to horses in the charters, perhaps because it was not easy

(London, 1995), 3–21. A. V. Murray ('The Army of Godfrey of Bouillon, 1096–1099: Structure and Dynamics of a Contingent on the First Crusade', *Revue belge de philologie et d'histoire* 70 (1992), 326–7) has suggested that Godfrey of Bouillon was carrying *deniers* he had just minted. This seems to be very unlikely.

[44] Antibes 62.
[45] See AA 572, 577–8; Chaise-le-Vicomte 6–7; Le Ronceray d'Angers 104.
[46] See for example GF 23, 28. [47] Paray-le-Monial 108. [48] St Jean d'Angély 33.111.

for religious houses to include them in a deal, but in agreements at the time of the First Crusade, Isnard of la Garenne, a possible crusader, got a horse worth forty *solidi*[49] and in return for their surrender of rights by the brothers who shared the lordship of the castle of Mezenc near Le Puy one man got a mule, another got 100 *solidi* and a horse worth 100 *solidi*, and a third forty *solidi* and another horse worth 100 *solidi*.[50]

Any estimate of the sum a recruit would be budgeting for in the spring of 1096 is a guess, but a reasonable one is that a poor knight would have to find at least four times his average annual income[51] and the raising of this sort of cash would have put a strain even on the affluent. The Burgundian castellan Achard of Montmerle pledged valuable property to the abbey of Cluny because 'he desired to go armed [to Jerusalem]', the inference being that he would have had no need to borrow if he had been going unarmed.[52] The German nobleman Wolfker of Kuffern entered into a pledge 'because he could not afford the costs' of the crusade;[53] the same was true of the archbishop of Cologne's *ministerialis* Frumold;[54] and in 1120 the crusader Guy Tortus of Rochefort-sur-Loire admitted to being in the same predicament.[55] Pope Urban had asked the richer armsbearers to subsidize the less well-off[56] and the pockets of the magnates must have been stretched further, in some cases beyond breaking point. The relatively small number of charters relating to the crusade which are to be found in Languedoc, from where we know Raymond of St Gilles led a substantial force, may be a reflection of the assistance Raymond himself was prepared to give. I have already suggested that Normandy and Champagne may be similar cases. When subjects had to raise cash themselves, their lords, who would be spared the granting of subsidy and could anyway benefit from *douceurs* paid in return for their consent to the disposal of property,[57] would do what they could to ease their knights' own arrangements. When Robert Michael sold some land, 'Nivelo son of Fulcher, at that time lord of Fréteval [and Robert Michael's lord and crusade leader], and his brother Hamelin confirmed the sale. And

---

[49] St Pere de Chartres 2.516.   [50] St Chaffre du Monastier 141.
[51] Riley-Smith, *The First Crusade*, 43.   [52] Cluny 5.51.
[53] Göttweig 194.[54] 'Chronicon Brunwylarense' 152.
[55] Marmoutier (Anjou) 66.   [56] RR 729.
[57] See, for example, Marmoutier (Dunois) 139, 142; St Jean d'Angély 30.114.

Nivelo sent his uncle Gerard. . .to divide and set limits to the aforesaid land, meadow, and water.'[58]

At any rate it is not surprising to find in the cartularies of religious communities many examples of the steps taken by crusaders and their families to provide themselves with cash.

RENUNCIATIONS FOR CASH

In a lawless and violent age it was common for lords who believed they had some right to lands, rents or customs to hold them back or extort them by force. One measure, which seems to have been attractive to them once they had decided to crusade, was the settlement of the disputes which had resulted. As penitent pilgrims they were reluctant to leave behind men and women, and particularly religious, with grudges or complaints against them; indeed they could be threatened with excommunication and forbidden to go if they did not make peace.[59] Renunciations were quite commonly made by them, as will be seen, but in some cases religious communities could be persuaded to part with money in exchange. The benefits to the crusader were multiplied, because once he had come to terms with the religious house concerned he could leave with a clearer conscience and also with a contribution towards his expenses, although when making a deal of this kind Stephen of Neublans wanted to assure those who would read his charter of his best intentions: 'Although I have done this [his renunciation] especially for my soul, I have received ... fifty *solidi* and two of the best mules.'[60]

Some lords had been extremely rough during the squabbles which were resolved by the charters of renunciation. The co-owners of the castle of Mezenc, in dispute with the monks of St Chaffre du Monastier, had made their point by plundering

the poor living in our villages, taking everything that belonged to them to a loaf's crust, as the saying goes. Now some of them, taking the road to Jerusalem to fight the barbarians, have promised, together with all the other knights in the castle, to demand in future no bad custom whatsoever from the men living in the farms and villages [of St Chaffre], neither in

---

[58] Marmoutier (Dunois) 140. Robert of Flanders entered into deals with vassals that freed properties, held in fief of him, to give away or pledge. Flanders 63, 64.
[59] St Hilaire-le-Grand de Poitiers (1847) 128; St Laon de Thouars 44. See also Reims (admin) 1.286.
[60] Cluny 5.90.

pack-animals, nor in demanding lodging, nor in food, nor in oxen, whether
for ploughing or for bearing burdens, nor in any other custom of this sort,
but all have sworn an oath on the sacred altar, in the presence of the abbot,
to exact nothing further of such a kind ... The bishop of Le Puy was asked
to absolve them from their crime. Wondering at their cruelty, he absolved
them from the crime they had committed because they were hastening to
join the expedition to Jerusalem and had promised amendment and
correction.[61]

The castellan Nivelo of Freteval had acted in much the same way.

I had harshly worn down the land of [the abbey of] St Père [de Chartres],
that is to say Emprainville and the places around it, in the way that had
become customary, by seizing the goods of the inhabitants there ... This
was the rough nature of this custom. Whenever the onset of knightly
ferocity stirred me up, I used to descend on the aforesaid village, taking
with me a troop of my knights and a crowd of my attendants, and against
nature I would make over the goods of the men of St Père for food for my
knights.[62]

Some quarrels had lasted for years. The father of Bertrand, the
castellan of Moncontour, had become a monk of La Trinité de
Vendôme in 1081 and as his entry gift had endowed the monks with a
lot of property at Coulommiers, for which he was a vassal of the
castellan of Beaugency. Bertrand had not been present when the gift
had been made and when he had heard of it he had made it clear
that he did not accept it. He had gained the backing of Count
Geoffrey Jordan of Vendôme and with his help had seized two-thirds
of the property by force. In 1092, deprived of the count's support,
Bertrand had settled out of court for one-third, but by the time of the
First Crusade he seems to have reoccupied the two-thirds he had
held earlier. Now, believing that his crusade 'would most certainly be
of no profit to him' otherwise, he summoned the abbot, acknowledged his fault and handed over the land. He received 1,800 *solidi*
from the abbey, with a further 100 *solidi* going to his wife, four
pounds to his eldest son and twelve *denarii* to each of his three
younger sons, one of whom was still a baby. His lord, Ralph of
Beaugency, who was also going on crusade, got twenty *solidi*.[63]
    These compositions were often expressed in grovelling terms,

---

[61] St Chaffre du Monastier 140.   [62] St Père de Chartres 2.428.
[63] La Trinité de Vendôme Cart 2.104–7; P. D. Johnson, *Prayer, Patronage and Power: The Abbey of
La Trinité, Vendôme 1032–1187* (New York, 1981), 79, 94–5. The date of 1098 given for the
renunciation must be in error. Ralph of Beaugency was referred to as being in Poitou,
whereas in 1098 he was with the crusade in Syria.

more humiliating to the lords than those involving free renunciations which were contrite enough; perhaps this was demanded by the religious in return for their money. Nivelo of Fréteval, who by his own admission had been behaving very badly over Emprainville, allowed his charter-writer to refer to him, quoting from Pope Gregory I, as being 'raised in a nobility of birth which produces in many people an ignobility of mind', and to his claims as

the oppressive behaviour resulting from a certain bad custom, handed on to me not by ancient right but from the time of my father, a man of little weight who first harassed the poor with this oppression. Thereafter I had constantly maintained it in an atrociously tyrannical manner.[64]

The fact that at least fourteen of these agreements survive from the time of the First Crusade,[65] with one from 1107,[66] three from 1120[67] and possibly another from 1129,[68] suggests that some churchmen also fastened on them as good ways of ending what must have been exhausting and stressful contests. But renunciations could only play a part in meeting costs. Property might well also have to be pledged or sold.

PLEDGES AND SALES

Evidence survives for thirty (possibly thirty-two) pledges made at the time of the First Crusade[69] and for another in 1120.[70] The figures for sales or agreements involving counter-gifts are: thirty-

[64] St Père de Chartres 2.428. For other renunciations by Nivelo, see Marmoutier (Blésois) 56–7, 58–9.
[65] St Chaffre du Monastier 88, 139–41; La Trinité de Vendôme Cart 2.104–7; Chamalières 16–18; St Vincent du Mans 1.293, 384; Paray-le-Monial 107–8; St Philibert de Tournus (Juénin) 135; Marmoutier (Dunois) 141; St Père de Chartres 2.428–9; St Jean d'Angély 33.110; Cluny 5.87–91; Laurence of Liège 498.
[66] Vigeois 61–2.
[67] Angers 166; Marmoutier (Anjou) 66; St Marcel-lès-Chalon-sur-Saône 45–6.
[68] St Laon de Thouars 44–5.
[69] 'Départ d'un seigneur normand pour la première croisade' 28–9; Valenciennes (595); Cluny 5.51–3, 59, 108; St Hubert-en-Ardenne 1.85 ('Triumphus Sancti Lamberti de castro Bullonio' 499); Göttweig 194–6; OV 4.338; 5.26, 32, 208, 278–80 (Hugh of Flavigny 475; William of Jumièges 274–5; *Regesta regum Anglo-Normannorum* 2.403); St Pierre de la Réole 140–1, 141, 141–2, 142, 142–3; Tulle 416–18 (276–7); Molesme 2.64–5, 229; Flanders 64–5; St Victor de Marseille (Rolland) 26–7; Aureil 113–14; Grenoble 165–6; 'Actes constatant la participation des Plaisançais à la première croisade' 399; La Charité-sur-Loire 88–9; Carcassonne 1.83; Savigny 1.457–8; St Jean d'Angély 30.384–5, 391; Roussillon 111; Marcigny 164–5; GAD 101; and possibly Auch 65; St Mont 121–2. For proposals for another pledge, see OV 5.280 (WMGR 2.379; Robert of Torigni 202 which is confused).
[70] Noyers 265–7.

eight (possibly forty-five) for the First Crusade,[71] four for 1107[72] and three for 1129.[73] All the pledges appear to have been *vifgages*, in which the lenders did not receive interest but occupied the properties concerned, enjoying the revenues from them until their loans had been repaid. In a charter dated 9 September 1096 William of Le Vast pledged his land for three silver marks to the abbey of Fécamp. A clause specified that while William could enjoy the rents taken this year – the harvest would just have been in – the abbey would have the rents in the year of the pledge's redemption.[74] In another more unusual *vifgage*, Bernard Morel, who was probably an early crusader and was anyway intending to spend a few years away helping to defend the Holy Land, pledged a farm to the nuns of Marcigny

on condition that while he remains in Jerusalem, where he was wanting to go, the nuns of Marcigny should take half the fruits of the land as their own and should put the other half on one side and should keep an account of how much that half is worth so that, if he returns, he should receive his share.[75]

Since no interest was technically payable the employment of *vifgages* may have avoided the taint of usury, but a disadvantage for crusaders and their families was that the property passed out of their control until the pledges were redeemed.

Most pledges involved land, but loans were also raised on churches, tithes and glebe lands,[76] on rights of market justice,[77] on a castle[78] and on offices and advocacies.[79] Some pledge-charters

---

[71] St Hubert-en-Ardenne 1.86; Burgundy (Perard) 201–2; Laurence of Liège 498; St Chaffre du Monastier 88–9, 89; St Victor de Marseille (Guérard) 1.167–8; 2.568–9; 'Chronicon Brunwylarense' 151–3; St Lambert de Liège 1.46–8; Dinant 1.13–14; St Vincent du Mans 1.190–1, 266–7, 301 (291); Sauxillanges 882, 884; Le Ronceray d'Angers 95, 104; Marmoutier (Tourangeau) 40–1; St Martial de Limoges 347; Marmoutier (Dunois) 139–40, 141–2; Aureil 85; Lérins 311–12 (although the payment was nominal); Azé et Le Genéteil 60–1 (Anjou (Halphen) 330); *Die Reichskanzler* 3.88–9; St Jean d'Angély 30.113–14, 260–1; 33.111–13; St Maixent Chartes 16.215–16; Montpellier 545, 550–1; Conques 368; Noyers 262, 275–6; Domène 248–9; Morigny 11; OV. 5.324 (Philip I 368 n.1); St Laon de Thouars 32; Talmont 197–8; Cluny 4.254; and possibly Auch 65; Savoy 2, Preuves, 27; St Vincent du Mans 1.222–3; Domène 91; St Jean d'Angély 30.388; St Amant de Boixe 111; St Père de Chartres 2.516.
[72] Cluny 5.199, 202–3; Vigeois 62; St Père de Chartres 2.274–7.
[73] St Aubin d'Angers Cart 1.145; Eenaeme 28–9; Angers 258–60.
[74] 'Départ d'un seigneur normand' 28–9.
[75] Marcigny 164.
[76] St Pierre de la Réole 141, 142; St Jean d'Angély 30.384–5; Tulle 416–18 (276–7); 'Actes constatant la participation des Plaisançais' 399; Grenoble 165–6; Noyers 265–7.
[77] St Pierre de la Réole 140–1.   [78] St Hubert-en-Ardenne 1.85.
[79] OV 4.338; Valenciennes (595); Flanders 64–5.

specified that only the borrower himself,[80] or his successors or very close relations,[81] could redeem the loan, but occasionally redemption was available to all members of the family.[82] In one case it was laid down that there should be no redemption until the prior of the community making the loan, who was the borrower's brother, had died.[83] Normandy was *vifgaged* for five years.[84] The abbey of St Victor de Marseille would only permit a loan to be redeemed after four years.[85] The community at Göttweig allowed redemption only in the fifth year of the loan.[86]

It was common for some kind of additional inducement to be offered to the lenders. The property concerned, or part of it, was often left to the lender after the borrower's death, whether on crusade or otherwise,[87] although Achard of Montmerle, who did not in fact survive, specified that this was to happen only if he died without an heir.[88] Ramnulf of 'Tuinac' was to get back from the abbey of St Jean d'Angély only half of the property he had pledged; but it was ecclesiastical and his rights to it must have been doubtful anyway.[89]

Most of the sales consisted, as one would expect, of lands, vineyards, mills, rents and serfs. Some properties were substantial: the abbacy of Etampes and the viscounty of Bourges (both to King Philip I),[90] part of the county of Chalon[91] and the castle of Couvin.[92] Two lesser fiefs were sold to the crusaders' own lords.[93] Allods, the freeholds which were so valuable to their possessors,[94] were disposed of, together with local taxes,[95] and, again, churches, tithes and

---

[80] Cluny 5.52, 59; St Pierre de la Réole 140–1; St Victor de Marseille (Rolland) 27; Roussillon 111; and probably Savigny 1.457–8; La Charité sur Loire 88.

[81] St Pierre de la Réole 141; Flanders 64–5; St Hubert-en-Ardenne 1.85.

[82] St Pierre de la Réole 142–3; 'Départ d'un seigneur normand' 29.

[83] St Pierre de la Réole 141–2.

[84] OV 5.26, 32, 208, 278–80. But Hugh of Flavigny (473) reported that the agreement was for three years.

[85] St Victor de Marseille (Rolland) 27.   [86] Göttweig 194.

[87] La Charité-sur-Loire 88; Tulle 417–18 (277); Marcigny 164; Cluny 5.59, 108; St Victor de Marseille (Rolland) 26; Molesme 2.65, 229; St Jean d'Angély 30.384; Savigny 1.457; Roussillon 110–11.

[88] Cluny 5.52.   [89] St Jean d'Angély 30.384–5.

[90] Morigny 11; OV 5.324 (Philip I 368 n.1).   [91] Burgundy (Pérard) 201–2.

[92] St Lambert de Liège 1.46–8; Dinant 1.12–15.

[93] St Vincent du Mans 1.190–1; Angers 258–60.

[94] St Hubert-en-Ardenne 1.86; Lérins 311–2; St Chaffre du Monastier 89; Montpellier 550–1; Eenaeme 28–9.

[95] Marmoutier (Dunois) 141–2.

beneficed land.[96] A high proportion of the agreements relating to these involved counter-gifts, in which sales were expressed in terms of mutual giving, often with the assurance that the layman was actually disposing of the property as an act of charity. This was obviously done to evade the accusation of simony at a time when the Church's disapproval of the buying and selling of ecclesiastical property was a live issue. One man had already surrendered some of the tithes he owned, perhaps under pressure from reformers.[97] In Lorraine the first crusader Quino recognized the merit attached to restoring a church benefice to its possessor by ancient right.[98] In the Chartrain in 1129 William of La Ferté-Vidame admitted that he had held a church 'against God and the safety of his soul'.[99] The use of counter-gifts technically combined the benefits of an endowment and a sale, but at least one family tried to go further and was turned down sharply by the monks it approached. Geoffrey and Engelelmus of St Savin and their brothers wanted the land they were going to alienate, on which there was a ruined chapel, to become a religious foundation.

They wanted to require the abbot and monks [of Noyers] to found a village there and rebuild the church, but the monk Lancelin [with whom they were negotiating] replied that no agreement of this sort could be made, but that it would be in the power and will of the abbot and monks whether they constructed a village there or not.[100]

ENDOWMENTS, FREE RENUNCIATIONS AND WILLS

Apprehension enveloped the last stages of preparation like a cloud. Over and above their alienations for cash, many crusaders felt the need to make endowments to religious communities or to renounce claims against them close to or at the moment they were leaving, or in the early stages of the march. Stephen of Blois's anxiety was all too apparent when he gave a wood to the abbey of Marmoutier,

so that God, at the intercession of St Martin and his monks, might pardon me for whatever I have done wrong and lead me on the journey out of my homeland and bring me back healthy and safe, and watch over my wife Adela and our children.[101]

[96] Noyers 262, 276; Lérins 311–12; Azé et Le Genéteil 60 (Anjou (Halphen) 330); Le Ronceray d'Angers 95, 104; St Victor de Marseille (Guérard) 2.568–9; St Vincent du Mans 1.266–7, 301; St Jean d'Angély 30.113–14, 260–1; and possibly St Jean d'Angély 30.388; Domène 91.
[97] St Vincent du Mans 1.266.   [98] St Mihiel 191.   [99] St Père de Chartres 2.511.
[100] Noyers 276.   [101] Marmoutier (Dunois) 81.

Robert Burgundio of Sablé expressed the same desire when giving Marmoutier vineyards and a farm, 'so that God may keep me healthy and safe in going and returning',[102] sentiments which were echoed in other charters for Marmoutier drawn up on behalf of one of his knights, Ardouin of Vione,[103] and a knight of Rillé called Herbert of 'Campus Marini'.[104] Robert of Flanders withdrew his opposition to the grant his sister had made to the abbey of St Thierry-lèz-Reims 'for the remission of my sins and my safety and the safety of my wife Clemency'.[105] In 1120 Rainald of Martigné, the bishop of Angers, gave permission to the abbot of St Nicolas d'Angers to place twelve monks in the almonry of Le Genéteil. The abbey promised to appoint an ordained monk to say Mass 'so that God would lead me [the bishop] and my count [of Anjou] out [on crusade] and lead us back healthy and safe'.[106]

When Robert Burgundio reached Marmoutier on an early stage of his journey, he asked the monks to pray for him.[107] Miles of Bray made the same request of the monks of his father's foundation of Longpont-sous-Montlhéry.[108] Hugh of Chaumont-sur-Loire and Aimery of Courron endowed the abbey of Pontlevoy on condition that the monks pray each Thursday for their souls and for those of the soldiers killed in the battle of Pontlevoy eighty years before.[109] Robert of Flanders and Bernard Ato of Béziers made gifts to the canons of St Pierre de Lille and the monks of St Guilhem du Désert respectively, in order that God would favour the enterprise in which they were engaged.[110] Raymond of St Gilles made an endowment to the cathedral of Le Puy, 'so that as long as I live a candle should burn for me incessantly day and night on the altar before the revered image of the Mother of God [the sacred statue and object of a famous cult at Le Puy]'.[111] Hugh of Rougemont gave part of a tithe to the abbey of Molesme 'when he wished to become a *Jerosolimitanus* but was uncertain about his return'.[112] A cleric, Raymond Eic, gave the abbey of Lézat half of a church on condition that if he returned safe from Jerusalem he would get his gift back to hold of the abbey; if he wished to become a monk the abbot and the community would receive him;

---

[102] Marmoutier (Manceau) 2.87.   [103] Marmoutier (Manceau) 91.
[104] Marmoutier (Anjou) 39.   [105] Flanders 67.
[106] Azé and Le Geneteil 64.   [107] Marmoutier (Manceau) 90.
[108] Longpont 184.   [109] Anjou (Halphen) 326.
[110] Flanders 63; Gellone 248.   [111] HGL 5.747.   [112] Molesme 2.217.

and if he died the whole of the divine office would be said for him
and for all his relations and his name would be inscribed in the
obit book among those of the abbey's dead members.[113] In 1101
Eudes of Burgundy, making a gift to the abbey of Molesme, asked
'the brothers to remember him in their prayers to God, so that the
vow and journey he was making to Jerusalem should have a good
result'[114] and he made a will in favour of the abbey, 'so that the
brothers should take care assiduously to pray to the Lord for the
prosperity of his body and soul'.[115] In 1129 Hugh III of Le Puiset
gave Tiron a rent of wine each year, which he wanted to be drunk
by the brothers on Trinity Sunday, and 'when they hear of my
death they will keep my anniversary each year and this wine,
which the brothers shall drink on the feast-day of their church
during my lifetime, they will have on my anniversary after my
death'.[116]

As we have seen, one way of benefiting from prayers was to put a
young relative into a community as an oblate, thus assuring that the
family shared in the merits of the office and the community's Masses.
At the time of the First Crusade Arnald of Aigurande left 'my
nephew Humbald in monastic habit at La Chapelle-Aude in the
hands of Eudes the prior'. He also provided Humbald's entry gift.[117]
Even more efficacious was to make a monastic foundation or
establish a church, as eleventh-century pilgrims had done. In 1096
Gilbert of Aalst founded the nunnery of Merhem for his sister
Lietgard 'so that he should find a better inheritance in the heavenly
Jerusalem'.[118] In 1129 Matthew Giraud, who may have been a
crusader, established a parish church at Belle-Noue.[119]

The crusaders' worries help to explain the large number of gifts
they made. Leaving aside their foundations of churches, seventy-
eight (possibly eighty) records of endowments made before or on
departure between 1096 and 1101 survive,[120] with a further two in

---

[113] Lézat 17.188–9.   [114] Molesme 2.143.   [115] Molesme 2.13.
[116] Tiron 1.127–8. See also Savoy 2, Preuves, 27.   [117] La Chapelle-Aude 82–3.
[118] Afflighem 11–13.   [119] Angers 271–3.
[120] Auch 57–8; Aureil 21, 51–2 (see 32), 114, 170, 178–9, 192, 199–200; Bèze Chron 392 (Bèze
Liber 614); St Flour cxxxv–vi; 'Cantatorium Sancti Huberti' 338–40; Carcassonne 5.155
(2.237); La Charité-sur-Loire 104–5; *Chronique de Parcé* 10; Chaise-le-Vicomte 7; Dinant 1.13;
Forez 1.1 (no. 1); Gellone 248; HGL 5.747–8, 749; Anjou (Halphen) 326; LA 580–1; Leire
230; Lézat 17.188–9; Longpont 93, 109–10, 184–5; Lérins 289–90, 311–12; 'Chronicon
Affligemense' 415; Marmoutier (Anjou) 39; Marmoutier (Dunois) 56–7 (and see 75), 79–82
(69), 137; Marmoutier (Manceau) 2.87–9, 90–1 (456–7); Molesme 2.84, 143, 217; Brittany
(Morice) 1.488, 491; Morigny 19–20; Néronville 310; Noyers 268, 269–70, 273–4; St Florent-

1107,[121] six in the early 1120s[122] and three in 1129.[123] Sixteen free renunciations of rights unjustly claimed or exercised are known from the time of the First Crusade,[124] three from 1120[125] and three from 1129.[126] There are twenty-four wills made by crusaders before they left for the First Crusade[127] and two in 1120.[128] Some crusaders put together a package, with elements of the property concerned to be held by the beneficiary immediately and parts of it to be surrendered after the donor's death. In the Limousin Peter of La Vue gave the priory of Aureil some land. He willed more land, a rent of rye, which had been included in his wife's dowry – this would go to Aureil after her death – and his bed, with blanket, pillow, mattress, bed-clothes and curtain.[129]

The charters of endowment tended to be expressed in terms of penitence and humility. So were the charters of renunciation, only more so. In 1101 Eudes of Burgundy, followed by an entourage of his greatest vassals,

entered the chapter of St Bénigne de Dijon and, with the monks sitting round the room and many members of their household standing by, I corrected the injuries which I had been accustomed to inflict until now. I recognized my fault and, having sought mercy, I asked that I should be

lès-Saumur (Normandes) 688–9; St Georges de Rennes 269–70; St Jean d'Angély 30.260–1; 33.82–3; St Philibert de Tournus (Juënin) 135 (St Philibert de Tournus (Chifflet), Preuves, 335); St Pierre de la Réole 141; St Père de Chartres 2.628; St Victor de Marseille (Guérard) 1.230; St Vincent de Mâcon 315; St Vincent du Mans 1.87, 200; Savigny 1.433–4; Sauxil-langes 971, 1045; La Trinité de Vendôme Cart 2.158; Uzerche 195, 242, 287, 315, 316, 440; Laurence of Liège 498; Flanders 62–3 and possibly 68–70; Vigeois 51, 64, 67–8; A. Wauters, *Table chronologique des chartes et diplômes imprimés concernant l'histoire de la Belgique* (Brussels, 1866–1965), 1.602; Riant, 'Un dernier triomphe', 252–4; and probably Valenciennes (600).

[121] Marcigny 79–80; Marmoutier (Anjou) 54.
[122] Cart Temp 5–6; Oberalteich 110–11; Marmoutier (Manceau) 2.473–4; Noyers 329–32; Le Ronceray d'Angers 1861, 214–15; St Julien de Tours 87–8.
[123] Burgundy (Pérard) 224; St Cybard d'Angoulême 93–6; St Père de Chartres 2.610
[124] Valenciennes (594–7); Flanders 60-2, 66–7; HGL 5.743–6; Brittany (Morice) 1.484 (491); Uzerche 95; St Mihiel 191; St Avit d'Orléans 54; Marmoutier (Dunois) 56–7, 123; St André-le-Bas de Vienne 281; St Bénigne de Dijon 2.174–7; Cluny 5.156–9; Burgundy (Plancher) 1, Preuves, xliii–xliv; St Martin de Pontoise 21; and probably Nîmes 293–4. See Chaise-le-Vicomte 25, 347: a right given by a crusader's father and only confirmed on the crusader's deathbed in the East.
[125] Tiron 2.23–4; St Hilaire-le-Grand de Poitiers (1847) 122 (128); Reims (admin) 1.286.
[126] Bar 1.42–4 (St Lambert de Liège 1.58-60); Cart Temp 8–10; St Père de Chartres 2.511–12.
[127] Aureil 192, 193, 199; Chaise-le-Vicomte 6; Huesca 1.148–50; Lérins 311–12; Longpont 121–2, 189–90; Molesme 2.13, 18, 64, 229; Morigny 40; Noyers 271, 274; Roussillon 110-11; St Jean d'Angély 30.384–5, 391; 33.78–9; St Victor de Marseille (Rolland) 26–7; Sauxillanges 1045; Sens 2.18; Tulle 416–18 (276–7); Vigeois 51; Uzerche 242.
[128] Le Ronceray d'Angers 215–17; Mauléon 15–16.
[129] Aureil 21, 170, 193, 199; and see 192.

absolved. And I promised amendment in future if I should happen to return [from the crusade].[130]

He seems to have arranged another melodramatic ceremony at Gevrey-Chambertin during which he renounced claims he had unjustly imposed on the Cluniac monks there.[131] At about the same time William II of Nevers sought pardon and absolution from Abbot Robert of Molesme for a fire he had started in the village of Molesme.[132] Solemn renunciations appealed to the flamboyance of the age and could be expressed with verve. In 1096,

so that it should be clear to all with how much devotion he had made [this renunciation], Nivelo of Fréteval made his prévôt Ascelin swear on the relics of the saints that he would knowingly exact or receive no custom or tax from any property belonging to the said obedience [of Marmoutier] or knowingly be violent with respect to anything belonging to it.[133]

As the moment of departure approached the power that lay in the hands of churchmen, who by excommunicating a recruit could prevent him leaving and nullify all his preparations, led crusaders to give away more than perhaps they would have wanted to surrender in a more normal situation. Anselm II of Ribemont had been in dispute with the abbey of St Amand over rights in what seem to have been newly established peasant settlements. The monks had appealed to the count of Flanders, whose court had found in their favour. Anselm had ignored the judgement and had compounded his offence by building a mill which took custom away from the mills of the monks, by diverting water from the river to run it and by imposing dues on the villagers passing down a nearby road. He had, moreover, pledged this part of what he considered to be his lordship to his seneschal for 120 silver marks. The monks had responded by excommunicating him and by adopting an old last measure when faced by a recalcitrant lord, the humiliation of their relics, in order that Anselm 'should be more and more frightened'. The relics of St Amand and other saints were brought out of the church and exposed, covered with thorns, 'on the ground' in the open air, in the belief that the saint would feel so insulted that he would demand severe retribution from God. What makes this case particularly interesting is that Anselm was no ordinary noble bully. He was a man with a reputation for generosity and probity and he must have felt that he had a good

---

[130] St Bénigne de Dijon 2.175.   [131] Cluny 5.156–9.
[132] Molesme 2.42.   [133] Marmoutier (Dunois) 56.

case for what he had done in spite of the court judgement against him. Nevertheless he was brought to heel, probably because he was anxious to crusade; it was said that he was in a hurry to leave for Jerusalem. He was made to come before St Amand's body bare-footed, to prostrate himself and to beg mercy for his sin. He was absolved and on the next day he formally renounced his claims. The monks agreed to cancel the pledge-agreement with his seneschal by redeeming it on Anselm's behalf; they were to be repaid within three years from the following Christmas.[134]

On the other hand, the bustle and hurry, and the general atmosphere of penitence and humility, did not prevent some recruits from adopting quite a hard-headed approach to their giving. Bruno of Ré specified in his will that if he should wish to become a monk the property he had left should be treated as his entry gift.[135] Boso of La Chèze gave away a portion of his wife's dowry; presumably he felt he could part with it more easily than with patrimony.[136] Rossello left the chapter of Elne a freehold which he had retained after his grandfather and father had already left it to the chapter in their wills, but he specified that it would pass to the canons only if he died without legitimate heirs. He went further and pledged land, which by rights belonged to it already, to the chapter.[137]

RELIGIOUS COMMUNITIES

Over the winter of 1095–6, news reached Everard II of Breteuil, who had now been a monk at Marmoutier for eighteen years, that his nephew, Everard III of Le Puiset, 'wanted to go in the army to Jerusalem against the pagans'. The monk Everard sought permission from his abbot to look for his nephew, in order to persuade him to augment an existing Le Puiset endowment for the abbey, and a meeting was arranged near Blois. His journey was made in February 1096 at the latest.[138] His nephew, whose mother was one of the Montlhéry sisters, may have witnessed Pope Urban's proclamation of

---

[134] Valenciennes (594–7). For the humiliation of relics, see Geary, *Furta Sacra*, 23. For Anselm's reputation, see GN Gesta 218; RC 680.

[135] St Jean d'Angély 33.78–9.

[136] Aureil 170.

[137] Roussillon 110 11. When Matthew Giraud established his parish church, he retained half the revenues in his own hands; an example of the rights still claimed by lay patrons in the late 1120s. Angers 271–3.

[138] Marmoutier (Dunois) 137. The meeting took place during the year before the abbey church was dedicated by Urban II on 10 March 1096. See Becker, *Papst Urban*, 2.446. From dating

war in the field outside Clermont in the previous November, or the news could have reached him at Chartres late in December, or he could have been attending the meeting summoned by the king to Paris in February. He had obviously made up his mind quickly. It would have been no surprise to him to have discovered that an elderly monk, who happened to be closely related, was scouring the countryside for him and wanted him to be generous to a community with which his family was already closely associated. Once a man had decided to take the cross kinsmen who were churchmen often seem to have been quickly drawn in, especially if they were monks; being celibate they could themselves have no personal claims on family property, whatever their institutions might covet. Before the First Crusade Ramnulf Silvain, archpriest and monk of St Jean d'Angély, was very active when his brother Berald was raising money from his abbey[139] and Gerald of Landerron's brother Auger, who was prior of St Pierre de la Réole, not only arranged a loan to Gerald from his community, but also agreed to 'hold Gerald's castles and freeholds and woods and the rest with his sons, whom he would rear until the time that he himself would make them knights'.[140] In 1129 William of La Ferté-Vidame renounced claims he had been making against St Père de Chartres in the chamber of his uncle, who was dean of Chartres and monk of St Père; his brother Hugh, who was provost of Chartres cathedral, also played a part in the proceedings.[141] On the other hand, Josbert Alboin, who was probably a crusader in 1107, had deceived his uncle, the abbot of Vigeois, and had broken an agreement he had made with him. He now came before his uncle and 'recognized that he had treated him badly'.[142]

Monks who were friends could find themselves involved. The advice of Lancelin, a monk of Noyers resident nearby, was sought by Geoffrey and Engelelmus of St Savin when they wanted to sell property to finance their crusade.[143] But like the monk Everard of Breteuil religious could be pushy. It looks as though the abbot of Marmoutier made a special journey to Brittany and Anjou while the First Crusade was being planned, visiting Ancenis and Sablé; 'while he was resting in his house there' the lord, Robert Burgundio, made

clauses in other charters (Marmoutier (Dunois) 56, 139, 141; Marmoutier (Vendômois) 255, 59), it is clear that the abbey dated the year from the day of this dedication.
[139] St Jean d'Angély 33.111–13.   [140] St Pierre de la Réole 141–2.
[141] St Père de Chartres 2.511–12.   [142] Vigeois 62.   [143] Noyers 275–6.

an endowment for the abbey.[144] When in the spring of 1101 William of Aquitaine's army was mustering near Poitiers, a monk from St Aubin d'Angers asked Herbert of Thouars for a cloak of precious cloth, worth 300 *solidi*, which Herbert was intending to take with him as an easily disposable asset. Herbert had already sought the prayers of the monks of his favourite abbey, St Florent-lès-Saumur, and he refused, but when the monk began to withdraw shamefacedly, he exclaimed : 'We go on the way of God and the 300 *solidi* would have been quickly spent. It would be better to give it up so that we may be helped by the prayers of St Aubin and the monks.'[145]

It goes without saying that the decision to pledge or sell property was an extreme measure. Its disposal to a church or religious community was a last resort, a point graphically made in 1100 by Fortun Sanchez and his wife, who were going on pilgrimage to Jerusalem and sold freeholds to the bishop and canons of Huesca, 'because no one would give us as much as we thought the freeholds were worth, neither relations nor friends, Christian, Jewish, or Muslim'.[146] But, as Fortun's charter shows, it was often only churches and religious communities which had the funds available, because they were rich or because they could realize cash from the disposal of valuables treasurized in their shrines. The canons of Chalon stripped the silver from the altar table of the shrine of St Vincent in their cathedral to provide Savary of Vergy, the uncle of the crusader Geoffrey II of Donzy, with some of the cash he needed to buy his nephew's fief.[147] William of England forced the churches in his kingdom to disgorge their treasures to raise the huge sum of 10,000 silver marks for the *vifgage* of Normandy.[148] Bishop Richer of Verdun, whose brother Bencelinus of Brie took the cross, confiscated valuables from the churches in his diocese.[149] So did Bishop Obert of Liège. Obert's acquisition of the castles of Bouillon and Couvin from Godfrey of Bouillon and Baldwin of Mons brought, he maintained, honour to his diocese. His purpose, he wrote, was 'to assure peace and tranquillity for ever, because malefactors living there were vexing the diocese dreadfully with their plundering, robbing and other annoyances'.[150] His method of raising the money infuriated the monks of St Hubert-en-Ardenne, to whom he seemed to be

---

[144] Brittany (Morice) 1.488; Marmoutier (Manceau) 2.87.   [145] Chaise-le-Vicomte 7.
[146] Huesca 1.106.   [147] Burgundy (Pérard) 201–2.
[148] Tyerman, *England and the Crusades*, 16–18.   [149] Laurence of Liège 498.
[150] St Lambert de Liège 1.47; Dinant 1.12–13; 'Triumphus Sancti Lamberti' 499.

concerned with his own glory ... He showed the greatest hostility to St Hubert, for through the appropriators he sent he stripped the gold covering from the altar and stole three gold crosses, studded with precious stones.[151]

He took a silver altar from the abbey of Lobbes.[152] One of his charters, however, provides details of how at least one community was partly repaid. It relates how in exchange the bishop gave the 'poor little church' of SS Marie et Perpétue de Dinant, which had contributed 34 marks, some tolls and rents of his own, together with a yard and a rent the crusader Cono of Montaigu had been persuaded to donate. The bishop also agreed to the purchase of a sales tax on wine which the community had made from another crusader, a man called Walter.[153] Presumably this was only one of many similar arrangements he made with establishments in his diocese.

The material on the rôle of churchmen as financiers at this early date is inadequate. The religious communities and cathedrals to which crusaders turned are widely scattered, and the number of deals made are in most cases very few. During the preparations for the First Crusade, for which we have enough material to make some comparisons, St Jean d'Angély, St Pierre de la Réole and St Vincent du Mans stand out as centres of finance, with Cluny, Marmoutier, St Chaffre du Monastier and St Victor de Marseille a little way behind. St Jean, Cluny, Marmoutier and probably St Vincent had been visited by Pope Urban in the course of his journey through France, and Cluny, Marmoutier, St Jean and St Victor were major abbeys. Benedictine communities had taken the lead in putting themselves forward as 'asylums of the penitent' for laymen, but that these all happened to be Benedictine houses may be misleading, because Dr Bull has shown that reforming houses of canons regular in the Limousin were also centres of crusading enthusiasm.[154]

Nearly seventy religious communities are known to have benefited from the gifts of the first crusaders on departure. They are scattered widely and there is evidence for only a few making substantial gains. Aureil, Marmoutier, Uzerche, Longpont-sous-Montlhéry, Molesme, Noyers and St Jean d'Angély head the list, although many of the entries in the cartularies of the Limousin houses of Aureil and Uzerche may refer to pledges and sales under the guise of endow-

---

[151] 'Cantatorium Sancti Huberti' 340.   [152] 'Gesta abbatum Lobbiensium' 318.
[153] Dinant 1.12–15.   [154] Bull, *Knightly Piety*, 259–62.

ments. Somewhat lower down come Sauxillanges, Vigeois, Chaise-le-Vicomte and St Hubert-en-Ardenne. Apart from those mentioned, no community appears to have been a major beneficiary; indeed known centres of crusading fervour like Cluny hardly rate at all, although it should be remembered that Marmoutier, Longpont-sous-Montlhéry, Sauxillanges and Vigeois were Cluniac and several other Cluniac abbeys and priories also benefited. When it came to making gifts it seems that crusaders thought chiefly of the intercession of local saints, neighbouring monks and family foundations. In this, as in so many things, their extraordinary initiative was rooted in their daily life and perceptions.

Only three communities, Marmoutier, St Jean d'Angély and St Vincent du Mans, were prominent both as financiers and bene-ficiaries, and of these Marmoutier was outstanding. This abbey, where Pope Urban had presided over a cross-taking ceremony in the spring of 1096,[155] had at least 114 priories by 1100 and was compar-able in size and influence to Cluny, from which it had been reshaped a hundred years before. It was a centre of monastic reform, but it was nevertheless able to maintain close relations with its secular patrons, the counts of Blois, and to nurture others with the more recent masters of Tours, the counts of Anjou.[156] Such a cosy association with lay nobles must have been unusual in a reforming house – a feature of monastic reform was the impulse to break free from secular influence – and it may have made Marmoutier particularly susceptible to the crusade ideal, especially as Count Stephen of Blois was committed to the enterprise and Count Fulk IV of Anjou was also in favour of it. At any rate, it seems to have been an important centre for crusaders and in 1106 it was to include all the faithful engaged in fighting in Palestine in its society of prayer.[157]

The First Crusade was preached during an agricultural depres-sion, the consequence of several years of drought, and land values, already low, were weakened further as properties were put on the market by those intending to go.[158] It has often been said that ecclesiastical institutions were therefore the real beneficiaries of the early crusading movement, because they could pick up land rela-tively cheaply. There are grounds for questioning whether they were

[155] GAD 101.
[156] S. Farmer, *Communities of St Martin: Legend and Ritual in Medieval Tours* (Ithaca and London, 1991), 65–186; for the number of priories see p. 123.
[157] Marmoutier (Tourangeau) 45–6.   [158] GN Gesta 141; OV 5.16.

conscious of this at the time. It is noticeable that crusaders showed extreme reluctance to enter into financial arrangements with the religious houses founded by their own families. Magnates could occasionally treat these foundations roughly. Just before leaving in 1096 Godfrey of Bouillon restored the priory of St Dagobert de Stenay, which had been wrecked by his own forces,[159] and a consequence of the pledging of Bouillon to the bishop of Liège by him was the bishop's expulsion of the monks of St Hubert-en-Ardenne from the priory there, which had been founded by his grandfather. When his mother, Ida of Lorraine, discovered this, she sent for the abbot of St Hubert, who played on her distress, threatening Godfrey and his uncle, who had agreed to the bishop's decision, with excommunication, a sentence that could well have prevented Godfrey leaving. Ida's response was to give St Hubert the church of Sansareux to erect into a priory and she endowed it with another church as well.[160] But founders or descendants tended to be exceptionally attached to their foundations. In one of his charters for the abbey of Marmoutier Stephen of Blois described his family's involvement with the community at length and averred rather touchingly that 'if thus far I have not protected or helped the abbey as assiduously as I ought, I have taken care not to offend it seriously; nor have I molested it much'.[161] The only example I have found of a man raising money from a house of this sort, and it is by no means certain, involved Duke Alan Fergent of Brittany, who had inherited a close family relationship with the monks of Ste Croix de Quimperlé, which had been founded by his grandfather, Alan of Cornouaille. Alan Fergent exchanged some land with the monks of Ste Croix for a counter-gift, 'because on the day I gave them this I needed money'; his charter is undated, but the arrangement was perhaps linked to his preparations for the First Crusade.[162] Otherwise, in every case for which I have evidence – relating to the communities of Chaise-le-Vicomte, Longpont-sous-Montlhéry, Marmoutier, Morigny, Nogent-le-Rotrou, St Laud d'Angers, St Michel de Cons and St Saveur de Lohéac – crusaders from the founding families confined themselves to making endowments in return for prayer or leaving property in their wills. Although it is possible that some of the charters of endowment were masking sales, it looks as though

[159] Lorraine 502–3.   [160] 'Cantatorium Sancti Huberti' 338–40.
[161] Marmoutier (Dunois) 80.
[162] Brittany (ducs) 61. For his relations with Ste Croix, see Brittany (ducs) 44–5, 52–4, 58–61.

crusaders desisted from entering into financial arrangements with *their* communities and this suggests that they thought such deals would harm them. In the long run, of course, the religious must have benefited, but in the short they may have perceived only over-extension and economic damage. Perhaps they entered into the agreements they did because they had been encouraged by the pope to do so.

A reluctance on the part of patrons and friends to risk the finances of religious communities, together with the natural desire of land-owners to prevent property passing into church hands and out of the land market for ever, helps to explain why 16 per cent (five, perhaps six) of the surviving pledges of the time of the First Crusade[163] and at least 13 per cent (six, perhaps seven) of the sales[164] were agreed not with churchmen at all but with lay men and women. The number of deals may not seem impressive, but it should be remembered that the surviving records are almost entirely ecclesiastical and that it would have been rare for an agreement negotiated among lay people to have surfaced in them. This indicates quite a lot of activity in the secular world devoted to raising money for the crusade and makes one wonder whether we are not glimpsing the tip of an iceberg. If so, we may have overestimated the part played by churchmen as financiers at this time.

FAMILIES

Ten per cent (three, perhaps four) of the pledges[165] and at least 9 per cent (four, perhaps five) of the sales[166] involved the close relations of crusaders. It is notable that some of these were female, including sisters who could perhaps call on their husbands' assets at a time when the male members of the family were short of cash. The lands of a family from the Savanès near Auch, which had been divided in the late eleventh century between three brothers and two sisters, had been reconsolidated in the hands of Bertrand of St Jean, the son of

[163] GAD 101; Cluny 5.108; Valenciennes (595); OV 4.338; 5.26, 32, 208, 278–80 (William of Jumièges 274–7; Hugh of Flavigny 475); and possibly Auch 65.
[164] Burgundy (Pérard) 201–2; Montpellier 545, 550–1 (557); Morigny 11; OV 5.324 (Philip I 368 n.1); St Laon de Thouars 32; and possibly Auch 65.
[165] GAD 101; Cluny 5.108; OV 5.26, 32, 208, 278–80 (William of Jumièges 274–5; Hugh of Flavigny 475); and possibly Auch 65.
[166] Burgundy (Pérard) 201–2; Montpellier 545, 550–1; St Laon de Thouars 32; and possibly Auch 65.

one of the sisters called Saure, by the time he joined the crusade of 1147. A chain of accidents had brought this about, among them the decisions of two of his uncles to go to Jerusalem, perhaps because they had taken the cross; one had sold his share to Saure and the other had pledged his land to her.[167]

The influence of families on recruitment, and the culture of dependence and cooperation which flourished in them, was bound to involve kindred in the raising of cash. The disposal of property was anyway something that directly involved them all, since what was being alienated was patrimony in which they had an actual or potential interest; this is clear enough in the way they would record their agreement in pledge- and sales-charters. The lists of their names confirm the conclusions already reached in a study of the *laudatio parentum* in Touraine.[168] They are nearly all of close relations, those whom the pilgrim Fortun Sanchez and his wife referred to as 'totos nostros meliores parentes et amicos':[169] mothers, wives, brothers and sisters (and their spouses), children, uncles and close cousins. *Douceurs* had sometimes to be offered to assure their agreement.

The terms of some endowments were so involved that they could have led to trouble. Gerald of 'Tuda', a knight of Montmoreau who was going on the 1101 expedition, left St Jean d'Angély a bordery in his will. But no sooner had he departed than his brother Itier, who also took the cross, gave the bordery outright to the abbey with the agreement of a third brother called Peter, at the same time pledging two others. The new agreement specified that Gerald could not recover the original bordery, which he had had no intention of handing over in his lifetime, unless his brother Peter repaid half the loan.[170] We do not know the results of this arrangement, but the potential for future disputes is obvious. Even in more straightforward cases families could make difficulties and question the arrangements which had been made. While one mother sold property on her son's behalf,[171] another was reluctant to sanction a borrower's pledge.[172] Hugh II of Matheflon held back tithes which his father had sold for 1,100 *solidi* to the abbey of St Nicolas d'Angers.[173] The son of Robert Dalmace of Collanges, who crusaded in 1107, struggled for twenty years to retain a *mansus* his father had sold to Cluny.[174] Peter of

---

[167] Auch 65–6.   [168] White, *Custom, Kinship and Gifts to Saints, passim.*
[169] Huesca 1.106.   [170] St Jean d'Angély 30.391.
[171] *Die Reichskanzler* 3.88–9.   [172] Noyers 266.   [173] Azé et Le Geneteil 60–1.
[174] Cluny 5.199, 355–6.

Chevanville seized a vineyard his crusading brother Raimbert had given the priory of Longpont-sous-Montlhéry and pledged it; the monks had to spend ten *solidi* to get it back.[175] Sometimes one has the impression that members of a family were determined to squeeze what they could out of a situation. When William Miscemalum sold a tithe, his lord and his mother got douceurs, but a cousin, Achard of Born, himself probably a crusader needing cash, complained that the tithe had been sold without his permission and had to be given 100 *solidi*.[176] When Joscelin of Lèves sold serfs with their land to the abbey of St Père de Chartres, he arranged payments for his brothers, but the youngest of them, a boy who had at first agreed, objected later to the amount he had been given.[177]

Opposition could be even more vehement when it came to gifts or testamentary bequests, which were often made in an emotional state and must sometimes have reduced the kindred to despair. A family could respond generously on hearing of a crusader's death, as in the case of the mother of Guy Pinellus, who had left two shops to Longpont.

Affected by great sadness as the mother of a son, she took care to carry out diligently what her son had ordered her to do when he left. Coming before the altar of St Mary she handed over the shops.[178]

But the news could set off passionate, even hysterical, resistance. The widow of Geoffrey Jordan of Vendôme repossessed a church which Geoffrey had given 'out of his patrimony' and with her consent to the abbey of La Trinité de Vendôme; she had to be excommunicated to force her to release it.[179] Berald Silvain had made elaborate arrangements to cover the agreement of his kindred when he sold mills, which were already pledged, to St Jean d'Angély.

The monks of St Jean held what had been sold to them without challenge while Berald Silvain lived and remained in this region. But after he had taken the road [to Jerusalem] and had died there arose Bertrand son of Gerard, who was married to Berald's daughter, and he challenged everything.

Bertrand refused to accept the jurisdiction of the abbot in the case and it had to be transferred to the local seigneurial court.[180] Wills

[175] Longpont 109–10.　　[176] St Jean d'Angély 30.114.
[177] St Père de Chartres 2.274–7. For another example of a dispute, see St Hilaire-le-Grand de Poitiers (1847) 128–30.
[178] Longpont 121.　　[179] La Trinité de Vendôme Cart 2.159–60.
[180] St Jean d'Angély 33.111–13.

could cause particular trouble, perhaps because the relations had hoped the crusader would survive, perhaps because they were used to ignoring testamentary provisions anyway. Garsadon of Etréchy had left the village of Gomerville, which was already in pledge, to the abbey of Morigny. The report of his death sparked a furious reaction in spite of the fact that the abbey had been founded by his father. His mother Adelaide, who had approved of his will, now changed her mind. His first cousin's husband Stephen took up post in the village, swearing angrily that he would kill the monks. His brother-in-law Bovard fired Gomerville and went on to burn down a grange and barns with cattle in them which belonged to the monks.[181]

There was obviously a need to consult members of a family fully and to involve them in one's decisions. This is illustrated in two charters of Robert I Burgundio of Sablé. Robert had made two gifts to Marmoutier, one of them on departure. It looks as though he had wanted to add further donations but had been prevented by his younger son, another Robert, whom he was leaving in charge of Sablé. When Robert I stopped at Marmoutier on his way to the East he confirmed his earlier gifts, presenting the prior, who was in charge while the abbot was away, with a gold ring given him by his daughter, but he then added fresh endowments – obviously those he had wanted to give while he was still at home – stating that they should be separately listed 'because my son Robert has not conceded them'. The gifts, in other words, were qualified by the need for the younger Robert's consent and Robert I sent letters to his son, asking him to confirm them. He wanted it to be recorded that since his elder son, Rainald, had agreed to authorize all alms gifts he should make on this journey his younger son would have no fee for confirming the new benefaction. The prior handed the ring back to him, as a symbol to remind those who were present of his new gift. The passing back and forth of the ring was typical of the time; a little ceremony of this sort underlined for witnesses the seriousness of Robert's spontaneous decision.[182]

The close interest taken by kindred is demonstrated by the facts that of the surviving agreements with churchmen, 22 per cent (seven) of the pledges and at least 25 per cent (eleven, possibly thirteen) of the sales made by first crusaders were of churches,

---

[181] Morigny 40.   [182] Marmoutier (Manceau) 2.86–91.

tithes, and other ecclesiastical property, as were, incidentally, at least 21 per cent (seventeen) of their endowments.[183] I have already pointed out that the ownership of these was becoming precarious as the movement for church reform gathered pace. An eighth pledge concerned property to which the lender already had claims[184] and a ninth related to land which had already been left the lender in a brother's will.[185] At least 11 per cent (five) of the sales were of lands already pledged which, if *vifgaged*, would no longer have been in family hands anyway.[186] If one also takes into account the renunciations of disputed claims, at least 43 per cent of all surviving disposals for cash at the time of the First Crusade were of assets of doubtful value. So it seems that sensible policies were being adopted when it came to alienation. In the terms expressed in the charters we must be hearing echoes of conferences of the family summoned to decide whether assets could be saved and, if not, what type of property should be offered for pledge, or sale, or as a gift. When Guy Tortus of Rochefort-sur-Loire sold his fief to a nephew in 1120 he averred that he had no closer relation, but he had presumably decided, after discussion with the kin, to sell his property within the family.[187] One conference is recorded in a Breton document. The first crusader Thibald of Ploasme informed his brother William that if he was not helped financially he would have to sell his inheritance. William did not want Thibald's share of the estate to be lost, so he raised money from the monks of St Nicolas d'Angers by selling part of his share of a mill which was already pledged.[188] Apparent acts of generosity by relations may have been made to prevent the degradation of patrimonies. In southern Italy Tancred Marchisus was subsidized by his guardian and so did not have to sell his inheritance.[189] Before Fantin and his son Godfrey left in the crusading force led by Herbert of Thouars in 1101 they came to a complicated arrangement by which Fantin left some land to his wife

---

[183] La Trinite de Vendôme Cart 2.158; Vigeois 67; Anjou (Halphen) 326; Molesme 2.217; Lézat 188–9; Carcassonne 5.155; Savigny 1.433–4; LA 580–1; Gellone 248; HGL 5.749; Noyers 268; St Georges de Rennes 269–70; Forez 1.1 (no.1); St Jean d'Angély 1.260–1; St Père de Chartres 2.628; St Vincent du Mans 1.200; Sauxillanges 1045. For similar donations after 1102, see Le Ronceray d'Angers 186, 214; Noyers 329–32; St Julien de Tours 87–8; Burgundy (Pérard) 224. For ecclesiastical property pledged and sold, see above notes 76, 96.
[184] Roussillon 110—11.   [185] St Jean d'Angély 30.391.
[186] St Vincent du Mans 1.190–1 (193); Brittany (Morice) 1.490; St Jean d'Angély 30.113–14; 33.111–13; Cluny 5.202–3. A high proportion of the wills made during the crusade concerned pledged property and churches and tithes.
[187] Marmoutier (Anjou) 66.   [188] Brittany (Morice) 1.490.   [189] RC 606.

and to Godfrey, who then sold his share of it to his mother.[190]
Maternal uncles often had an interest in protecting their sisters'
children, as opposed to paternal uncles who were potential compe-
titors. Savary of Vergy bought the fief of his nephew, the crusader
Geoffrey II of Donzy, and then pledged it for no less than 8,000
solidi, at the same time renouncing rights he had claimed, to raise
the money to pay him.[191] The co-lord of Amboise, Hugh of
Chaumont-sur-Loire, pledged his lordship to the husband of an
aunt on his father's side of the family, Robert of Roches-Corbon,
but in addition was given a substantial cash sum by his maternal
uncle.[192]

It is clear that the costs of the venture were a cause for concern for
the crusaders' families and that they approached the issue of the
disposal of patrimonial land with care. But in their preparations did
they believe that future material benefit would justify an investment
of this sort? A reason commonly given nowadays for the crusading
impulse, rooted in a historical interpretation of the attitudes which
are believed to have prevailed in the European countryside, is that it
was an economic safety valve. Rising population, it is maintained,
was forcing land-owning families to take measures to prevent the
subdivision of their estates, either through the practice of primogeni-
ture or through a primitive method of birth-control by which only
one male in each generation was allowed to marry. These family
strategies destabilized society and led to a surplus of young men with
no prospects, for whom adventure, spoil and land overseas were
attractions. Individuals were encouraged to make themselves scarce
and crusading was an appropriate way for someone to reduce the
burdens his family was facing. This explanation of recruitment is
intelligent supposition, but no more than that, and the evidence does
not support it.[193] There is not even any justification for the proposition that younger sons went on crusade more commonly than older
ones. The picture of a family strategy centring on the departure of
unwanted males is probably a myth, because having a crusader in it
must have cost a family more than it would have had to spend if the
individual had stayed at home; and even if anyone had been fool
enough to think in 1096 that crusading would be a profitable and

---

[190] St Laon de Thouars 32.   [191] Burgundy (Pérard) 201–2.   [192] GAD 101.
[193] A throw-away remark by G. Duby (*La société aux XIe et XIIe siècles dans la région maconnaise*
(Paris, 1971), 334–5) has been amazingly influential, considering the fact that it rests on the
basis of one family and two charters (Cluny 5.59, 475–82), and is itself unprovable.

relatively painless venture, such an attitude would have been considered madness after the experiences the early armies underwent in Asia. The only family strategy revealed by the evidence is one evolved after the decision to crusade had been made and it was designed collectively by the kindred, including relations on the mother's side, to reduce the costs as far as possible and somehow to keep land to which there was good title in family hands.

SECURITY AT HOME

Family loyalty and support was a two-way affair, of course. The crusader himself could not ignore his responsibilities to his dependants and kindred, however fired up or worried he was by the prospect ahead, and issues which concerned any well-to-do landowner were the care and safety of his relations and the management of his estates while he was away. I will suggest in the next chapter that in 1095-6 it was feared that disorder would spread in the absence of so many of the great lords on whom the maintenance of stability depended, but the nature of society also meant that problems could arise very close to home, within families themselves, in which instincts of cooperation could be at war with ambitions for property and standing, particularly if the head of the family was unlucky enough to have bred only a daughter. In 1120 Baldwin of Vern d'Anjou, who was off to Palestine with Count Fulk, came to a carefully worded arrangement with his brother Rual 'concerning his land and all his things and his wife with his only daughter', Esteial. While he was away his lands and rents, which were detailed exhaustively, were to be divided between his brother on one side and his wife and daughter on the other. If he, Baldwin, should die on the crusade, his wife was to enjoy her share of the estate until she remarried or until their daughter married. If his wife should remarry before the daughter, her new husband would have charge of the land and the girl, provided her choice had been governed by 'the advice and agreement of friends and lords'. But as soon as the daughter should marry all the property, except for the dowry of Baldwin's mother, which Baldwin seems to have shared with her, was to be divided between Esteial and Rual; and the mother's dower land was also to be shared by them after her death. If Esteial should die while Baldwin was on crusade, all the property would pass to Rual, although Baldwin's wife was to have the lands settled on her on marriage. Rual promised always to deal faithfully with Baldwin and the two women, never to try to take away property to which they had a right and to aid them against anyone who injured them 'even to making war himself'. The agreement, which demonstrates clearly the threat posed by a younger, and probably unmarried, brother to a crusader's wife and daughter and the need to take steps to counter it while the crusader was thousands of miles away, was witnessed by ten men and was guaranteed by Baldwin's immediate lord.[194]

The fact was that although Pope Urban had obliged the Church to protect crusaders' lands (and probably their families) it was not yet, and indeed was never to be, strong enough to do this effectively. And anyway its responsibilities and functions had not been properly defined. In 1107 the crusader Hugh II of Le Puiset felt extremely threatened by a castle thrown up on an estate, partly allodial, partly a tenancy in his lordship, by Rotrou of Perche, the count of Mortagne who had himself been on the First Crusade; Rotrou was disputing Hugh's rights over this property. Because the resolution of such a case involved a judicial duel and the Church was barred from making that sort of judgement, Bishop Ivo of Chartres remitted it to the court of the county of Blois, where Hugh lost. But matters got worse, violence ensued, and Hugh's tenant was captured by Rotrou, who claimed that the case had nothing to do with a crusader's rights. Hugh appealed to the pope, but the confusion in ecclesiastical circles was manifest. Ivo of Chartres, one of the greatest canonists of the age, was clearly at sea. Instead of dealing with the matter himself, he had handed it over to a secular court and when the pope reallocated the case to him he pointed out that churchmen could not agree on a sentence, 'stating that this law of the Church protecting the goods of knights going to Jerusalem was new; and that they did not know whether the protection applied only to their properties or also applied to their fortifications'.[195] The importance of this issue is underlined by the fact that the First Lateran Council legislated on it in 1123, taking crusaders' 'houses, families, and all their goods into the protection of St Peter and the Roman church, as was established by our lord Pope Urban' and threatening to excommunicate those who disturbed them.[196]

---

[194] Le Ronceray d'Angers 215–17.
[195] Ivo of Chartres, 'Epistolae', cols. 170–4, 176–7. The pope was in Chartres in April 1107. *Regesta pontificum Romanorum* 1.729.
[196] *Conciliorum Oecumenicorum Decreta* 167–8.

Crusaders anyway felt safer taking their own measures. The count of Maine, Helias of La Flèche, who took the cross in 1096, stayed behind in the end to defend his lands from a threat posed by King William II of England, who was now in control of Normandy.[197] In 1120 Fulk of Anjou seems to have put his county under the protection of King Henry I of England, with whom he had entered into a marriage alliance.[198] Geoffrey of Le Louet put his wife into the care of the nuns of Le Ronceray d'Angers for a fee, drawn from her own marriage settlement; he became a *confrater* of the nunnery and promised a supplement to the sum as an entry gift should she wish to become a nun herself.[199] Fulk of Le Plessis-Macé gave rents and a tithe to the nuns in return for their agreement to look after his daughter for three years. If he should not return, they were to allow her to marry or become a nun 'according to her will and that of her brothers and other friends'. If she should decide not to enter the community he promised the nuns one of his nieces as an oblate and he guaranteed her entry gift.[200] A touching arrangement was negotiated by Hugh Rufus of Champallement, a recruit to the crusade of 1147, who had a very sick or disabled brother called Guy. Hugh made a grant of property to the monks of Corbigny, from the rents of which Guy was to be provided with a pension in cash and kind, payable at fixed times in the year. The monks would bury him in their cemetery should he die.[201]

Just as vital to the interests of crusaders were the arrangements they had to make for the administration of their estates in what were bound to be long absences. If the terms of their pledge agreements have anything to do with their expectations, they were realistic in planning for a long campaign in 1096. In 1120 Fulk of Le Plessis-Macé was allowing for the fact that he might be away for three years; so was the Poitevin knight R. Gabard.[202] When senior ecclesiastics were going colleagues could help out: in 1101 Bishop Peter of Limoges took charge of the diocese of Périgueux in Rainald of Thiviers's absence[203] and William of Montfort-l'Amaury, the bishop of Paris, left his diocese in the charge of three of his senior clergy.[204] Threats to local churches, in fact, could come from those who should have been most concerned to protect them. While the bishop of Angers was on crusade with the count of Anjou in 1120, the count's

---

[197] OV 5.228–32.   [198] WMGR 2.495.   [199] Le Ronceray d'Angers 213.
[200] Le Ronceray d'Angers 213–15.   [201] Corbigny 6–7.   [202] Mauléon 15–16.
[203] Limoges 18–19.   [204] Paris 1.153–4.

own prévôts broke a long-standing agreement that adulterers and usurers (technically subject to courts Christian) should be judged jointly by the prévôt and the archdeacon and that the profits of justice should be shared between them.[205] As far as the laity were concerned, members of the family or neighbours or vassals could be made responsible. During the First Crusade Raymond of St Gilles left his eldest son in charge of his lands,[206] as did Eudes of Burgundy,[207] Rainald of Château-Gontier[208] and Miles of Bray; in 1101 Miles entrusted his estate to Guy Trousseau of Montlhéry, who had run away from Antioch three years before.[209] In 1129 Fulk of Anjou and his companion Hugh of Chaumont-sur-Loire[210] made similar arrangements; like Raymond of St Gilles in 1096, neither intended to return. On the other hand, Hugh Guernonatus, the prévôt of Blois, crusaded in 1096 in company with his eldest son Guarin and left his second son, Peter, in charge of his estate.[211] Robert Burgundio of Sablé also left his second son, Robert, in control; his elder son Rainald did not crusade with him, but he was already established in his wife's fief of Craon and seems to have retained some say in his younger brother's decisions.[212] Aimery Michael was to look after the lands of his brother Robert, who was planning to crusade in the following of Nivelo of Fréteval.[213] The brothers Geoffrey and Engelelmus of St Savin entrusted their affairs to their two other brothers, Aimery and Hugh,[214] and Gerald of Landerron, as we have seen, left his castles and sons in the care of his brother Auger, the prior of St Pierre de la Réole.[215] In 1096 Hugh of Chaumont-sur-Loire left his castle at Amboise in the custody of his aunt's husband.[216]

Guy Pinellus, who seems to have been a townsman, gave his mother the power to administer his property.[217] It was quite common for wives to manage estates in their husbands' absences. Adela of England ruled the dominions of Stephen of Blois and Stephen wrote to her regularly. Two of his letters survive, in one of which he reminded her 'to act well and manage your land excellently and treat your children and subjects honestly, as becomes you'.[218]

---

[205] Angers 246-7.   [206] Hill, *Raymond IV de Saint-Gilles*, 22, 34.
[207] Cluny 5.157; St Bénigne de Dijon 2.175.   [208] CGCA 'Additamenta' 149.
[209] Longpont 184.   [210] GAD 115-6.   [211] Marmoutier (Dunois) 141.
[212] Marmoutier (Manceau) 87-91.   [213] Marmoutier (Dunois) 139-40.
[214] Noyers 275-6.   [215] St Pierre de la Réole 141-2.   [216] GAD 101.
[217] Longpont 121.
[218] Kb 152; the letters are on pp. 138-40, 149-52. See Kb 138, where there is a reference to a letter which must have been lost. For an example of Adela in charge, see Marmoutier (Dunois) 147.

Clemency of Burgundy, the wife of Robert of Flanders, had charge of his county while he was away, although she seems to have been a less successful regent than Adela.[219] In 1107 Walter of Montsoreau's wife managed his estate; Walter wrote to her from Apulia, validating his message with 'certain signs'[220] In 1120 Eremburge of Maine ran the county of Anjou while her husband Fulk was on crusade.[221]

On the other hand, in 1101 Guy of Bré gave custody of his land and the hand of his daughter Stephana to a neighbour, Oliver of Lastours, whose father and uncle had been on the expedition of 1096–9. In this case departure on crusade gave Guy, who had plenty of relations, the opportunity to settle property on his daughter and her future husband.[222] Geoffrey of Issoudun left his castle in the hands of one of his vassals.[223] Hugh I of Gallardon entrusted his castle and daughter to his subjects.[224] In 1120 a Poitevin knight left his lands under the patronage of St Peter and in the custody of the bishop of Poitiers.[225] Sometimes, therefore, there was no one in a family considered capable or trustworthy enough to take over, but in general it is the collective decision-making and cooperation within the kindred which stand out. Family traditions may have triggered the crusaders' original responses. Group loyalty within the family created the conditions which made it easier for them to carry out what they had promised.

DEPARTURE

Occasionally we catch glimpses of men just before or at the point of leaving: Stephen of Blois with his wife 'at the castle called Coulommiers, wishing to go to Jerusalem with the army of the Christians ... [and] preparing what was necessary for my journey';[226] Robert Burgundio in his castle at Sablé, 'when I wished to go to Jerusalem

---

[219] See, for instance, Kb 142–3; Afflighem 19–20. For problems in Flanders, see below pp. 145–6.
[220] Noyers 275. See Marmoutier (Anjou) 54. When Norgeot I of Toucy fell ill in Jerusalem, probably on pilgrimage in 1110, he confessed his sins to the patriarch, in particular an oppressive custom he had imposed against the interests of the monks of Fleury, 'but, hearing that penitence was fruitless unless it was followed by amendment, he sent letters to his wife and men, ordering them to abstain from imposing these bad customs'. *Gallia Christiana* 12, Instrumenta, 107–8.
[221] OV 6.310.   [222] Uzerche 210, 362, 927. See Bull, *Knightly Piety*, 278.
[223] Aureil 161.
[224] St Martin de Pontoise 470 n. 920. See also the careful arrangements made by Philip of Le Perche-Goët before his departure in 1140. St Pierre de la Couture 55–6.
[225] Mauléon 15–16.   [226] Marmoutier (Dunois) 80.

and was preparing what was needed for my journey';[227] Boso of La
Chèze and his brother Rainald 'in the tower of Laron on the day
[they] set off for Jerusalem';[228] Peter of La Vue outside the choir of
the priory church of Aureil;[229] Astanove of Fézensac in the chapter
of the canons of the cathedral of Auch;[230] Miles of Bray in the
chapter-house of his family's foundation of Longpont-sous-
Montlhéry;[231] and in 1120 Landolt, a knight of the bishop of
Eichstätt, before St Peter's altar in the abbey of Oberalteich.[232]
According to the crusading chaplain Fulcher of Chartres many
leave-takings were tearful, with husbands assuring their wives that
they would return and their wives convinced that they would not.[233]
When Herbert of Thouars was ready to leave his castle in 1101 he
received the abbot of St Florent-lès-Saumur. He asked for the
prayers of the monks, of whom he was a *confrater*, and he confirmed a
will he had made in favour of his family's foundation of Chaise-le-
Vicomte, a daughter house of St Florent; he desired to be buried
there. After this he went to Poitiers to be given the symbols of
pilgrimage by the bishop. The meetings at Thouars and Poitiers
were emotional, with everyone in tears. Herbert then proceeded to
the 'Royal Meadow' near Poitiers where the Poitevin army of
William of Aquitaine was gathering.[234]

We sometimes come across other crusaders travelling to the
mustering stations. Ansellus and Hugh of Méry and their cousin
Simon dined with the monks at their family's foundation of Lassi-
court, near Bar-sur-Aube,[235] which suggests that from Méry-sur-
Seine they had followed the river south to Troyes and were now
going on to Chaumont, perhaps to join other parties at Dijon or
Besançon. Hugh and Norgeot of Toucy lodged at Châtillon-sur-
Seine,[236] which meant that they had been riding east from their
home; probably they now intended to turn south and make for
Dijon. Robert Burgundio rode, as we have seen, from Sablé to
Marmoutier near Tours.[237]

The Flemish army probably mustered in 1096 at Lille, where
Count Robert issued a charter which was witnessed by a large
number of castellans and lords, some of whom must have come to

---

[227] Marmoutier (Manceau) 2.87. In 1129 Hugh III of Le Puiset was at the castle of Le Puiset
with 'all the court of Le Puiset, which was then plenary'. Tiron 1.128.
[228] Aureil 170.   [229] Aureil 21.   [230] Auch 57.
[231] Longpont 184.   [232] Oberalteich 110.   [233] FC 162–3.
[234] Chaise-le-Vicomte 341.   [235] Molesme 2.229.   [236] Molesme 2.84.
[237] Marmoutier (Manceau) 2.88–91.

see him off, others to travel with him: among them were four of those who can be found a few days later in his company when he stopped at the abbey of St Thierry near Rheims.[238] But we can only guess about the places where most of the contingents gathered. Presumably Robert of Normandy, who led a force including Normans, Bretons and English,[239] summoned men to Rouen, Raymond of St Gilles's forces mustered at St Gilles and Stephen of Blois's knights at Chartres.

One can trace the lines of the march to Constantinople of some of the larger contingents. Perhaps it was the army of Raymond of St Gilles and Adhémar of Monteil which was seen passing through Cremona during October 1096.[240] It had opted to take the old pilgrim road through Dalmatia to the via Egnatia, although the journey proved hard, with progress slowed by the large numbers of the poor accompanying the army and by the need to take precautions against harassment by bandits. Raymond of St Gilles, who was elderly, was always the last to reach camp, frequently in the middle of the night, after spending the day riding up and down the column rounding up stragglers.[241]

After the sight we had of Robert of Flanders near Rheims he is next to be found at Pontarlier. By then he had been joined by the forces of the brothers-in-law Robert of Normandy and Stephen of Blois[242] the most suitable meeting point would have been Besançon – and the three leaders probably crossed the Alps by the Great St Bernard Pass. Once in Italy, they intended to march south and cross the Adriatic before joining the via Egnatia. They proceeded to Lucca, where they met the pope and received his blessing, and to Rome, where they were attacked by supporters of the anti-pope Wibert of Ravenna while praying in St Peter's Basilica. They then travelled through Campagna and southern Italy to Bari, where they venerated the relics of St Nicholas.[243] By now it was late November and they had been on the road for at least two months. The forces of Bohemond of Taranto and of Hugh the Great of Vermandois, who had also come from France by way of Rome, had already crossed the Adriatic. Robert of Flanders

[238] Flanders 63. The four were Baldwin of Ghent; Roger of Lille, castellan of Lille; Onulf, Robert's seneschal; and Cono, Robert's chaplain.
[239] FC 159 60.   [240] 'Annales Cremonenses' 800.   [241] RA 36–7.
[242] Hugh of Flavigny 475. Does the grant in Cluny 5.63–4, in the presence of Eudes of Burgundy and William of Nevers at Autun, date from the mustering of the crusade of 1101?
[243] FC 163–7.

followed them at once, after sending home relics he was given by Duke Roger of Apulia.[244] Robert of Normandy and Stephen of Blois decided to winter in Calabria and only embarked on Easter Day (5 April) 1097. They put to sea 'to the sound of many trumpets', in a noisy display which would be repeated many times in the course of crusading history.[245]

Godfrey of Bouillon's army of Lorrainers and northern Frenchmen followed the third traditional pilgrim route to Constantinople, one already taken by the earlier crusade armies of Walter Sansavoir and Peter the Hermit, the old 'Bavarian road' through southern Germany and Hungary into Byzantine territory at Belgrade and then through the Balkans. This itinerary and that through Italy to Bari and across the Adriatic were to be used again by crusade forces in 1100–1,[246] but the earliest of the armies of the third wave, that of the Lombards, took a new road, marching through Carniola to follow the river Save to Belgrade.[247]

Whichever pilgrim road they marched, as the crusaders left western Europe they disappeared from sight. There were occasional letters or messages home.[248] From as early as the summer of 1096, when the first armies were broken up in Hungary, a stream of deserters was trickling back. Sometimes this must have become a flood, as when large numbers of the poor left southern Italy in the autumn; 'fearing future poverty, they sold their bows and took up again their pilgrims' staffs and ignobly returned home'.[249] Others deserted in the following April, demoralized by a disaster that occurred when they were embarking at Bari and one of the ships, which must have been grossly overloaded, broke up just after sailing.[250] The most significant group of defectors consisted of those who fled from Antioch in the summer of 1098 and helped to persuade the Emperor Alexius to return to Constantinople from central Asia Minor with his army of Greeks and western reinforcements.[251] It must have been in the interest of these men to paint a very pessimistic picture of the way things were going.

But in truth no one in the West knew much of what was happening. A man who had witnessed the surmounting of the crisis in

[244] Kb 142–3.   [245] FC 167–72.
[246] Garsadon of Etréchy died at Cluses, near Chambéry, and the army he was with must have been intending to cross the Alps by the Mont Cenis Pass. Morigny 19.
[247] AA 559–60. See Runciman, *A History*, 2.19.
[248] Kb *passim*; Noyers 275; Longpont 184; Afflighem 19–20.
[249] FC 168.   [250] FC 169–71.   [251] Riley-Smith, *The First Crusade*, 59, 71–2.

Antioch in June 1098 and must have left Syria in July had reached Lucca by October;[252] even those in Italy, therefore, would be getting news that was already three months' stale. The crusaders might almost have been on the moon for all their relations could tell.

[252] Kb 165–7.

CHAPTER 6

Returning from crusades

On the first Sunday after his return home in 1100 Rotrou of Perche, the count of Mortagne, visited his family's foundation, the abbey of Nogent-le-Rotrou, where his father, who had died while he was away, was buried.[1] Rotrou had left France over three years before in the company of Robert of Normandy.[2] He had shared the disorientation, the exhaustion and starvation, the disease and sickening cruelty, the loss of pack animals and horses and therefore of rank, the disintegration of morale and order, the stories of apparitions and ghostly armies, the penitential liturgies and hysterical religiosity, the discovery of relics and the euphoria of the final miraculous and bloody triumph at Jerusalem. He was portrayed in the epic poem, *La Chanson d'Antioche*, distinguishing himself during the siege of Antioch, where he had been one of those under Bohemond of Taranto's command who had clambered up ladders to break into the city just before dawn on 3 June 1098.[3] He had been a line commander in the Battle of Antioch three weeks later.[4] Now, surrounded by several of his nobles and all the monks, he applied to become a *confrater* of Cluny, Nogent-le-Rotrou's mother house. He confirmed the endowments of his ancestors and promised to protect the community, and he placed the charter of his confirmation on the church's altar, together with the palm fronds he had brought back from Jerusalem, the evidence that he had fulfilled his vow.[5] These palms had great emotional significance for the crusaders, as they had for pilgrims – the last wish of a dying knight called Olgerius was that the palms he had collected at Jericho should be laid on the altar of the abbey church of Bèze, of which he was a *confrater*[6] – and it was reported that after the liberation of Jerusalem and the defeat of the

---

[1] OV 6.394. [2] OV 5.34; WT 191. [3] Ch d'A 1.160, 166, 194, 199, 244, 307.
[4] WT 330. See Ch d'A 1.441. [5] Nogent-le-Rotrou 36–9. See OV 6.394.
[6] Bèze Liber 574.

Egyptian army of relief at Ascalon the survivors of the crusade abandoned most of their weapons and returned home carrying their palms 'as a sign of victory'.[7]

Ralph of Beaugency came back at about the same time as Rotrou, with whom he may have shared a camp during the siege of Antioch.[8] Ralph had also gravitated towards Bohemond's company[9] and he had been one of those chosen by Bohemond to guard the gates of Antioch on the night of 10 June 1098, when panic was sweeping through the army.[10] Accompanied by what seems to have been his entire household, at least two of them his companions-in-arms since they were designated *Jerosolimitani*, titles inherited by crusaders from pilgrims and given to those who had been to Jerusalem, he endowed the monks of La Trinité de Vendôme who served in the church of the Holy Sepulchre built by his father at Beaugency with the tithes of his corn and vine harvests. He handed the charter of endowment to the abbot 'with great devotion and on his knees', before placing it on the church's altar.[11]

Rotrou and Ralph had shared in the euphoric liberation of Jerusalem. Guy II of Rochefort, a leading member of the Montlhéry clan, had taken part in the disastrous sequel which in 1101 had been thrashed by the Turks in Asia Minor. Nevertheless, he was given a triumph, or rather a series of them, when he came home. He sent a messenger ahead to announce his arrival. The abbot of Morigny went out to meet him and he was received at the abbey by a procession of monks, together with many of his subjects. The following day, a Sunday, he moved on to St Arnoult-en-Iveline, where another procession and many other nobles were waiting for him.[12]

Events such as these, marking in a traditional way the end to pilgrimages, must have been taking place throughout western Europe. But the formal welcomes must also have been expressions of a heartfelt desire that the violence which had been prevalent while the magnates were away could be brought to an end. Flanders had been unsettled while Count Robert was on crusade, with serious street-fighting in Bruges; it had needed the intervention of the town

---

[7] AA 499–500. [8] Ch d'A 1.166. [9] BB 21 note. [10] BB 65 note; GAD 101.
[11] La Trinité de Vendôme Cart 2.108-9. Although not dated, the presence of the *Jerosolimitani* makes it certain that this was describing a ceremony on Ralph's homecoming. See Angers 152 for an example of the eleventh-century use of the title *Jerosolimitanus*.
[12] Morigny 41.

clergy to limit the damage there.[13] The chronicle of Morigny graphically reveals how chaotic parts of the royal domain around Paris had been in the absence of its castellans. Violence had broken out while Guy of Rochefort was in the East – 'scarcely anyone could be brought to justice' – and his return seems to have been punctuated with appeals for his intervention. A very bad case of disorder was only brought to the notice of the viscount of Etampes once he was back.[14] In Lorraine the abbey of St Hubert-en-Ardenne felt itself to be gravely exposed to predators once its natural protectors, Godfrey of Bouillon and his nobles, had gone to the East.[15] It has often been suggested that in preaching the First Crusade Pope Urban was trying to bring peace to western Europe by canalizing the warlike energies of knights abroad, but anarchy in the absence of the magnates must have been anticipated by him and by other leading churchmen, and the peace decrees issued at the council of Clermont and elsewhere must have been promulgated because it was known that there would be problems while so many nobles were away.

The first crusaders, or at any rate those who had persevered to the end, came back in triumph. Their successors all too often returned weighed down by their own inadequacy, a sentiment expressed in blunt terms by King Conrad III of Germany in May 1149, shortly after he had landed near Venice on his way home from a disastrous crusade.

The city of Edessa had been taken by the pagans and with the encouragement and advice of the most holy Pope Eugenius and also of Bernard, the most religious abbot of Clairvaux, we set out on a journey to liberate the Christians, but on account of our sins we had little success and after adoring the relic of the living and salvatory cross in Jerusalem we returned to our own land.[16]

But success or failure, the crowds, the curiosity, the prestige and the excitement could not hide the fact that many men and women had not come home at all. Some of those who learnt the worst from companions bringing the bad news back with them[17] had to find

---

[13] 'Ex miraculis S. Donatiani Brugensibus' 858. See 'Annales Blandinienses' 27.
[14] Morigny 40–1.   [15] 'Cantatorium Sancti Huberti' 340.
[16] Conrad III, *Urkunden*, 358.
[17] For wills made by men ill or dying on crusade and drawn up in the West on the basis of the survivors' reports, see Longpont 250; Molesme 2.105; Aureil 113–14, 126, 179; Vigeois 68–9; Redon 318–20; Chaise-le-Vicomte 7–8, 25, 347; St Cyprien de Poitiers 67–8; Bèze Chron 392 (Bèze Liber 614); Solignac fol. 23v. For other gifts, see Longpont 184, 250; Noyers 274–5; Uzerche 171.

security somewhere. The widow of one crusader became a nun of the priory of Marcigny.[18] The husband of another widow had left the priory of La Charité-sur-Loire some land; the monks agreed to provide her with half the rents they would get from buildings erected on it.[19] The most unbearable cases must have been those in which a husband, father or son was missing and there was uncertainty whether he had died or not. Ida of Louvain combined a pilgrimage to Jerusalem in 1106 with a search for her husband, Baldwin of Mons, who had disappeared in Asia Minor on a mission from Antioch to Constantinople eight years before.[20]

Of the survivors some, perhaps many, were not well. Hugh of Chaumont-sur-Loire came home a sick man.[21] Peter Jordan of Châtillon had fallen ill at Antioch, probably during an epidemic of typhoid or malaria which had broken out in July 1098. In this state he had been received and tonsured by a monk 'in the name and to the honour of God and St Paul', which suggests that he had been professed into the Greek monastery of St Paul which had been established for a long time in the city. Recovering his health, he forgot his profession and continued with his crusade. But a few days after he had got home he began to feel ill again; this looks like malaria. Believing the return of illness to be a sign from God, he sent for monks of the abbey of Cormery, which seems to have been the nearest to him dedicated to St Paul, and asked to be received into their community.[22] The knight Pons the Red died almost as soon as he returned, leaving the church of St Paul de Lyon 100 *solidi* and a banner which perhaps he had carried on crusade.[23]

Others were exhausted. Guy Trousseau of Montlhéry, who was one of those who fled from Antioch in the summer of 1098, came home worn out by his journey and unable to come to terms with the fact that his courage had left him.[24] Guigo of 'Mara' rested for some days with the community of St Julien de Tours and was so impressed by the monks' kindness to him that he gave them a church.[25] The return journey, after everything the crusaders had been through, must have been very hard. Those with funds seem to have taken ship

[18] Cluny 5.152.   [19] La Charité-sur-Loire 104–5.
[20] Gislebert of Mons 45. See AA 626.   [21] GAD 102.
[22] Cormery 104. For the monastery of St Paul in Antioch, see C. Cahen, *La Syrie du Nord à l'époque des croisades et la principauté franque d'Antioche* (Paris, 1940), 131, 323, 334 n.19, although Cahen knew of no evidence that it was still occupied in 1098.
[23] Lyon 2.106.   [24] Suger of St Denis, *Vita*, 36.   [25] St Julien de Tours 72–3.

if they could,[26] but there are several references to deaths at sea and the Mediterranean voyage, which was always to frighten their descendants, was a worrying experience. A graphic description is to be found in a collection of miracles attributed to St Nicholas. The story was apparently told to a monk of Bec by a Norman crusader called Richard son of Fulk of Aunou, who was one of more than 1,400 passengers crammed into a large ship at Jaffa. Cruising north, and therefore taking advantage of the current up the Levantine coast, it ran into a storm and was wrecked near Tartus. The town was in ruins and depopulated, but the travellers ransacked it for what they could find. Concerned that they might be attacked by Muslims, nearly 100 of them boarded another boat, which was Armenian and was bound for Cyprus. It met another storm and was sinking when it was apparently saved by the intervention of the saint.[27] Bertrand of Bas, a canon of Le Puy who had seen the ghost of his bishop in the later stages of the crusade,[28] felt unwell on board another ship and renounced tithes he had held personally.[29] Stephen of Vitry-sur-Seine fell so ill at sea that he despaired of surviving, and made a will, leaving half a church to Longpont-sous-Montlhéry. He recovered and got home safely, but gave up the half church anyway.[30] There was a later tradition at Neumoustier that Count Cono of Montaigu, his son Lambert and Peter the Hermit were returning on a boat which was also carrying some townsmen from Huy. Tossed by a storm and believing that they were in great danger they vowed to build a church if God would save them. The storm immediately abated, leaving 'the sea so tranquil and the air so serene that the sky could be compared to the purest sapphire.[31]

In the circumstances it is surprising to find some men who had returned from the expedition which left in 1096 rejoining the armies which marched to the East in 1100–1. But of the less than a dozen individuals known to have done this, Hugh the Great of Vermandois, Stephen of Blois and his chaplain Alexander, Ivo of Grandmesnil and Hugh of Toucy had through flight or bad luck not yet reached Jerusalem and fulfilled their vows. It is not known why Miles of Bray and Simon and William of Poissy went again. Miles could have fled

---

[26] See AA 504; also probably 'Qualiter reliquiae B. Nicolai episcopi et confessoris ad Lotharingiae villam, quae Portus nominatur, delatae sunt' 293.
[27] 'Miracula S. Nicolai conscripta a monacho Beccensi' 427–9.
[28] RA 119–20.   [29] Chamalières 54.
[30] Longpont 250.   [31] Neumoustier 815. See Giles of Orval 93.

from Antioch with his son Guy Trousseau or he could have been convinced that the dishonour of that desertion needed expiation; his brother Guy of Rochefort also went.

There is very little evidence for the crusaders coming home wealthy. Guy of Rochefort was said to have returned 'in glory and abundance', whatever that might mean.[32] A knight called Grimbald, who had been on the First Crusade and was passing by Cluny, became a *confrater*, made a will in the abbey's favour and presented it with an ounce of gold.[33] Hadvide of Chiny, who had crusaded with her husband Dodo of Cons-la-Grandville, gave the monks of St Hubert-en-Ardenne a complete set of vestments in black cloth worked with gold and a chalice made with 9 ounces of gold and adorned with jewels.[34] Guy of 'Insula Bollini', dying on the journey, left the abbey of Bèze 6 ounces of gold.[35] These are the only references I know which could be interpreted as evidence for riches gained on the expeditions and it is not likely that there are many more to be found, although the rulers of the new Latin settlements seem to have played on a myth of oriental splendour, perhaps to attract settlers: Bohemond plundered Antioch in order to cut a dash on his tour of Europe in 1106.[36]

All crusaders had faced potentially crippling expenses and they and their families had pledges to redeem. Some may also have been weighed down by the repayment of ransoms: a knight in Poitou made arrangements to deal with such an eventuality before the crusade of 1120.[37] Of course it cannot be denied that the survivors had gained honour and the title *Jerosolimitanus* meant a lot to them and their contemporaries.[38] The prestige they enjoyed was demonstrated on Bohemond of Taranto's journey through France in 1106, as we have seen. In 1119 Robert of Flanders was referred to by his son as a man who 'with God's cooperation and with the other princes of the army of the Christians subdued with his weapons the Lord's Sepulchre and Jerusalem'.[39] Amid the dangers and hardships

---

[32] Suger of St Denis, *Vita*, 38. [33] Cluny 5.118.
[34] St Hubert-en-Ardenne 81–2. [35] Bèze Chron 392.
[36] RC 713–14. [37] Mauléon 15.
[38] Crusaders who were definitely referred to by this title were Robert II of Flanders ('De genere comitum Flandrensium notae Parisienses' 259), Fulk V of Anjou (St Aubin d'Angers Cart 2.409–10), and posthumously Baldwin of Mons (St Waudru de Mons 1.9; Cysoing 39) and Rainald III of Château-Gontier (St Aubin d'Angers Cart 2.175).
[39] St Bertin (Haigneré) 1.52.

of a crusade, moreover, close association with a great magnate could lead to advancement, as in the case of a man called William of the *Camera*, who had served with Duke William of Aquitaine. The duke loved him dearly and on their return made him prévôt of Poitiers. But he began to puff himself up, at least according to a highly partisan account written by the monks of Nouaillé, to press on his inferiors and to act aggressively towards his superiors. Among his other tyrannies, he took control by force of mills which the monks believed belonged to them. They complained to Hugh of Lusignan, who had also come back from the East, and Hugh appealed to the duke on their behalf. The result was a judicial duel to decide the matter, which was won by David Four Bones, the monks' champion.[40]

The prestige the survivors enjoyed must have been enhanced by the relics some of them brought back. These were tiny and portable, but they were of immense religious significance to them and their contemporaries and the crusaders showered European churches with them: pieces of the True Cross, presumably from the fragment 'discovered' in Jerusalem shortly after the city's capture,[41] stones from the Holy Sepulchre[42] and the site of the Ascension,[43] hair torn from her head by Our Lady as she witnessed the Crucifixion,[44] a hair from Christ's beard,[45] and relics of SS John the Baptist,[46] Nicholas,[47] and possibly Cleophas and Sergius.[48] After Raymond of St Gilles's death in Syria in 1105 Bishop Herbert of Tripoli, who had been his chaplain, sent the relics Raymond had carried with him on crusade to his home priory of Chaise-Dieu, to embellish the tomb of St Robert there.[49] At least one sliver from the Holy Lance – the lump of metal purporting to be the tip of the spear which had pierced Christ's side while he was on the cross – found its way to western Europe before the Lance itself was lost in Asia Minor in 1101. Its hiding place under the floor of the old cathedral in Antioch had been revealed to the poor servant Peter Bartholomew in visions, during one of which St Andrew had carried him at night into

[40] Nouaillé 292–4. For William, see also Montierneuf de Poitiers 63.
[41] CSPVS 184–8; Redon 318–19; LA 626; Notre-Dame de Chartres 3.83.
[42] CSPVS 184–8; Redon 318–19; Giles of Orval 93.   [43] LA 626.
[44] OV 5.170; Eadmer, *Historia Novorum in Anglia*, 179–81.   [45] LA 626.
[46] Giles of Orval 93.   [47] 'Qualiter reliquiae B. Nicolai' 293–4; CSPVS 184–8.
[48] J. Baumel, *Histoire d'une seigneurie du Midi de la France – Naissance de Montpellier (985–1213)* (Montpellier, 1969), 86; W. K. zu Isenburg, F. Freytag von Loringhoven et al., *Europäische Stammtafeln*, 2nd edn (Marburg and Berlin, 1980ff), 13, table 129A.
[49] *Acta SS Aprilis* 3.330.

Antioch, which was then still in Muslim hands, and had shown him where it was buried. It was found only after Peter himself had jumped down into a trench which had been dug all day and had pulled it from the soil. Some of the leaders were very doubtful, but its discovery had an extraordinary effect on the army's morale at a crucial moment.[50]

The most famous relic after the True Cross and the Holy Lance was the arm of St George, who played a significant rôle on the First Crusade as a secondary patron; other relics of him were also picked up and the occupation of his tomb at Lydda was marked by the appointment of the first Latin bishop in Palestine and the holding of a service to ask for his intercession.[51] The arm was given to the abbey of Anchin by Robert of Flanders and the story of its translation is quite revealing about attitudes during the campaign.

Somewhere in Asia Minor or northern Syria Gerbault, a priest from Lille in Robert of Flanders's contingent, accompanied by a lay companion, was engaged in the most normal crusader activity: foraging for food. The two men came upon a monastery, where they were hospitably received and fed. During their stay Gerbault made himself as pleasant as he could while keeping an eye open for any particularly important relics. The monks, who were good-natured and simple-minded, hid nothing from him and showed him a locked marble chest in which they kept their most precious possession, St George's arm together with his shoulder and ribs. Gerbault managed to get hold of the key, persuaded his companion to steal the relic and made off with it. As he took flight he was struck by blindness and was forced to return to the monastery where he confessed what he had done. The very unlikely result, according to a narrative written by a man in Flanders who claimed to have known him personally from childhood, was that the monks forgave him and, on the recovery of his sight, made him a present of the relic.

He returned to his contingent, but he fell ill again – in the narrator's view for not paying due respect to the relic in his charge – and there began a macabre procession of custodians as each man, to whom the arm was passed like some unlucky charm, fell ill and died: Gerard of Buc, the second castellan of Lille, and after him a canon of

---

[50] LA 626. See Riley-Smith, *The First Crusade*, 95–8. For other relic gifts, see Poly, *La Provence*, 268 n.120; 'Chronicon Brunwylarense' 2.153; Barnwell 46–7; St Maixent Chron 170; and possibly 'Pancharta Caduniensis seu Historia sancti Sudarii Jesu Christi' 300–1.

[51] Riley-Smith, *The First Crusade*, 105. See also CSPVS 184–8; LA 626.

Lille called Gunscelin. At this point Count Robert, who had heard of the circumstances of Gerard's death, intervened and demanded that the relic be surrendered to him, together with Gerard's other possessions. He entrusted it to a series of custodians, who all fell ill in turn, until one of his chaplains took charge of it. It went with Robert to Jerusalem and was nearly lost in a shipwreck on the voyage home before it was presented to Anchin.[52]

The standing of the crusaders who had fulfilled their vows could well have helped to ease the financial burdens they faced. In an age when family fortunes could be improved by marriage, they might well, for instance, have found that they could arrange more advantageous matches for their sons and daughters, although this is hard to demonstrate. But prestige has rarely been able to pay all one's bills and a pressing need for cash led some men to try to lessen the damage by resorting to whatever measures were available to them. Achard of Born gave property and rights in a forest to St Jean d'Angély in repayment for 200 *solidi* which he owed the abbey.[53] When Fulk of Matheflon came back from the East he apparently tried to exact a toll on a bridge he had built from the tenants of the monks of St Serge d'Angers, who claimed exemption through frankalmoin,[54] and to levy another on the transport of pigs,[55] and he certainly turned to his advantage an old dispute with the nuns of Le Ronceray d'Angers. Early in the eleventh century the village of Seiches-sur-le-Loir had been given to the nuns by Countess Hildegarde of Anjou. The castle of Matheflon had then been built in the parish and within its enceinte a wooden church had been constructed. But the population had grown and Fulk and Le Ronceray had agreed to replace it in stone. The new church had been built and Fulk, whose father had already consented to the gift to the nuns of the tithes of Matheflon itself, had agreed to surrender other tithes he held in Anjou and to fund a priest, although he was paid 100 *solidi* (and his wife ten) 'not because this was a sale but out of charity', a clause that must have been inserted to avoid the charge of simony. He had not kept his side of the bargain, however, and had held on to

---

[52] 'Narratio quomodo relliquiae martyris Georgii' 248–52. See also 'Sigeberti continuatio auctarium Aquicinense' 395; 'Genealogia comitum Flandriae' 323; 'Historia monasterii Aquicinctini' 586; 'Annales Aquicinctini' 503; Dunes 3. For a reference to Robert as 'the son of St George', see 'Genealogia regum Francorum' 250.

[53] St Jean d'Angély 30.153. He reserved hunting rights.

[54] Laval 1.70–1, although it is possible that this dispute took place before the crusade.

[55] St Laud d'Angers 7.

the tithes, so that he and the nunnery were at odds up to the time he left on the First Crusade. While he was away his son Hugh came to recognize the strength of the nuns' case and made over the tithes. Hugh was given sixteen pounds, his wife twenty *solidi* and a cow, and his uncle ten *solidi*, but he agreed to return the money if Fulk refused to accept what he had done. When Fulk got back he wanted, or pretended to want, to nullify the agreement, but he was persuaded to endorse it for 100 *solidi* of Le Mans and a further 100 of Angers, together with other sums for relations; and he got another 312 *solidi* for confirming the nuns' possession of the tithes of Matheflon.[56]

Fulk's share of the tithes of Seiches had cost the nuns a great deal, which may be why they took a strict line in a related case. This concerned a man called Geoffrey Le Râle, who had sold the tithes of the mill of Seiches to Le Ronceray when raising money for his crusade. On his return he wanted the nuns to make a contribution, in proportion to the value of the tithes they held, towards the purchase of new mill-stones and he was furious with the abbess when she refused. He seized the mill, but he was hauled into the abbess's court, where he pleaded guilty and was fined.[57]

It is hard to penetrate the minds of the survivors. Of course they must have been grateful for their safe return and some made further pilgrimages of thanksgiving. Robert of Normandy went to Mont St Michel[58] and Godric of Finchale came home to England by way of Compostela.[59] Others made additional donations, among which one finds again a high proportion of churches and tithes.[60] An unusual but revealing case concerned Count Guy of Pistoia and a man in his company called Raimondino. In November 1100 Guy gave Raimondino the freehold of a fief he had held of him 'for the benefit of his [Guy's] soul and for the service Raimondino had performed on the Jerusalem journey'. Raimondino immediately transferred the property, which was now his to give, to the canons of Pistoia for the benefit of his soul and those of his wife and children and of the

---

[56] Le Ronceray d'Angers 92–5.   [57] Le Ronceray d'Angers 104.
[58] OV 5.300.   [59] Reginald of Durham 34.
[60] For gifts on return: Longpont 250; St Hubert-en-Ardenne 1.81–2; Cluny 5.117–18; Cormery 104–5; Nogent-le-Rotrou 36–9; Pistoia 7.242–3; Pébrac 17; St Julien de Tours 72–3; St Martial de Limoges 340–1; OV 6.310; and probably La Trinité de Vendôme Cart 2.108–9. For churches and tithes among these, see Pébrac 17; Longpont 250; St Julien de Tours 72–3; Cluny 5.117–18; and probably La Trinité de Vendôme Cart 2.108–9.

count. It looks as though he had been seeking from the count not material advancement but the reward of prayer.[61]

Others made foundations. While on crusade Robert of Flanders decided to refound a monastery near Bruges dedicated to St Andrew in gratitude for the help given by the apostle to the crusaders at Antioch: he was thinking of St Andrew's revelation to Peter Bartholomew of the whereabouts of the Holy Lance. He sent letters to his wife Clemency, asking her to get the necessary licence from the bishop of Tournai, and when he came home the new community was put under the control of the abbey of Afflighem.[62] The community at Neumoustier, an Augustinian abbey near Huy dedicated to the Holy Sepulchre and St John the Baptist, believed that their house had been founded by Cono and Lambert of Montaigu and Peter the Hermit in fulfilment of the vow they had made during the storm on their voyage home. Peter lived in the community until his death in 1115 and was buried in the church. There developed the very unlikely tradition at the abbey that the patriarch of Jerusalem and the canons of the Holy Sepulchre had granted Peter the privilege that men and women who could not fulfil their vows to pilgrimage to Jerusalem for good cause could gain the same benefits by visiting Neumoustier.[63] The priory of Landécourt was founded by the Lorrainer lord Bencelinus of Brie on his return in 1100.[64] The priory of Crisenon in Burgundy had been founded before the First Crusade by Hugh of Toucy, one of those first crusaders who deserted. When he came back his affection for his foundation grew and he built a church for it, but, conscious that his vow had not been fulfilled, he left for the East again in 1101, putting Crisenon under the protection of the bishop of Auxerre.[65]

Some of the survivors became priests or monks. At least two, Peter Jordan of Châtillon and Raymond of Aguilers,[66] had taken the step during the First Crusade itself, and others were ordained or professed on their return to Europe. One of them was Eudes Arpin, who had sold his viscounty of Bourges to the king of France to raise money for his crusade. He was captured during the battle of Ramle in 1102 and was held a prisoner in Cairo until he was freed through the intervention of the Byzantine emperor. On his way home he visited Pope Paschal, into whose mouth a contemporary put a speech which

[61] Pistoia 7.241–3.   [62] Afflighem 19–21.
[63] Neumoustier 815; Giles of Orval 93.   [64] Lorraine 513–14.
[65] Molesme 2.84; and see 1.138–9.   [66] Cormery 104; RA 108.

stressed the satisfactory nature of the penance Eudes Arpin had undertaken and the merit of his subsequent sufferings; never again should he risk his soul in the world. It is clear that Eudes Arpin had already experienced some kind of inner conversion. He returned to France and became a monk at Cluny.[67] These men may have found their vocations out of their experiences, but there was anyway such a close association in people's minds between crusading and the religious life that one could lead naturally to the other. For example, Maurice of Glons, who was preparing to leave for the crusade of 1147, came to an agreement with the abbey of St Jacques de Liège. He transferred to the monks a *mansus* he had held of the abbey, receiving in return a counter-gift, but he specified that his mother should get a lifetime annuity of forty *solidi* drawn from half of it and that if he was alive once the crusade was over he was to be received into the community 'either as a servant or as a monk'; presumably he feared that he might not pass a literacy test. He obviously saw crusading as a natural penitential preparation for entry into the religious life.[68]

An extraordinary story current in the Limousin several decades later suggests that Gouffier of Lastours brought a tame lion back with him from the East.[69] This would have been an exotic reminder of his adventures, but for him and for most men their return marked a re-entry into a disordered society with which they had to come to terms and one which often seems to have become more disordered because of their absence. In fact there was no way once they were home that lords could avoid being drawn into the constant disputes over property and rights that regularly punctuated life. I have already described how within six years of the liberation of Jerusalem Bishop Ivo of Chartres had to deal with a case arising from the way Rotrou of Perche-Mortagne had thrown up a castle on land which a crusader believed was his and how the dispute had degenerated into violence.[70] Another case troubling Ivo involved Raimbold Croton

---

[67] OV 5.324, 342–52. Others who had a vocation included Adiutor of Vernon (after a period in the Holy Land: *Acta SS Aprilis* 3.824), Drogo of Chaumont-en-Vexin (St Martin de Pontoise 362), Frumold ('Chronicon Brunwylarense' 153), Godric of Finchale (Reginald of Durham, 57–8), Richard son of Fulk of Aunou ('Miracula S. Nicolai' 429) and the almoner of Tournemire who became a monk at Aurillac (St Flour ccvii).

[68] St Jacques de Liège 442–3; and see also Bèze Chron 473.

[69] GV 12.428.

[70] See above p. 136. In the Limousin Gerald Malefaide of Noailles and his brother were imprisoned by the canons of St Etienne de Limoges for holding on to church lands and tithes to which they had no right. St Etienne de Limoges 186–90.

from Chartres, a hero who had distinguished himself at Antioch[71] and had been the first, or one of the first, over the walls of Jerusalem in July 1099.[72] Within a year or two of his return Raimbold had had a monk of the abbey of Bonneval, who must have been in charge of one of its granges, beaten up and castrated because the abbey's servants had been stealing his crops; presumably this was another case of disputed rights. Ivo imposed fourteen years' penance, but Raimbold used all the influence he could to get an exemption from the prohibition against bearing arms during that period. He had lost a hand during the attack on Jerusalem[73] and was probably incapable of fighting anyway, but the effect of the ban on his standing in society would have been disastrous.[74] Before Hugh of Chaumont-sur-Loire had left in 1096 he had been involved in a violent quarrel originating in his belief that the count of Anjou was setting up his cousin, Corba of Thorigné, as a co-heiress of Amboise with the complicity of his uncle Lisois, who had had wardship of his estate in his minority. Part of the plan had been to marry Corba off to a man called Aimery of Courron. Hugh had reacted fiercely to the threat to his inheritance, but the count had intervened and the quarrel had been patched up. Hugh and Aimery had taken the cross and had left together, but Aimery had died at Nicaea. Returning at Easter 1100, Hugh found that the count, in return for a substantial sum, had married Corba to an elderly man called Achard of Saintes without informing her relations and that there was a new threat to his possession of his lordship. Achard fled with his young wife to Tours, but he was followed by Hugh's subjects, one of whom made contact with Corba and planned her abduction when she went to pray in a church nearby. One day she was bundled out of the church and on to a horse, and was handed over to a party of her kinsmen, who were led by Robert of Roches-Corbon, Hugh's uncle by marriage and protector. Achard died of illness and sorrow soon afterwards.[75]

An extreme case is that of Thomas of Marle. Thomas was a cruel and exceptionally violent man and he had already shown these traits before the First Crusade. It is possible that his personality had been damaged by the hatred his father, Engelrand of Boves, felt towards him. Engelrand seems to have doubted whether Thomas was indeed

[71] BB 49 note, 71 note; AA 410; WT 310. See also Ch d'A 1.71 , 208–11, 306, 442, 527–8.
[72] BB 102 note; HP 218–19; RC 688–9; OV 6.158. See Ivo of Chartres 144.
[73] RC 688–9.   [74] Ivo of Chartres 144–5.
[75] GAD 99–102. See Duby, *The Knight*, 245–7.

his son. He had wanted to disinherit him and his feelings of hostility were inflamed by the jealousy and vindictiveness of his second wife.[76] Thomas was married to Ida of Hainault, the daughter of Baldwin of Mons, but he did not march with the forces from Flanders or Lorraine. Together with another lord from northern France he joined the Swabian count Emich of Flonheim and took part in the persecution of the Jews in the Rhineland and in a ravaging march to the Hungarian borders.[77] After Emich's army had disintegrated, he went to Italy and by the summer of 1097 was in the Christian camp before Nicaea.[78] He distinguished himself in the battle of Dorylaeum,[79] and took part in the battle of Antioch[80] and the siege of Jerusalem.[81] Thomas, 'the valiant ... whose heart was loyal',[82] was to become a hero of the writers of the *chansons*; his character must have been suited to that brutal, alienated world.

Ida of Hainault died during or soon after the crusade and on his return Thomas married Ermengarde of Montaigu, whose castle – a very strong one – became a centre for a spectacular pillaging campaign in the region of Laon, Rheims and Amiens. A league was organized against him in 1103 under the leadership of his father and some of the most influential local lords, including Ebles of Roucy, but it came to nothing when the king intervened.[83] In Thomas's case the crusade seems to have been merely an interlude in a savage vendetta against a father who loathed him, in an internal family feud which rocked much of northern France.

In August 1099 those crusaders who had decided to remain in Palestine were occupying only Jerusalem itself and a corridor of land stretching to Jaffa on the coast. Three hundred miles to the north there were Christian enclaves around Albara and Ma'arrat-an-Nu'man, and further still, around Antioch and Edessa. Their hold on the newly conquered territories in the Levant was precarious. Jerusalem is awkwardly placed geographically, has never had much economic importance and could not be held in isolation. Control had to be established over the region around it and there had to be a relatively secure line of communications back to Antioch and

---

[76] See Suger of St Denis, *Vita*, 30-4, 174-8; GN Vita 328, 362-72, 396-416; OV 6.258, 290.
[77] AA 293-5; WT 156-7.   [78] AA 295, 315 (Ch d'A l.69, 94).
[79] AA 332 (WT 217).   [80] AA 422 (WT 330; Ch d'A 1.441, 450-1); RR 833; Gilo 775.
[81] AA 464, 468 (WT 410).   [82] Ch d'A 1.171,450 and *passim*.
[83] Suger of St Denis, *Vita*, 30-4.

beyond. Enlargement began almost at once and the coastal ports
were progressively reduced in a strategy which dominated the next
twenty-five years. In the north, the settlements at Antioch and Edessa
expanded and met, and the Christians occupied the coast and much
of its hinterland as far south as Baniyas. Meanwhile the gap from
Baniyas to Beirut was bridged by the establishment of the county of
Tripoli and by 1124 the Christians held the whole of the Levantine
coast from Alexandretta to Gaza, with the sole exception of the city
of Ascalon and its territory. Reinforcements who wished to travel
overland now had an assured route once they had crossed Asia
Minor, and smaller contingents, which it was practicable to transport
by sea, had a more secure passage, because the Egyptian galley fleet,
the only really effective military arm left to the Fatimid caliphs in
Cairo, was deprived of ports to take on water and did not have the
range to operate effectively against the northern Mediterranean
shipping lanes.[84] The settlers embarked on a massive building
programme: of port facilities, castles, town fortifications, monasteries
and churches, above all in and around Jerusalem where, it has been
suggested, they were trying to mirror the heavenly city in stone.[85]
But there were never enough of them to assure security,[86] and it is
not surprising to find western knights who, although not crusaders in
the technical sense, had committed themselves to periods of religious
exile to help defend the Holy Land. They were soon to be followed
by the brothers of the military orders.

   The first men who were prepared to put aside a few years to serve
in the East were some crusaders who in 1099 delayed their departure
for home. They included William V of Montpellier,[87]Adiutor of
Vernon,[88] Ilger Bigod,[89] and probably Rainald II of Burgundy[90] and
Ralph of Montpincon.[91] These para-crusaders should not be confused with the mercenaries who were being employed in Palestine
and Syria from their conquest.[92] They performed their service as a
devotion and in doing so were establishing a tradition which lasted as

[84] J. Pryor, *Geography, Technology and War* (Cambridge, 1988), 112–34.
[85] Hamilton, 'The Impact of Crusader Jerusalem', 699–711.
[86] Although more than there used to be thought. See R. Ellenblum, *Frankish Rural Settlement in Crusader Palestine* (forthcoming).
[87] AA 507; Baumel, *Histoire d'une seigneurie*, 86.   [88] *Acta SS Aprilis* 3.824.
[89] Eadmer, *Historia novorum in Anglia*, 179–81.   [90] AA 583.
[91] AA 531. For *milites ad terminum* in general, see G. Ligato, 'Fra Ordini Cavallereschi e crociata: "milites ad terminum" e "confraternitates" armate', *'Militia Christi' e Crociata nei secoli XI–XIII* (Milan, 1992), 645–97.
[92] See AA 545.

long as crusading did; their heirs were the men who were to travel to fight in support of the Teutonic Knights and the Hospitallers in Prussia, Rhodes and Malta in the fourteenth, fifteenth and sixteenth centuries. Their ethos was summarized by a biographer of Charles the Good of Flanders, who wrote that after Charles had reached manhood and had been belted as a knight he vowed to go to Jerusalem,

and there, bearing arms against the pagan enemies of our faith ... he fought vigorously for Christ the Lord for a considerable time and ... consecrated to him the first fruits of his labours and deeds.

Since he had been born between 1080 and 1086 Charles would have been about fifteen in 1100, which leads one to suppose that his majority would have occurred soon after the First Crusade. He seems to have spent most of the first decade of the twelfth century in Palestine, because he returned to Flanders shortly before the death of Count Robert II in 1111.[93]

It must have been common for knights like Charles to attach themselves to some institution in or around Jerusalem. Before 1127 Robert Burgundio of Sablé, a grandson of the first crusader of the same name, had been associated with the church of St Stephen outside the walls of the city.[94] In 1130 it was known that secular knights, called *milites ad terminum*, were serving for fixed terms with the Templars,[95] who themselves may have originated in such a group; there was a tradition in Palestine later in the century that the earliest Templars had been attached to the church of the Holy Sepulchre.[96] A sad case concerned a Burgundian knight called Guy Cornelly of Til-Châtel. His wife, who had borne him three daughters, had contracted leprosy and he decided, perhaps in a fit of despair, to go to Jerusalem 'and there in the Temple of the Lord to pursue his career as a knight in the service of God to the end of his life'. Before leaving he arranged for his wife and daughters to be cared for by the abbey of St Bénigne de Dijon.[97] There was a tendency for those who had served temporarily in the East to join a

---

[93] Walter of Thérouanne, 'Vita Karoli Comitis Flandriae', 540–1.

[94] Anjou (Chartrou) 366.

[95] *Die ursprüngliche Templerregel* 142–3. This occurs in an addition to the Rule, made in Jerusalem in c.1130.

[96] See K. Elm, 'Kanoniker und Ritter vom Heiligen Grab', *Die geistlichen Ritterorden Europas*, ed. J. Fleckenstein and M. Hellmann (Sigmaringen, 1980), 159–66.

[97] Cart Temp 19.

military order eventually. Hugh I of Troyes spent the years 1104–8 in the Holy Land,[98] and he pilgrimaged again in 1114[99] and in 1125, when he became a Templar.[100] Robert Burgundio ended up as master of the same order.[101] Bernard V Gros of Uxelles, who may have spent the years 1110–16 in Palestine, joined the crusade of 1147 and became a Hospitaller.[102]

With the foundation of the Templars the crusading ideal was transferred on to a different plane. These warrior-religious originated in a decision made during the winter of 1119–20 by some knights in Jerusalem who, under the leadership of a noble from Champagne called Hugh of Payns and in the atmosphere of crisis that followed the catastrophe of the Field of Blood, formed themselves into a brotherhood with the aim of securing the pilgrim roads to and from the holy places, which were still very unsafe. They took vows of poverty, celibacy and obedience and their establishment was approved by the patriarch of Jerusalem. They attracted the patronage of King Baldwin II of Jerusalem, who gave them part of his palace in the Temple compound to be their headquarters, and they were probably recognized at a church council which met in Nablus in January 1120. Their foundation was confirmed by the Church at large in 1129 at a council at Troyes presided over by a papal legate, which, exploiting a wealth of experience of the religious life available to it, drew up a Rule for them.[103] They were soon being granted property in Europe; Templar brothers, perhaps itinerant at first, were active in Provence from possibly 1124, Flanders from perhaps 1125, Languedoc and Iberia from 1128, and Burgundy and Champagne from *c.*1130.[104]

The concept of a military order was as unprecedented in Christian thought as had been the idea of warfare as a penance which provided the basis for its existence. Thomas Aquinas made the association

---

[98] Molesme 2.321–3.

[99] Montier-la-Celle 14–18, 284–7; Montiéramey 30–1, 42; Reims (admin) 1.269; Reims (ville) 3.728–9; Epernay 2.118; Laurence of Liège 504.

[100] Bernard of Clairvaux, 'Epistolae', 7.85-6. See Cart Hosp 1.78; Notre-Dame de Josaphat (Delaborde) 44.

[101] Mayer, 'Angevins *versus* Normans', 6–7; M.-L. Bulst-Thiele, *Sacrae Domus Militiae Templi Hierosolymitani Magistri* (Göttingen, 1974), 30–40.

[102] Cluny 5.246-8, 456, 473–4; Bouchard, *Sword, Miter, and Cloister*, 304–5. A 'transalpine' knight called Hugh, who later became a monk in the East, came out to Palestine 'militiae gratia' early in the twelfth century. *Duodecima Centuria* 1606.

[103] See M. Barber, *The New Knighthood* (Cambridge, 1994), 6–18.

[104] Cart Temp 1–3, 7–8, 12, 19–23.

between penitential violence and the military orders clear 150 years later when he defended their rôle by pointing out that: 'To make war in the service of God is imposed on some as a penance, as is evident from those who are enjoined to fight in aid of the Holy Land.'[105] With the Templars and the brothers of the other military orders warfare as a temporary act of devotion became warfare as a devotional way of life. Whereas crusaders were laymen directing their everyday skills for a time into a holy cause, Templars were religious as permanently at war as their colleagues in other more conventional orders were at prayer. They were members, they and their apologists admitted, of a new kind of order of the church, although they insisted that its foundation had been foreshadowed, and therefore justified, in scripture.

This kind of new order originated, we believe, in the holy land of the East through the holy scriptures and divine providence. That is to say that this armed company of knights can kill the enemies of the cross without sinning. For this reason we judge you to be rightly called knights of the Temple, with a probity which is both meritorious and beautiful.[106]

Wearing the cross as crusaders did, they appropriated for themselves the monastic, and then crusading, title of 'knights of Christ'. They took up a theme already present in early crusade propaganda, the comparison of the new knight, saving his soul in a worthy cause, with the old violent reprobate.

Oh, this is a truly holy and secure knighthood and it is certainly free from that double peril which often and habitually endangers one sort of man, in so far as he fights for some other cause than Christ. For how often do you who fight the knighthood of the world come to grips with a most dread situation, in which either you may kill the enemy in body while in fact killing your own soul, or by chance you may be killed by him and die in body and soul simultaneously.[107]

They were motivated by love.

Like true Israelites and warriors most versed in holy battle, on fire with the flame of true love, you carry out in your deeds the words of the gospel, in which it is said *Greater love than this no man hath, that a man lay down his life for his friends.*[108]

---

[105] Thomas Aquinas, *Summa Theologiae*, 2a2ae, qu.188, art.3.
[106] *La Règle du Temple* 58–9.
[107] Bernard of Clairvaux, 'De laude novae militiae ad milites Templi liber', 215. See also the prologue to the Rule. *Die ursprüngliche Templerregel* 130.
[108] *Papsturkunden für Templer und Johanniter* 205–6.

They died as martyrs.

How glorious are the victors who return from battle! How blessed are the
martyrs who die in battle! Rejoice, courageous athlete, if you live and
conquer in the Lord, but exult and glory the more if you die and are joined
to the Lord. Life indeed is fruitful and victory glorious, but according to
holy law death is better than either of these things. For if those are *blessed
who die in the Lord*, how much more blessed are those who die for the
Lord?[109]

But the early Templar documents, the apologies of Bernard of
Clairvaux, the Temple's most eloquent supporter, and Hugh of St
Victor, written with a greater force and clarity than the Templars
themselves could ever have expressed, and *Omne datum optimum*, Pope
Innocent II's charter for them, cannot hide the fact that the
founding of a religious order, the professed members of which took
familiar vows, listened to the office and then rode out to kill their
enemies, was considered to be abhorrent in some circles. And
anyway the idea and practice of penitential warfare had been
applied until now to laymen; the proposition that fighting was a
charitable activity for religious on an equivalent level to actions such
as the care of the sick was quite another matter. What is surprising
is that the section of clerical opinion which disapproved was not
larger. In fact, so small, or so discreet, was the opposition to the
Templars that we do not even have the names of any of their critics;
we know only of their existence from the reactions to their views in
the apologias.[110]

A reason for this may have been that the Templars quickly gained
powerful support, not only from the king of Jerusalem and others in
the eastern settlements, but also in the West. The approval of a
prestigious figure like Bernard of Clairvaux was obviously a major
advantage[111] and although the real growth of their estates in Europe
came after Hugh of Payns's recruiting campaign in 1128-9, the
Templars had the favour of leading nobles from early on. Fulk V of
Anjou became closely associated with them while on crusade in 1120,
perhaps being received as a *confrater* within months of their foundation. He apparently had to get their permission to return to his
county in France and when he did so he established an annual
subvention of thirty pounds of the money of Angers for them and

---

[109] Bernard of Clairvaux, 'De laude novae militiae', 215.
[110] See the discussion in A. J. Forey, *The Military Orders* (London, 1992), 10–17.
[111] William Dandozille, the archbishop of Auch, became a *confrater* in 1126 × 30. Cart Temp 4.

encouraged other magnates to do the same.[112] Alfonso I of Portugal became a *confrater* in 1129.[113] Hugh of Troyes renounced his county and, as we have seen, entered the order as a fully professed brother in 1125, as did Raymond Berengar III of Barcelona in 1131,[114] the year of Alfonso I of Aragon's notorious and abortive will in which he left his kingdom to the Templars, the Hospitallers and the canons of the Holy Sepulchre.[115]

One sign that the ideal of the Templar brother knight struck a chord with contemporaries is the speed with which it was imitated. The Hospital of St John had been founded in Jerusalem to care for poor pilgrims, particularly when they were sick. The first evidence that it was beginning to diversify into military activities comes in a charter recording a gift made to it on 17 January 1126 by the constable of the lordship of Jaffa in the presence of witnesses who included six Hospitallers, among them a brother who also had the military title of constable. Given the date of this endowment we can be certain that the men present to witness it were serving in a Christian army which was advancing into territory controlled by Damascus.[116] Two years later the master of the Hospital, Raymond of Le Puy, was to be found in a royal army devastating the territory of Ascalon.[117] So it looks as though within six years of the Templars' foundation the Hospitallers were starting along the road they had taken. Ten years later, in 1136, the king of Jerusalem entrusted them with the strategic castle of Bait Jibrin in southern Palestine; presumably they intended to garrison it with mercenaries. From 1144 comes the first evidence for a brother-knight, a man called Peter Loup who was based at St Gilles in southern France. In the same year the Hospitallers were given the castle of Crac des Chevaliers, which carried with it responsibilities for the defence of a stretch of the frontier of the county of Tripoli, and in 1148 they may have taken part in the crusade which at that time was campaigning in the East.[118]

[112] OV 6.308–10.   [113] Cart Temp 17.
[114] Cart Temp 25. See Barber, *The New Knighthood*, 28.
[115] See Barber, *The New Knighthood*, 26–9.
[116] Cart Hosp 1.71. The main engagement of this campaign was fought on 25 January. Ibn al-Qalanisi, *The Damascus Chronicle of the Crusades*, 175–7.
[117] Cart Hosp 1.78.
[118] Cart Hosp 1.97–8, 116–18, 129. J. S. C. Riley-Smith, *The Knights of St John in Jerusalem and Cyprus c.1050–1310* (London, 1967), 52–8. For the date of the acquisition of Crac des Chevaliers, see J. Richard, *Le comté de Tripoli sous la dynastie toulousaine (1102–1187)* (Paris, 1945), errata slip.

It is no coincidence that the recruitment of nobles into the Hospitaller brotherhood followed these first steps towards militarization. Although the early brethren cannot have been peasants, their origins and connections – even those of the first two masters – are uncertain; only two brothers, Peter Abon from Gap in *c*.1110[119] and Winther from Austria in 1128,[120] are known to have come from the class of knights. The first recruit from a leading noble family, Count Robert II of Auvergne whose mother was the sister of King Roger II of Sicily, had entered the order by 1141. At that time he was entitled seneschal. The office of seneschal of the central convent did not persist – indeed Robert was the only brother in the central Middle Ages to hold it – but in the secular world it was a high-ranking one. It looks as though the master had made Robert his second-in-command and Robert was listed receiving the important gift of Crac des Chevaliers immediately after him.[121] In 1148, as has been seen, Bernard Gros of Uxelles, a major Burgundian lord, joined the order, and it was also in the 1140s that the first noble *confratres* are to be found: Rainald I of Bailleul, who had crusaded in Spain in 1125,[122] and Count Guigo II of Forcalquier.[123]

The militarization of the Hospital proceeded quite slowly and with opposition from the popes, which may be why in the middle years of the twelfth century the Temple gained more in the way of endowments than it did.[124] The fact is that the ethos of a military order was attractive to western armsbearers. Although most sons of nobles and knights entered the ranks of the secular clergy or conventional monastic communities, some of them found in the Templar life a way of expressing their longing for a religion more in accordance with the culture of the society from which they came than were the traditional and new forms of monasticism. The Templars foreswore the ostentation and glamour of the world, but there was in their ethos enough concurrence with the world's values to make it, and not simply the prospect of fighting for Christ in the East, appealing. In 1138 a Provençal lord called Hugh of Bourbouton entered the order and gave it all his land. His son joined him as a professed brother and his wife became a nun. Ownership of Hugh's lordship was split

---

[119] Cart Hosp 1.4–5.   [120] Cart Hosp 1.76.
[121] Cart Hosp 1.113, 118.   [122] Cart Hosp 1.125. For his crusade, see OV 6.402.
[123] Cart Hosp 1.146.
[124] M. Gervers, 'Pro defensione Terre Sancte: The Development and Exploitation of the Hospitallers' Landed Estate in Essex', *The Military Orders*, ed M. Barber (Aldershot, 1994), 3–20 *passim*. For papal opposition, see Riley-Smith, *The Knights of St John*, 76–7.

between several branches of his family, but most of it had come into Templar hands by 1147. By that year at the latest Hugh had become master of the commandery of Richerenches created out of the estate and he ran it until his death in 1151. The commandery's extraordinarily rich documentation gives us glimpses of him at such regular intervals that one can be confident that from the time of his reception he can hardly ever have gone to Palestine; he certainly could not have stayed there for more than a year. He had been relatively old when he had responded to the spirituality of the new knights of Christ and he remained living a religious life he must have found satisfying on his old estate, content to manage the lands there for the benefit of the fighting convent in the East.[125]

The military service of laymen in the East and the emergence of the military orders must be set against the fact that appeals to crusade between 1102 and the opening of St Bernard's preaching campaign in 1146 for the so-called Second Crusade attracted only sporadic interest in most of western Europe. In 1107 Bohemond of Taranto was followed, as one might expect, by a group of men from southern Italy, Normandy and Britain, and other crusaders came from Iceland, Norway, Berry, Languedoc, Flanders, French and imperial Burgundy, northern Poitou, Anjou, the Ile-de-France, the Chartrain, where Bohemond himself had preached the crusade, and probably the Limousin. Men joined Pope Calixtus' crusade of 1120–4 from Maine, Poitou, Flanders, the northern Ile-de-France, Anjou, French and imperial Burgundy, Venice and Germany.[126] In 1128 Hugh of Payns recruited many crusaders in England for the expedition of the following year, as we have seen, and others have been identified who came from Flanders, Angoulême, Berry, Champagne, Poitou, Lorraine, the Chartrain and again Anjou, from where Count Fulk V was travelling to Palestine to marry the heiress to the kingdom of Jerusalem.

The lists I have compiled of participants in these minor crusades are not very long. Although I have no idea of the total numbers involved, they came nowhere near those taking part from 1096 to 1103 or from 1147 to 1149 and it seems that often only isolated individuals of significance were inspired to join. And in contrast to the practice of multiple crusading of a century later, once an early

---

[125] *Cartulaire de la Commanderie de Richerenches de l'Ordre du Temple (1136-1214) passim.*
[126] See Ekk C 262.

crusader was home he was very unlikely to crusade again. The most impressive group of second-timers comprised the first crusaders Gaston IV of Béarn, Centule II of Bigorre, Bernard Ato of Béziers, William IX of Aquitaine and William V of Montpellier from south-western France, and Rotrou of Perche-Mortagne from the southern borders of Normandy, who fought in the early Spanish crusades.[127] Leaving them aside, one finds only the following. Accompanying Bohemond of Taranto in 1107 were his half-brother Guy of Haute-ville, who had been in the Byzantine army that had turned back half way across Asia Minor in 1098, and Ralph the Red of Pont-Echanfray, a semi-professional soldier who had been with Bohemond in Antioch soon after it fell to the crusaders; he had served Bohemond's father and probably felt loyalty to the family. Godric of Finchale, who also took the cross for a second time, seems to have been one of those who went directly to the East.[128] The first crusader Stephen of Neublans probably went again on Pope Calixtus' crusade in 1120 and in 1129 Fulk of Anjou, who had already crusaded in 1120, had in his household the first crusader Hugh of Chaumont-sur-Loire. Only three of the many participants in the crusade of 1147 had taken the cross before.[129]

So it is clear that most crusaders did not feel the urge to crusade again. A number of them, on the other hand, subsequently made peaceful pilgrimages to Jerusalem: of the first crusaders, Gerard of Gournay-en-Bray in 1104,[130] Ralph of Montpinçon and Norgeot of Toucy in 1110,[131] Hugh Dalmace of Semur in 1118[132] and Rotrou of Perche-Mortagne before 1144; he gave the relics he carried with him to his foundation of La Trappe.[133] Walter of Montsoreau, who was on the crusade of 1107, was a pilgrim in 1122.[134] So their enthusiasm for Jerusalem as a cult centre and their concern for the Holy Land

---

[127] See Bull, *Knightly Piety*, 99–107, and for William of Montpellier, Maguelonne 1.76–81. Peter I of Aragon also took the cross for the First Crusade.

[128] Reginald of Durham 53–8.

[129] Conrad III of Germany, Thierry I of Flanders and Rainald I of Bar-le-Duc. Other recruits had made pilgrimages to Jerusalem before.

[130] William of Jumièges 278.

[131] Ralph of Montpinçon: OV 3.166. Norgeot of Toucy: *Gallia Christiana* 12, Instrumenta, 107–8; *Papsturkunden in Frankreich* 6.115–16.

[132] Marcigny 96; Bouchard, *Sword, Miter, and Cloister*, 360.

[133] La Trappe 579. The Ralph of Beaugency who witnessed a charter of 1124–5 (St Sépulcre de Jerusalem 213) among the burgesses of Jerusalem cannot have been the first crusader.

[134] Tours 37.286 note, although he may in fact have been on crusade again.

had not dimmed, even if taking part in another crusade was, for one reason or another, not an attractive proposition for most of them.

An associated feature of the period is that the interest aroused in Europe by the crusades of 1107 and the 1120s was localized, being in most regions sporadic or non-existent. The Limousin, where there had been great enthusiasm for the First Crusade, provides us with the name of only one crusader for the period from 1102 to 1131, and he is doubtful.[135] It is not as though concern for the Holy Sepulchre had evaporated; indeed it looks as though the old eleventh-century tradition of pilgrimages to Jerusalem had reasserted itself. The Limousin generated many pilgrims in the period[136] and the intense emotional attachment to Jerusalem still in evidence was demonstrated in 1119 when Robert of Roffignac was planning to go on pilgrimage there with Viscount Bernard of Comborn. When Robert attended a meeting at the abbey of Tulle at which the pilgrims were probably making plans, the monks raised with him a dispute they had with him over property. He refused to listen to them, but later, when the monks were in the refectory, he burst into the hall with his son and grandson and surrendered his claims there and then.[137] No crusader has been identified in the period between 1103 and 1147 from Provence, where there had again been an enthusiastic response in 1096, but there were many pilgrims to Jerusalem, especially from the nobles in the district of Marseilles.[138] Much the same picture is to be found in Champagne, which had sent many men to the East between 1096 and 1102. Few crusaders can be found before 1147, but there was enthusiasm for pilgrimages to Jerusalem, the lead being taken by Count Hugh I of Troyes, as we have seen.[139]

---

[135] Josbert Alboin.

[136] It is not impossible that one or two were first crusaders, but most seem to have been pilgrims. Gerald of Le Mont (Aureil 27), Peter lord of Noailles,the nephew of the abbot of Vigeois and brother of the abbot of Uzerche (Uzerche 399; Vigeois 155; Bull, *Knightly Piety*, 211, 268), Adhémar of Roffignac (Tulle 99), Robert of Roffignac (Tulle 157), Hugh of Soulier (Tulle 213), Robert of Lagarde-Enval (Tulle 241), Guitard of Tulle (Tulle 306), Garsias of Malemort (Tulle 158), Viscount Bernard of Comborn (Tulle 88, 157), William of Chanac (Tulle 45, 55), Gerard of Chanac (Tulle 65), Walter of Condat (Uzerche 294), Roger of Courson (Uzerche 275; see Bull, *Knightly Piety*, 210–11), Bernard Goscelm (Aureil 106), Guy of Bujaleuf (Aureil 105–6), Hugh Artmand (Tulle 68–9, 71, 439–40) and two members of the family of Ligonnat (Uzerche 323).

[137] Tulle 157–8. See Bull, *Knightly Piety*, 216.

[138] They included William Hugh of Les Baux (St Rémy de Provence 111–12; St Paul de Mausole 15–17), Hugh Geoffrey of Marseilles (St Victor de Marseille (Guérard) 1.451–2; 2.45) and Ismidon of Sassenage (*Acta SS Septembris* 7.847).

[139] Other pilgrims were Guy I of Dampierre-sur-l'Aube (Notre-Dame de Josaphat (Delaborde) 42), Erard I of Brienne (Montiérender 190, 200), Walter II of Brienne (St Etienne de

One is left with the impression that in much of western Europe the crusading idea proper became dormant after all the efforts associated with the First Crusade. To many armsbearers that expedition must have seemed a unique chance to engage in a particularly appropriate meritorious activity. Now they turned back to their traditional devotions, to be recalled to crusading only in 1146, when Bernard of Clairvaux preached the new enterprise as another once-and-for-all opportunity of self-help on one's passage to heaven.

[God] puts himself into a position of necessity, or pretends to be in one, while all the time he wants to help you in your need. He wants to be thought of as the debtor, so that he can award to those fighting for him wages: the remission of their sins and everlasting glory. It is because of this that I have called you a blessed generation, you who have been caught up in a time so rich in remission and are found living in this year so pleasing to the Lord, truly a year of jubilee.[140]

The result was a fiasco and it was to be another forty years before crusading became an everyday expression of the aspirations of the armsbearing classes. The idea of the crusade was still too radical. It needed to be diluted and to become more conventional before it could be regularized and institutionalized.

Vignory 180; possibly in 1119 when a Henry of Brienne was in Jerusalem) and Andrew of Baudement, who pilgrimaged twice (Notre-Dame de Josaphat (Kohler) 113; Notre-Dame de Josaphat (Delaborde) 32).
[140] Bernard of Clairvaux, 'Epistolae', 8.314.

CHAPTER 7

Crusading and the Montlhérys

Among those who maintained an enthusiasm for the Christian hold on Palestine and Syria in the first third of the twelfth century, and were sporadically involved in crusading as well, were the members of a circle of families from central and northern France. For a brief period, indeed, it must have seemed as if they were going to take the movement over and with the collapse of their ambitions the first stage of its history ended.

On 31 January 1120 King Baldwin II confirmed the privileges of the chief Marian shrine in Jerusalem, the abbey of St Mary of the Valley of Jehoshaphat. The ruins of St Mary lie in the valley below the city walls, over a shaft which leads down to the site of a tomb from whence the Blessed Virgin Mary is believed to have been assumed into heaven. The tomb has, therefore, an equivalence as the site of a resurrection to the Holy Sepulchre, even if it is of less importance. In his charter Baldwin referred to the abbot-elect, Gilduin of Le Puiset, as his blood-relation.[1] Gilduin was in fact the king's first cousin. He had only recently arrived in Palestine from the Cluniac community of Lurcy-le-Bourg, where he had been prior, and he joined a number of members of his family already in the East. His brother Waleran was a magnate in the county of Edessa,[2] which was ruled by another first cousin, Joscelin of Courtenay. Yet another cousin was William of Bures-sur-Yvette, the lord of Galilee.[3] Gilduin's nephew, Hugh of Le Puiset, was lord of Jaffa.[4]

What bound these men together was descent from Guy I of

---

[1] Notre-Dame de Josaphat (Delaborde) 33–5. See H. E. Mayer, *Bistümer, Klöster und Stifte im Königreich Jerusalem* (Stuttgart, 1977), 265, 278, 313, 332, 339, 363.

[2] Tractatus de reliquiis S. Stephani Cluniacum delatis', 317–18. See also FC 651–2, 659, 692; WT 567, 570; Notre-Dame de Josaphat (Kohler) 121–2.

[3] See M. Rheinheimer, *Das Kreuzfahrerfürstentum Galiläa* (Frankfurt-am-Main, 1990), 46–8, 287.

[4] Two other early settlers, Frederick and Herbert of Corbeil (Genoa (Iur) 1.102; Notre-Dame

Montlhéry and his wife Hodierna of Gometz. Guy had been a powerful figure in the Ile-de-France, mainly because of the castles he possessed. In 1104 his great-granddaughter was to marry one of King Philip's younger sons, and one of his granddaughters, born to his son Guy of Rochefort who was the king's seneschal from 1091 to 1095 and again after 1104, was to be betrothed to Philip's heir, the future Louis VI, although that marriage never took place.[5] Montlhéry was one of those troublesome castellan families – others were Beaugency, Montfort, and Le Puiset – which in the eleventh century had come to dominate the territories round Paris at the king's expense. They all bred crusaders and so must have shared some of the features which predisposed kindreds to respond to the appeal. This was especially the case with the Montlhérys. Guy I had been pious and, attracted to Cluniac monasticism, had founded the Cluniac priory of Longpont-sous-Montlhéry; he ended his days as a monk there.[6] A streak of religiosity ran in the family. His grandson, Baldwin II of Jerusalem who as Baldwin of Le Bourcq had been a first crusader and count of Edessa, was a noted *dévot*; it was later said that his hands and knees were calloused through frequent prayer and penitential discipline.[7] But another impression one has of the family is how ruthless its members could be. They carried this ruthlessness with them to the East. Several decades after the First Crusade, an indigenous observer, the Armenian Matthew of Edessa who must have known them well, described Baldwin as devout, modest and morally pure, but also mean and greedy: '[his] good qualities were offset by his ingenious avariciousness in seizing and accumulating the wealth of others, his insatiable love for money and his deep lack of generosity';[8] this was a criticism which was also to be made by his subjects in Jerusalem.[9] 'He harassed [moreover] those Armenian princes who were still free from the domination of the ferocious Turks, and with unheard of cruelty compelled all of them to go into exile.'[10] When Joscelin of Courtenay became count of Edessa he abandoned 'his former cruel nature'.[11]

---

de Josaphat (Delaborde) 36), could have been related through the marriage of Gilduin's brother Everard III of Le Puiset to Alice of Corbeil.

[5] A. Fliche, *Le règne de Philippe Ier, roi de France* (Paris, 1912), 91, 114, 321–5; E. Bournazel, *Le gouvernement capétien au XIIe siècle 1108–1180: structures sociales et mutations institutionelles* (Limoges, 1975), 31–4, 46.

[6] Fliche, *Le règne de Philippe I*, 320 note 4.   [7] WT 551.

[8] Matthew of Edessa, *Chronicle*, 221–2.   [9] Galbert of Bruges, 'Passio Karoli comitis', 564.

[10] Matthew of Edessa 220.   [11] Matthew of Edessa 225.

Two of Guy and Hodierna's sons, the husbands of two of their daughters, six grandsons, a granddaughter and her husband, and the husband of another granddaughter, a great-grandson and the husband of a great-granddaughter took part in the First Crusade. This extraordinary record was due largely to the offspring of Guy and Hodierna's four daughters, the legendary Montlhéry sisters whose procreativity was mentioned with awe by the twelfth-century historian William of Tyre.[12] They were married into the families of St Valéry and Le Puiset-Breteuil, which each sent three first crusaders, Le Bourcq of Rethel, which sent two, and Courtenay which provided one. If one adds to this the contribution from an array of closely related families – Chaumont-en-Vexin, Broyes and Pont-Echanfray – two generations of this clan produced twenty-six, perhaps twenty-eight, crusaders to and settlers in the East.

The mother of Baldwin of Le Bourcq, later to be King Baldwin II, was one of the Montlhéry sisters. Baldwin was also related to the families of the counts of Burgundy and of Boulogne, one of his paternal grandmothers, Ida of Boulogne, being the aunt of Godfrey of Bouillon and Baldwin of Boulogne. Belonging to the Lorrainer nobility, he marched from Europe in Godfrey's force and seems to have been a trusted and prominent member of that contingent. He accompanied Baldwin of Boulogne on a raid into Cilicia and he distinguished himself during the siege of Jerusalem, where he was wounded.[13] A short while later, perhaps early in 1100, he was sent north to Antioch to serve Bohemond of Taranto in what looks like paid military service.[14] Meanwhile, Godfrey had become the first ruler of Jerusalem and Baldwin of Boulogne count of Edessa. When news reached Baldwin of Boulogne in late August 1100 of Godfrey's death he summoned Baldwin of Le Bourcq from Antioch and handed the county of Edessa over to him before travelling south to claim the succession.[15]

Baldwin of Le Bourcq was to hold Edessa for the next eighteen years, in the course of which he arranged for his sister Cecilia to be married to Roger of Salerno, the prince-regent of Antioch,[16] and brought in at least two of his cousins. In about 1103 he gave Joscelin of Courtenay, who had also taken part in the First Crusade, an enormous and strategically situated fief, centred on Tilbashir and comprising most of the frontier with the principality of Antioch,[17]

---

[12] WT 547.   [13] AA 306, 310, 343, 350, 464, 468; FC 278; WT 161, 171, 174, 410.
[14] AA 527.   [15] FC 353; AA 527.   [16] See FC 622.   [17] WT 483.

and in 1117 he granted Waleran of Le Puiset the important fief of
Bira, on the Euphrates.[18] Late in 1112, however, he quarrelled with
Joscelin, whom he accused of disloyalty. He imprisoned and then
exiled him, depriving him of his lands. Joscelin made the journey
down to Palestine where Baldwin of Boulogne, now Baldwin I of
Jerusalem, granted him the important lordship of Galilee, on the
frontier with Damascus.[19] Joscelin soon granted a rear-fief in Galilee
to another Montlhéry cousin, William of Bures-sur-Yvette, who had
settled in the East in 1114 'as an act of penance', presumably to
expiate some act of violence perpetrated during the unsuccessful
rebellion of a league of castellans against the king of France.[20]

Meanwhile other Montlhérys had arrived. Hugh II of Le Puiset,
who had taken the cross for Bohemond of Taranto's crusade in 1107
– his wife, who accompanied him, was Bohemond's niece – reached
Palestine perhaps in 1108, certainly before 1110, and was given by
King Baldwin the other main strategic lordship in his kingdom, that
of Jaffa, which faced the Egyptian beachhead at Ascalon. Hugh was
dead by the middle of 1112 and a marriage was arranged for his
widow; the idea seems to have been to keep the lordship warm for
Hugh's son, another Hugh, who had been born in Apulia in 1106 or
1107.[21]

Hugh II of Le Puiset may have been accompanied to Palestine by
a man called Barisan the Old, who by the time he first comes into
view in 1115 had become constable of Jaffa.[22] Barisan was the
progenitor of the Ibelins, a family which was to be the most
prominent noble house in Palestine in the thirteenth century. By
then the Ibelins had some memory of descent from the Le Puisets,
because their pedigree opens with the following statement: 'Balian
[Barisan] the Frenchman was the brother of Count Guilin of
Chartres.[23] There never was a count of Chartres of that name and
this has always been rejected as myth. Barisan's origins have been
thought to have been obscure, one suggestion being that he was a
knight from northern Italy.[24] But the name Guilin in the pedigree is
perhaps an echo of that of Abbot Gilduin of St Mary of the Valley of

[18] Matthew of Edessa 220.   [19] WT 528–9.
[20] APC 430; Rheinheimer, *Das Kreuzfahrerfürstentum Galiläa*, 46–8. William's brother or uncle,
    Guy II of Rochefort, made the pilgrimage with him. Tiron 1.17.
[21] H. E. Mayer, 'The Origins of the County of Jaffa', *Israel Exploration Journal* 35 (1985), 40–5.
[22] Notre-Dame de Josaphat (Delaborde) 29.
[23] 'Les Lignages d'Outremer' 448.
[24] See P. W. Edbury, *The Kingdom of Cyprus and the Crusades 1191–1374* (Cambridge, 1991), 39.

Jehoshaphat, not himself a viscount of Chartres but the son and brother of viscounts. Barisan could have been Gilduin's illegitimate brother; or he could have been a brother-in-law, perhaps the brother of Hugh II's wife Mabel of Roucy; her mother had been a daughter of Robert Guiscard of Apulia and the Roucys, who commemorated this through the use of the names Guiscard and Robert Guiscard in subsequent generations,[25] could also have adopted another name with south Italian connotations, like Barisan. It is most likely, however, that Barisan was indeed Gilduin's brother, and therefore Hugh II's brother as well. This would have made him a first cousin of Baldwin of Le Bourcq, who was king after 1118. It is suggestive that two of Barisan's charters were witnessed by Montlhérys, one of them by two Montlhéry visitors from western Europe, Guy of Le Puiset and Guy I of Dampierre-sur-l'Aube.[26] He seems to have moved in exalted circles for a rear-vassal. He was, for instance, one of the few laymen referred to by name as being among those present at the important church council held at Nablus in 1120; he was probably there as regent for Hugh, the new and very young lord of Jaffa, who would have been his nephew.[27]

At any rate, by 1118 members of the Montlhéry kindred were well placed in the Latin settlements in the Levant. Everyone seems to have been aware of the relationships between them, which were constantly referred to in charters and narrative accounts. They held, or could claim rights to, the two most important frontier lordships in the kingdom of Jerusalem – it is surely no coincidence that in the 1120s these frontier marches were the only lordships to have had constables among their lords' officials[28] – and among the vassals in these seigneuries their relations were also prominent. In the north, the count of Edessa and one of his most powerful magnates were members of the kin, while the count's sister was the wife of the prince-regent of Antioch.

The death of Baldwin I of Jerusalem on 2 April 1118 as he withdrew with his army from Egypt provided the Montlhérys with the opportunity to stage a *coup d'état*. On Palm Sunday (7 April), the day the king's body was brought into Jerusalem to be buried,

[25] Isenburg, Freytag von Loringhoven *et al.*, *Europäische Stammtafeln* 3, table 677.
[26] Notre-Dame de Josaphat (Delaborde) 41–2; Cart Hosp 1.71.
[27] *Sacrorum Conciliorum Nova et Amplissima Collectio* 21.263. See also RRH nos. 127, 137a.
[28] J. S. C. Riley-Smith, *The Feudal Nobility and the Kingdom of Jerusalem, 1174–1277* (London, 1973), 19.

Baldwin of Le Bourcq arrived suddenly and unannounced. He had
come down from Edessa on pilgrimage to celebrate Easter and had
heard of the king's death on the way. The vassals and leading
churchmen of the kingdom met at once, presumably in what was
later to be called a *parlement*, to discuss to whom the succession should
be offered. There was a division of opinion, with a party headed by
Joscelin of Courtenay and the patriarch, Arnulf of Chocques, an able
but corrupt man who had come out as one of Robert of Normandy's
chaplains, proposing that Baldwin of Le Bourcq should be offered
the throne. Baldwin, Joscelin argued, was present in the East, was
related to the previous king and had shown himself to be the kind of
person who would make a good ruler. But the majority seems to
have decided that the legitimate heir was the late king's eldest
brother, Count Eustace of Boulogne, who had returned home after
the First Crusade, and an embassy was immediately despatched to
western Europe. After it had left a second meeting of the *parlement*
was demanded by Joscelin. This second assembly, in the absence of
at least some of Eustace's partisans, reversed its earlier decision and
Baldwin was anointed king on Easter Day, although he was not
crowned for another twenty-one months. The speed at which events
had moved must have taken everyone's breath away: there had been
two meetings of the *parlement*, the departure of an embassy to Europe
and the sacring of a new king in the space of a week. Eustace and the
mission from Jerusalem had reached Apulia on the journey East
when the news reached them. The envoys were indignant, but
Eustace, who had not been enthusiastic, turned back to avoid
scandal.

It has been suggested that Baldwin I, knowing that Eustace was
unlikely to accept the throne, had sent for Baldwin of Le Bourcq to
discuss the succession with him, which would account for the latter's
apparently sudden journey south. But there can be no doubt that
Joscelin of Courtenay, who as lord of Galilee was the greatest
magnate in the kingdom, had manipulated a *parlement* to get his first
cousin the throne. His relationship with Baldwin of Le Bourcq may
have soured when he had been expelled from Edessa five years
before, but it was still one of blood and he, and the rest of the kin,
were soon rewarded, as they had to be, given the importance to a
new king whose legitimacy was open to question of having his
'natural friends' in positions of trust. Joscelin was granted the county
of Edessa in the late summer of 1119 and William of Bures-sur-Yvette

was made lord of Galilee in his place.[29] In 1119 two other members of the family arrived in the East, no doubt hurriedly sent to bolster the king's position. The Cluniac prior Gilduin of Le Puiset was, as we have seen, at once made abbot of St Mary of the Valley of Jehoshaphat and the young Hugh of Le Puiset, the son of Hugh II and Mabel of Roucy who had spent his childhood in Apulia, had taken possession of Jaffa by January 1120 when he witnessed King Baldwin's grant to his uncle Abbot Gilduin, although he was 'not yet a knight'; in other words, he was still a minor.[30] The recognition of the lordship of a boy who cannot have been more than thirteen years old over one of the most strategically important frontiers of the kingdom is an indication of the king's reliance on his relations, but it may not have been as rash a move as it sounds, because Barisan the Old was constable of Jaffa and must have taken charge until the young man came of age. Later in his reign Baldwin II strengthened his position further by marrying one daughter to the new prince of Antioch and probably betrothing another to the son of the count of Tripoli.[31]

The way the Montlhéry *coup d'état* in Palestine had evoked an immediate response in support from the kindred in Europe demonstrates the strength of the ties which bound the settlers in the East to their families in the West 2,000 miles away, although in that case the kinsmen in Europe must have been expecting patronage; Joscelin of Courtenay had been penniless when he arrived in the East. Another illustration of the bonds of sentiment which chained the settlers to their old homelands is to be found in an account of the sending of a relic of St Stephen to the abbey of Cluny. In 1120 Gilduin of Le Puiset left Jerusalem with King Baldwin for Edessa; on their way they were joined by Gilduin's brother Waleran. At Edessa the party met its Latin archbishop, who over a decade earlier – certainly before 1109 – had stopped at Cluny on the way from Flanders to the East and had been made a *confrater* of the community by Abbot Hugh. The archbishop asked Gilduin for the latest news of the Cluniac congregation in Europe. The meeting and the conversation about Cluny and her daughter houses had a profound effect on him,

---

[29] WT 547–50; FC 615–16, 635; AA 709–10; Mayer, *Mélanges*, 73–89; Rheinheimer, *Das Kreuzfahrerfürstentum Galiläa*, 45–6.

[30] Notre-Dame de Josaphat (Delaborde) 35; WT 651; Mayer, 'The Origins', 43–4.

[31] H. E. Mayer, 'The Succession to Baldwin II of Jerusalem: English Impact on the East', *Dumbarton Oaks Papers* 39 (1985), 140.

for they gave rise to a number of vivid dreams – he believed they
were visions – in which he was instructed to give the relic to Gilduin
for transmission to Cluny.[32]

Writing several decades later, William of Tyre drew attention to
the questionable nature of the events of 1118.[33] It seems that
Baldwin's government was never entirely assured: when he was
captured by the Muslims in 1123 and held by them for a time,
Charles the Good of Flanders, who had experienced conditions in
Palestine, as we have seen, was offered the throne in his place by
what appears to have been a party of quite prominent individuals
who thought that Baldwin had been miserly and had not governed
well.[34] In 1129, at the time of the marriage of the king's daughter to
Fulk V of Anjou, Pope Honorius II took the trouble to recognize in
writing the validity of his succession.[35] But papal backing had been
manifest from the beginning. Baldwin faced a military crisis almost
as soon as he came to the throne, because on 28 June 1119 there
occurred the catastrophe for the Christians in northern Syria, the
Battle of the Field of Blood. The new king hurried north to take
charge of the principality of Antioch and on 23 January 1120 the
subject of a formal appeal to the West was discussed by the church
council held at Nablus, at which the king was present. Embassies
were then sent to the pope and the doge of Venice,[36] but there must
have been an earlier appeal for help from Baldwin directly to the
pope, whose response to it adds to the picture of a family network in
operation.

News of the battle had reached the West by the autumn of 1119. At
that time, Pope Calixtus II was travelling through France. While he
was in Poitiers in August, he excommunicated a man called Chalo
the Red of Vivonne, who had unjustly usurped land belonging to the
church of St Hilaire-le-Grand. 'After this, the pope forbade with
apostolic authority Chalo, who after his departure [from Poitiers]
had rashly dared to take the cross for the pilgrimage to Jerusalem, to
make the journey he intended.' Chalo repented and renounced his
usurpation before St Hilary's tomb. This story is evidence that
Calixtus had already proclaimed a crusade before the end of 1119,
because Chalo 'took the cross'.[37] The pope had reacted very quickly.

---

[32] 'Tractatus de reliquiis S. Stephani', 317–20.   [33] WT 550.
[34] Galbert of Bruges 564.   [35] *Papsturkunden für Kirchen im Heiligen Lande* 142.
[36] Riley-Smith, 'The Venetian Crusade', 340.
[37] St Hilaire-le-Grand de Poitiers (1847), 122, 128–9.

Of course he would have been inclined to do so anyway, given the reverence with which everyone regarded the Holy Land and the anxiety with which any threat to it would be greeted. He came, moreover, from the family of the counts of Burgundy which had shown itself to be strongly predisposed to crusading, as we have seen. But he was also, as one of his letters pointed out, Baldwin's kin.[38] It is not certain how the two men were related. It may have been through Calixtus' mother Stephanie, the origins of whom have never been discovered;[39] alternatively, it could have been established through the marriage of the king of France's son Philip to Elizabeth of Montlhéry and that of his elder brother King Louis VI to Calixtus' niece Adelaide of Maurienne. What matters is that Calixtus was himself conscious of kinship and that at this crucial moment the Montlhérys had a natural ally on the papal throne, who responded to the threat to Latin rule in the East, and therefore to the family, by instantly preaching a crusade, the first to be formally proclaimed since that of 1107. It must be significant that this crusade never seems to have been intended to engage itself in Syria, where the westerners had been defeated, but went instead to the Holy Land, 400 miles to the south, where Baldwin's seat of government was.

The insecurity of Baldwin's position, made worse by the fact that he and his wife bred only daughters, and the need to prove himself before Latin Christendom and perhaps especially in the eyes of his European relations, help to explain why in the middle 1120s he adopted a remarkably aggressive strategy towards his Muslim adversaries, Sunni Damascus and Shii Egypt. Damascus, the chief city of Syria, was in a chaotic state, wracked by problems which resulted from the focusing of Ismaili Assassin ambitions on it.[40] Fatimid Egypt had been visibly weakening for some time. The last major Egyptian expedition by land approached the kingdom of Jerusalem in 1118, shortly after Baldwin's accession. A large army, supplied from the sea, mustered on the southern border, where it was joined by a force from Damascus. The Christians took up position opposite it and the two sides faced it out for three months before the Egyptians withdrew.[41] An even greater humiliation had to be endured by Egypt six years later. The city-port of Tyre acknowl-

---

[38] *Papsturkunden für Kirchen im Heiligen Lande* 129.
[39] Bouchard, *Sword, Miter, and Cloister*, 273.
[40] M. G. S. Hodgson, *The Order of Assassins* (The Hague, 1955), 104–5.
[41] FC 617–19; WT 552–3.

edged Fatimid suzerainty and although a governor from Damascus had been installed at the citizens' request in 1112, the Fatimid caliph al-Amir had regained direct control ten years later by the expedient of kidnapping him. In 1123, however, the most effective force still at Egypt's disposal, its galley fleet, was so badly damaged by the Venetian ships which had arrived on crusade that when in 1124 the crusaders and the army of the kingdom of Jerusalem laid siege to Tyre, al-Amir had to admit to Damascus that he did not have the means to defend it. Damascus did what it could, but with no supporting action from Cairo, Tyre fell on 7 July.[42] The Egyptian government had shown itself to be powerless and the loss of Tyre severely reduced the range of operations of its galley fleet, because the ships were now deprived of any harbour north of Ascalon where they could take on water.[43]

In the summer of 1126, now refurbished and its sortie well publicized in advance, the fleet cruised north again, nosing from port to port as far as Beirut, looking without success for weaknesses it could exploit in its search for water. Baldwin, in an apparently rash move, ignored the news that the Egyptians were about to sail and marched north with part of his army to meet a Muslim threat to the borders of Antioch. This was justified as the confrontation of the greater of two dangers, but it may be that Baldwin did not take the war plans of the Egyptians very seriously, although he must have known that their recapture of one of the ports in Christian hands would have threatened his lines of communication to the West since a more northerly watering place would have increased the galleys' range sufficiently for them to have caused havoc in the crowded sea lanes near Cyprus.[44] He must have assumed that the cruise of the fleet was made more for public consumption than anything else.

Nevertheless, Egyptian troops held on to the beachhead at Ascalon, to which the Fatimid government sent reinforcements four times a year[45] and from which raids could be launched to ravage Christian territory and threaten traffic on the roads almost as far as Jerusalem: two took place in 1124.[46] Our knowledge of what transpired is sketchy, but the course of events seems to have been as

---

[42] Ibn al-Qalanisi 128–30, 142, 165–6, 170–2; Ibn al-Athir 1.356–9. For the fall of Tyre, see Runciman, *A History*, 2.168–71.
[43] Pryor, *Geography*, 115–16.   [44] FC 800–5; WT 612. See Pryor, *Geography*, 116–22.
[45] WT 607.   [46] FC 697–8, 731–2; WT 595, 599–600.

follows. The fall of Tyre in 1124 was followed in the autumn of 1125 by a descent by Baldwin on Ascalon, using troops he had already assembled to raid the territory of Damascus, during which the garrison, which had just been reinforced, was severely mauled.[47] This was a pre-emptive strike, giving Baldwin the freedom to turn on Damascus in January 1126 without apparently worrying about his southern frontier. All fief-holders and others throughout the kingdom were summoned to his army by an *arrière ban*, and troops from Jaffa, Ramle and Lydda, who might normally have been expected to hold the line against Ascalon, were mentioned marching north to the muster.[48] The king seems to have adopted a similar high-risk strategy two years later. Early in April 1128 his army was devastating the countryside around Ascalon. The crops would have been quite mature by this time and their destruction, and the consequent food shortages, would probably have meant that the garrison at Ascalon had to be temporarily reduced in size.[49] The *chevauchée* was followed by another attack on Damascus in 1129 in conjunction with the new crusade which had now reached Palestine.[50]

More light is thrown on Christian strategy by three charters granted to two religious institutions which seem to have been especially favoured by the Montlhéry kindred in Palestine. One of them was the abbey of St Mary of the Valley of Jehoshaphat where, as has been mentioned, a member of the clan was abbot. The other was the Hospital of St John, which from before 1126 had embryonic commanderies in Jaffa and Tiberias, the chief towns in those lordships with active frontiers against the Muslims ruled by members of the kindred.[51] The charters were associated with or were issued in the name of Hugh of Jaffa, who had now come of age. They recorded gifts made in 1126 and probably 1127 by the constable Barisan and Hugh himself of properties well within 'the territory or lordship' of Ascalon, 'for the condition of Christianity' and for the redemption of the souls of Hugh's parents and all his relations, and 'so that God should hand over the rebel city of Ascalon to the Christians'.[52] The endowments for St Mary and the Hospital had the blessing of the

---

[47] FC 773–4; WT 607–8.   [48] FC 784–5; WT 608.   [49] Cart Hosp 1.78.

[50] WT 620–2; Ibn al-Qalanisi 195–200; Ibn al-Athir 1.385–6; Henry of Huntingdon, *Historia Anglorum*, 251.

[51] Cart Hosp 1.71, 73.

[52] Cart Hosp 1.71, 72–3; Notre-Dame de Josaphat (Kohler) 119–20 (wrongly dated: it must date from the same period as the other charters). *Cf.* Mayer, *Bistümer*, 151–60.

king, who confirmed the gift to St Mary in 1130,[53] even though it had previously been assumed that Ascalon would be part of the royal domain once it had been taken.[54] It looks as though in the autumn of 1125, at the time of his first *razzia* into the region, or at any rate just before his expedition to Damascus in January 1126, Baldwin had given Hugh lordship over Ascalon in advance of its conquest, possibly in return for him keeping up pressure on it or perhaps even organizing its occupation by force. Such an arrangement on the Christian marches may not have been unusual. The Hospitallers were to be given other territories outside Christian control when they were endowed with Crac des Chevaliers in 1144 and other castles on the frontiers of Tripoli and Antioch in 1168, 1184 and 1186.[55]

In the seven years from 1124, therefore, Tyre had been occupied; the two chief Muslim enemies, Cairo and Damascus, had been taken on at the same time, with major attacks on Damascus or its territory being launched in 1126 and 1129; two raids into the countryside around Egyptian Ascalon had been accompanied by the granting of it to the closest Christian marcher lord, Hugh of Jaffa, who was the king's cousin. It must be indicative that no record has survived of any action, or threat of action, by Muslim raiders from Ascalon between 1126 and 1132. And it may also be that now an Egyptian government sued for peace.

The Fatimid caliph al-Amir was assassinated in 1130. His son, only a few months old, was proclaimed his heir, but was soon murdered and a death from natural causes was announced by al-Amir's cousin and future successor, the regent al-Hafiz. But al-Hafiz was himself imprisoned by the new wazir, Abu Ali Ahmad ibn al-Afdal, known as Kutayfat, the son of the wazir al-Afdal who had tried to retake Palestine from the First Crusade in 1099. Kutayfat had retained the loyalty of his father's regiment and so was able to seize power, but he was not a caliph and the Friday sermons in the mosques did not name one. Rather, since the direct line of the Fatimid dynasty had been extinguished, the Egyptian empire was placed under the sovereignty of the Hidden Imam. It is noteworthy that the Imam regarded as being in occultation – in hiding until he would reappear on the Last Days – was the Twelfth, the mahdi of the Imamis, and it has been pointed out that this effectively abolished Ismailism as

---

[53] Notre-Dame de Josaphat (Delaborde) 47.   [54] Urkunden Venedig 1.88, 92–3.
[55] Riley-Smith, *The Knights of St John*, 55–7, 66–8.

Egypt's state religion. The *katibs* had to declaim a grandiloquent list of titles accorded by Kutayfat to himself as protector of the rights of the Hidden Imam.

Kutayfat was murdered by guards loyal to the Fatimids in December 1131.[56] In his short period of government he had taken the unprecedented step of appointing or replacing the four chief *qadis* in Cairo – of the Shafiis, Malikis, Ismailis and Imamis: 'the like of this had never been heard of before in the faith of Islam' – and he also allowed a new Coptic patriarch to be consecrated after a six-year vacancy in the patriarchate.[57] Although the details of his rule seem to have been expunged from the Fatimid records, it may be that he had instituted a policy of religious toleration to gain support, although it was said later that he had proclaimed the religion of anti-Shiism and had persecuted the Ismailis.[58]

Three months before his death he sent an embassy to Jerusalem. The evidence for this is to be found in a memorandum in the cartulary of the college of St Laud in Angers, which had been founded by Count Geoffrey Martel of Anjou some time before 1060 and was favoured by his successors. The memorandum, written in the 1130s by the dean, Guy of Athée, detailed some of the rights enjoyed at St Laud by the counts. Among them is the following:

When a count who has been newly created comes to the church he should be received solemnly in procession by the chapter and clerks of St Laud and furthermore whenever the count – ... or the countess or their children – returns from a long pilgrimage or period away they should be received by the dean or by him who will be superior of the church with gospel book and thurible and holy water, and ... the dean should solemnly hand the count the ivory *tau* which Fulk, king of Jerusalem and count of the Angevins, gave this church. Fulk had it [the *tau*] from the sultan of Babylon [Egypt] when Christ raised him to be king of Jerusalem.

I, Guy of Athée, with the whole chapter of the church and the clerks, have received the count of the Angevins often in this way. And King Fulk gave the *tau* to our church for this reason – that we should receive the counts in this way – and he ordered and wished that this should signify that the counts of the Angevins are lords and abbots of the church of St Laud before all other churches.[59]

[56] Ibn al-Athir 1.390–1, 393–5; S. M. Stern, 'The Succession to the Fatimid Imam al-Amir, the Claims of the Later Fatimids to the Imamate, and the Rise of Tayyibi Ismailism', *Oriens* 4 (1951), 193–255.

[57] I am grateful to Dr Michael Brett for providing me with this information.

[58] Stern, 'The Succession', 199–200.

[59] St Laud d'Angers 4–5. For the college, see St Laud d'Angers vi–xiii.

The St Laud memorandum provides evidence for a visit by Egyptian envoys at the time of, or shortly after, the coronation of Fulk of Anjou and Melisende of Jerusalem on 14 September 1131, three weeks after Baldwin II's death. Contemporary descriptions of Egyptian embassies often refer to the gifts they brought with them: in the autumn of 1126 an ambassador brought to Damascus 'magnificent robes of honour and costly Egyptian presents' and another in September 1147 brought 'a gift of horses and money'.[60] The ivory *tau* must have been only one of a number of presents. Some historians have confused it with the famous relic of the True Cross which Fulk also sent St Laud, but it is clear that the *tau* was a T-shaped staff. Ivory *tau* staffs were quite commonly carved in the medieval East and a number of examples of them survive.[61] Fulk obviously intended it to be used in much the same way as were those sceptres which denoted lordship when presented to property owners. He wished it to be a symbol of the authority of the son he had left behind and of his future descendants in the county of Anjou, and an expression of their patronage of a family religious foundation. His reaction on receiving it – to think of some use for it at home – was predictable. What proved to be less predictable was his policy on becoming king.

Since his coronation was held so soon after Baldwin's death, the Egyptian embassy may well have been originally intended to address the latter. It could have signalled the success of Baldwin's aggressive policy towards the Muslims, but if it came offering terms, these must have been refused,[62] although it could be that al-Hafiz, who assumed power in Egypt after Kutayfat's assassination and was a far more able ruler than his predecessors, took a more aggressive line against the Latin settlers from the start. The first sign of a renewed Christian anxiety about the Muslim garrison at Ascalon is to be found in 1132, probably early in the year when King Fulk was absent in the north, and so within months of the visit of the Egyptian embassy. The patriarch and citizens of Jerusalem built a castle, Chastel Hernaut, in the foothills of the Judaean hills to protect the road to their city from Egyptian raiders.[63] By 1136 the threat from Ascalon to the kingdom

[60] Ibn al-Qalanisi 179, 280.
[61] A. Maskell, *Ivories* (London, 1905), 193. For the relic, see A. Frolow, *La relique de la Vraie Croix* (Paris, 1961), 322.
[62] For the principles behind and the methods of making truces between Christians and Muslims, see M. A. Köhler, *Allianzen und Verträge zwischen fränkischen und islamischen Herrschern im Vorderen Orient* (Berlin and New York, 1991), 390–418.
[63] WT 640.

was so great that Fulk had begun to construct a ring of fortresses round it to contain its garrison; they included the one he granted to the Hospitallers.[64]

Fulk's acceptance of the hand of Melisende had followed long negotiations, the matters at issue being the legitimacy of Baldwin's position and Melisende's status as an heiress to the throne, which would have been on everyone's mind because of the parallel case of Mathilda of England, another woman whose succession was raising doubts. Mathilda had been betrothed to Fulk's son Geoffrey in the summer of 1127 and she had married him on 17 June 1128, shortly after Fulk had taken the cross for the new crusade. It has been suggested that the English precedent, in which King Henry I declared her to be his heir on 1 January 1127, was echoed in Palestine in the recognition of Melisende as *heres regni*, an act which overcame any doubts that Fulk might have had about his future.[65]

But why had Fulk been approached at all? It could have been simply that he was a relatively powerful nobleman, was free to marry since his first wife had died, and had shown himself to be an enthusiastic supporter of the Latin settlements in the Levant; he had paid for 100 knights to serve in the Holy Land at the end of his first crusade in 1120[66] and had been closely associated with the Templars.[67] But there probably was more to it than that. The 'rightful heir' of 1118, Eustace of Boulogne, had died in 1125, but in that year his daughter and heiress, another Mathilda, had married Stephen of Blois, who took the title of count of Boulogne and was to underline the Boulogne inheritance by naming his first son Eustace. Stephen, who was a younger son of the first crusader Stephen of Blois and had been brought up and favoured by his uncle Henry of England, was also a claimant for the English throne – after the death in 1128 of Robert of Normandy's son William Clito, a strong claimant – and in the end resolved to compete for that. There is no evidence, as far as I am aware, for him seriously considering a bid for the throne of Jerusalem on the basis of his wife's inheritance, but the mere fact of Mathilda of Boulogne's marriage must have caused anxiety in Palestine and Stephen would inevitably have been seen as a threat to Melisende's future succession. This may have persuaded Baldwin

---

[64] WT 659–61; Cart Hosp 1.97–8.   [65] Mayer, 'The Succession', 143–6.

[66] WT 633; although Mayer ('The Succession', 145 n.35) was worried by the fact that William appeared to be referring to a second pilgrimage by Fulk.

[67] OV 6.310.

and his advisers to make their proposal to Fulk, a man who, they must have known, had already taken on Stephen on the borders of Normandy in one of the petty wars which plagued French political life and had defeated him.[68]

At any rate the offer of Melisende's hand was carried to France by the Montlhéry William of Bures-sur-Yvette and the crusade of 1129 which followed was encompassed, like the *coup d'etát* in 1118, by Montlhéry activity. In 1127 Guy I of Dampierre-sur-l'Aube, whose mother was a Montlhéry,[69] appeared in the East, together with another cousin, Guy of Le Puiset.[70] In 1128 Stephen of Chartres, the abbot of St Jean-en-Vallée of Chartres who was referred to by William of Tyre as Baldwin's blood relation and was a member of the family of the vidames of Chartres which must have been related to the Le Puisets, came to Palestine on pilgrimage. He was waiting for a ship home when the patriarch of Jerusalem died. He was promptly elevated to the patriarchate, although this move was not a success, because his desire to reclaim what he believed to have been the rights of the patriarchate led to a bitter quarrel with the king.[71] By March 1129 Guitier of Rethel, the son of Baldwin's sister Mathilda of Le Bourcq, had arrived in the East; he witnessed a charter of his uncle's, with his cousins Melisende of Jerusalem, Gilduin of Le Puiset and Hugh of Jaffa, in the presence of his cousin the patriarch.[72] Then Viscount Hugh III of Chartres, the head of the Le Puiset family, crusaded.[73] If he travelled with Count Fulk and the Angevins, which is likely, Fulk arrived in Palestine flanked by two Montlhérys, because William of Bures-sur-Yvette returned with him.[74] It looks as though the choice of Fulk was a Montlhéry device to shore up the government established in 1118.

Even more to the point, the crusade of 1129 which accompanied Fulk to Palestine was a Montlhéry creation and must be viewed as an exercise to reinforce the status quo. William of Tyre, who wrote several decades later but was chancellor of the kingdom of Jerusalem and had access to governmental records, looked on the departure on a preaching tour of the West by the master of the Templars, Hugh of Payns (who owed so much to Baldwin's favour that he could be

---

[68] C. W. Hollister, 'The Anglo-Norman Succession Debate of 1126: Prelude to Stephen's Anarchy', *Journal of Medieval History* 1 (1975), 19–41.
[69] Isenburg, Freytag von Loringhoven *et al.*, *Europäische Stammtafeln* 3, table 51.
[70] Notre-Dame de Josaphat (Delaborde) 42.   [71] WT 619–20.
[72] St Sépulcre de Jérusalem 93 (in which he witnessed as *sororius* of King Baldwin II).
[73] Suger of St Denis, *Vita*, 170; Tiron 1.128.   [74] WT 618.

regarded as the king's creature), as a consequence solely of a decision made by Baldwin and his advisers. Hugh and certain other churchmen, including the archbishop of Tyre and the bishop of Ramle, 'were sent to the western princes in order to arouse people to come to our aid and especially to call on the powerful to join a siege of Damascus.'[75] The rôle of Pope Honorius II, who certainly knew of the crusade since in one of his letters he referred to recruitment in Anjou,[76] seems to have been passive. There is no evidence of papal initiative or of papal legates at work.

The Montlhéry enterprise foundered, however, on Fulk's independence of mind. It is clear that from the start of his reign he was determined to change the direction in which the kingdom had been moving and to reverse the policies of the 1120s. He signalled this by choosing to be crowned not in Bethlehem, as his two predecessors had been, but in Jerusalem, under the Sepulchre rotunda. This may have been because the date chosen for his coronation was 14 September, the Feast of the Exaltation of the Holy Cross, commemorating the discovery of the True Cross;[77] or it may have reflected his personal dévotion to the cross. But whatever it meant, his coronation marked a clean break with the predilections of his predecessors.

Upsetting a family enterprise is never easy, as two contemporaries, of different religious persuasions and two thousand miles apart, testified. In Normandy the monk-historian Orderic Vitalis reported that Fulk

looked less wisely to the future than he should and changed governors and other officials too quickly and unreasonably. As a new ruler he banished from his household the lords who from the first had fought strenuously against the Turks ... and replaced them with Angevin strangers and other newly-arrived unsophisticates...So there arose great rancour.[78]

In Damascus Ibn al-Qalanisi made almost the same charge.

[Fulk] was not sound in his judgement nor was he successful in his administration, so that by the loss of Baldwin [II] they [the settlers] were thrown into confusion and discordance.[79]

Both these authors referred to trouble and in fact there was a revolt early in the reign, involving Hugh of Jaffa, whom Fulk had

[75] WT 620. [76] *Papsturkunden für Kirchen im Heiligen Lande* 139, 142.
[77] H. E. Mayer, 'Das Pontifikale von Tyrus und die Krönung der lateinischen Könige von Jerusalem', *Dumbarton Oaks Papers* 21 (1967), 154.
[78] OV 6.390–2. [79] Ibn al-Qalanisi 208.

accused of treason. William of Tyre was later to suggest that it was the rumour that Hugh was having an affair with Melisende – they were, of course, both Montlhérys, as William knew – that led to bad blood between him and the king. It may be, however, that the 'familiaria colloquia' which Hugh and Melisende were suspected of having were family discussions about how to retrieve a situation that was getting out of hand. At any rate, with the support of a dispossessed lord of Transjordan Hugh rebelled, refused to appear for a judicial duel and, faced by the confiscation of his fief, sailed down the coast to Ascalon, where he made a treaty with the Egyptian garrison. The Egyptians raided Christian territory as far as Arsuf. When Fulk responded by besieging Jaffa, Hugh's leading vassals, including Barisan, deserted him. After mediation by the patriarch, Hugh accepted the judgement that he and his supporters should be exiled for three years, during which time the crown would enjoy the revenues from his fiefs. But after three years Jaffa would be restored to him, and it is clear that the king had little public support, while Hugh enjoyed much, particularly after a Breton knight had tried to assassinate him.[80]

Hugh's sentence was an extraordinarily light one, given the fact that an *établissement* on the confiscation of fiefs, which dated from Baldwin II's reign, had decreed permanent disinheritance for anyone who entered into possession of a fief 'using Muslim force, against his lord's will and without judgement of court',[81] which is precisely what Hugh had envisaged doing. The historian William of Tyre inveighed against the enormity of Hugh's crime, but William had been a child in the 1130s and was writing many years later. It has been suggested, on the basis of Orderic Vitalis's comments, that the real cause of Hugh's rebellion was the king's determination to bring in new men of his own to replace the old household officials.[82] One can also speculate that the revolt, which followed relatively shortly after the visit to Jerusalem of the Egyptian embassy, was connected in some way with Fulk's reaction to whatever the Egyptians had proposed. It is possible that Kutayfat, whom, incidentally, the St Laud memor-

---

[80] WT 651–6. Both William of Tyre and Ibn al-Qalanisi (215) seem to assign Hugh's revolt to late 1132. Professor H. E. Mayer ('Studies in the History of Queen Melisende of Jerusalem', *Dumbarton Oaks Papers* 26 (1972), 102–5) has dated it, however, to the second half of 1134.

[81] *Le Livre au roi* 177–84. For the date, see J. S. C. Riley-Smith, 'Further Thoughts on Baldwin II's *Etablissement* on the Confiscation of Fiefs', *Crusade and Settlement*, ed. P. W. Edbury (Cardiff, 1985), 176–80.

[82] Mayer, 'Angevins *versus* Normans', 1–25.

andum was nearly correct in describing as sultan – he actually referred to himself as *malik* or prince[83] – had been feeling so isolated and threatened that he was prepared to surrender the beachhead at Ascalon. If so, Ascalon would have been almost within Hugh's grasp, since his rights to it had already been recognized by Fulk's predecessor. What seems to be certain is that Hugh was representing the interests of the Montlhérys, who were now being deprived of influence by a king they had put on the throne. The dominance of a family of middle-ranking French nobles, who had taken over the Latin East and had been responsible for initiating one, and perhaps two, crusades, was coming to an end.

Since the Montlhérys were the first clan to exploit the movement in this way they present us with a model. The concentration of first crusaders in the family suggests that it must have been predisposed in some way to respond to the earliest calls to crusade. Armsbearers had to finance themselves, unless lucky enough to find a magnate to subsidize them, and had to engage in lengthy and protracted preparations. They were, therefore, exceptionally dependent on family support and this gave the kindred influence at a crucial stage in the development of crusading and no doubt reinforced collective commitment to it. Two Montlhérys were among the first settlers, and one of them was independently related to the greatest figures in the Latin East and was talented enough to be rewarded by them with lordship. He in turn patronized other relations, including new arrivals. Members of the family were, therefore, well placed when in 1118 they were provided with an opportunity to seize the ultimate power. And the characteristic way the instinct for cooperation and mutual assistance would bring a whole kindred-group, or a substantial part of it, into line behind an initiative is demonstrated by the attempts by the family, in the West as well as in the East, to lend support to Baldwin of Le Bourcq through settlement, influence or visits to Palestine. It should be remembered that although the additional inducement of advancement through family patronage must have played a part, it cannot have been responsible for all the activities of the kinsmen, because some, who came to the kingdom of Jerusalem for short periods and then returned home, had nothing obvious to gain from their visits.

---

[83] Ibn al-Athir 1.394.

The crusading movement was susceptible to exploitation of this kind because it relied on individual responses which might provide opportunities for anyone to shine and on support for those responses from relations and lords. It, and the settlements in Palestine and Syria it established and helped to maintain, fed on enthusiasms within a western European society in which kindred networks were rampant. Crusading, particularly in the earliest period when it was still inchoate and uncontrolled, was so dependent on the reactions of committed European kin-groups that it could be manipulated by them relatively easily.

Conclusion and postscript

In this book I have tried to argue the following. Crusading drew on the traditions of pilgrimage to Jerusalem, whether as a penance or a devotion, and of pious violence. These traditions did not merge gradually together, but were fused by Pope Urban II in 1095. He was able to do this because the radical idea that war could be penitential had surfaced in Gregorian circles in the early 1080s. The First Crusade was, therefore, a truly revolutionary event, because the pope presented the faithful with an idea which had been unprecedented in Christian thought. The response of the armsbearers to it, however, was to be as important as the idea itself, because the proposal for a campaign to liberate Jerusalem was dependent on their cooperation. Their reaction naturally reflected their own preoccupations, so that in some ways they interpreted Urban's message in a manner that must have horrified him and in others viewed it in a conservative light, but there can be no doubt that they seized on the central theme: that they could contribute to their own salvation by engaging with the world in a crusade rather than abandoning it for the religious life. Their response was at the same time spontaneous and preconditioned. Some families had become predisposed to react positively to an appeal of this sort and although the assumption of the cross must often have been the result of a sudden, independent decision, the practical difficulties involved in fulfilling the vow – the raising of cash, the purchase of animals and equipment, the choice of household, arrangements for the management of the estates in his absence, endowments for prayer on his behalf – meant that the volunteer was dependent not only on local religious communities, but also on his lord and especially on his family, the cooperation of which in the preliminary stages was essential. This accounts for the clusters of crusaders which can be found in kindred groups. It bred a collective commitment which in the early twelfth century could manifest itself not so much in crusading, although it sometimes did, as in support for the new settlements in the East. I have concluded that the movement was so dependent on the support and enthusiasm of networks of kindred that it was open to domination by them and I have provided the example of the Montlhéry clan. One reason, incidentally, for the initiative of King Louis VII of France, which helped to lead to the crusade of 1147, may have been the fear that if he did not personally respond to the news of the disaster which had overtaken the county of Edessa, which was still a Montlhéry lordship, the kindred might do something themselves.

POSTSCRIPT: THE LUSIGNANS

I have confined my arguments to the first few decades of the crusading movement, but I am inclined to believe that, although conditions changed, nothing was ever able to prevent well-organized families from taking advantage of crusading if the opportunity arose for them to do so. For example, fifty years after the Montlhérys' bid had failed, another western family made its first move, in a way that could hardly have been more dramatic.

In an account purportedly written by someone close to the events and in a history composed by an English priest who was in Palestine ten years later there are references to a scandal involving Sibylla, the sister of King Baldwin IV of Jerusalem and therefore Baldwin of Le Bourcq's great-granddaughter. Aimery of Lusignan, who had a reputation as a fighting man, had settled in Palestine, where he had married the daughter of Baldwin of Ibelin, a descendant of Barisan the Old and one of the leading nobles. He had become the lover of Agnes of Courtenay, Sibylla's mother and Joscelin of Courtenay's granddaughter, and he had been appointed constable of the kingdom. He and Agnes set about persuading Sibylla, who had recently been widowed, to consider marrying his brother Guy, whom Aimery went to France to fetch. Sibylla at once fell in love with Guy and shared his bed. This forced the king to agree to their marriage, which, according to William of Tyre, took place in the Easter season of 1180 'against custom'; in other words, it was a hurried affair.[1]

Chance had again brought another seigneurial family of moderate

---

[1] Ernoul, *Chronique*, 59–60; *Gesta regis Henrici secundi* 1.343; WT 1007.

status to the foreground. It was one which, like the Montlhérys, had shown a predisposition to crusading from the start and by the late twelfth century it had developed traditions of commitment to the cause of the Latin East. The great-grandfather of Guy and Aimery, Hugh VI of Lusignan, and a horde of relations, including their great-great-uncles Raymond of St Gilles and Herbert and Geoffrey of Thouars, had been on the First Crusade. Both their grandfathers, Hugh VII[2] and Geoffrey III of Rancon,[3] had taken part in the crusade of 1147 and their father, Hugh VIII, had been captured in Syria in 1164 and had died a prisoner of the Muslims.[4]

Baldwin IV, who suffered from leprosy, succumbed to the disease in 1185 and his successor, Sibylla's eight-year-old son by a previous marriage, died in 1186. In spite of opposition from a party of nobles of whom Count Raymond III of Tripoli was the most prominent, an opposition generated partly by Guy's poor performance as regent during one of Baldwin's periods of incapacity, Sibylla and Guy engineered their joint succession to the throne. On 4 July 1187, however, Guy led the largest army ever put into the field by the kingdom of Jerusalem to annihilation by Muslim forces under Saladin. He was held prisoner by the Muslims until the summer of 1188. By then all of Palestine had been lost except for Tyre, which had been saved by a new arrival, Conrad of Montferrat, a member of a much grander family than the Lusignans: he was related to both the German emperor and the king of France. Refused entry to Tyre by Conrad, Guy marched south in April 1189 to lay siege to Acre, the most important port on the Palestinian coast. This courageous act decided the course the crusade of 1189 (the Third Crusade) would take.[5]

I have already described how the first crusaders Hugh of Lusignan and Raymond of St Gilles shared the same mother, Almodis of La Marche. Her life casts a shadow across the crisis-events of the late 1180s and early 1190s. Guy of Lusignan, Raymond of Tripoli, Guy's leading opponent before 1187, and Richard I of England, Guy's staunchest ally after his arrival in the summer of 1191 and the Lusignans' lord in Poitou, were all descended from her; and the

[2] 'Historia gloriosi regis Ludovici VII' 126.
[3] 'Historia gloriosi regis Ludovici' 126; Eudes of Deuil 114, 122, 128; Suger of St Denis, 'Epistolae', 502.
[4] Louis VII, 'Epistolarum regis Ludovici VII et variorum ad eum volumen', 62; WT 873, 875; St Hilaire-le-Grand de Poitiers (1847) 214.
[5] See Riley-Smith, *The Feudal Nobility*, 109–14.

marriage of Richard's father, Henry II, who was Sibylla of Jerusalem's first cousin, to Eleanor of Aquitaine, through whom descent from Almodis passed, meant that Sibylla herself was distantly related to the Lusignans. Contemporaries were aware of these ties of kinship. Raymond of Tripoli's supporter William of Tyre must have been conscious of them, because in his *Chronicle* he referred to Hugh VI of Lusignan as the brother of Raymond of St Gilles.[6] As for Richard of England, events at home would have brought the genealogy of the Lusignans forcefully to his attention.

Richard had governed Aquitaine on behalf of his father. In December 1177 the last count of La Marche of the house of Charroux, whose only son was dead and whose daughter was infertile, had sold his county to Henry of England for an insignificant sum. There were rumours that Henry had put pressure on him to do so. Geoffrey of Lusignan, an elder brother of Guy and Aimery who headed the family on behalf of his youthful nephew Hugh IX, claimed La Marche for himself and his brothers 'by hereditary right'. This must have meant by virtue of descent from Almodis's eldest son, Hugh VI of Lusignan, whereas Henry's wife, Eleanor of Aquitaine, could claim descent, and therefore hereditary rights to La Marche, only through a daughter of Almodis's third son. Geoffrey tried to take La Marche by force. He failed, but the Lusignans did not give up their claims and by the early 1180s were denying Richard control of the county. They eventually got it by kidnapping the aged Eleanor of Aquitaine in 1199 and holding her until it was surrendered to them.[7]

That was after the crusade of 1189-92, but during it Richard showed the Lusignans exceptional marks of favour. Sibylla died in 1190, as did the daughters she had borne Guy, and a challenge was made to Guy's kingship by Conrad of Montferrat and his new wife Isabella of Jerusalem, Sibylla's half-sister.[8] By this time the Lusignans

---

[6] WT 476.

[7] GV 12.446–7; *Gesta regis Henrici secundi* 1.196–7; Roger of Howden, *Chronica*, 2.147–8; Robert of Torigni 274–5; Ralph of Diceto, 'Ymagines Historiarum', 1.425; *Chroniques de Saint-Martial de Limoges* 188–9; Painter, 'The Lords of Lusignan', 41–3; W. L. Warren, *Henry II* (London, 1973), 585. The editor of GV (447 note b) thought that the claim to La Marche was based on Hugh IX of Lusignan's marriage to Mahaut of Angoulême, a niece of Pontia of La Marche. But Hugh did not marry Mahaut until 1194. The marriage would not anyway have given the other Lusignans any claims. For the marriages of Hugh IX, see Isenburg, Freytag von Loringhoven et al., *Europäische Stammtafeln* 3, table 816.

[8] For this and the politics of the Third Crusade in Palestine, see Riley-Smith, *The Feudal Nobility*, 114–20.

were strongly represented in Palestine and one has the impression of members of the family gearing themselves up in support of the break-through that chance had brought one of them, although in this case the representation was much less extended than it had been with the Montlhérys, being confined to brothers and a nephew. Hugh IX of Lusignan was in Richard of England's crusading force which wintered in Sicily and conquered Cyprus before reaching Palestine on 8 June 1191. Geoffrey had already joined Guy and Aimery in the East, and Geoffrey and Guy sailed to meet Richard in Cyprus, asked for his help and recognized his leadership. For his part, Richard welcomed Guy 'because he was from a very well-born family with well-known relations'. He lent him 2,000 marks in cash and a quantity of gold and silver, and he put him in command of a large part of the army with which he was reducing the island.[9] After Acre had fallen to the Christians on 12 July, Richard and King Philip II of France, who was also on crusade, agreed to adjudicate between the two claimants for the throne of Jerusalem. They judged that Guy should retain it for life and that Conrad and Isabella should in the meantime hold the northern part of the kingdom, but they also proposed that the royal apanage of Jaffa and Ascalon, with, perhaps, overlordship of Caesarea, should be granted to Geoffrey of Lusignan, the man, it should be remembered, who had claimed La Marche, had tried to seize it by force in 1178 and had been a thorn in Richard's side in Poitou. Jaffa and Ascalon were not yet back in Christian hands, of course. When they were, the southern frontier would have to be secured and Geoffrey was a notable soldier. Nevertheless, with Guy in possession of Acre (even if Philip of France had handed Conrad of Montferrat half its rents), Aimery as constable and Geoffrey holding an enormous fief in the south, the Lusignans' rôle in the kingdom would be guaranteed even after Guy's death and the passing of the throne to Conrad.[10] Their standing was beginning to look like that built up by the Montlhérys in the 1120s.

The opposition to Guy of a section of the local nobility and by the French crusaders in Palestine was so strongly expressed that the arbitration of the western kings proved to be unworkable. After eight months Richard had to agree to Guy's surrender of government to Conrad, but he proceeded to compensate Guy in an extravagant

---

[9] Ambroise, *L'Estoire de la Guerre Sainte*, cols. 46–7, 53–4; *Itinerarium peregrinorum et Gesta regis Ricardi* 195, 199, 201–2; *Gesta regis Henrici secundi* 2.165–6.

[10] *Gesta regis Henrici secundi* 2.183–4; *Itinerarium peregrinorum* 235–6; Ambroise col. 135.

way. He had originally sold Cyprus, which was known to be rich,[11] cheaply to the Templars, to whom he was close, but they had had difficulty holding it. The costs of war meant that crusaders' appetites for cash were virtually unquenchable and Richard had a reputation as a hard bargainer where money was concerned. It is, therefore, astonishing that he should have agreed when Guy asked if he might buy the island from him for the same sum of 100,000 besants negotiated with the Templars. Since the authors of the lawbook, *Le Livre au roi*, which was written shortly after this, assumed that a knight in Palestine could be enfeoffed for an annual rent of 300 besants,[12] the cost of Cyprus to Guy was the equivalent of maintaining *c.*330 knights for one year, which was not much in the circumstances. Guy made a down-payment of 60,000 besants. He never paid the rest, but on the other hand Richard had already had 40,000 from the Templars.[13]

Later in the 1190s Richard again ostentatiously showed favour to the Lusignans. Hugh IX's brother Ralph of Lusignan was given the hand of the heiress of the count of Eu and became the lord of great estates in Normandy and England.[14] But Richard was holding on to La Marche and it is probable that his staunch support for Guy's claim to the throne of Jerusalem long after it had become obvious that this was not acceptable in Palestine, the creation of a great lordship for Geoffrey and the sale of Cyprus on very advantageous terms to Guy were at least partly motivated by a desire to pacify their family, the claims of which to La Marche he could not satisfy.

At any rate the Lusignans, like the Montlhérys before them, found outside support at a crucial time and they were to establish a royal dynasty which ruled Cyprus (and laid claim to Jerusalem) for nearly three centuries. In the 1120s the Montlhérys had had the advantage of an extended cousinhood and the support of two popes. In the 1190s the Lusignans exploited family, although from a narrower base, and benefited from the anxieties of a European king. Both families demonstrate a kind of *blitzkrieg* mentality. Drawing on their natural instincts for mutual solidarity and cooperation, and in some cases with an eye on a share of the rewards, kindred would range themselves behind any one of their number fortunate or talented

[11] Edbury, *The Kingdom of Cyprus*, 14.   [12] *Le Livre au roi* 233.

[13] *La Continuation de Guillaume de Tyr* 136–9. For Richard's relations with the Templars, see Barber, *The New Knighthood*, 119.

[14] Painter, 'The Lords of Lusignan', 42.

enough to have found a way to power. The Lusignans were not the last middle-ranking European family to try to seize control of the eastern end of the crusading movement – the Briennes were to attempt something similar in the thirteenth century – and like the Montlhérys they demonstrate how prone a movement depending on spontaneous reactions, individual enterprise and collective support was to determined initiatives.

Preliminary list of crusaders

The list which follows is arranged chronologically and subdivided into those who I am certain, or relatively certain, took the cross, those who I think probably did and those who possibly did. The argument in the book has drawn only on evidence relating to the first two of these categories. Toponyms are given in modern forms. Each entry includes a guide to the evidence I have found to support an entry, except with respect to the best-known of the leaders – references to secondary works seemed to be sufficient in their cases – and a reference number which will help the reader find the crusader's place of origin on the maps. Those whose places of origin are unknown have the words 'Not located' entered after the number. No 'possible' crusader is referred to in the maps. I must stress that what has qualified a man or woman for entry is evidence for the taking of the cross, not actual participation, although most of those referred to here did join one or other of the armies. I have not distinguished between the various waves of the First Crusade, except in the cases of men who went on two of them, since it is usually impossible to establish the date when a man or woman volunteered.

I have trawled through all the narrative sources and many of the cartularies and other collections of documents, but this is a report of work in progress and many more names are likely to be discovered in future. I have not made use of the poems *Jérusalem* and *Chétifs* in the cycle of crusade epics, although they may well contain authentic material, and, mindful of the demolition of the historicity of the cycle of crusade *chansons* by Robert Cook (*'Chanson d'Antioch', Chanson de Geste, passim*), I have treated only as possibilities most of the uncorroborated names in the North French recension of *Antioche* and the early fragment of the Provencal version of it. And, with a few exceptions, I have not included names from the Spanish translation of the Provençal version in the *Gran Conquista de Ultramar*, because it is very corrupt, although no doubt there is also real evidence buried in it somewhere. I have also ignored the names to be found in the very late Chronicle of Zimmern, unless there is corroboration elsewhere, but I have included the three Zimmern brothers; two of them as 'possibles', and the third, Frederick, about whom circumstantial details are provided in the Chronicle, as a 'probable'.

Abbreviations

abb abbot (of); adv advocate (of); archbp archbishop (of); archd archdeacon (of); bp bishop (of); but butler (of); can canon (of); cast castellan (of); chap chaplain (of); cl cleric; con constable (of); ct count (of); d duke (of); e emperor; k king (of); kt knight; l lord (of); m monk (of); n noble; pl papal legate; pr priest (of); sen seneschal (of); st-b standard-bearer (of); vct viscount (of); vid vidame (of); w wife (of).

THE FIRST CRUSADE, 1096–1103

Certainties, or nearly so

Abo of St Bonnet (75)
    Chamalieres 54.
Achard of Marseilles, archbp Arles (1643)
    St Victor de Marseille (Guérard) 2.151-2; Poly, *La Provence*, 268 n. 120.
Achard of Montmerle, cast Montmerle (435)
    Cluny 5.51–3; GF 5, 88–9; PT 135; RA 141; AA 317, 468–9; BB 98–9; RR 865; GN Gesta 224; Gilo 795; OV 5.160-2; WT 398; Ch d'A 1.167, 441; Ch d'A Pr 491.
Adalbero of Luxembourg, archd Metz (390)
    AA 370–1.
Adam son of Michael (25 Not located)
    AA 365, 366, 426; Ch d'A 1.471.
Adelolf (26)
    AA 481.
Adhémar of Felez, pr St Germain (1476)
    Vigeois 68; Solignac fol. 23v.
Adhémar of Las Gaydias (1475)
    Uzerche 315; Vigeois 68.
Adhémar of Monteil, bp Le Puy (375)
    J. H. and L. L. Hill, 'Contemporary Accounts and the Later Reputation of Adhémar, Bishop of Puy', *Mediaevalia et Humanistica* 9 (1955), 30–8; J. A. Brundage, 'Adhémar of Puy: The Bishop and his Critics', *Speculum* 34 (1959),

201–12; H.. E. Mayer, 'Zur Beurteilung Adhémars von Le Puy', *Deutsches Archiv* 16 (1960), 547–52.

Adiutor of Vernon, kt (124)
  Acta SS Aprilis 3.824.

Aimery Bernard (1489)
  Vigeois 68; Aureil 179.

Aimery Brun, kt (4620)
  St Martial de Limoges 347.

Aimery, chap Chasseneuil (3782)
  St Amant de Boixe 159.

Aimery of Courron, co-l Amboise (174)
  Anjou (Halphen) 326; GAD 100–1.

Ainard of La Croix (4609)
  St Martial de Limoges 340–1.

Airard (29 Not located)
  RC 641.

Alan Fergent of Brittany, d Brittany (267)
  AA 316; BB 50 note; WT 191; Ch d'A 1.70; Ch d'A Pr 476; and probably Brittany (ducs) 61.

Alan of Gaël (283)
  BB 33; OV 5.58.

Alan, sen archbishop of Dol (30)
  BB 33; OV 5.58.

Alard of 'Spiniacum' (545)
  Kb 145.

Albert, kt (23)
  'Qualiter reliquiae B. Nicolai' 293–4.

Albert of Biandrate, ct Biandrate (111)
  AA 559, 561–2, 568–9, 582, 591, 603; Caffaro, 'De liberatione', 112; OV 5.326, 336; (Ch d'A 1.71, 160 – erroneous and called Thierry of Biandrate).

Albert of Parma, ct Parma (457)
  AA 559, 568; Riant, 'Un dernier triomphe', 249–55.

Alexander, pr, pl, chap Stephen of Blois (22)
  1096: Kb 152; CSPVS 184–8.
  1101: CSPVS 184–8.

Amanieu III of Albret, l Albret (653)
  The references in GC 122, 127, 155, 195 seem to be confirmed by the confusion of his name with that of Amanieu of Loubens in PT 'Var Ms' 98.

Amanieu of Loubens, kt (382)
  St Pierre de la Réole 140–1; PT 129; HP 210.

Anonyma, leader of a sect which followed her goose (4727 Not located)
  GN Gesta 251. See AA 295.

Anonyma, nun of Sta Maria ad Horrea, Trier (560)
  AA 327–8.

Anonymous, armiger of Baldwin of Le Bourcq (5491 Not located)
  AA 469.

Anonymous, author of the *Gesta Francorum* (38)
GF *passim*, esp 27, 40, 47, 57, 73, 82–92.
Anonymous, cl (5490 Not located)
AA 415–16.
Anonymous, kt (5492 Not located)
GN Gesta 248–50.
Anonymous, kt, 'king of the Tafurs' (797)
GN Gesta 242; Ch d'A 1.169–70, 218–21, 223, 227–18, 317–8, 407, 438, 475, 527.
Anonymous, m Cerne (1655)
Anselm of Canterbury 4.85.
Anonymous of La Mote (2668)
La Sauve-Majeure fol. 25 (information provided by Dr Bull).
Ansellus of Cayeux (184)
Kb 145.
Ansellus of Méry (411)
Molesme 2.229.
Anselm II of Ribemont, cast Bouchain, l Ostrevant and Valenciennes (497)
Valenciennes (594–601); Kb 144–6, 156–60, 176; GF 85; PT 131; RA 108–9; FC 270; RC 680–1; AA 315, 424, 452, 456; GN Gesta 218–19, 251; BB 93; RR 744n, 857; HP 211, 215; OV 5.150; WT 330, 365; 'Sigeberti continuatio auctarium Aquicinense' 394–5; 'Sigeberti continuatio auctarium Ursicampinum' 471; Ch d'A 1.69, 83, 94, 160, 440, 478, 481.
Anselm of Buis, archbp Milan, pl (169)
Landulf the Younger 22; Ekk H 28; AA 559, 561–2, 568, 573–4; GN Gesta 244; RC 709; Caffaro, 'De liberatione', 112; OV 5.326.
Anselm Rascherius (799)
Genoa (Church) 41; Caffaro, 'De liberatione', 102.
Ardouin of St Mars, kt (3484)
St Julien de Tours 82; AA 579.
Ardouin of Vione, 'procer' of Sablé (3583)
Marmoutier (Manceau) 2.89, 91–2.
Arnald of Aigurande (3638)
La Chapelle-Aude 83.
Arnald Tudebode, kt (562)
PT 116.
Arnold II of Ardres, cast Ardres (50)
Flanders 67 (Arnulf of Ardea); LA 625–7.
Arnulf, bp Martirano (401)
GF 93–4; PT 144; RA 152, 154, 156; RC 683; BB 106–7; HP 216; OV 5.178; WT 421–2, 424–5, 436.
Arnulf, cl (677)
Kb 177.
Arnulf Malecouronne of Chocques, pr, pl, chap Robert II of Normandy (217)
R. Foreville, 'Un chef de la première croisade: Arnoul Malecouronne',

Bulletin philologique et historique du comité des travaux historiques et scientifiques (1953–4), 377–90.
Arnulf of Hesdin, l Chipping Norton (337)
    'Chronica monasterii de Hida' 301–2; WMGP 438.
Arnulf of 'Tirs', kt (567)
    AA 317, 371.
Arnulf son of Villicus (52 Not located)
    AA 574.
Arvedus Tudebode, kt (563)
    PT 97.
Ascelin of Grandpré (315)
    Neumoustier 804.
Attropius, kt (56 Not located)
    RC 614.
Aubrey of Cagnano (183)
    GF 8; BB 21; Monte Cassino 477; HP 177, 187; OV 5.36; WT 177.
See Jamison, 'Some Notes', 203.
Aubrey of Grandmesnil, kt (312)
    GF 56–7; PT 97; BB 64; GN Gesta 194; RC 662; HP 200; OV 5.34, 98; WT 310, 312.
Aufan of Agoult, bp Apt (41)
    RA 89–90, 119, 135. See Poly, *La Provence*, 268.
Aznar Exemenones of Oteiza (4757)
    Leire 272.

Baldric, sen Godfrey of Bouillon (64)
    AA 300, 412, 481.
Baldwin, abb, chap Godfrey of Bouillon (65)
    GN Gesta 182–3, 251; WT 472.
Baldwin Chauderon, kt (185)
    Kb 145; AA 315, 320–1; WT 203; WT Fr 1.118; Ch d'A 1.69, 77–8, 80, 86, 88–9, 91,95, 99–100, 526; and probably Valenciennes (600).
Baldwin I of Guines, ct Guines (319)
    LA 580–1.
Baldwin of Boulogne (141)
    Mayer, *Mélanges, passim*.
Baldwin of Ghent, adv St Pierre-au-Mont-Blandin, Ghent, l Aalst (287)
    Flanders 67; Kb 139, 145; AA 315, 321; 'Annalista Saxo' 730; WT 203; Ch d'A 1.69, 86–8, 90–2, 94, 99–100.
Baldwin of Grandpré, kt (316)
    AA 563, 569; Laurence of Liège 499.
Baldwin of Hestrud (340)
    AA 591, 593.
Baldwin of Le Bourcq, l Le Bourcq (150)
    FC 278; GN Gesta 254; AA 299, 306, 310, 315, 332, 343, 350, 422, 464, 468–9; WT 138, 161, 171, 174, 217, 219, 330, 410; Ch d'A 1.281.

Baldwin of Mons, ct Hainault (325)

St Lambert de Liège 1.46–8; Dinant 1.12; GF 2; RC 642; AA 305, 315, 332, 366, 424, 434–5; WT 138, 161, 252, 278, 343; GN Gesta 147, 208; BB 17, 20; RR 744; Sigebert of Gembloux, 'Chronica', 367; Gilo 701; Giselbert of Mons 37, 43–5; Monte Cassino 476; HP 174; OV 5.34; 'Annalista Saxo' 730; Anonymus Florinensis, 'Brevis Narratio Belli Sacri', 371; Henry of Huntingdon, 'De captione Antiochiae a Christianis', 374; Ch d'A 1.69, 441.

Bartholomew Boel of Chartres, vid Chartres (205)

Genoa (Church) 41 (Kb 156); GF 8; RA 64; BB 21; RC 654–5; Gilo 765; Monte Cassino 477; HP 177; OV 5.36; WT 177; Ch d'A Pr 478, 494.

Bartholomew, cl (69 Not located)

Consecrated archbishop of Misis (Mamistra) at Christmas 1099 (RC 704; HP 227) so must have been on the crusade.

Bego of La Rivière (496)

PT 129; HP 210.

Bellacosa (5229)

Genoa (Church) 41.

Bencelinus of Brie (5362)

Lorraine 513–14 (*PL* 157.439–40). See Laurence of Liège 497.

Benedict, cl (97 Not located)

Consecrated archbishop of Edessa at Christmas 1099 (RC 704; HP 227) so must have been on the crusade.

Berald Silvain (3953)

St Jean d'Angély 33.111–13.

Berengar of Narbonne (680)

St Victor de Marseille (Guérard) 2.151–2.

Berengar Peter of Gignac (644)

HGL 5.749.

Berlai of Passavant-sur-Layon (1650)

Chaise-le-Vicomte 7–8.

Bernard (100)

Cluny 5.59.

Bernard Ato of Béziers, vct Béziers and Carcassonne (109)

Gellone 248; Carcassonne 5.155; St Victor de Marseille (Guérard) 2.151–2.

Bernard II of Besalù, ct Besalù (197)

Papsturkunden in ... Katalonien 2.287–8.

Bernard II of Bré, co-l Bré (1482)

Vigeois 51; Aureil 179.

Bernard le Baile (102)

Aureil 126.

Bernard of 'Pardilum' (454 Not located)

HP 193.

Bernard (of Scheyern, ct Scheyern) (540)

Ekk H 32. See Ekkehard (Hagenmeyer) 248 note 15.

Bernard of St-Valéry (531)
    AA 316; BB 33; RC 693; HP 221; OV 5.58; Ch d'A 1.70, 85, 152, 401;
Ch d'A Pr 473.
Bernard of Valence, pr, chap Adhémar of Monteil (568)
    WT 340.
Bernard Raymond of Béziers, n (110)
    RA 51.
Bernard Veredun (577)
    Cluny 5.108.
Berthold, ct (of Neuffen) (442)
    OV 5.28, 38; Zimmern 23, 29. But *cf.* Murray, 'The army of Godfrey of
Bouillon', 319–20.
Bertrand of Bas, pr, can Le Puy (71)
    Chamalières 54; RA 119–20.
Bertrand of Marseilles (1639)
    St Victor de Marseille (Guérard) 1.169–70.
Bertrand of Moncontour, cast Moncontour (419)
    La Trinité de Vendôme Cart 2.104–7.
Bertrand of 'Scabrica' (469 Not located)
    HP 181.
Bertrand of Taillecavat (2654)
    St Pierre de la Réole 141.
Bertrand Porcellet, lay sacristan of the church of Arles (478)
    Gallia Christiana 1, Instrumenta, 97. Poly (*La Provence*, 262–4, 268)
suggested that he travelled East with Achard of Marseilles.
Bohemond of Taranto, l Taranto (334)
    R. B. Yewdale, *Bohemond I, Prince of Antioch* (Princeton, 1924), 34–105.
Bonfilius, bp Foligno (276)
    Acta SS Septembris 7.523.
Boniface, can (Le Puy?) (73)
    Chamalières 54.
Boso of La Chèze (103)
    Aureil 126, 170.
Brunet of Treuil, can Aureil (379)
    Aureil 29.
Bruno (275)
    AA 568.
Bruno, n, can (165)
    Ekk H 32.
Bruno, n, can (166)
    Ekk H 32.

Caffaro de Caschifelone (780)
    Caffaro, 'De liberatione', 121.

Centule II of Bigorre, l Bigorre (87)
BB 17; OV 5.30; WT 139, 182.
Chalo VII of Aulnay, vct Aulnay (4782)
Notre-Dame de Saintes 139–40; and probably Montierneuf de Poitiers 45.
Clarembald of Vendeuil, l Vendeuil (574)
AA 293–5, 299, 304–5, 398; RR 833; GN Gesta 206; Gilo 775; WT 156, 168, 291; Ch d'A 1.69, 440, 450–1.
Conan of Lamballe (155)
AA 316, 422, 463; RC 648; BB 28, 33; OV 5.54, 58; WT 191, 330, 410; Ch d'A 1.70, 526. See C. W. David, *Robert Curthose Duke of Normandy* (Cambridge, Mass., 1920), 222.
Cono of Montaigu, ct Montaigu (420)
Dinant 1.13; 'Cantatorium Sancti Huberti' 340, 371; AA 306, 310, 317, 366, 385, 464, 495, 504; RC 632, 637, 639, 641; OV 5.110, 166–8; WT 161, 171, 174, 252, 410; Neumoustier 804, 815. See 'Document inédit' 100.
Cono, pr (695 Not located)
GN Gesta 250.
Cono, pr, chap Robert II of Flanders (4534)
Flanders 67.
Conrad, once con the emperor Henry III (228)
AA 562, 568, 570, 573–4, 582–3, 591, 593–5, 649–50.
Conrad, son of Taio (5226)
Genoa (Church) 41.
Constantine son of Bernard (613)
Cluny 5.108.
Corba of Thorigné, co-l Amboise (173)
GAD 86–7, 102–3.

Daimbert, archbp Pisa (696)
B. Hamilton, *The Latin Church*, 14–16.
Dithmar, ct (246)
Mainz Anonymous, 'Narrative of the Old Persecutions', 100.
Dodo de Advocato (806)
Caffaro, 'De liberatione', 102.
Dodo, kt (247 Not located)
AA 574.
Dodo of Clermont-en-Argonne, l Clermont-en-Argonne (220)
AA 563, 569.
Dodo of Cons-la-Grandville (229)
St Hubert-en-Ardenne 1.81–2; AA 299, 317; WT 161.
Drogo I of Mouchy-le-Châtel, l Mouchy-le-Châtel (418)
AA 422; OV 5.30; WT 330; Ch d'A 1.70, 307.
Drogo of Nesle (443)
AA 299, 304–5, 315, 398, 442; RR 833; Gilo 775; WT 168, 291; Ch d'A 1.86, 90–1, 93–5, 440, 450–1, 488; Ch d'A Pr 473.

Durand Bovis (77)
  Chamalières 54.

Edgar Atheling (646)
  WMGR 2.309–10.
Ekkehard of Aura, m Michelsberg, Bamberg (58)
  Ekk H 29–30 and *passim.*
Elvira of Leon-Castile, w Raymond IV of St Gilles (599)
  GN Gesta 150.
Emeline, w Fulcher of Bullion (135)
  AA 436. For her name see St Martin des Champs Chartes 1.112–13.
Emerias of Altejas (35)
  HGL 5.757.
Emich ct Flonheim (372)
  Ekk H.20; AA 292–5, 299; Mainz Anonymous 107; Solomon ben Simson,
'Chronicle', 28, 70; WT 156 158; Zimmern 23; also Ekk C 261.
Emma of Hereford, w Ralph I of Gaël (645)
  OV 2.318.
Engelrand of Châlons-sur-Marne (202)
  AA 574.
Engelrand of Coucy, bp Laon (230)
  AA 563, 568, 573, 582–3, 600; GN Gesta 243.
Engelrand of St Pol (527)
  RA 109; BB 47 note, 76 note; AA 315, 372–3, 422, 451; RC 681; HP 215;
WT 161, 330, 357; Ch d'A 1.63, 70, 82–3, 92, 95, 149–52, 155–6, 160, 163,
200, 244–6, 307, 313, 315–16, 401–2, 437, 441, 526, 530.
Engilbert of Cysoing, adv Cysoing, l Petegem, st-b Robert II of Flanders (237)
  Flanders 63. For his office in Flanders, see E. Warlop, *The Flemish Nobility
before 1300* (Kortijk, 1975–6), 4, table 169.
Engilbert of Tournai (557)
  AA 472, 477; RC 693; HP 221; BN 515; WT 409.
Erald of Châlons-sur-Marne (203)
  AA 574.
Ermengald of Roussillon, bp Elne (515)
  HP 176, 189; Monte Cassino 477.
Eudes (101)
  Cluny 5.59.
Eudes Arpin of Bourges, vct Bourges (151)
  'Excerptum Historicum' 158; AA 544, 591, 593–5; GN Gesta 244–5; OV
5.324, 344–52; (Ch d'A 1.35, 39, 49–50, 52, 508, 523–4 – erroneous).
Eudes (Odo), bp Bayeux (85)
  St Bénigne de Dijon 2.167; GN Gesta 232–3; 'Chronica monasterii de
Hida' 296, 300; OV 4.118; 5.34, 208–10.
Eudes I of Burgundy, d Burgundy (178)
  St Bénigne de Dijon 2.173–7, 180; Molesme 2.13, 18, 143; Cluny 5.156–9;

St Etienne de Dijon 11; Burgundy (Pérard) 82–4, 202–3; OV 5.324 (mis-named), 338.

Eudes of Beaugency, st-b Hugh the Great of Vermandois (89)
    RR 831; Gilo 775; Ch d'A 1.426–7, 442 (as Eudes of Beauvais).

Eudes of St Mars, abb Preuilly (3485)
    St Julien de Tours 82.

Eudes of Verneuil (579)
    Kb 145.

Eustace, but Robert II of Flanders (4533)
    Flanders 67.

Eustace III of Boulogne, ct Boulogne (144)
    Kb 161–5; GF 90, 93, 95; PT 71, 118–19, 139–40, 143, 145–6; AA 314–15, 398, 424, 448, 451, 472, 477, 491, 495; BB 17, 20, 28, 34–5, 100 note, 102, 105, 108, 110 note; GN Gesta 147, 226, 234–5; Gilo 797; RC 632; 'Notitiae duae Lemovicenses' 351; 'Gesta triumphalia Pisanorum in captione Jerusalem' 369; Henry of Huntingdon, 'De captione', 374; WT 138, 191, 215, 252, 276, 278, 330, 332, 354, 407, 409, 426, 434, 453; Ch d'A 1.69, 85–6, 262, 307, 441, 515, 519, 526. See St Bertin (Guérard) 229.

Everard III of Le Puiset, vct Chartres (373)
    Marmoutier (Dunois) 137; GF 5; AA 362, 365, 383, 410, 422; RR 796, 833; BB 17, 21 note; RC 697–8; Morigny 11; Gilo 751, 774; HP 223; OV 5.30; Suger of St Denis, *Vita*, 130; WT 139, 242, 275, 310, 330; Ch d'A Pr 473, 491; Ch d'A 1.70, 194 , 196, 199, 206, 307, 450–1.

Everard, pr (258 Not located)
    RA 117–18, 121.

Everard Venator, huntsman (573)
    GF 78; PT 122; RR 847; BB 85 note; Gilo 782; HP 208.

Fantin Incorrigiatus (354)
    St Laon de Thouars 32.

Farald of Thouars (351)
    RA 75.

Florina of Burgundy, w Sven of Denmark (179)
    AA 377.

Folkmar, pr (277)
    Ekk H 12, 20. See Cosmas of Prague 103.

Fortun Iniguez, l Grez (4738)
    Leire 230.

Franco I of Mechelen, cast Brussels (395)
    AA 413; WT 317; Wauters, *Table chronologique*, 1.602.

Frederick of Bogen, adv Regensburg (128)
    'Probationes ad tabulam chronologicam ad Stemmatographiam comitum de Bogen' 41, 76.

Frumold, ministerialis of the archbishop of Cologne (282)
    'Chronicon Brunwylarense' 151–3.

Fulcher of Bullion, kt (134)
    AA 436 (called Folbert). See Emeline, above.
Fulcher of Chartres, kt (206)
    RA 64; AA 281, 283, 286, 288, 357, 442; RR 799–800, 805; RC 654–5;
Gilo 765; OV 5.90; WT 15; Ch d'A Pr 491.
Fulcher of Chartres, pr, chap Stephen of Blois, chap Baldwin of Boulogne
(208)
    FC 153, 160-206 and *passim*; GN Gesta 250, 252.
Fulk Doon of Châteaurenard, l Châteaurenard (1628)
    Lérins 311–12.
Fulk I of Matheflon, cast Matheflon (1559)
    Azé et Le Genéteil 60; Anjou (Halphen) 330; Le Ronceray d'Angers 93–5.
Fulk of Guines (320)
    LA 580–1; 'Versus de viris illustribus diocoesis Tarvanensis qui in sacra
fuere expeditione' 540.
Fulk of Solliès (1638)
    St Victor de Marseille (Rolland) 26–7. See St Victor de Marseille (Guérard)
1.169.
Fulk the Lombard of Grasse, l Grasse (1624)
    Antibes 62–3.

G. of Las Gaydias, pr (3875)
    Uzerche 315.
Galdemar Carpenel of Dargoire, l Dargoire (188)
    RA 141; RA Cont 307–8; PT 135; WT 397–8.
Garin of Gallardon (3297)
    St Martin des Champs Liber 98; St Martin des Champs Chartes 1.123–6.
Garnier Marchio (5493 Not located)
    RC 642.
Garnier of Grez, ct Grez (317)
    AA 299, 301, 310, 315, 365, 383–4, 422, 424; WT 138, 161, 275, 330; Ch
d'A 1.69. See 'Document inédit', 100.
Garsadon of Etrechy (3326)
    Morigny 19, 40-1.
Gaston IV of Béarn, vct Béarn (88)
    St Vincent de Lucq 19–20; GF 92, 95; PT 78, 110, 141, 145–6; RA 145–6;
RR 874; AA 316, 332, 422, 442, 460, 462–4, 504; BB 162 note, 108; GN
Gesta 228–9, 235; Gilo 799; HP 193; WT 139, 182, 217, 331, 377–8, 399, 410;
Ch d'A Pr 474, 492.
Geoffrey Burel, co-l Amboise (172)
    GAD 86–7, 102–3.
Geoffrey Chotard (218)
    Brittany (Morice) 1.488.
Geoffrey, doctor (1652)
    Chaise-le-Vicomte 8.

Geoffrey Guarin, kt (4723)
 Marmoutier (Dunois) 141–2.
Geoffrey I Jordan of Vendôme, ct Vendôme (575)
 La Trinité de Vendôme Cart 2.159–60; Marmoutier (Blésois) 106; Marmoutier (Vendômois) 315; Marmoutier (Manceau) 2.427; FC 437; WMGR 2.450; AA 593; BN 533–4; GAD (198); Ch d'A 1.70 (erroneous).
Geoffrey II of Donzy, ct Chalon-sur-Saône, l Donzy (1566)
 Burgundy (Pérard) 201–2 (Chalon-sur-Saône Preuves 46).
Geoffrey III of Roussillon, ct Roussillon (516)
 Papsturkunden in ... Katalonien 2.287–8; GF 8, 9; PT 41; BB 21; HP 176, 189; Monte Cassino 477; OV 5.36, 44; WT 177.
Geoffrey III of Thouars (352)
 Chaise-le-Vicomte 6–8, 25, 347.
Geoffrey Le Râle (4326)
 Le Ronceray d'Angers 104.
Geoffrey of Issoudun, l Issoudun (3891)
 Aureil 161.
Geoffrey of Montescaglioso (428)
 GF 8, 21, 61; PT 55, 102; BB 21, 35, 68; GN Gesta 162; HP 177, 183, 202; Monte Cassino 477, 480; OV 5.36, 62, 102; WT 177. See Jamison, 'Some notes', 191, 200–1.
Geoffrey of Riveray (3901)
 Nogent-le-Rotrou 39.
Geoffrey of Signes, kt (294)
 St Victor de Marseille (Guérard) 1.167–8.
Geoffrey Parented of Segré (193)
 OV 5.90.
Geoffrey son of Deriadoc (632)
 Brittany (Morice) 1.484, 491.
Geoffrey son of Geoffrey of 'Perolium' (633)
 Brittany (Morice) 1.484, 491.
Gerald Malefaide of Noailles, l St Viance, l Noailles (394)
 Uzerche 95; *Documents historiques inédits tirés des collections manuscrits* 3.437; HP 193; GC 127.
Gerald of Landerron, cast Landerron (2656)
 St Pierre de la Réole 141–2.
Gerald of 'Tuda', kt (3944)
 St Jean d'Angély 30.390–1.
Gerard, abb Schaffhausen (538)
 'Monachi anonymi Scaphusensis de reliquiis sanctissimi crucis et dominici sepulchri Scaphusam allatis' 337; Bernold of St Blasien 467. See also Berthold of Zwiefalten, 'Chronicon', 108.
Gerard Barson (68 Not located)
 AA 593.

Gerard, bp Ariano (51)
    HP 176–7; Monte Cassino 477; FC 327; GN Gesta 255.
Gerard, household cl Baldwin of Boulogne (304 Not located)
    AA 395, 446.
Gerard I of Quierzy, l Quierzy (483)
    AA 315, 331–2, 467–8, 494; WT 139, 217, 291; Ch d'A 1.94, 441.
Gerard of Avesnes, kt (61)
    AA 499.
Gerard of Buc, cast Lille (168)
    'Narratio quomodo relliquiae martyris Georgii' 250–1.
Gerard of Gournay-en-Bray (311)
    AA 316; BB 33; OV 5.34, 58; Ch d'A 1.94, 441.
Gerard of Roussillon (514)
    HP 176; AA 316, 422, 464; Monte Cassino 477; WT 139, 177, 182, 331,
410; Ch d'A 1.489(?).
Gerard the Old of Meleone (406)
    RR 833; Gilo 776; Ch d'A 1.450–1.
Gerbault of 'Castellum Winthinc' (192)
    AA 591, 593, 595.
Gerbault of Lille, pr (380)
    'Narratio quomodo relliquiae martyris Georgii' 248–50.
Gerento of Le Béage, l Le Béage (114)
    St Chaffre du Monastier 89 (HGL 5.751). See also Chamalières 17–8.
Gervase of St Cyprian, abb St Savin (522)
    Acta SS Aprilis 2.226.
Gilbert, abb Admont (27)
    Henry of Breitenau, 'Passio S. Thiemonis Juvavensis archiepiscopi', 203,
205; 'Annales Mellicenses auctarium Garstense' 568; 'Annales Admuntenses'
577; 'Annales Sancti Rudberti Salisburgenses' 774.
Gilbert, bp Evreux (259)
    OV 4.118; 5.210.
Gilbert of Aalst, kt (1393)
    Afflighem 13.
Gilbert of Clermont, ct Clermont (221)
    AA 350; WT 219, 229.
Gilbert of Traves (559)
    AA 316, 468–9; WT 398.
Gilbert Payen of Garlande, sen King Philip I of France (290)
    AA 320; WT 139, 201; Ch d'A 1.161.
Girbert of Mézères (72)
    Chamalières 54.
Girismannus (308)
    Landulf the Younger 22.
Godehilde of Tosny, w Baldwin of Boulogne (142)
    AA 302, 358; WT 221.

Godfrey Burel (171)
   AA 277–8, 281, 286, 288.
Godfrey Incorrigiatus (355)
   St Laon de Thouars 32.
Godfrey of Bouillon, d Lower Lorraine (145)
   J. C. Andressohn, *The Ancestry and Life of Godfrey of Bouillon* (Bloomington,
1947), 47–111; Mayer, *Mélanges*, 10–48.
Godfrey of Esch-sur-Sûre, n, kt (54)
   AA 299–300, 306–7, 366; WT 161–2. See 'Document inédit' 100.
Godric of Finchale, merchant, pirate (715)
   Reginald of Durham 33–4; AA 595.
Godschalk, pr (310)
   AA 289–91, 300; Ekk H 12, 20; WT 153–5, 157, 161, 163.
Gottman of Brussels (167)
   AA 591, 594.
Gouffier of Lastours, l Lastours (370)
   GF 79; PT 78, 123; RA 97–8; BB 85; GN Gesta 213; RR 847–8; Gilo 783;
GV 12.422, 428; HP 193, 206, 209; OV 5.138; 'Notitiae duae Lemovicenses'
351; WT 341, 354–5; Ch d'A Pr 492–3; Ch d'A 1.441; Tenant de la Tour,
L'Homme et la Terre, 357–60; Ch d'A 2.171–2.
Gozelo of Montaigu (421)
   AA 317, 358–9; WT 240, 242; Ch d'A 1.144–6.
Grimbald (318 Not located)
   Cluny 5.117–18
Grimoald of Maule (642)
   OV 3.200.
Guarin Guernonatus (4719)
   Marmoutier (Dunois) 141.
Guarin, kt (291 Not located)
   RC 614.
Guarin of 'Petra Mora' (465)
   RR 857; Gilo 792.
Guarin of 'Tanea' (1654)
   WMGR 2.460–1.
Guigo of 'Mara' (398)
   St Julien de Tours 72–3.
Gunscelin, pr, can Lille (322)
   'Narratio quomodo relliquiae martyris Georgii' 250.
Guy, co-l Mezenc (3841)
   St Chaffre du Monastier 88, 139–41.
Guy II of Rochefort, ct Rochefort, sen King Philip I of France (432)
   Suger of St Denis, *Vita*, 38–40; AA 563, 568, 573; Morigny 40–1.
Guy of Biandrate, kt (112)
   AA 559, 568.

Guy of Bré (1483)
   Aureil 179; Uzerche 210, 341, 362; Vigeois 67–9; Solignac fol. 23v.
Guy of Escorailles (1658.)
   St Flour cxxxv, ccvii.
Guy of Guines (1336)
   LA 580–1.
Guy of Hauteville (335)
   GF 63–5; PT 105–7; HP 203–4; RR 816–7; GN Gesta 200–1; BB 72–3, 80
note; OV 5.76, 106–8; WT 321; Ch d'A 1.350–2.
Guy of Pistoia, ct Pistoia (5295)
   Pistoia 241–3.
Guy of Possesse, l Possesse (480)
   AA 315, 320, 322; Kb 145 (as Guy of Vitry); WT 139, 201, 203; Ch d'A
1.69, 81, 91, 93, 95, 99–100.
Guy of Roumoulès (1623)
   Lérins 289–90.
Guy of Sarcé, kt (537)
   St Vincent du Mans 1.190–1, 200.
Guy of Signes (295)
   St Victor de Marseille (Guérard) 1.167–8.
Guy of Thiers, ct Chalon-sur-Saône (201)
   Paray-le-Monial 107–8.
Guy Trousseau of Montlhéry, l Montlhéry (433)
   GF 56–7; PT 97–8; HP 200; RC 650; GN Gesta 194; BB 64; OV 5.30, 98;
Suger of St Denis, *Vita*, 36–8; WT 312.
Guynemer of Boulogne, pirate (139)
   AA 348–9, 380, 447, 500–1; WT 228, 362–3, 371.

Hadvide of Chiny, w Dodo of Cons-la-Grandville (4158)
   St Hubert-en-Ardenne 1.81–2.
Hamo, abb Cerne (1656)
   Anselm of Canterbury 4.85.
Hamo of La Hune (367)
   St Vincent du Mans 1.266–7.
Hartmann of Dillingen-Kybourg, ct Dillingen-Kybourg (245)
   AA 299, 322, 427; Bernold of St Blasien 466; WT 156, 203, 338; Zimmern 23.
Helias of La Flèche, ct Maine (366)
   OV 5.228–32.
Henry Contarini, bp Castello (817)
   'Historia de translatione' 255–81 *passim*; Martin da Canal, *Les Estoires de
Venise*, 24–6.
Henry, ct (341)
   AA 576.
Henry II of Regensburg, burgrave of Regensburg (493)
   Göttweig 196–7; Ekk H 32.

Henry of Esch-sur-Sûre, cast Esch-sur-Sûre (55)
    AA 299, 305, 322, 328, 365–6, 369, 413, 422, 424, 427, 435; WT 138, 161–2, 171, 203, 316–17, 330, 338, 344. See 'Document inédit' 100.
Henry of Grandpré, ct Grandpré (630)
    Laurence of Liège 497.
Heraclius I of Polignac, vct Polignac, st-b Adhémar of Monteil (377)
    RA 82, 119–20; Ch d'A Pr 492. See Chamalières 16–18.
Herbert II of Thouars, vct Thouars (353)
    Chaise-le-Vicomte 6–8, 25, 347. See Ch d'A Pr 474, 491 (erroneous).
Herbert of 'Campus Marini', kt (4315)
    Marmoutier (Anjou) 39.
Herbert of Chaise-Dieu, prior of Prevezac (45)
    Acta SS Aprilis 3.330
Herbrand of Bouillon, kt (137)
    AA 317, 440. See 'Document inédit' 100.
Herluin, pr, interpreter (342 Not located)
    GF 66–7; PT 108; RR 825–7; GN Gesta 204; BB 74; HP 204; OV 5.108; WT 326; Caffaro, 'De liberatione', 1.107; Ch d'A 1.364 , 367–9.
Hermann of Canne (187)
    GF 7; BB 21; HP 187; Monte Cassino 477; OV 5.36; WT 177; Jamison, 'Some notes', 198–9.
Hervey son of Dodeman (344 Not located)
    BB 33; OV 5.58.
Hildebert, ct (345 Not located)
    OV 5.28.
Hilduin of Mazingarbe (405)
    Kb.145.
Host of 'Castellum Ruvra' (191 Not located)
    AA 593.
Hugh, archbp Lyons, pl (244)
    Savigny 1.433–4; Hugh of Flavigny 487, 494; RA Cont 307–8; Ch d'A 1.47 (li vesques del Forois; erroneous).
Hugh Bardolf II of Broyes, l Broyes (157)
    AA 563, 568, 573.
Hugh Bochard, cast Trivy (127)
    St Philibert de Tournus (Juënin) 2.135 (St Philibert de Tournus (Chifflet) 335).
Hugh Botuns (133 Not located)
    AA 591, 593.
Hugh Bunel (170 In exile in Islamic territory)
    OV 5.156–8.
Hugh Guernonatus, prévôt of Blois (4717)
    Marmoutier (Dunois) 141.
Hugh I of Gallardon, l Gallardon (3296)
    St Martin de Pontoise 470 note 920; St Martin des Champs Liber 98.

Hugh II of Empurias, ct Empurias (198)
Papsturkunden in ... Katalonien 2.287–8.
Hugh II of St Pol, ct St Pol (528)
AA 315, 372, 422, 463; BB 28, 33; RC 642; OV 5.34, 54, 58; WT 138 ,161, 213, 278, 330, 357, 410; Ch d'A 1.69, 82, 92, 95, 150–2, 160, 163, 194–8, 200, 281–2, 315, 321, 401, 437, 441, 530; Ch d'A Pr 473.
Hugh III of Juillé (361)
St Vincent du Mans 1.293.
Hugh Lo Forsenet (or 'The Mad') (358 Not located)
GF 61; PT 102; BB 68; GN Gesta 197; HP 202; OV 5.102. See RR 824.
Hugh of 'Almaz' (33)
AA 593.
Hugh of Amboise, kt (634)
Marmoutier (Tourangeau) 40–1.
Hugh of Apigné (40)
St Georges de Rennes 269–70.
Hugh of 'Bellafayre' (96)
HP 181.
Hugh of Burgundy, archbp Besançon (104)
St Philibert de Tournus (Juënin) 144; Calixtus II, *Bullaire*, 1.4–5, 39, 205, 380; 2.14. See Bouchard, *Sword, Miter, and Cloister*, 274.
Hugh of 'Calniacum' (635)
Kb 145.
Hugh of Chaumont-sur-Loire, co-l Amboise (175)
Anjou (Halphen) 326; GAD 100–2; BB 17 note, 21 note, 33 note, 65 note.
The documents in Marmoutier (Blésois) 72, 87 probably relate to his crusade.
Hugh of Guines (1337)
LA 580–1.
Hugh of Méry, kt, l Méry-sur-Seine (412)
Molesme 2.229.
Hugh of 'Montbeel' (427 Not located)
AA 559, 561, 568.
Hugh of Pierrefonds, bp Soissons (464)
AA 563, 573; GN Gesta 243.
Hugh of Rethel (Le Bourcq), ct Rethel (147)
AA 593.
Hugh of Rheims (495)
Kb 145.
Hugh of St Hilaire (2222)
Sauxillanges 882.
Hugh of St Omer, l Fauquembergues (260)
AA 531; 'Versus de viris illustribus' 540. See 'Les Lignages d'Outremer' 455; Rheinheimer, *Das Kreuzfahrerfürstentum Galiläa*, 41–2.
Hugh of Toucy, co-l Toucy (553)
1096 and 1101: Molesme 2.84; and see 1.138–9.

Hugh the Great, ct Vermandois (280)

1096: Kb.145, 153–5, 160; Anna Comnena 2.213–15, 225–6; RA 79; GF 5–6, 18–20, 68, 70, 72; PT 37–8, 51–4, 110–12; FC 155–6, 194–5, 255; AA 304–5, 316, 366, 422, 424–5, 434–5; GN Gesta 148–50, 152, 155, 160–1, 196, 200, 205–8, 241; BB 17, 20–1, 33–5, 44 note, 50 note, 75, 77, 79, 80 note; Gilo 732, 745–6, 748, 777; OV 5.30, 34, 36, 58, 60–2, 110, 114, 128; WT 138, 167–8, 191, 202, 215, 252, 276, 278, 288, 330–2, 336, 341, 343, 465; Ch d'A 1.20, 70, 94, 161, 220–1, 224, 261, 281, 299, 307, 341, 388–9, 391, 393, 425–7, 440, 444, 449, 472, 489, 508–9, 513, 518, 520, 526, 530.

1101: Molesme 2.13; FC 430, 433; GN Gesta 200, 243, 259; WT 465, 467.

Hugh Verdosius (4639)

St Cyprien de Poitiers 68.

Hugh VI of Lusignan, l Lusignan (389)

1101: Nouaillé 293; AA 591; FC 438; BN 532–4, 561; WMGR 2.447–8, 450; WT 476. He is possibly referred to on the expedition of 1096 to 1099 as 'lo dux de Laconha' in Ch d'A Pr 491. His seneschal certainly took part then (PT 135), but it is unlikely that he went twice himself.

Humberge of Le Puiset, w Walo II of Chaumont-en-Vexin (810)

RR 795–6; Gilo 750–1.

Humbert II of Savoy, ct Maurienne, Savoy, and Turin (2217)

Savoy 27.

Humphrey son of Ralph (349)

GF 7–8; BB 21; HP 176; OV 5.36; Monte Cassino 477; WT 177.

Husechinus (350 Not located)

AA 341.

Ida of Cham, w Markgraf Leopold II of Austria (59)

Ekk H 32; AA 579–81; 'Annales Mellicenses' 500; 'Historia Welforum Weingartensis' 462.

Ilger Bigod, con Tancred Marchisus (113)

OV 5.170.

Ingo Flaonus (820)

Caffaro, 'De liberatione', 102.

Isoard I of Die, ct Die (243)

RA 132, 144; WT 138, 330, 411.

Isoard of Ganges, n, kt (289)

RA 60.

Isoard of Mouzon (426)

GF 5; Henry of Huntingdon, 'De captione', 375.

Itier I of Toucy, co-l Toucy (554)

Molesme 2.84, 105; and see 1.138–9.

Itier of 'Tuda' (3945)

St Jean d'Angély 30.391.

Ivo of Grandmesnil, sheriff of Leicester (313)
    1096: PT 97; AA 398?, 410; RC 662; HP 200; BN 501; OV 4.338; 5.34;
WT 310; Ch d'A 1.307?.
    1101: OV 4.338.

John, chamberlain (824 Not located)
    Caffaro, 'De liberatione', 109.
John Michiel (823)
    'Historia de translatione' 255, 262.
John of Nijmegen (445)
    AA 317; Ch d'A Pr 491.
Jordan of Le Breuil (1501)
    Vigeois 68; Solignac fol. 23v.
Josbert of Les Murs (3913)
    Aureil 203.
Josbert of St Hilaire (2221)
    Sauxillanges 882.
Joscelin of Courtenay (234)
    OV 5.324.
Josceran of Vitrolles (1627)
    St Victor de Marseille (Guérard) 1.229–31. See Poly, *La Provence*, 267.

Lagman of Man, k Man (5482)
    Chronicle of the Kings of Man 8, 62.
Lambert (368 Not located)
    AA 279.
Lambert (625 Not located)
    In Palestine late in 1099, so must have been a crusader. AA 510.
Lambert, doctor (5231)
    Genoa (Church) 41.
Lambert Ghezo (826)
    Caffaro, 'De liberatione', 118.
Lambert Magus (5225)
    Genoa (Church) 41.
Lambert of Montaigu (422)
    AA 317, 422, 464, 495; WT 330, 410; Ch d'A 1.84, 146 and probably 441,
526; Neumoustier 804, 815.
Lambert the Poor (222 Not located)
    GF 56–7; PT 97; BB 64; HP 200; OV 5.98; Henry of Huntingdon, 'De
captione' 377; WT 312.
Lanfranc Drubesci or Roza (828)
    Genoa (Church) 41; Caffaro, 'De liberatione', 102.
Leger (1653)
    Chaise-le-Vicomte 8.

Lethold of Tournai, kt (558)
  GF 91; PT 140; AA 472, 477; BB 102; RR 867; GN Gesta 226–7; RC 693;
BN 515; Gilo 798; HP 221; OV 5.168; WT 409; Neumoustier 811.
Lisiard of Flanders (271)
  Kb.145.
Louis, archd Toul (556)
  AA 375–6.
Louis of Mousson, ct Mousson (425)
  AA 317, 422, 464; WT 330, 410; Ch d'A 1.441; Neumoustier 804.

Mainfinit, sen Alan Fergent of Brittany (631)
  Brittany (Morice) 1.484, 491.
Mala-Corona, servant of Bohemond of Taranto (393 Not located)
  GF 45–6; PT 85; BB 55; HP 196.
Manasses, bp Barcelona (107)
  AA 582, 584–5.
Manasses of Clermont (223)
  Kb.145.
Manasses Robert of Guines (1335)
  LA 580–1.
Matthew, kt (402)
  GN Gesta 183–4; OV 5.28.
Mauro de Platea Longa (778)
  Caffaro, 'De liberatione', 118.
Miles Louez, kt (386 Not located)
  AA 316.
Miles of Bray, cast Bray, vct Troyes (434)
  1096: Longpont 93; OV 5.30.
  1101: Longpont 184, 184–5; OV 5.324, 346; AA 563, 568.

Nivelo of Fréteval, cast Fréteval (448)
  St Père de Chartres 2.428–9; Marmoutier (Dunois) 56–7, 76 and probably
75.
Norgeot, bp Autun (5498)
  Hugh of Flavigny 487.
Norgeot I of Toucy, co-l Toucy (555)
  Molesme 2.64, 84; and see 1.138–9.
Norman of Morvilliers (3442)
  St Père de Chartres 2.628–9.

Oliver of Jussey, kt (362)
  AA 317, 494; Ch d'A 1.91, 94, 166.
Onulf, sen Robert II of Flanders (4532)
  Flanders 67.
Opizo Mussus (832)
  Caffaro, 'De liberatione', 102.

Osbert Bassus de Insula (834)
    Caffaro, 'De liberatione', 102.
Osbert son of Lambert de Marino (833)
    Caffaro, 'De liberatione', 102.
Otto Altaspata (34)
    AA 559, 568, 591.
Otto, bp Strasbourg (549)
    Bernold of St Blasien 466–7; 'Annalista Saxo' 730; OV 5.28; Zimmern 22.
Otto, cl (5230)
    Genoa (Church) 41.

Pagano of Volta (779)
    Caffaro, 'De liberatione', 118.
Paschale Noscentius Astor (835)
    Caffaro, 'De liberatione', 102.
Payen of Beauvais (94)
    RR 833; Gilo 775; Ch d'A 1.450–1.
Payen Peverel, st-b Robert II of Normandy (466)
    Barnwell 46–7, 54–5.
Payen, sergeant (453)
    BB 5 + note, 56, 79 note; HP 196; OV 5.90; GF 46; PT 86.
Peter, abb Maillezais (392)
    BB 5, 8.
Peter Airoveir, l Trouillas (4602)
    See *Gallia Christiana* 6.979.
Peter Bartholomew, servant of William Peyre of Cunhlat (70)
    Kb 159, 166; GF 59–60, 65; PT 100–1, 107–8, 122,, 131 note; RA 68–137
    passim; FC 235–41; AA 419–20, 452; RC 676–8, 682–3; GN Gesta 196–7,
    203–4, 218; BB 67–8, 74; RR 822–3; BN 502, 507; NF 357; HP 201–2; OV
    5.100–2, 110; WT 324–5, 367; Ch d'A 1.358–9.
Peter Bastard, kt, co-l Mezenc (78)
    St Chaffre du Monastier 88, 139–41.
Peter, bp Glandèves (5382)
    St Victor de Marseille (Guérard) 2.152.
Peter Desiderius, pr, chap Isoard I of Die (242)
    RA 116–17, 131–4, 144.
Peter Fasin (266)
    St Maixent Chron 170.
Peter Fortis (4636)
    St Cyprien de Poitiers 68.
Peter I of Aragon, k Aragon (4752)
    Coleccion diplomatica de Pedro I de Aragon y Navarra 113 note 6. See Ch d'A
Pr 492.
Peter II of Pierre-Buffière, cast Pierre-Buffière (1500)
    Vigeois 68; Aureil 179.

Peter Jordan of Châtillon, l Châtillon (3795)
    Cormery 104.
Peter Lombard, kt (385)
    In Palestine late in 1099, so must have been a crusader. AA 509.
Peter of Alifa, kt (57)
    GF 25–6; PT 60; BB 39; GN Gesta 168; RR 769; HP 185; OV 5.66.
Peter of Castillon, vct Castillon (194)
    GF 26; PT 61, 78, 129; BB 39; GN Gesta 168; HP 193, 210; OV 5.68.
Peter of Dampierre-le-Château, ct Astenois, l Dampierre-le-Château (238)
    AA 299, 301, 310, 317, 343, 365–6, 422, 424; WT 161, 219, 330; Laurence
of Liège 494; Ch d'A 1.129, 404–5.
Peter of Fay, co-l Fay-le-Froid (263)
    St Chaffre du Monastier 88–9; and perhaps Pébrac 17.
Peter of Friac (1490)
    Vigeois 68; Solignac fol. 23v.
Peter of La Garnache (1649)
    Chaise-le-Vicomte 8.
Peter of Mercœur, pr (74)
    Chamalières 54.
Peter of Narbonne, pr, consecrated bp al-Barah during the crusade (441)
    RA 91–2, 97–100, 102, 104–5, 111,120–1, 124, 128, 146, 153; GF 75; PT 117,
131 note; FC 239; BN 507; HP 207; RR 840; BB 83; GN Gesta 210; WT 352–3,
356, 358–9, 364, 369, 411, 422, 424. See also 'Canonici Hebronensis tractatus
de inventione sanctorum patriarcharum Abraham, Ysaac et Jacob' 309.
Peter of 'Picca', pr, chap Bertrand of 'Scabrica' (468 Not located)
    HP 181.
Peter of Roaix (500)
    GF 26; PT 61; BB 39; GN Gesta 168; OV 5.68; Henry of Huntingdon,
'De captione', 376; GC 157, 165.
Peter of Vallières, l La Narce (2219)
    Sauxillanges 884.
Peter Raymond of Hautpoul, l Hautpoul (336)
    GF 26; PT 61, 78; RA 69; BB 39; GN Gesta 168; HP 189, 193; OV 5.68.
Peter Raynouard (488)
    RA 38; PT 44; HP 178.
Peter son of Gisla (463 Not located)
    AA 410; WT 310.
Peter the Hermit (423)
    See H. Hagenmeyer, *Peter der Eremite* (Leipzig, 1879), *passim*.
Peter Tudebode, pr (564)
    PT *passim*, esp. 138
Philip the Grammarian of Montgomery, pr (431)
    OV 4.302; 5.34; WMGR 2.460.
Pisellus (596)
    AA 446.

Pons, co-l Mezenc (3842)
St Chaffre du Monastier 88, 139–41.
Pons II of Fay, co-l Fay-le-Froid (264)
St Chaffre du Monastier 88–9.
Pons of 'Balazun' (Balazuc?), n (63)
RA 35, 75, 107; PT 131; RR 857; Gilo 792; HP 211; WT 365.
Pons of Grillon, chap Raymond Decan (744)
St Victor de Marseille (Guérard) 2.152.
Pons Raynouard, kt (489)
PT 44; RA 38; HP 178.
Pons the Red, kt (5358)
Lyon 2.106.
Primo Embriaco (781)
Caffaro, 'De liberatione' 110–11, 116.

Quino son of Dodo (4950)
St Mihiel 191.

Raimbold Croton, kt (235)
AA 410; RC 688–9; BB 49 note, 71 note, 102 note; Ivo of Chartres 144–5; HP 218–19; OV 5.168; WT 310; Ch d'A 1.71, 208–11, 306, 442, 527–8.
Raimbold II of Orange, ct Orange (450)
AA 317, 422, 463–4; WT 138, 182, 330, 410; Ch d'A 1.441.
Raimondino son of Donnucci (5296)
Pistoia 7.241–4.
Rainald (484)
GF 3–4; PT 34–6; GN Gesta 144–5; RR 732–4; BB 18–19; HP 174–5; OV 5.32, 38.
Rainald II of Burgundy, ct Burgundy and Mâcon (105)
AA 583; Ch d'A 1.440, 480 (erroneous).
Rainald III of Château-Gontier, l Château-Gontier and Segré (3471)
Azé et Le Genéteil 55; CGCA 'Additamenta' 149; St Aubin d'Angers Cart 2.175.
Rainald of Beauvais, kt (93)
AA 316, 332, 363, 422; Gilo 775; Ch d'A Pr 473, 492; WT 217, 330; Ch d'A 1.70, 441, 474.
Rainald of Broyes, kt (158)
AA 277, 281, 286, 288; WT 152.
Rainald of La Chèze (1521)
Aureil 170.
Rainald of the Principate (330)
GF 7; BB 21; HP 176; Monte Cassino 477; OV 5.36; WT 177.
Rainald of Thiviers, bp Périgueux (461)
Limoges 18–19; GV 12.430. See 'Ex fragmento de Petragoricensibus episcopis' 391.

Rainald Porchet, n, kt (479 Not located)
PT 79–81; HP 192, 194; Ch d'A 1.205, 212–17, 221, 224, 229–33, 528.
Rainald, sen Hugh VI of Lusignan (485)
PT 135.
Rainaldo de Rudolpho (838)
Caffaro, 'De liberatione', 118.
Rainer, cl, chap Robert II of Flanders (4535)
Flanders 67.
Ralph Dolis (841 Not located)
BB 65 note.
Ralph I of Gaël, l Gaël (284)
BB 28, 33; AA 422; William of Jumièges 287; OV 2.318; 5.34, 54 , 58.
Ralph of Aalst (24)
Ch d'A 1.86 (called Baldwin of Ghent's brother; actually he was his
uncle). See AA 591, 593.
Ralph of Beaugency, ct Beaugency (91)
St Avit d'Orléans 54; BB 17 + note, 21 note, 47 note, 65 note; OV 5.30;
GAD 101; WT 138; Ch d'A 1.94, 166; probably Anna Comnena 2.226–8,
230 and La Trinité de Vendôme Cart 2.108–9.
Ralph of Escorailles (1659)
St Flour cxxxv, ccvii.
Ralph of Fontaines, kt (278)
AA 410; BB 65 note; RC 662; WT 310.
Ralph of 'Scegonges', n (533 Not located)
AA 579.
Ralph the Red of Pont-Echanfray (476)
Genoa (Church) 41 (Kb 156); Ch d'A Pr 478.
Raymond Bertrand of L'Isle-Jourdain (359)
RA 103.
Raymond Decan, lay dean of the Church of Arles, l Posquières (660)
Gallia Christiana 1, Instrumenta 97; St Sépulcre de Jérusalem 186–7; Poly,
La Provence, 253–4, 268, 330. His chaplain, Pons of Grillon, was already in
the East by January 1103.
Raymond IV of St Gilles, ct Toulouse (524)
See Hill, *Raymond IV de Saint-Gilles*, 21–143.
Raymond of Aguilers, pr, chap Raymond IV of St Gilles (28)
RA *passim*, esp 35, 72, 75–6, 81–2, 89, 107–8, 119, 121, 123–4, 131–3.
Raymond of 'Castellum' (189)
Kb 146.
Raymond of Curemonte, kt (4420)
Tulle 276–7; 416–18.
Raymond of Les Baux (747)
Gallia Christiana 1, Instrumenta 97; St Sépulcre de Jérusalem 187; Poly, *La
Provence*, 221, 267.
Raymond of Turenne, vct Turenne (566)

Tulle 276–7, 416, 418; GF 83–4, 87–8; PT 78, 129, 134–5; BB 91, 97; RR 854, 863–5; 'Notitiae duae Lemovicenses' 351; GN Gesta 216, 223; GV 12.428; HP 193, 206, 210; OV 5.146, 158.

Raymond Pilet, l Alès (471)

GF 73–4, 83–4, 87–9; PT 115, 129, 134–6; RA 122–3, 141–2; AA 316, 422, 452; RR 838, 845, 854, 863–5; BB 81–2, 84–5, 91, 97–8; GN Gesta 209, 216, 223–5; Gilo 778–80, 789, 794–5; HP 206, 210; OV 5.130–2, 138, 146, 158, 160–2; WT 182, 330–1, 361, 398, 411.

Raymond the Chamberlain (1502)

Vigeois 68.

Reinhard III of Toul, ct Toul (239)

GF 69; PT 111; AA 299, 301, 317, 343, 365–6, 398, 422, 424, 442, 494; GN Gesta 206; BB 77, 78 note; RR 831; HP 205; Laurence of Liège 494; OV.5.34, 110, 112; WT 161, 219, 252, 291, 330; Ch d'A 1.129, 404–5, 420–1; and perhaps Ch d'A Pr 478, 494.

Reinhard of Hamersbach, kt (326)

AA 422, 424, 435; WT 330, 344.

Reinhold, n (494)

Die Reichskanzler 3.88–9.

Reinhold of 'Firmamentum', vct 'Firmamentum' (270 Not located)

AA 563

Richard 'Carus Asini', kt (4722)

Marmoutier (Dunois) 141–2.

Richard (of Caiazzo and Alife) son of Count Ranulf (331)

GF 8; BB 21; HP 176; Monte Cassino 477; OV 5.36; WT 177. See Jamison, 'Some notes', 197–8.

Richard of the Principate, ct Salerno (332)

GF 5, 7, 13, 20; PT 54; AA 349–50; GN Gesta 152, 161; RR 744; BB 17, 21, 25; RC 638–9; *Acta SS Novembris* 3.159–60, 164–5, 177–8, 180–1; Anna Comnena 2.215–16, 220; HP 176, 180, 182, 198; Monte Cassino 477, 479; OV 5.36, 50; Henry of Huntingdon, 'De captione', 375; WT 177, 219, 229; Ch d'A Pr 478, 494; Ch d'A 1.136.

Richard son of Fulk the elder of Aunou, kt (498)

'Miracula S. Nicolai' 429.

Richard the Pilgrim (499 Not located)

Ch d'A 1, *passim*, esp. 442–3; LA 626–7. But see Cook, *'Chanson d'Antioche', Chanson de Geste* 23–7.

Riou of Lohéac (383)

Redon 318–21; BB 33; OV 5.58.

Robert I Burgundio of Sablé, l Sablé-sur-Sarthe (2529)

Azé et Le Genéteil 55; Marmoutier (Manceau) 2.86–91, 456–7.

Robert II of Flanders, ct Flanders (302)

See M. M. Knappen, 'Robert II of Flanders in the First Crusade', *The Crusades and Other Historical Essays Presented to Dana C. Munro*, ed. L. J. Paetow (New York, 1928), 79–100.

Robert II of Normandy, d Normandy (449)
  See David, *Robert Curthose*, 89–119.
Robert Marchisus (327)
  BB 33; RC 611.
Robert Michael (414)
  Marmoutier (Vendômois) 254–8 (Marmoutier (Dunois) 139–40).
Robert of Anzi (39)
  Genoa (Church) 41 (Kb.156); GF 7, 20; PT 53; AA 350; BB 21; HP 182;
Monte Cassino 477; OV 5.36; Henry of Huntingdon, 'De captione', 375;
WT 177, 219, 229. See Jamison, 'Some notes', 203.
Robert (of Buonalbergo) son of Gerard, con and st-b Bohemond of Taranto
(504)
  GF 36–7; PT 72; AA 316, 422; GN Gesta 178; BB 47; RC 668; HP 176,
182, 191; Monte Cassino 477, 479; OV 5.78; Henry of Huntingdon, 'De
captione', 376; WT 330; Ch d'A Pr 478, 494; GC 136, 141, 171. See Jamison,
'Some notes', 201–2.
Robert (of Molise) son of Tristan, l Limosano (506)
  GF 7; BB 21; HP 176; Monte Cassino 477; OV 5.36; WT 177. See
Jamison, 'Some notes', 204–5.
Robert of Nevers (416)
  AA 577.
Robert of Paris (455)
  Kb 145; Notre-Dame de Paris 1.373; AA 329–30; Anna Comnena 2.229–
30; 3.18; WT 215.
Robert of Rouen, pr, consecrated bp Lydda during the crusade (513)
  AA 461; GF 87; PT 134; RA 136; FC 277; BB 96, 110 note; GN Gesta
222–3; WT 374, 479.
Robert of Sourdeval, l Torosse? (543)
  Genoa (Church) 41 (Kb 156); GF 7; BB 21; HP 176; Monte Cassino 477;
OV 5.36; WT 177; Ch d'A Pr 494; GC 165, 171. See Jamison, 'Some notes',
207.
Robert son of Godwin, kt (505)
  WMGR 2.310, 449.
Roger, abb, chap Anselm II of Ribemont (508)
  Kb 145.
Roger, cl (510 Not located)
  Consecrated archbishop of Tarsus at Christmas 1099 (RC 704; HP 227)
so must have been on the crusade.
Roger of Barneville (67)
  Kb 159; GF 15–16; RA 66; AA 320, 362–3, 365–6, 381, 407–8, 411; RR
808–9; BB 28; Gilo 769–70; HP 181, 198; OV 5.54, 90, 102; WT 139, 191,
201, 242, 304, 308, 311; Ch d'A 1.330–2, 526. See Jamison, 'Some notes',
207–8.
Roger of Bétheniville (108)
  Kb 159.

Roger of Lille, cast Lille (509)
   Flanders 63, 67; Kb 159.
Roger of Mirepoix, l Mirepoix (4606)
   Carcassonne 4.78 (HGL 5.778–9).
Roger of Rozoy (517)
   AA 358–9; Ch d'A 1.70, 153, 162, 442.
Rossello (4594)
   Roussillon 110–11.
Rothold, kt (512 Not located)
   In Palestine late in 1099 so must have been a crusader. AA 509.
Rotrou of Perche, ct Perche, ct Mortagne (460)
   Nogent-le-Rotrou 36–9, 165; OV 5.34; 6.394; WT 138, 191, 330, 632; Ch
   d'A 1.70, 114, 160, 166, 194, 199, 244, 307, 441. See La Trappe 579.
Rudolf, ct (of Sarrewerden?) (348)
   AA 316, 332. See Zimmern 23, 29.
Ruthard son of Godfrey (520 Not located)
   AA 316, 332, 442; WT 330.

Sancho Iniguez of Cinnito (4739)
   Leire 230; Huesca 1.148–50.
Sannardus, pr, chap Robert II of Flanders (536)
   'Narratio quomodo relliquiae martyris Georgii' 251.
Saswalo of Phalempin (649)
   Flanders 64.
Sichard, kt (541 Not located)
   PT 129; HP 210.
Sigemar of Mechelen (396)
   AA 413; WT 317.
Simon (413)
   Molesme 2.229.
Simon, chap? Raymond IV of St Gilles (542 Not located)
   RA 89.
Simon of Ludron (384)
   Redon 318.
Simon of Poissy (472)
   1096: OV 5.28
   1101: OV 5.346.
Stabelo, chamberlain of Godfrey of Bouillon (546)
   AA 300, 481–2.
Stephen Bonin, l Ars (131)
   St Vincent de Mâcon 315. (This could possibly refer to the crusade of
1120.)
Stephen I of Burgundy, ct Burgundy and Mâcon (106)
   AA 563, 565, 568–9, 573, 582–3, 591, 593–4; FC 430, 438, 443; GN Gesta
244; BN 532–4; Henry of Breitenau 205; OV 5.324.

Stephen I of Neublans, cast Neublans (444)
    Cluny 5.87–91.
Stephen of Aumale, ct Aumale (31)
    AA 316; RC 642; WT 138, 191, 330; Ch d'A 1.70, 171, 441.
Stephen of Blois, ct Blois and Chartres (126)
    1096 and 1101: See J. A. Brundage, 'An Errant Crusader: Stephen of
Blois', *Traditio* 16 (1960), 380–95.
Stephen of Lioriac (76)
    Chamalières 54.
Stephen of Valence, pr (569)
    PT 98–100, 110, 112; GF 57–8; RA 72–4, 118–19, 127–8; FC 245–7; RR
821–2; BB 66; GN Gesta 195; BN 502; HP 201.
Stephen son of Richilda (547 Not located)
    OV 5.326.
Sven of Denmark (241)
    AA 376–7; 'Annalista Saxo' 730 (with two bishops).

Tancred Marchisus (328)
    See R. L. Nicholson, *Tancred* (Chicago, 1940).
Thibald of Ploasme (652)
    Brittany (Morice) 1.490.
Thiemo, archbp Salzburg (535)
    Ekk H 32; Henry of Breitenau *passim*; 'Passio prior Beati Thiemonis'
passim; 'Passio altera Beati Thiemonis' *passim*; 'Annales Mellicenses' 500;
'Vita Chunradi archiepiscopi Salisburgensis' 64–5, 67; 'Genealogia Wel-
forum' 734; 'Annales Reicherspergenses' 450; 'Casus monasterii Petrihu-
sensis' 656; Zimmern 22.
Thomas of Marle, l Marle and La Fère (233)
    AA 293–5, 315, 332, 422, 464, 468; RR 833; Gilo 775; WT 139, 156, 217,
330, 410; Ch d'A 1.69, 94, 155–6, 160, 171, 307, 441, 450-1, 526.
Turonicus of St Martin, kt (525)
    BB 65 note.

Udelard of Wissant, n, kt (597)
    AA 358.
Ulric Bucel, kt (3850)
    La Trinité de Vendôme Cart 2.157–8, 177.
Ulrich, bp Passau (458)
    'Probationes ad tabulam chronologicam' 41, 76.

Walbert of Laon, cast Laon (369)
    AA 563, 568–9. See Ch d'A 2.172.
Walbricus, kt (588 Not located)
    AA 410.
Walker of Chappes, l? Chappes (204)
    AA 316.

Walo II of Chaumont-en-Vexin, con King Philip I of France (214)
   Kb 159; AA 316, 332, 363, 422; GN Gesta 252; RR 795–6, 798; Gilo 750–1; WT 139, 217, 330; Ch d'A Pr 492; Ch d'A 1.70, 441.
Walo of Lille (381)
   AA 322; WT 203.
Walter II of Poissy, l Boissy-sans-Avoir (473)
   OV 5.28, 30.
Walter of Berga (99 Not located)
   AA 593.
Walter of Breteuil (154)
   AA 278, 281, 286, 288.
Walter of Couches, bp Chalon-sur-Saône (5499)
   Hugh of Flavigny 487.
Walter of St-Valéry, adv St Valéry-sur-Somme, vct Domart-en-Ponthieu (532)
   AA 316, 382, 422, 424; BB 33; OV 5.34, 58; WT 330; Ch d'A Pr 473; Ch d'A 1.70, 85, 152, 161, 401, 441.
Walter of 'Verra', kt (578 Not located)
   AA 459; WT 372.
Walter of Verveis (580 Not located)
   AA 317.
Walter Sansavoir of Poissy, kt (474)
   AA 274–6, 283, 286, 288; GF 4; PT 36; FC 159; RR 735; BB 20; GN Gesta 145–6; Fulk IV of Anjou 346; HP 175; OV 5.28, 38; Fulco, 'Historia gestorum viae nostri temporis Jerosolymitanae' 704; WT 103, 140–3, 149, 152.
Walter son of Walter (5332)
   Dinant 1.13–14.
Welf IV of Bavaria, d Bavaria (82)
   Ekk H 29, 32; AA 579–83; 'Annales Mellicenses' 500; 'Historia Welforum' 462; 'Annales Augustani' 135; 'Genealogia Welforum' 734; 'Annales Weingartenses Welfici' 308; 'Passio altera Beati Thiemonis' 217.
Welf, kt (590)
   AA 346, 349, 362; WT 224.
Wicher the German, ministerialis of Fulda (592)
   BB 47 note, 50 note, 92 note; RR 867–8; Gilo 798; Ch d'A Pr 489–90; Ch d'A 1.62, 71, 180, 200, 233, 262, 316, 427–8, 442, 446, 449, 452–3; Metellus of Tegernsee, *Expeditio Ierosolimitana*, 125–8; John of Würzburg, 'Descriptio Terrae Sanctae', 154; Neumoustier 811.
William Amanieu II of Bezaume, vct Bezaume and Bezanne, l Albret (387)
   BB 17; WT 139, 182, 331.
William, bp Pavia (459)
   Ekk H 28.
William Bonofilius, kt (132)
   RA 121.

W(illiam) Boterat of Flée (5249)
   Brittany (Morice) 1.491.
William Botinus, kt (182 Not located)
   PT 129; HP 210.
William Caputmalei, consul of Genoa (5497)
   Caffaro, 'Annales Ianuenses', 1.11.
William, co-l Mezenc (3840)
   St Chaffre du Monastier 88, 139–41.
William de Bono Seniore (851)
   Caffaro, 'De liberatione', 102.
William Ermingareus (254)
   HP 209.
William Hugh of Monteil (376)
   RA 42, 128, 130, 144.
William I Embriaco (251)
   RA 146–7; Caffaro, 'De liberatione', 110–11, 116; WT 400.
William I of Sabran, l Sabran (521)
   GF 88; PT 78, 135; RA 141; BB 98; RR 865; HP 193; OV 5.160; WT 398,
411; and probably Nîmes 293–4.
William II of Nevers, ct Nevers (417)
   Molesme 2.42; AA 574–8, 582; Ch d'A 1.70, 166 (erroneous).
William III of Forez, ct Forez and Lyon (279)
   Forez I. n I, p. I; AA 315, 321–2; WT 138, 182, 203; Ch d'A 1.70.
William IX of Aquitaine, d Aquitaine (42)
   See J. L. Cate, 'A Gay Crusader', *Byzantion* 16 (1942–3), 503–26.
William Jordan of Cerdagne, ct Cerdagne (196)
   Papsturkunden in ... Katalonien 2.287–8; Ch d'A Pr 476.
William Maluspuer, kt (397)
   RA 121.
William Marchisus (329)
   GF 5, 21; PT 38, 55; AA 330; RC 611, 623–5; RR 742; BB 21, 33, 35; GN
Gesta 152, 162; HP 176, 183; Monte Cassino 480; OV 5.36, 62; WT 215;
Ch d'A 1.117–20.
William of Apremont (1651)
   Chaise-le-Vicomte 8.
William of Baffie, bp Clermont (62)
   AA 581.
William of Bayeux (86)
   BB 33; OV 5.58.
William of 'Bernella' or 'Archis', kt (48 Not located)
   GF 56 note, 63 note; PT 97; HP 200.
William (of Bohemia) (5500)
   Gilo 775; RR 831.
William of Ferrières (268)
   BB 33; OV 5.58.

William of Grandmesnil (314)
   Kb 166; GF 56–7; PT 97; RA 74; AA 414–15, 417; GN Gesta 194; BB 64; RC 662; HP 200; OV 5.98; WT 312, 319, 321, 323; Ch d'A 1.139–40.
William of Le Breuil (1543)
   Vigeois 64.
William of Les Murs (3912)
   Aureil 203.
William of Le Vast (572)
   'Depart d'un seigneur normand' 28–9.
William of Montfort-l'Amaury, bp Paris (456)
   Paris 1.153–4; GN Gesta 243.
William of 'Nonanta', st-b William II of Nevers (415)
   AA 577.
William of Orange, bp Orange (451)
   Kb 176; GF 80; PT 125; RA 46, 75–6, 97, 132, 152; RR 850; BB 76 note, 86; Gilo 785; HP 209; OV 5.140; Fulco 700, 702; WT 137–8, 182, 220, 355, 422.
William of Poissy (475)
   1096: OV 5.28.
   1101: OV 5.346.
William of the Camera (4647)
   Nouaillé 292–3.
William Peyre of Cunhlat, l Cunhlat (236)
   RA 71, 105; WT 358.
William Pichard, n, kt (470)
   GF 85; PT 131; RR 857; BB 93; Gilo 792; HP 211; OV 5.150.
William son of Richard (593 Not located)
   PT 97; HP 200.
William the Carpenter of Melun, vct Melun (407)
   GF 33–4; PT 68–9; AA 294–5, 305, 414–15, 417; BB 43–4; GN Gesta 173–5; RR 781–2; RC 650; HP 188–9; OV 5.30, 74; WT 156, 168, 312; Ch d'A 1.69, 515, 526.
William V of Montpellier, ct Montpellier (436)
   Montpellier 214; GF 26, 78; PT 61 note, 78, 123; AA 316, 422, 447; BB 39, 85; RR 847; GN Gesta 168, 213; Gilo 782; HP 193, 208; OV 5.68, 138; Henry of Huntingdon, 'De captione', 378; WT 139, 182, 331, 353; Ch d'A 1.477.
William VI of Auvergne, ct Auvergne, Clermont and Velay (2641)
   St Victor de Marseille (Guérard) 1.151–2.
Wolfker of Kuffern, n (364)
   Göttweig 194–6.

Probable

Achard of Born (3933)
   St Jean d'Angély 30.153–4.

Achard of Bully (3747)
  Savigny 1.478.
Adam I of Béthune, cast Béthune (2078)
  'Les Lignages d'Outremer' 463. See Warlop, *The Flemish Nobility*, table
21.
Adhémar Chatard (1474)
  Aureil 52.
Ado of Quierzy (482)
  Active in the East in 1102. AA 593.
Aimery (4803)
  Noyers 271.
Aimery Bislingueas (115)
  St Maixent Chartes 1.215–16.
Aimery I Durnais (1503)
  Uzerche 314.
Aimery II Durnais (1505)
  Uzerche 314.
Aimery of 'Bullium' (5001)
  Talmont 197.
Aimery of Pont-roy (3897)
  Uzerche 440; Aureil 85.
Airald Bardo (3949)
  St Jean d'Angély 33.83.
Aldo, bp Piacenza (467)
  'Actes constatant la participation des Plaisançais' 398–401.
Andrew Raina (4652)
  Domène 91.
Anfredus, pr (667 Not located)
  Already settled, with property in Jerusalem, during the rule of Godfrey of
Bouillon. Cart Hosp 1.21.
Anonymous, almoner of Tournemire (1663)
  St Flour ccvii.
Anonymous father of Mainente Arcicoco (609)
  'Actes constatant la participation des Plaisançais' 400.
Archimbaud Chauderon (286 Not located)
  Ch d'A Pr 491.
Arnold II of Vierzon, cast Vierzon (583)
  Ch d'A Pr 473.
Astanove II of Fézensac, ct Fézensac (269)
  Auch 57–8.
Autran of Agoult, kt (60)
  Apt 248–9. See Poly, *La Provence*, 267.

Berengar (98 Not located)
  Cluny 5.152.

Berengar Raymond II of Barcelona, ct Barcelona (2264)

The version of his death, apparently on crusade, in *Gesta comitum Barcinonensium* 7, 37 may be confirmed by the references to him in Ch d'A Pr 476, 492.

Bernard Durnais (1504)
    Uzerche 314.
Bernard Morel (438)
    Marcigny 164–5.
Bernard of St Amand (3867)
    Uzerche 195.
Bruno of Ré (3951)
    St Jean d'Angély 33. 78–9.
Burchard of Marmande (4795)
    Noyers 269–70.

Chatard (209)
    Savigny 1.457–8.
Constantius of Diénay (4560)
    Bèze Chron 392.

Drogo of Chaumont-en-Vexin, l Trie-Château (213)
    St Martin de Pontoise 21.
Durand Cheuvre (215)
    St André-le-Bas de Vienne 281.

Engelelmus of St Savin (4827)
    Noyers 275–6.
Engilbert (3761)
    St Maixent Chartes 16.266.
Eudes Betevin (4716)
    Marmoutier (Dunois) 123.
Eudes of Vert-le-Grand (3824)
    Longpont 189–90.
Eustace I Garnier (293)
    'Versus de viris illustribus' 540.

Frederick of Zimmern, co-l Herrenzimmern (604)
    Zimmern 24–36.
Fulcher of Brousse (3908)
    Aureil 199–200.
Fulcher of Faverges (262)
    Grenoble 165–6.
Fulk of Pontoise, vicar of Pontoise (3355)
    St Martin de Pontoise 37.

Gaucher I of Châtillon-sur-Marne, cast Châtillon-sur-Marne (212)
AA 574.
Geoffrey (296 Not located)
Godfrey of Bouillon's chamberlain in the summer of 1100. AA 526.
Geoffrey II of Clervaux, l Clervaux (219)
Chronique de Parcé 10.
Geoffrey of St Savin (4826)
Noyers 275–6.
Gerald (298)
St Victor de Marseille (Guérard) 2.568–9.
Gerald of Bériu, pr (1529)
Aureil 114.
Gerald of St Junien-la-Bregère (1527)
Aureil 114–15
Gerald Pincre (1531)
Aureil 114.
Guy III of Lastours, l Lastours (1472)
GV 12.422.
Guy Le Duc (160)
St Vincent du Mans 1.384.
Guy of 'Insula Bollini', kt (4558)
Bèze Chron 392.
Guy of Pers-en-Gâtinais (5400)
Néronville 310.
Guy Pinellus (3812)
Longpont 121.

Helias of Cray, l Cray (606)
Cluny 4.254.
Helias of Malemort (3873)
Uzerche 287.
Herbert Vigers (3865)
Uzerche 171. He could have been on any crusade between 1096 and 1147.
Hervey son of Arnold (4783)
Notre-Dame de Chartres 3.83 (for date, see 1.99); Sens 2.10.
Hugh II of Usson-en-Forez, l Usson-en-Forez (2224)
Sauxillanges 1045.
Hugh of Bully (3748)
Savigny 1.478.
Hugh of Equevilley, kt (4559)
Bèze Chron 392.
Hugh of Rougemont (3663)
Molesme 2.217–18.
Humbald the White of Hubans (5032)
La Charité-sur-Loire 88.

Humbert of Le Dognon (1532)
    Aureil 113–14.

Itier of La Rivière (1528)
    Uzerche 316.
Itier of La Vue (1538)
    Aureil 170.

John of Draché (4788)
    Noyers 262.
John, pr (3940)
    St Jean d'Angély 30.260–1.
Josbert Cabrun (4812)
    Noyers 273–4.
Joscelin, provost Chartres cathedral (5360)
    Sens 2.18.

Lantelmus, gonfalonier (adv) of Piacenza cathedral (626)
    'Actes constatant la participation des Plaisançais 400–1, and see 396.
Leodegar, can Chartres (4787)
    Notre-Dame de Chartres 3.132; Sens 2.15.
Leteric of Châtillon, l Châtillon (5039)
    La Charité-sur-Loire 104.

Matthew (403 Not located)
    Godfrey of Bouillon's seneschal in the summer of 1100. AA 526.
Miles of Clermont, kt (224)
    A member of Godfrey of Bouillon's household in the first half of 1100.
AA 522.

Otto, abb Ilsenburg (5510)
    Theodore, 'Annales Palidenses', 72; 'Annales Rosenveldenses' 102.

Payen of Mondoubleau (301)
    St Vincent du Mans 1.384.
Peter, bp Anagni (36)
    Acta SS Augusti 1.237.
Peter Gaubert (1512)
    Aureil 192.
Peter of Coudes, cl (2223)
    Sauxillanges 971.
Peter of La Vue (587)
    Aureil 21, 193, 199.
Peter Robert of Champagne (4655)
    Domene 248.

Philip of Briouze (4355)
St Florent-lès-Saumur (Normandes) 688–9.
Pons (299)
St Victor de Marseille (Guérard) 2.568–9.

Raimbert of Chevanville (195)
Longpont 109–10.
Rainald Superbus (4792)
Noyers 268–9.
Ralph of Montpinçon, kt (437)
A member of Godfrey of Bouillon's household in the summer of 1100.
AA 531.
Ralph of 'Monzon', kt (409 Not located)
A member of Godfrey of Bouillon's household in the summer of 1100.
AA 526, 531.
Ramnulf of 'Tuinac' (3941)
St Jean d'Angély 30.384–5.
Raymond (303)
St Victor de Marseille (Guérard) 2.568–9.
Raymond Eic, cl (3720)
Lézat 1.189.
Raymond of Gensac (2658)
St Pierre de la Réole 142–3.
Richard, abb St Victor de Marseille, cardinal (755)
St Victor de Marseille (Guérard) 2.151.
Richard of Chaumont-en-Vexin (811)
Ch d'A 1.35, 39–40, 44, 46, 48–50, 52, 523–4.; GC 15.
Rigaud IV of Tournemire, l Tournemire (1662)
St Flour ccvii.
Robert, vicar (581)
St Vincent du Mans 1.301, and see 291, 306–7.
Rostagn Dalmace (4529)
Montpellier 545, 550–1; and see 557.

Simon son of Herbert (769)
Ch d'A 1.70, 160, 164. Is he the 'Symon, ducis filius' of RRH no 59? See
also RRH nos 52, 68a, 76b, 79.
Stephen Adrachapel (3830 Not located)
Longpont 250.
Stephen of Vitry-sur-Seine, kt (3828)
Longpont 250.
Stephen Walter (3870)
Uzerche 242.

Walter, cl (5049)
St Jean d'Angély 30.260–1.

William Arnold of Nerpoy, l Luppé (4556)
  Conques 368; and probably St Mont 121–2.
William Miscemalum (3926)
  St Jean d'Angély 30.113–14.
William of Forz (3954)
  St Jean d'Angély 33.110.
William of Les Moulières (1530)
  Aureil 113–14.
William of Percy, l Topcliffe and Spofforth (648)
  Whitby 1.2. See AA 701.
William Peter (3948)
  St Jean d'Angély 30.388.
Winrich of Flanders (273)
  Godfrey of Bouillon's butler in the first half of 1100. AA 522, 526.

Possible

Adhémar III of Limoges, vct Limoges (2272)
  Ch d'A 1.71. See Bull, *Knightly Piety*, 252–3.
Aimery Garaton (793)
  Ch d'A 1.70.
Alard of Clisson (225)
  Ch d'A Pr 491.
Albert of St Quentin (529)
  Ch d'A Pr 473.
Albert of Zimmern, co-l Herrenzimmern (602)
  Zimmern 24–6, 29, 31.
Aliis of Veurne (794)
  Ch d'A 1.156.
Andrew of Clermont (795)
  Ch d'A 1.70.
Angerius son of Robert (37)
  St Vincent du Mans 1.87.
Anonymous, d 'Bonberc'? (130)
  Ch d'A Pr 476.
Anonymous Gaubert (1511)
  Aureil 192.
Anonymous, l St Thierry? (530)
  Ch d'A Pr 474 (Is this meant to be Ebles of Roucy?).
Ansellus of 'Valbetons' (798)
  Ch d'A 1.526.
Anselm of Chantemesle (118)
  Acta SS Aprilis 3.825.
Anselm Parented (671)
  See above p. 102 note 139.

Antelme of Avignon (800)
    Ch d'A 1.199.
Arnald the Lorrainer (53)
    Ch d'A 1.441.
Arnold of Beauvais (801)
    Ch d'A 1.35, 40.

Baldwin of Beauvais (802)
    Ch d'A 1.35, 39–40, 47–8, 50, 52, 523.
Baldwin Tauns, kt (679)
    In the East by the summer of 1100. AA 530.
Bernard L'Etranger (378)
    In Cilicia in 1101. AA 581–2.
Bertrand of Prévenchières, bp Lodève (643)
    HGL 3.480.
Bracas of Valpin (570)
    Ch d'A Pr 494.

Charles the Good of Flanders (5215)
    Walter of Thérouanne 540.
Cherfron the German (647)
    Ch d'A 1.71.
Conrad of Zimmern, co-l Herrenzimmern (603)
    Zimmern 23–5, 29, 31.

Daniel (5496)
    Ch d'A 1.81.
Dodo Donat (248)
    Auch 65.
Doon the Young of Montbéliard (424)
    Ch d'A Pr 492.
Drogo (le Frison?) (371)
    Ch d'A Pr 476.

Ebles of 'Torviars' (1550)
    Ch d'A Pr 491.
Erkenbald (700)
    Active in the East in 1101. AA 549.
Eudes of Montfaucon (430)
    Ch d'A Pr 491.
Eudes of Port-Mort (122)
    Acta SS Aprilis 3.825.
Eudes the Bastard (656)
    See St Vincent du Mans 1.191 note 1.

Eudes the Breton (807)
  Ch d'A 1.489.
Eudon of St-Valéry (804)
  Ch d'A 1.70, 156
Eürvin of Creil (808)
  Ch d'A 1.377–9.
Everard (3571)
  St Vincent du Mans 1.292 (in which witnessed document of *c*.1097 as a *Jerosolimitanus*).

Faucon of Vierzon (584)
  Ch d'A Pr 492.
Fulcher of Alencon (618)
  Ch d'A 1.307, 371, 442.
Fulcher of 'Coversana' (5501)
  Ch d'A Pr 474.
Fulcher of Melan, kt (628)
  Ch d'A 1.39–40, 50, 52, 523.
Fulcher the Orphan (321)
  Ch d'A 1.304–5, 442.
Fulk of Clermont (619)
  Ch d'A 1.526.

Gandier (288)
  Ch d'A Pr 494.
Garin son of Milson of 'Verzels' (Vercel-Villedieu?) (576)
  Ch d'A Pr 492.
Gaston of Béziers (620)
  WT 410; a possible reduplication of Gaston IV of Béarn's name.
Geoffrey (655)
  See St Vincent du Mans 1.191 note 1.
Geoffrey of Montgin (812)
  GC 136. See Ch d'A 2.192.
Geoffrey son of Droon (297)
  Ch d'A Pr 491.
Gerald of 'Ponti' (477)
  Ch d'A Pr 473.
Gerard, cl (305)
  Abbot of Mt Thabor from 1101. See Mayer, *Bistümer*, 49.
Gerard of Donjon (637)
  Ch d'A 1.442.
Gerard of St Gilles (813)
  Ch d'A 1.137 note.
Gilbert of Entraigues (253)
  Ch d'A Pr 492.

Gilbert of Rheims (621)
   Ch d'A 1.160.
Godfrey Parented (1671)
   See above p. 102 note 139.
Godschalk (714)
   Ch d'A 1.70, 160, 164.
Gontier of Aire, squire of Robert II of Flanders (814)
   Ch d'A 1.173–5, 307.
Gouffier of Bouillon (136)
   Ch d'A Pr 491.
Guarin of Clisson (226)
   Ch d'A Pr 491.
Guiraut of Hirson (346)
   Ch d'A Pr 491.
Gunter, kt (323)
   In Jerusalem in the summer of 1100. AA 526.
Guy of Château-Landon (210)
   Ch d'A Pr 491.
Guy of Chaumont-en-Vexin (119)
   Acta SS Aprilis 3.825.
Guy of Morlay (4494)
   Beaurain 326; and see 257–8.

Hamelin (3572)
   St Vincent du Mans 1.422. A *Jerosolimitanus*.
Heliodore of Blaru (116)
   Acta SS Aprilis 3.825.
Henry of Préaux (123)
   Acta SS Aprilis 3.825.
Herbert (leader of the Basques?) (722)
   Ch d'A 1.70,160, 164.
Hubert of Cergy (200)
   St Martin de Pontoise 62.
Hugh (654)
   See St Vincent du Mans 1.191 note 1.
Hugh Dalmace of Semur, l Dyo and Couzon? (240)
   Ch d'A Pr 489 (count Dalmatz).
Hugh of Dijon (623)
   Ch d'A 1.441.
Hugh of Les Baux (818)
   GC 127.
Hugh of Liège (819)
   Ch d'A 1.86 note.
Hugh of Morentin (439)
   Ch d'A Pr 473.

Hugh of Robecq (501)
  'Versus de viris illustribus' 540.
Hugh of Salagnac, l Salagnac (1535)
  Uzerche 328.

Ingelbald (356)
  St Vincent du Mans 1.69.
Isnard of La Garenne (3513)
  St Père de Chartres 2.516.

John (92)
  Ch d'A Pr 473.
John of 'Alis' (822)
  Ch d'A 1.35, 39–40, 50, 52.
John of Bréval (117)
  Acta SS Aprilis 3.825.
Josbert (5381)
  La Trinité de Vendôme Cart 2.109.
Joscelin, cl (825)
  Ch d'A 1.492.

Leofranc Donat (249)
  Auch 65.
Leomer Musart (440)
  St Vincent du Mans 1.222–3.
Lithard of Cambrai (186)
  Active in the East in 1102, so perhaps came in 1099. AA 593, 621–2;
BN 534. See RRH no. 134.

Mahuis of Clermont (830)
  Ch d'A 1.441.
Mainard (3570)
  St Vincent du Mans 1.259, 267. A *Jerosolimitanus*.
Martin, ct (400)
  Ch d'A Pr 474.
Mer son of Garin (410)
  Ch d'A Pr 473.
Miles (3849)
  La Trinité de Vendôme Cart 2.109.
Morellus, cl (734)
  Secretarius in the household of Daimbert, the patriarch of Jerusalem, in
the summer of 1100. AA 524, 538.

Oliver of Venise (831)
  Ch d'A 1.71.

Payen of 'Camelli' (636)
   Ch d'A 1.442.
Payen of Chevré (216)
   St Vincent du Mans 1.423.
Peter of Courtigny (120)
   Acta SS Aprilis 3.825.
Peter of Vihiers (586)
   Angers 140–1.
Peter Postels (809)
   Ch d'A 1.377–8.
Philip of Bouillon (138)
   In the East by 1102. AA 593.

Raimbold of Commercy (837)
   Ch d'A 1.166.
Rainald (486)
   Ch d'A Pr 494.
Rainald of Nivelles (839)
   Ch d'A 1.160.
Rainer (3591)
   St Aubin d'Angers Cart 2.175. A *Jerosolimitanus*.
Ralph (3573)
   St Vincent du Mans 1.422. A *Jerosolimitanus*.
Ralph of Simas (490)
   Ch d'A Pr 491.
Raymond William (595)
   Aniane 358–9.
Richard of Harcourt (121)
   Acta SS Aprilis 3.825.
Richard of Mâcon (391)
   Ch d'A Pr 492.
Richard of Pavia (842)
   Ch d'A 1.50.
Richard of 'Valpin' (571)
   Ch d'A Pr 478.
Richard of Verdun (751)
   Ch d'A 1.166. Is he the same man as the settler Reinhard of Verdun
referred to in AA 623?
Robert of 'Durenzan' (250)
   Ch d'A Pr 491.
Roger the Emperor (843)
   Ch d'A 1.69, 84, 160.

Seguin of Mauléon (404)
   Ch d'A Pr 491.

Seguin of Nevers (4915)
St Etienne de Nevers 79–80.
Stephen Gasteuil (3780)
St Amant-de-Boixe 111. He could have been on the crusade of 1107 or that of 1120.
Symeon (847)
Ch d'A 1.492.

Telin?, ct (551)
Ch d'A Pr 473.

Vassalis of Roaix (836)
GC 155–7.

Waleran of Bavaria (848)
Ch d'A 1.71.
Walter (589)
Ch d'A Pr 478.
Walter (849)
Ch d'A 1.81.
Walter (3705)
Redon 267, 320, 330. A *Jerosolimitanus*.
Walter, kt (776)
In the East by the summer of 1100. AA 530.
William (788)
Active in the East in 1101. AA 549.
William of Beauvais (95)
Ch d'A 1.427, 442.
William of Bréteau, l Dangeul (152)
See St Vincent du Mans 1.191 note 1; and perhaps the charter in *ibid.* 419–20.
William of Senlis (853)
Ch d'A 1.438.

Zaizolfus, chap Gerard of Schaffhausen (629)
Berthold of Zwiefalten 108. But this was at a later date in the East.

THE PLANNED 'CRUSADE' OF THE EMPEROR HENRY IV, 1103

Henry IV of Germany, western e (1240)
Ekk C 224–5; *Annales Hildesheimenses* 50–1; Otto of Freising 318.

THE CRUSADE OF BOHEMOND OF ANTIOCH-TARANTO, 1107–8

Certainties, or nearly so

Aimery Andrea (4823)
  Noyers 275.
Anonyma of Lèves, w Ralph the Red of Pont-Echanfray (1170)
  OV 6.104.
Arni Fjöruskeiv (5486)
  Riant, *Expéditions*, 178–9.
Aslak Hani (5485)
  Riant, *Expéditions*, 178–9.

Bohemond of Taranto, ruler of Antioch (334)
  Yewdale, *Bohemond*, 106–31.

Gastinellus of Bourgueil (4820)
  Noyers 275.
Geoffrey of 'Mali' (Mailly?) (5502 Not located)
  Anna Comnena 3.139.
Gerard, archbp York (5489)
  Quadripartitus 161–2.
Godfrey Brisard (4817)
  Noyers 274–5.
Godric of Finchale, hermit (715)
  Reginald of Durham 52–8. The date of Godric's second assumption of the cross must be before 1110, since he spent sixty years at Finchale before his death in 1170. Reginald of Durham 331.
Goldinellus of Curzay (4821)
  Noyers 275.
Guy (816 Not located)
  AA 651.
Guy of Hauteville (335)
  OV 6.102–4; Anna Comnena 3.102, 104, 107, 120; 'Secunda pars historiae Iherosolimitanae' 568.

Hamundr Thorvaldsson of Vatnsfjord (5487)
  Riant, *Expéditions*, 178–9.
Hervey son of Durand (4824)
  Noyers 275.
Hugh II of Le Puiset, vct Chartres, l Le Puiset (702)
  Ivo of Chartres 171–4, 176–7; OV 6.100, 104; NF 361; Anna Comnena 3.108; WT 651.
Hugh Sansavoir of Poissy (791)
  OV 6.70.

Humbert son of Ralph (5503 Not located)
    Anna Comnena 3.139.

Joscelin of Lèves (1169)
    St Père de Chartres 2.275.
Josceran of Vitry (1597)
    Cluny 5.202–3.

'Koprisianos' (5504 Not located)
    Anna Comnena 3.102.

Mabel of Roucy, w Hugh II of Le Puiset (886)
    WT 651. See Mayer, 'The Origins', 40.
Maurice Bourdin, bp Coimbra (2099)
    'Qualiter tabula S. Basili continens in se magnam dominici ligni portionem Cluniacum delata fuerit, tempore Pontii abbatis' 296.

Payen, ct (Kontopaganos) (5505 Not located)
    Anna Comnena 3.104–5, 109.
Philip of Montoro (763)
    NF 361.

Ralph 'Licei' (4819)
    Noyers 275.
Ralph of Caen, kt (1657)
    See *RHC Oc* 3.xxxix.
Ralph Rabaste (4818)
    Noyers 275.
Ralph the Red of Pont-Echanfray (476)
    OV 6.70, 100, 104.
Renier Brun (762 Not located)
    NF 361.
Richard (of Le Puiset) (5507)
    Anna Comnena 3.108–9. A brother of a Hugh, who must be Hugh II of Le Puiset. But it is possible that this is Richard of Chaumont-en-Vexin (see above p. 231), a brother of Hugh's brother-in-law who had died on the First Crusade.
Richard of the Principate (332)
    Anna Comnena 3.102, 134, 138.
Robert Dalmace of Collanges, l Collanges (1598)
    Cluny 5.199 (355–6); Marcigny 79–80.
Robert of Maule (790)
    OV 6.70.
Robert of Montfort-sur-Risle, con King Henry I of England (792)
    OV 6.100–4.

Robert of Vipont (759)
    NF 361.

'Sarakenos' (5508 Not located)
    Anna Comnena 3.104–5.
Siger, abb St Pierre au Mont-Blandin (5183)
    'Annales Blandinienses' 27.
Sigurd Jorsalafara, k Norway (845)
    FC 543-8; AA 675; Snorri Sturluson, *Heimskringla*, 688–99; WT 517–19;
Riant, *Expéditions*, 173–215.
Simon of Anet (789)
    OV 6.70, 100.
Simon of Nouâtre (4822)
    Noyers 275.

Walchelin II of Pont-Echanfray (774)
    OV 6.70, 100, 104.
Walter, monk (4816)
    Noyers 274–5.
Walter of Montsoreau (4316)
    Marmoutier (Anjou) 54; Noyers 274–5.
William Claret (850 Not located)
    AA 651; Anna Comnena 3.116.
William of Ghent (5509)
    Anna Comnena 3.138.
William of Normandy, illegitimate son of Robert II of Normandy (785)
    OV 5.282.

Probable

Halldor Skaldri (5488)
    Riant, *Expéditions*, 178–9.

Josbert Alboin (3915)
    Vigeois 61–2.
Peter Rostagn of 'Poncianum' (4554)
    Béziers 149.

Possible

Barisan the Old (2052)
    See above p. 172.

Garcia Livar Castro (4764)
    Leire 301.

Godfrey I of Louvain, ct Louvain, d Lower Lorraine (4552)
   Joannes Molanus, *Historiae Lovanensium libri XIV*, 1.414.

Robert of Matheflon (4318)
   Marmoutier (Anjou) 54.
Roger of Choiseul, l Choiseul (3656)
   Molesme 2.73.

THE 'CRUSADE' OF BERTRAND OF ST GILLES, 1108–9

Ansaldo Corso, n (670)
   Genoa (Church) 43 (Ansald Caput de Burgo); Caffaro, 'De liberatione',
120, 124; WT 508.

Bertrand of St Gilles (690)
   AA 664–9, 671–2, 677–9, 682–3; Caffaro, 'De liberatione', 122–3; WT
507–8; Genoa (Church) 42–3.

Hugh I Embriaco, n (725)
   Caffaro, 'De liberatione', 123–4; WT 508–9.

Ingo de Pedegola (730)
   Genoa (Church) 43.

Oberto Usu de Mar (735)
   Genoa (Church) 43.
Ordelafo Falier, doge of Venice (2199)
   WT 576–81; Martin de Canal 26. See Urkunden Venedig 1.86, 91.

William I Embriaco (251)
   Genoa (Church) 43.

THE CRUSADE OF POPE CALIXTUS II, 1120–4

Certainties, or nearly so

Baldwin of Vern d'Anjou (4340)
   A Le Ronceray d'Angers 215–17.
Bellay II of Montreuil-Bellay (3596)
   Angers 166.

Chalo the Red of Vivonne (4932)
   St Hilaire le Grand de Poitiers (1847) 122, 128–30.
Conrad (III of Germany) (1374)
   Ekk C 262.

Domenico Michiel, doge of Venice (1803)
   Urkunden Venedig 1.84-94; FC 669-72, 693-8; WT 573-9, 601; Martin da Canal 26-36; Andrea Dandolo, *Chronica*, 232; 'Historia ducum Veneticorum' 73-4.

Fulk of Le Plessis-Macé, l Le Plessis-Macé (4335)
   Le Ronceray d'Angers 213-15.
Fulk V of Anjou, ct Anjou (951)
   Marmoutier (Manceau) 2.473; Le Ronceray d'Angers 213-14; St Julien de Tours 104; Angers 246-7; Cart Temp 5; APC 417; WMGR 2.495; Florence of Worcester 2.72; St Florent-lès-Saumur Chron 190; St Aubin d'Angers Chron 32; OV 6.308-10. See St Aubin d'Angers Cart 2.409-10.

Garsias of Le Bignon-du-Maine (3584)
   Marmoutier (Manceau) 2.473.
Geoffrey Fulcard of Loudun (4330)
   Le Ronceray d'Angers 186; Noyers 265-7.
Geoffrey of Le Louet (4333)
   Le Ronceray d'Angers 213.
Godfrey of Ribemont (4155)
   St Martin de Tournai 1.30.
Guy Tortus of Rochefort-sur-Loire, kt (4323)
   Marmoutier (Anjou) 66.

Rainald of Martigné, bp Angers (2266)
   Azé et Le Genéteil 63-4; Angers 246-7; Le Ronceray d'Angers 213-14; St Aubin d'Angers Chron 32.

Walter of Mayenne (3490)
   APC 417-18.
William Venator, huntsman (3486)
   St Julien de Tours 87-8.

Probable

Frederick of Châtillon (3814)
   Longpont 173-4.

Hugh of Ste Maure-de-Touraine, cast Ste Maure-de-Touraine (4843)
   Noyers 332.

Isaac of Veurne, chamberlain of Flanders (2090)
   Witnessed a charter in Jerusalem on 8 April 1124. St Sépulcre de Jérusalem 212.

Landolt, kt (5288)
    Oberalteich 109–11.

R. Gabard (3769)
    Mauléon 14–16.

Stephen I of Neublans, cast Neublans (444)
    St Marcel-lès-Chalon-sur-Saône 45–7.

Possible

Boleslaw III of Poland, d Poland (5192)
    'Annales Poloniae' 589; 'Annales Polonorum' 624–5. The cryptic state-
ments that Boleslaw crossed the sea do not necessarily refer to a crusade.

Guy IV of Vignory, l Vignory (3707)
    St Etienne de Vignory 181.

Hugh of Montmirail (3434)
    St Père de Chartres 2.471. (1101 × 29)
Hugh of St Aubin-du-Désert (3372)
    Tiron 2.23–4.

Pons Palatinus (3750)
    Savigny 1.495.

Rodulf (4939)
    St Marcel-lès-Chalon-sur-Saône 64.
Roger of Bouesse (3637)
    Bourbonnais 177–8.

Two members of the family of Ligonnat (3879–80)
    Uzerche 323.

William Calvus (3751)
    Savigny 1.495.

THE CRUSADE OF KING BALDWIN II, 1129

Certainties, or nearly so

Fulk V of Anjou, ct Anjou (951)
    Le Ronceray d'Angers 68; *Papsturkunden für Kirchen im Heiligen Lande* 142;
Cart Temp 6, 9; CGCA 69–70; GAD 115–16; APC 431; St Aubin d'Angers
Chron 33.

Geoffrey of 'Bello Mortario' (3588)
    St Aubin d'Angers Cart 1.145. (He could be a crusader of either 1139 or
1147.)

Hugh III of Le Puiset, vct Chartres, ct Corbeil (1005)
    Tiron 1.127–8; Suger of St Denis, *Vita*, 171.
Hugh of Chaumont-sur-Loire, l Amboise (175)
    Cart Temp 8–10; Anjou (Chartrou) 370–2; GAD 115–16.

Rainald I of Bar-le-Duc, ct Bar-le-Duc and Monçon (2609)
    Bar 1.44 (St Lambert de Liège 1.58–60).

Thierry of Chièvres (4696)
    Eenaeme 28–9.

William of La Ferté-Vidame (3496)
    St Père de Chartres 2.511–12,610–11. (He could have gone on the crusade
of 1120.)

Probable

Achard son of Leevin (5006)
    Talmont 268.
Albert Fortis of Vitry (5349)
    Burgundy (Pérard) 224.
Alo Albus of L'Isle (4906)
    St Cybard d'Angoulême 93–6.
Andrew of La Haye (3775)
    St Laon de Thouars 44–5.

Berthold of Sperberseck (544)
    Ortlieb of Zwiefalten, 'Chronicon', 89; Berthold of Zwiefalten 108, 119.

Gerard of Roucy (4542)
    Reims (admin) 1.285–7.

Henry Burgundio (1863)
    Cart Hosp 1.78. See Mayer, 'Angevins *versus* Normans', 7.

Robert of Buzançais (3602)
    Angers 258–60.
Walter Tirel III, cast Pontoise, vct Poix (2355)
    OV 5.294; Longpont 167–8.

Possible

Hugh II of Matheflon, l Matheflon (3542)
  Chronigue de Parcé 11.

Matthew Giraud (3605)
  Angers 271–3.

Robert Burgundio, kt (1976)
  See Mayer, 'Angevins *versus* Normans', 7.

APPENDIX II

Pedigrees

Underlined – Crusader, settler in, or visitor to the East: A and B, 1095–1131; C, 1095–1191.

A   COMITAL BURGUNDY

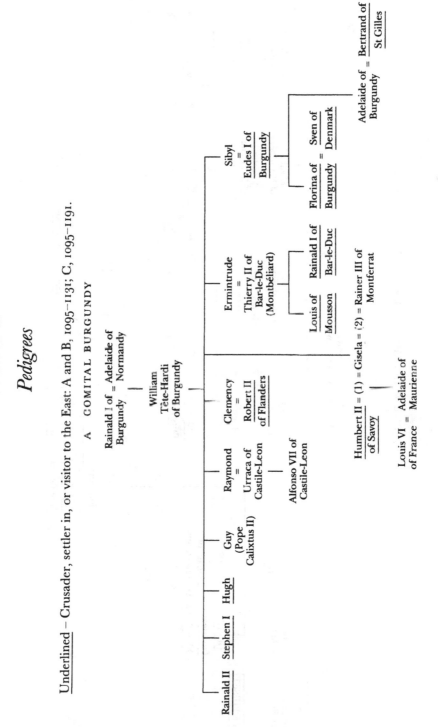

B   THE MONTLHÉRY CLAN

Montlhéry

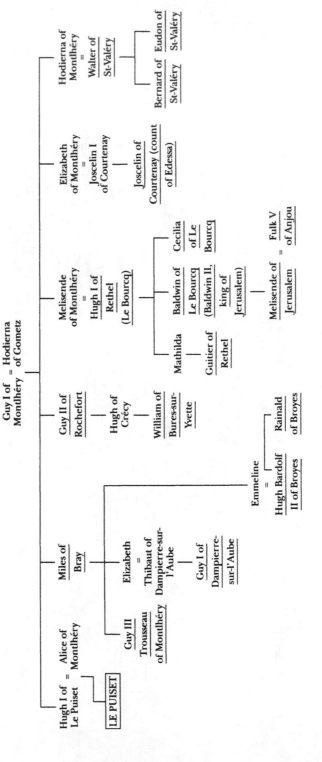

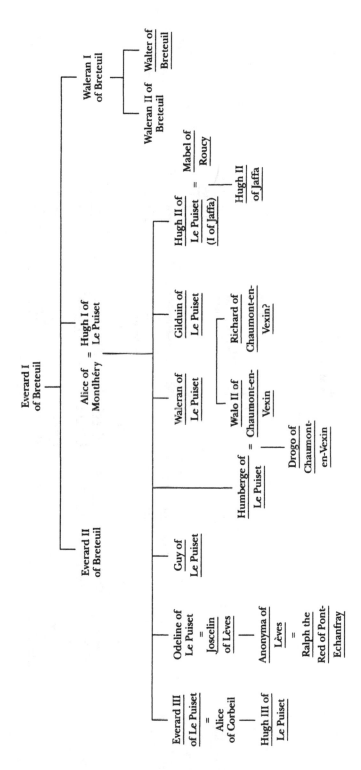

Le Puiset

C SOME DESCENDANTS OF ALMODIS OF LA MARCHE

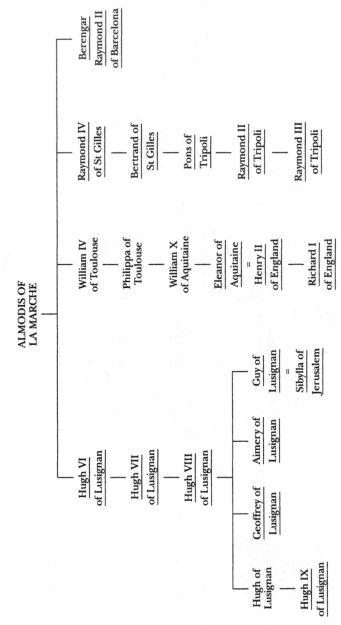

Bibliography of works referred to in the notes and appendix I

PRIMARY SOURCES

(Headed by abbreviations when appropriate)

AA   Albert of Aachen, 'Historia Hierosolymitana', *RHC Oc* 4.

Acta pontificum Romanorum inedita, ed. J. von Pflugk-Harttung, 3 vols. (Tübingen and Stuttgart, 1881–6).

Acta SS   Acta Sanctorum quotquot toto orbe coluntur, ed. Société des Bollandistes, 70 vols. so far (Antwerp, Brussels, Tongerloe, 1643ff).

'Actes constatant la participation des Plaisançais à la Première Croisade', ed. G. Tononi, *AOL* I (1881), 395–401.

Adhémar of Chabannes, *Chronicon*, ed. J. Chavanon (Paris, 1897).

Afflighem   *Cartulaire de l'abbaye d'Afflighem*, ed. E. de Marneffe (*Analectes pour servir a l'histoire ecclésiastique de la Belgique. Sér. 2. Cartulaires*, Louvain, 1894–1901).

Aimé of Monte Cassino, *Storia de'Normanni*, ed. V. de Bartholomaeis (Fonti per la Storia d'Italia 76, Rome, 1935).

Ambroise, *L'Estoire de la Guerre Sainte*, ed. G. Paris (Paris, 1897).

Andrea Dandolo, *Chronica*, ed. E. Pastorello (*RISNS* 12.1, Bologna, 1938)

Angers   *Cartulaire noir de la cathédrale d'Angers*, ed. C. Urseau (Paris, 1908).

The Anglo-Saxon Chronicle, tr. D. Whitelock, D. C. Douglas and S. I. Tucker (London, 1981).

Aniane   *Cartulaires des abbayes d'Aniane et de Gellone 2. Cartulaire d'Aniane*, ed. L. Cassan and E. Meynial (Montpellier, 1900–10).

Anjou (Chartrou)   J. Chartrou, *L'Anjou de 1109 à 1151* (Paris, 1928).

Anjou (Guillot)   O. Guillot, *Le comte d'Anjou et son entourage au XIe siècle*, 2 vols. (Paris, 1972).

Anjou (Halphen)   L. Halphen, *Le comte d'Anjou au XIe siècle* (Paris, 1906).

Anna Comnena, *Alexiade*, ed. and tr. B. Leib, 4 vols. (Paris, 1943–76).

'Annales Admuntenses', *MGHS* 9.

Annales Altahenses maiores, ed. E. L. B. Ab Oefele (*MGHS in usum scholarum*, Hanover, 1891).

'Annales Aquicinctini', *MGHS* 16.

'Annales Augustani', *MGHS* 3.

'Annales Besuenses', *MGHS* 2.

'Annales Blandinienses', *MGHS* 5.

'Annales Cremonenses', *MGHS* 18.

'Annales de Waverleia', ed. H. R. Luard, *Annales monastici* 2 (Rolls Series 36.2, London, 1865).

Annales Hildesheimenses, ed. G. Waitz (*MGHS in usum scholarum*, Hanover, 1878).

'Annales Mellicenses', *MGHS* 9.

'Annales Mellicenses auctarium Garstense', *MGHS* 9.

'Annales Poloniae', *MGHS* 19.

'Annales Polonorum', *MGHS* 19.

'Annales Reicherspergenses', *MGHS* 17.

'Annales Rosenveldenses', *MGHS* 16.

'Annales S. Benigni Divionensis', *MGHS* 5.

'Annales Sancti Disibodi', *MGHS* 17.

'Annales Sancti Rudberti Salisburgenses', *MGHS* 9.

'Annales Weingartenses Welfici', *MGHS* 17.

'Annalista Saxo', *MGHS* 6.

Anonymus Florinensis, 'Brevis Narratio Belli Sacri', *RHC Oc* 5.

Anonymus Haserensis, 'De episcopis Eichstetensibus', *MGHS* 7.

Anselm of Canterbury, 'Epistolae', ed. F. S. Schmitt, *S. Anselmi Cantuariensis archiepiscopi opera omnia* 3–5 (Edinburgh, 1946–51).

Antibes   *Recueil des actes des evêques d'Antibes*, ed. G. Doublet (Monaco and Paris, 1915).

AOL   Archives de l'Orient latin.

APC   *Actus pontificum Cenomannis in urbe degentium*, ed. G. Busson and A. Ledru (*Archives historiques du Maine* 2, Le Mans, 1901).

Apt   *Cartulaire de l'église d'Apt*, ed. N. Didier, H. Dubled and J. Barruol (Paris, 1967).

Auch   *Cartulaires du chapitre de l'église metropolitaine Sainte-Marie d'Auch*, ed. C. Lacave La Plagne Barris (Paris and Auch, 1899).

Aumônerie de St Martial de Limoges   'Premier et second cartulaires de l'Aumônerie de S. Martial', ed. A. Leroux, *Documents historiques bas-latins, provençaux et français concernant principalement La Marche et Le Limousin* 2 (Limoges, 1885).

Aureil   'Cartulaire du prieuré d'Aureil', ed. G. de Senneville, *Bulletin de la société archéologique et historique du Limousin* 48 (1900), 1–289.

Azé and Le Geneteil   *Cartulaire d'Azé et du Geneteil, prieurés de l'abbaye Saint-Nicolas d'Angers*, ed. E. C. du Brossay (*Archives historiques de Maine* 3, Le Mans, 1903).

Bar   *Actes des comtes de Bar*, ed. M. Parisse, 2 vols. (Pré-edition Université de Nancy II. *Actes des princes lorrains*, Nancy, 1972–4).

Bardo, 'Vita Anselmi episcopi Lucensis', *MGHS* 12.

Barnwell *Liber memorandorum ecclesie de Bernewelle*, ed. J. W. Clark (Cambridge, 1907).

BB Baldric of Bourgueil, 'Historia Jerosolimitana', *RHC Oc* 4.

Beaujeu *Cartulaire de l'église collégiale de Notre-Dame de Beaujeu*, ed. M. C. Guigue (Lyons, 1864).

Beaurain 'Essai sur les prieurés de Beaurain et de Maintenay et leur chartes', ed. R. Rodière, *Mémoires de l'académie d'Arras* sér. 2, 34 (1903), 235–390.

Bernard of Clairvaux, 'De laude novae militiae ad milites Templi liber', *Sancti Bernardi Opera*, ed. J. Leclercq *et al.*, 3 (Rome, 1963).

Bernard of Clairvaux, 'Epistolae', *Sancti Bernardi Opera*, ed. J. Leclercq *et al.*, 7–8 (Rome, 1974–7).

Bernold of St Blasien, 'Chronicon', *MGHS* 5.

Berthold, 'Annales', *MGHS* 5.

Berthold of Zwiefalten, 'Chronicon', *MGHS* 10.

Bèze Chron *Chronique de l'abbaye de Saint-Bénigne de Dijon, suivie de la Chronique de Saint-Pierre de Bèze*, ed. F. Bougaud and J. Garnier (*Analecta Divionensia* 9, Dijon, 1875).

Bèze Liber 'Liber memorabilium rerum seu etiam cartarum abbatiae Besensis', ed. L. d'Achéry, *Spicilegium*, 1st edn, 1 (Paris, 1665).

Béziers *Livre noir ou cartulaire du chapitre cathédral de Béziers*, ed. J. Rouquette (Paris and Montpellier, 1918).

Bibliotheca Sebusiana, ed. S. Guichenon (Lyons, 1660).

BN Bartolf of Nangis, 'Gesta Francorum Iherusalem expugnantium', *RHC Oc* 3.

Bonizo of Sutri, 'Liber ad amicum', *MGH Libelli de Lite Imperatorum et Pontificum* 1.

Bourbonnais *Les origines du Bourbonnais. 1. Catalogue des actes*, comp. M. Fazy (Moulins, 1924).

Brittany (ducs) *Recueil des actes inédits des ducs de Bretagne*, ed. A. Lemoyne de La Borderie (Rennes, 1888).

Brittany (Morice) *Mémoires pour servir de preuves à l'histoire ecclésiastique et civile de Bretagne*, ed. P. H. Morice, 3 vols. (Paris, 1742–6).

Bruno of Segni, 'Vita S. Leonis', *PL* 165.

Burgundy (Pérard) E. Pérard, *Recueil de plusieurs pièces curieuses servant à l'histoire de Bourgogne* (Paris, 1664).

Burgundy (Plancher) U. Plancher, *Histoire générale et particulière de Bourgogne*, 4 vols. (Dijon, 1739–81).

Busdorf in Paderborn *Die Urkunden des Stifts Busdorf in Paderborn*, ed. J. Prinz, 2 vols. (*Veröffentlichungen der Historischen Kommission für Westfalen* 37, Paderborn, 1975–84).

Caffaro, 'Annales Ianuenses', ed. L. T. Belgrano, *Annali Genovesi* 1 (*Fonti per la storia d'Italia* 11, Genoa, 1890).

Caffaro, 'De liberatione civitatum orientis', ed. L. T. Belgrano, *Annali Genovesi* 1 (*Fonti per la storia d'Italia* 11, Genoa, 1890).

Calixtus II, *Bullaire*, ed. U. Robert, 2 vols. (Paris, 1891).

'Canonici Hebronensis tractatus de inventione sanctorum patriarcharum Abraham, Ysaac et Jacob', *RHC Oc* 5.

'Cantatorium Sancti Huberti', ed. Baron de Reiffenberg, *Monuments pour servir à l'histoire des provinces de Namur, de Hainault et de Luxembourg* 7 (Brussels, 1844–74).

Carcassonne   *Cartulaire et archives de … diocèse … de Carcassonne*, ed. M. Mahul, 6 vols. (Paris, 1857–72).

Cart Hosp   *Cartulaire général de l'ordre des Hospitaliers de St Jean de Jérusalem*, ed. J. Delaville Le Roulx, 4 vols. (Paris, 1894–1906).

Cart Temp   *Cartulaire général de l'ordre du Temple 1119?–1150*, ed. G. A. M. J. A. d'Albon (Paris, 1913–22).

Cartulaire de la Commanderie de Richerenches de l'ordre de Temple (1136–1214), ed. Marquis de Ripert-Monclar (Paris, 1907).

'Casus monasterii Petrishusensis', *MGHS* 20.

CGCA   'Chronica de gestis consulum Andegavorum', ed. L. Halphen and R. Poupardin, *Chroniques des comtes d'Anjou et des seigneurs d'Amboise* (Paris, 1913).

Chaise-le-Vicomte   'Prioratus de Casa-Vicecomitis', ed. P. Marchegay, *Cartulaires du Bas-Poitou* (La Roche-sur-Yonne, 1877).

Chalon-sur-Saône   C. Perry, *Histoire civile et ecclésiastique ancienne et moderne de la ville et cité de Chalon-sur-Saône* (Chalon-sur-Saône, 1659).

Chamalières   *Cartulaire de Chamalières-sur-Loire en Velay*, ed. A. Chassaing (Paris, 1895).

La Chapelle-Aude   *Fragments du cartulaire de La Chapelle-Aude*, ed. M.-A Chazaud (Moulins, 1860).

La Charité-sur-Loire   *Cartulaire du prieuré de La Charité-sur-Loire (Nièvre)*, ed. R. de Lespinasse (Nevers and Paris, 1887).

Château-du-Loir   *Cartulaire du Château-du-Loir*, ed. E. Vallée, (*Archives historiques du Maine* 6, Le Mans, 1905).

Ch d'A   *La Chanson d'Antioche*, ed. S. Duparc-Quioc, 2 vols. (Paris, 1977-8).

Ch d'A Pr   'Fragment d'une Chanson d'Antioche en provençal', ed. P. Meyer, *AOL* 2 (1884), 473–509.

Christina of Markyate, *Life*, ed. C. H. Talbot (Oxford, 1959).

'Chronica monasterii de Hida juxta Wintoniam', ed. E. Edwards, *Liber monasterii de Hyda* (Rolls Series 45, London, 1866).

Chronicle of the Kings of Man and the Isles, ed. and tr. G. Broderick and B. Stowell (Edinburgh, 1973).

'Chronicon Affligemense', *MGHS* 9.

'Chronicon Brunwylarense', ed. G. Eckertz, *Fontes adhuc inediti rerum Rhenanarum*, 2 (Cologne, 1870).

'Chronicon S. Andreae castri Cameracesii', *MGHS* 7.

'Chronicon Trenorciense', *RHGF* 11.

'Chronicon Vindocinense seu de Aquaria', ed. P. Marchegay and E. Mabille, *Chroniques des églises d'Anjou* (Paris, 1869).

Chronique de Parcé, ed. H. de Berranger (Le Mans, 1953).

Chroniques de Saint-Martial de Limoges, ed. H. Duplès-Agier (Paris, 1874).

Cluny   *Recueil des chartes de l'abbaye de Cluny*, ed. A. Bernard and A. Bruel, 6 vols. (Paris, 1876–1903).

Coleccion diplomatica de Pedro I de Aragon y Navarra, ed. A. Ubieto Arteta (Zaragoza, 1951).

Conciliorum Oecumenicorum Decreta, ed. J. Alberigo *et al.* (Freiburg, 1962).

Conques   *Cartulaire de l'abbaye de Conques en Rouergue*, ed. G. Dejardins (Paris, 1879).

Conrad III, *Urkunden*, ed. F. Hausmann (*MGH. Die Urkunden der deutschen Könige und Kaiser* 9,Vienna, Cologne and Graz, 1969).

La Continuation de Guillaume de Tyr (1184–1197), ed. M. R. Morgan (Paris, 1982).

Corbigny   'Chartes de Corbigny', ed. C. A. Desplaces de Charmasse, *Mémoires de la société éduenne* NS 17 (1889), 1–39.

Cormery   *Cartulaire de Cormery*, ed. J. -J. Bourassé (Tours, 1861).

Cosmas of Prague, 'Chronica Boemorum', *MGHS* 9.

'The Council of Troyes, 23 May 1107', ed. U.-R. Blumenthal, *The Early Councils of Pope Paschal II* (Toronto, 1978), 82–97.

CSPVS   *Chronique de Saint-Pierre-le-Vif de Sens*, ed. R.-H. Bautier and M. Gilles (Paris, 1979).

Cysoing   *Cartulaire de l'abbaye de Cysoing*, ed. I. de Coussemaker (Lille, 1886).

Decreta Claromontensia, ed. R. Somerville, *The Councils of Urban II. 1 (Annuarium Historiae Conciliorum.* Supplementum 1, Amsterdam, 1972).

'De genere comitum Flandrensium notae Parisienses', *MGHS* 13.

'Départ d'un seigneur normand pour la première croisade', ed. L. V. Delisle, *Littérature latine et histoire du moyen âge* (Paris, 1890).

Dinant   *Cartulaire de la commune de Dinant*, ed. S. Bormans and L. Lahaye, 6 vols. (Namur, 1880–1906).

'Document inédit pour servir à l'histoire des croisades', ed. A. Van Hasselt, *Annales de l'académie archéologique de Belgique* 6 (1849), 93–102.

Documents historiques inédits tirés des collections manuscrits, ed. J. J. Champollion-Figeac, 4 vols, (Paris, 1841–8).

Domène   *Cartulare monasterii beatorum Petri et Pauli de Domina*, ed. C. de Monteynard (Lyons, 1859).

Dunes   *Chronica et cartularium monasterii de Dunis*, ed. F. Van de Putte (*Société d'émulation de Bruges. Recueil de chroniques etc.*, sér. 1, Bruges, 1844).

Duodecima Centuria, ed. Magdeburg Centuriators, *Ecclesiastica Historia* 7 (Basel, 1569).

Eadmer, *Historia novorum in Anglia*, ed. M. Rule (Rolls series 81, London, 1884).

Eberwin, 'Ex miraculis sancti Symeonis', *MGHS* 8.

Les Ecouges   'Cartulaire de l'ancienne chartreuse des Ecouges', ed. A. Auvergne, *Documents inédits relatifs au Dauphiné*, sér. 1, 2 (Grenoble, 1865), 81–267.

Eenaeme *Cartulaire de l'abbaye d'Eenaeme*, ed. G. J. C. Piot (Bruges, 1881).
Ekk C. Ekkehard of Aura, 'Chronicon Universale', *MGHS* 6.
Ekkebert, 'Vita sancti Haimeradi presbiteri', *MGHS* 10.
Ekkehard (Hagenmeyer) H. Hagenmeyer, *Ekkehardi Uraugiensis abbatis Hierosolymita* (Tübingen, 1877).
Ekk H. Ekkehard of Aura, 'Hierosolymita', *RHC Oc* 5.
Epernay A. Nicaise, *Epernay et l'abbaye Saint-Martin de cette ville*, 2 vols. (Chalons-sur-Marne, 1869).
Epistolae Karolini Aevi, ed. *MGH*, 8 vols. so far (Berlin, 1892–1989).
Ernoul, *Chronique*, ed. L. de Mas-Latrie (Paris, 1871).
Eudes of Deuil, *De Profectione Ludovici VII in Orientem*, ed. V. G. Berry (New York, 1948).
Eugenius III, 'Quantum praedecessores', ed. P. Rassow, 'Der Text der Kreuzzugsbulle Eugens III. vom 1. März 1146', *Neues Archiv* 45 (1924), 300–5.
'Excerptum Historicum', *RHGF* 11.
'Ex fragmento de Petragoricensibus episcopis', *RHGF* 12.
'Ex miraculis S. Donatiani Brugensibus', *MGHS* 15, 2.
FC Fulcher of Chartres, *Historia Hierosolymitana*, ed. H. Hagenmeyer (Heidelberg, 1913).
Flanders *Actes des comtes de Flandre 1071–1128*, ed. F. Vercauteren (Brussels, 1938).
Florence of Worcester, *Chronicon*, ed. B. Thorpe, 2 vols. (English Historical Society, London, 1848–9).
Forez *Chartes du Forez*, ed. G. Guichard, Comte de Neufbourg, ·E. Perroy and J. E. Dufour, 24 vols. (Mâcon, 1933–70).
Fulco, 'Historia gestorum viae nostrae temporis Jerosolymitanae', *RHC Oc* 5.
Fulk IV of Anjou, 'Gesta Andegavensium peregrinorum', *RHC Oc* 5.
GAD 'Gesta Ambaziensium dominorum' ed. L. Halphen and R. Poupardin, *Chroniques des comtes d'Anjou et des seigneurs d'Amboise* (Paris, 1913).
Galbert of Bruges, 'Passio Karoli Comitis', *MGHS* 12.
Gallia Christiana, ed. Maurists *et al.*, 16 vols. (Paris, 1715–1865).
GC *La Gran Conquista de Ultramar*, ed. P. de Gayangos (Madrid, 1858).
Gellone *Cartulaires des abbayes d'Aniane et de Gellone 1. Cartulaire de Gellone*, ed. P. Alaus, L. Cassan and E. Meynial (Montpellier, 1898).
'Genealogia regum Francorum', *MGHS* 13.
'Genealogia Welforum', *MGHS* 13.
'Genealogiae comitum Flandriae', *MGHS* 9.
Genoa (Church) *Liber privilegiorum Ecclesiae Ianuensis*, ed. D. Puncuh (*Fonte e studi di storia ecclesiastica* 1, Genoa, 1962).
Genoa (Iur) *I Libri Iurium della Repubblica di Genova*, ed. A. Rovera, 2 vols. so far (*Publicazioni degli Archivi di Stato. Fonti* 12, Rome, 1992).
Geoffrey, 'Historia coenobii Thetfordensis', *Monasticon Anglicanum*, ed. W. Dugdale, J. Caley, H. Ellis and B. Bandinell, 5 (London, 1825).

Geoffrey Malaterra, 'De rebus gestis Rogerii Calabriae et Siciliae comitis et Roberti Guiscardi ducis fratris eius', *RISNS* 5.1.

Geoffrey of Le Chalard, 'Dictamen de primordiis ecclesiae Castaliensis', *RHC Oc* 5.

Geoffrey of Vendôme, 'Epistolae', *PL* 157.

'Gesta abbatum Lobbiensium', *MGHS* 21.

Gesta comitum Barcinonensium, ed. L. Barrau Dihigo and J. Masso Torrents (*Croniques Catalanes* 2, Barcelona, 1925).

'Gesta episcoporum Tullensium', *MGHS* 8.

'Gesta episcoporum Virdunensium', *MGHS* 4.

Gesta regis Henrici Secundi, ed. W. Stubbs, 2 vols. (Rolls Series 49, London, 1867).

'Gesta triumphalium Pisanorum in captione Jerusalem', *RHC Oc* 5.

GF   *Gesta Francorum et aliorum Hierosolimitanorum*, ed. R. M. T. Hill (London, 1962).

Giles of Orval, 'Gesta episcoporum Leodicensium', *MGHS* 25.

Gilo, 'Historia de via Hierosolymitana', *RHC Oc* 5.

Gislebert of Mons, *Chronicon Hanoniense*, ed. L. Vanderkindere, *La Chronique de Gislebert de Mons* (Brussels, 1904).

GN Gesta   Guibert of Nogent, 'Gesta Dei per Francos', *RHC Oc* 4.

GN Vita   Guibert of Nogent, *De vita sua*, ed. E.-R. Labande (Paris, 1981).

Göttweig   *Die Traditionsbücher des Benediktinerstiftes Göttweig*, ed. A. F. Fuchs (*Fontes rerum Austriacarum* abt. 2, 69, Vienna, 1931).

Greg Ep Vag   *The Epistolae Vagantes of Pope Gregory VII*, ed. H. E. J. Cowdrey (Oxford, 1972).

Greg Reg   *Das Register Gregors VII*, ed. E. Caspar, 2nd edn. (*MGH Epistolae Selectae* 2, 2, Berlin, 1955).

Grenoble   *Cartulaires de l'église cathédrale de Grenoble*, ed. J. Marion (Paris, 1869).

GV   Geoffrey of Vigeois (Geoffrey of Brueil), 'Chronicon', *RHGF* 10.267-8; 11.288-9; 12.421-51; 18.211-23.

Hariulf, *Chronicon Centuliense*, ed. F. Lot, *Chronique de l'abbaye de Saint-Riquier* (Paris, 1894).

Helmold of Bosau, 'Chronica Slavorum', *MGHS* 21.

Henry of Breitenau, 'Passio S. Thiemonis Juvavensis archiepiscopi', *RHC Oc* 5.

Henry of Huntingdon, 'De captione Antiochiae a christianis', *RHC Oc* 5.

Henry of Huntingdon, *Historia Anglorum*, ed. T. Arnold (*Rolls Series* 74, London, 1879).

HGL   *Histoire générale de Languedoc*, 3rd edn, ed. J. Vaissète, C. Devic and A. Molinier, 16 vols.(Toulouse, 1872–1904).

Historia Compostellana, ed. E. Falque Rey (*Corpus Christianorum. Continuatio medievalis* 70, Turnholt, 1988).

'Historia de translatione sanctorum magni Nicolai ... ejusdem avunculi, alterius Nicolai, Theodorique ... de civitate Mirea in monasterium S. Nicolai de Littore Venetiarum', *RHC Oc* 5.

'Historia ducum Veneticorum', *MGHS* 14.

'Historia gloriosi regis Ludovici VII', *RHGF* 12.

'Historia monasterii Aquicinctini', *MGHS* 14.

'Historia mortis et miraculorum S. Leonis IX', *PL* 143.

'Historia Welforum Weingartensis', *MGHS* 21.

'Historiae Francicae Fragmentum', *RHGF* 12.

HP   'Historia peregrinorum euntium Jerusolymam', *RHC Oc* 3.

Huesca   *Collecion diplomatica de la catedral de Huesca*, ed. A. Duran Gudiol, 2 vols. (Zaragoza, 1965–9).

Hugh of Flavigny, 'Chronicon', *MGHS* 8.

Ibn al-Athir, 'Sum of World History', *RHC Or* 1–2.

Ibn al-Qalanisi, *The Damascus Chronicle of the Crusades*, tr. H. A. R. Gibb (London, 1932).

Ivo of Chartres, 'Epistolae', *PL* 162.

Italia pontificia, ed. P. F. Kehr *et al.*, 10 vols. (*Regesta Pontificum Romanorum*, Berlin and Zürich, 1966–75).

Itinerarium peregrinorum et Gesta regis Ricardi, ed. W. Stubbs, *Chronicles and Memorials of the Reign of Richard I* 1 (Rolls Series 38, London, 1864).

Joannes Molanus, *Historiae Lovanensium libri XIV*, ed. X. de Ram, 2 vols. (*Collection des chroniques belges*, Brussels, 1861).

John of Joinville, *La vie de Saint Louis*, ed. N. L. Corbett (Quebec, 1977).

John of Mantua, 'Tractatus in Cantica Canticorum', ed. B. Bischoff and B. Taeger, *Ioannis Mantuani in Cantica Canticorum et De Sancta Maria Tractatus ad Comitissam Matildam* (Freiburg, 1973), 25–155.

John of Würzburg, 'Descriptio Terrae Sanctae', ed. T. Tobler, *Descriptiones Terrae Sanctae* (Leipzig, 1874).

Jumièges   *Chartes de l'abbaye de Jumièges*, ed. J. -J. Vernier, 2 vols. (*Société de l'histoire de Normandie. Publications* 45, Rouen and Paris, 1916).

Kb   *Die Kreuzzugsbriefe aus den Jahren 1088–1100*, ed. H. Hagenmeyer (Innsbruck, 1901).

LA   Lambert of Ardres, 'Historia comitum Ghisnensium', *MGHS* 24.

Lambert of Arras, 'De primatu sedis Atrebatensis', *PL* 162.

Lampert of Hersfeld, *Opera*, ed. O. Holder-Egger (*MGHS in usum scholarum*, Hanover and Leipzig, 1894).

Landulf the Younger, 'Historia Mediolanensis', *MGHS* 20.

Laurence of Liège, 'Gesta episcoporum Virdunensium', *MGHS* 10.

Laval   A. B. de Broussillon, *La maison de Laval (1020-1605)*, 5 vols. (Paris, 1895–1903).

Leire   *Documentacion Medieval de Leire*, ed. A. J. Martin Duque (Pamplona, 1983).

Lérins   *Cartulaire de l'abbaye de Lérins*, ed. E. de Flamare (Nice, 1885).

Lézat   *Cartulaire de l'abbaye de Lézat*, ed. P. Ourliac and A.-M. Magnou (*Collection de documents inédits* 17–18, Paris, 1984–7).

Liber Pontificalis, ed. L. Duchesne, 3 vols. (Paris, 1886–1957); and *Studia Gratiana* 22 (1978), *passim*.

'Les Lignages d'Outremer', *RHC Lois* 2.

Limoges 'Un acte de l'évêque Pierre de Limoges (1101)', ed. J. Becquet, *Bulletin de la société archéologique et historique du Limousin* 112 (1985), 14–19.

Le Livre au roi, ed. M. Greilsammer (Paris, 1995).

Longpont *Le cartulaire du prieuré de Notre-Dame de Longpont de l'ordre de Cluny* (ed. A. Marion) (Lyons, 1879).

Lorraine A. Calmet, *Histoire ecclésiastique et civile de Lorraine*, 5 vols. (Nancy, 1728–51), 'Preuves'.

Louis VII, 'Epistolarum regis Ludovici et variorum ad eum volumen', *RHGF* 16.

Lupus Protospatharius, 'Annales Barenses', *MGHS* 5.

Lyon *Obituaires de la province de Lyon*, ed. J. Laurent and P. Gras, 2 vols. (*Recueil des historiens de France. Obituaires* 6, Paris, 1951–65).

Maguelonne *Cartulaire de Maguelonne*, ed. J. Rouquette and A. Villemagne, 3 vols. (Montpellier, 1912–22).

Maillezais A. Lacurie, *Histoire de l'abbaye de Maillezais* (Fontenay-le-Comte, 1852).

Mainz Anonymous, 'Narrative of the Old Persecutions', tr. S. Eidelberg, *The Jews and the Crusaders* (Madison, 1977).

Mainzer Urkundenbuch, ed. M. Stimming and P. Acht, 2 vols. (Darmstadt, 1968–72).

Le Mans Cart *Cartulaire de l'évêché du Mans*, ed. B. de Broussillon, 2 vols. (*Archives historiques du Maine* 1, 9, Le Mans, 1900–8).

Le Mans Liber *Chartularium insignis ecclesiae Cenomanensis quod dicitur Liber Albus capituli*, ed. A. Cauvin (Institut des Provinces de France, *Mémoires*, 2nd ser., 2, Paris, 1869).

Marcigny *Le cartulaire de Marcigny-sur-Loire*, ed. J. Richard (Dijon, 1957).

Marianus Scottus, 'Chronicon', *MGHS* 5.

Marmoutier (Anjou) 'Les prieurés de Marmoutier en Anjou', ed. P. Marchegay, *Archives d'Anjou* 2 (Angers, 1853).

Marmoutier (Blésois): *Marmoutier. Cartulaire blésois*, ed. C. Metais (Blois, 1889–91).

Marmoutier (Dunois) *Cartulaire de Marmoutier pour le Dunois*, ed. E. Mabille (Châteaudun, 1874).

Marmoutier (Manceau) *Cartulaire Manceau de Marmoutier*, ed. E. T. Laurain, 2 vols. (Laval, 1911–45).

Marmoutier (Tourangeau) *Marmoutier. Cartulaire tourangeau*, ed. L. P. Piolin and C. Chantelou (Tours, 1879).

Marmoutier (Vendômois) *Cartulaire de Marmoutier pour le Vendômois*, ed. M. de Trémault (Paris and Vendôme, 1893).

Martin da Canal, *Les Estoires de Venise*, ed. A. Limentani (Florence, 1972).

Matthew of Edessa, *Chronicle*, tr. A. E. Dostourian, *Armenia and the Crusades* (Lanham, 1993).

Mauléon 'Documents pour servir à l'histoire de l'abbaye de la Trinité de Mauléon', ed. B. Ledain, *Archives historiques du Poitou* 20 (Poitiers, 1889), 1–91.

Metellus of Tegernsee, *Expeditio Ierosolimitana*, ed. P. C. Jacobsen (Stuttgart, 1982).

MGH Monumenta Germaniae Historica.

MGHS MGH Scriptores in Folio et Quarto, ed G. H. Pertz *et al.*, 34 vols. so far (Hanover and Leipzig, 1826ff).

'Miracula S. Nicolai conscripta a monacho Beccensi', ed. Bollandists, *Catalogus Codicum Hagiographicorum Latinorum antiquiorum saeculo XVI qui asservantur in Bibliotheca Nationali Parisiensi* 2 (Brussels, 1890).

Molesme *Cartulaires de l'abbaye de Molesme*, ed. J. Laurent, 2 vols. (Paris, 1907–11).

'Monachi anonymi Scaphusensis de reliquiis sanctissimi crucis et dominici sepulchri Scaphusam allatis', *RHC Oc* 5.

Montacute *Two Cartularies of the Augustinian Priory of Bruton and the Cluniac Priory of Montacute*, ed. J. Batten *et al.* (*Somerset Record Society* 8, London, 1894).

Monte Cassino 'Chronica monasterii Casinensis', *MGHS* 34.

Montier-la-Celle 'Cartulaire de Montier-la-Celle', ed. C. Lalore, *Collection des principaux cartulaires du diocèse de Troyes* 6 (Paris and Troyes, 1882).

Montiéramey 'Cartulaire de l'abbaye de Montiéramey', ed. C. Lalore, *Collection des principaux cartulaires du diocèse de Troyes* 7 (Paris and Troyes, 1890).

Montiérender 'Chartes de l'abbaye de Montiérender' ed. C. Lalore, *Collection des principaux cartulaires du diocèse de Troyes* 4 (Paris and Troyes, 1878).

Montiérneuf de Poitiers *Recueil des documents relatifs à l'abbaye de Montierneuf de Poitiers (1076–1319)*, ed. F. Villard (*Archives historiques du Poitou* 59, Poitiers, 1973).

Montpellier *Liber instrumentorum memorialium; cartulaire des Guillems de Montpellier*, ed. A. Germain, 2 vols. (Montpellier, 1884–6).

Morigny *La Chronique de Morigny (1095–1152)*, ed. L. Mirot (Collection de textes 41, Paris, 1909).

'Narratio quomodo relliquiae martyris Georgii ad nos Aquicinenses pervenerunt', *RHC Oc* 5.

Néronville 'Recueil des chartes du prieuré de Néronville', ed. H. Stein, *Annales de la société historique et archéologique du Gâtinais* 13 (1895), 298–373.

Neumoustier 'Chronica Albrici monachi Trium Fontium a monacho Novi Monasterii Hoiensis interpolata', *MGHS* 23.

NF 'Narratio Floriacensis de captis Antiochia et Hierosolyma et obsesso Dyrrachio', *RHC Oc* 5.

Nîmes *Cartulaire du chapitre de l'église Notre-Dame de Nîmes*, ed. E. Germer-Durand (Nîmes, 1874).

Nogent-le-Rotrou *Saint-Denis de Nogent-le-Rotrou 1031–1789, Histoire et cartu-laire*, ed. H. J. G. de Souancé and C. Metais (Vannes, 1899).
Normandy *Recueil des actes des ducs de Normandie de 911 à 1066*, ed. M. Fauroux (*Mémoires de la société des antiquaires de Normandie* 36, Caen, 1961)
'Notitiae duae Lemovicenses de praedicatione crucis in Aquitania', *RHC Oc* 5.
'Notitiae fundationis monasterii Bosonis-Villae', *MGHS* 15.
Notre-Dame de Chartres *Cartulaire de Notre-Dame de Chartres*, ed. E. de Buchère de Lépinois and L. Merlet, 3 vols. (Chartres, 1862–5).
Notre-Dame de Josaphat (Delaborde) *Chartes de la Terre Sainte provenant de l'abbaye de Notre-Dame de Josaphat*, ed. H. F. Delaborde (Bibliothèque des Ecoles françaises d'Athènes et de Rome, sér. 1, 19, Paris, 1880).
Notre-Dame de Josaphat (Kohler) 'Chartes de l'abbaye de Notre-Dame de la vallée de Josaphat en Terre Sainte', ed. C. Kohler, *ROL* 7 (1900), 108–222.
Notre-Dame de Paris *Cartulaire de l'église Notre-Dame de Paris*, ed. B. E. C. Guérard, 4 vols. (Paris, 1850).
Notre-Dame de Saintes *Cartulaire de l'abbaye royale de Notre-Dame de Saintes*, ed. T. Grasilier (*Cartulaires inédits de la Saintonge* 2, Niort, 1871).
Nouaillé *Chartes de l'abbaye de Nouaillé*, ed. P. G. de Goislard de Montsabert (*Archives historiques du Poitou* 49, Poitiers, 1936).
Noyers 'Cartulaire de l'abbaye de Noyers', ed. C. Chevalier, *Mémoires de la société archéologique de Touraine* 22 (1872), 1–815.
Noyon O. Guyotjeannin, 'Noyonnais et Vermandois aux Xe et XIe s.', *Bibliothèque de l'Ecole des Chartes* 139 (1981), 143–89.
Oberalteich *Die Traditionen des Klosters Oberalteich* 1, ed. C. Mohr (*Quellen und Erörterungen z. bayerischen Geschichte*, NS 30, Munich, 1979).
Ortlieb of Zwiefalten, 'Chronicon', *MGHS* 10.
Otto of Freising, *Chronica*, ed. A. Hofmeister (*MGHS in usum scholarum*, Hanover and Leipzig, 1912).
Oulx *Le Carte della Prevostura d'Oulx*, ed. G. Collino (*Società storica subalpina. Bibliotheca* 45, Pinerolo, 1908).
OV Orderic Vitalis, *Historia aecclesiastica*, ed. and tr. M. Chibnall, 6 vols. (Oxford, 1969–79).
'Pancharta Caduniensis seu Historia Sancti Sudarii Jesu Christi', *RHC Oc* 5.
Papsturkunden für Kirchen im Heiligen Lande, ed. R. Hiestand (*Vorarbeiten zum Oriens Pontificius* 3, Göttingen, 1985).
Papsturkunden für Templer und Johanniter, ed. R. Hiestand, 2 vols. (*Vorarbeiten zum Oriens Pontificius* 1–2, Göttingen, 1972–84).
'Papsturkunden in Florenz', ed. W. Wiederhold, *Nachrichten von der Gesell-schaft der Wissenschaften zu Göttingen. Phil.-hist. Kl.* (1901), 306–25.
Papsturkunden in Frankreich, ed. J. Ramackers *et al.*, NS, 7 vols. (Göttingen, 1932–76).
Papsturkunden in Spanien. 1. Katalonien, ed. P. F. Kehr, 2 vols. (Berlin, 1926).

Paray-le-Monial   *Cartulaire du prieuré de Paray-le-Monial*, ed. C. U. J. Chevalier (Montbéliard, 1891) (also in *Collection de cartulaires dauphinois* (Lyons, 1869–1912) 8.2).

Paris   *Cartulaire général de Paris* 1, ed. R. de Lasteyrie (*Histoire générale de Paris*, Paris, 1887).

'Passio altera Beati Thiemonis', *RHC Oc* 5.

'Passio prior Beati Thiemonis', *RHC Oc* 5.

'Passio S. Cholomanni', *MGHS* 4.

Pébrac   *Cartularium sive terrarium Piperacensis monasterii*, ed. J. B. Payrard (Le Puy, 1875).

'Un pèlerinage à Jérusalem dans la première moitié du XIe siècle', ed. J. Doinel, *Bibliothèque de l'Ecole des Chartes* 51 (1890), 204–5.

Philip I   *Recueil des actes de Philippe Ier, roi de France (1059–1108)*, ed. M. Prou (Paris, 1908).

Pistoia *Regesta chartarum Pistoriensium: canonica di S. Zenone secolo XI*, ed. N. Rauty (*Fonti storiche pistoiesi* 7, Pistoia, 1985).

PL *Patrologiae Cursus Completus. Series Latina*, comp. J. P. Migne, 217 vols. and 4 vols. of indexes (Paris, 1841–64).

Polignac   *Preuves de l'histoire de la maison de Polignac*, ed. A. Jacotin, 5 vols. (Paris, 1898–1906).

'Probationes ad tabulam chronologicam ad Stemmatographiam Comitum de Bogen, hodie ab Arco', comp. H. Scholliner, *Neue historische Abhandlungen der churfürstlichen baierischen Akademie der Wissenschaften* 4 (1792), 11–310.

PT   Peter Tudebode, *Historia de Hierosolymitano itinere*, ed. J. H. and L. L. Hill (Paris, 1977).

PT 'Var Ms', *RHC Oc* 3.

Quadripartitus, ed. F. Liebermann (Halle, 1892).

'Qualiter reliquiae B. Nicolai episcopi et confessoris ad Lotharingiae villam, quae Portus nominatur, delatae sunt', *RHC Oc* 5.

'Qualiter tabula S. Basili continens in se magnam dominici ligni portionem Cluniacum delata fuerit, tempore Pontii abbatis', *RHC Oc* 5.

RA   Raymond of Aguilers, *Liber*, ed. J. H. and L. L. Hill (Paris, 1969).

RA Cont   Raymond of Aguilers, 'Var. Mss.', *RHC Oc* 3.

Ralph Glaber, *Historiarum Libri Quinque*, ed. and tr. J. France (Oxford, 1989).

Ralph of Diceto, 'Ymagines Historiarum', ed. W. Stubbs, *Radulfi de Diceto decani Lundoniensis Opera Historica*, 2 vols. (Rolls Series 68, London, 1876).

Ramsey Cart   *Cartularium monasterii de Rameseia*, ed. W. H. Hart and P. A. Lyons, 3 vols. (Rolls Series 79, London, 1884–93).

Ramsey Chron   *Chronicon Abbatiae Ramesiensis*, ed. W. D. Macray (*Rolls Series* 83, London, 1886).

RC   Ralph of Caen, 'Gesta Tancredi', *RHC Oc* 3.

Redon   *Cartulaire de l'abbaye de Redon*, ed. A. de Courson (Paris, 1863).

Regesta pontificum Romanorum, comp. P. Jaffé *et al.*, 2 vols. (Leipzig, 1885–8).

Regesta regum Anglo-Normannorum 1066–1154, ed. H. W. C. Davis *et al.*, 5 vols. (Oxford, 1913–69).

Reginald of Durham, *Libellus de Vita et Miraculis S. Godrici, Heremite de Finchale* (Surtees Society 20, London, 1847).

La Règle du Temple, ed. H. de Curzon (Paris, 1886).

Die Reichskanzler K. F. Stumpf-Brentano, *Die Reichskanzler*, 3 vols. (Innsbruck, 1865–83).

Reims (admin) *Archives administratives de la ville de Reims*, ed. P. J. Varin, 5 vols. (Paris, 1839–48).

Reims (ville) G. Marlot, *Histoire de la ville . . . de Reims*, 4 vols. (Reims, 1843–6).

RHC Recueil des historians des croisades, ed. Académie des Inscriptions et Belles Lettres (Paris, 1841–1906).

RHC Arm RHC Documents arméniens, 2 vols. (Paris, 1869–1906).

RHC Lois RHC Lois. Les Assises de Jérusalem, 2 vols. (Paris, 1841–3).

RHC Oc RHC Historiens occidentaux, 5 vols. (Paris, 1844–95).

RHC Or RHC Historiens orientaux, 5 vols. (Paris, 1872–1906).

RHGF Recueil des historiens des Gaules et de la France, ed. M. Bouquet *et al.*, 24 vols. (Paris, 1737–1904).

Rioja *Coleccion diplomatica medieval de la Rioja (923–1225)*, ed. I. Rodriguez de Lama, 3 vols. (Logrono, 1976–9).

RISNS Rerum Italicarum Scriptores. Nova Series, ed. G. Carducci *et al.*, 34 vols. so far (Città di Castello and Bologna, 1900ff).

Robert of Torigni, *Chronica*, ed. R. Howlett (*Chronicles of the Reigns of Stephen, Henry II, and Richard I* 4, Rolls Series 82, London, 1889).

Roger of Howden, *Chronica*, ed. W. Stubbs, 4 vols. (Rolls Series 51, London, 1868–71).

ROL Revue de l'Orient latin.

Romoald of Salerno, 'Annales', *MGHS* 19.

Le Ronceray d'Angers 'Cartularium monasterii beatae Mariae Caritatis Andegavensis', ed. P. Marchegay, *Archives d'Anjou* 3. *Angers, Cosnier et Lachèse* (Angers, 1854).

Roussillon *Cartulaire roussillonnais*, ed. B. Alart (Perpignan, 1880).

RR Robert of Rheims, 'Historia Iherosolimitana', *RHC Oc* 3.

RRH *Regesta regni Hierosolymitani 1097–1291*, comp. R. Röhricht (Innsbruck, 1893) *Additamentum* (Innsbruck, 1904).

Sacrorum Conciliorum Nova et Amplissima Collectio, ed. G. D. Mansi, 31 vols. (Florence and Venice, 1759–98).

St Amant de Boixe *Cartulaire de l'abbaye de Saint-Amant-de-Boixe*, ed. A. Debord (Poitiers, 1982).

St André-le-Bas de Vienne *Cartulaire de l'abbaye de Saint-André-le-Bas de Vienne*, ed. C. U. J. Chevalier (*Collection de cartulaires dauphinois* 1, Lyons, 1869).

St Aubin d'Angers Cart *Cartulaire de l'abbaye de Saint-Aubin d'Angers*, ed. A. Bertrand de Broussillon, 3 vols. (Paris, 1903).

St Aubin d'Angers Chron 'Chronicae Sancti Albini Andegavensis in unum congestae', ed. P. Marchegay and E. Mabille, *Chroniques des églises d'Anjou* (Paris, 1869).

St Avit d'Orléans   *Cartulaire du chapitre de Saint-Avit d'Orléans*, ed. G. Vignat (*Collection des cartulaires du Loiret* 2, Orléans, 1886).

St Bénigne de Dijon   *Chartes et documents de Saint-Bénique de Dijon*, ed. G. Chevrier and M. Chaume, 2 vols. (Dijon, 1943–86).

St Bertin (Guérard)   *Cartulaire de l'abbaye de Saint-Bertin*, ed. B. E. C. Guérard (Paris, 1841).

St Bertin (Haigneré)   *Les chartes de Saint-Bertin*, ed. D. Haigneré, 4 vols. (St Omer, 1886–99).

St Chaffre du Monastier   *Cartulaire de l'abbaye de Saint Chaffre du Monastier*, ed. C. U. J. Chevalier (*Collection de cartulaires dauphinois*, 8.1, Lyons 1869–1912).

St Cybard d'Angoulême   *Cartulaire de l'abbaye de Saint-Cybard*, ed. P. Lefrancq (Angoulême, 1930).

St Cyprien de Poitiers   *Cartulaire de l'abbaye de Saint-Cyprien de Poitiers*, ed. L. Rédet (*Archives historiques du Poitou* 3, Poitiers, 1874).

St Etienne de Dijon   *Chartes de l'abbaye de Saint-Etienne de Dijon de 1140 à 1155*, ed. M.Bourrier (Paris and Dijon, 1912).

St Etienne de Limoges   'Cartulaire du chapitre de Saint-Etienne de Limoges', ed. J. de Font-Réaulx, *Bulletin de la société archéologique et historique du Limousin* 69 (1922), 5–258.

St Etienne de Nevers   *Les chartes de Saint-Etienne de Nevers*, ed. R. de Lespinasse (*Bulletin de la société nivernaise des lettres, sciences et arts*, sér. 3. fasc. 1, Nevers, 1908).

St Etienne de Vignory   *Cartulaire du prieuré de Saint-Etienne de Vignory*, ed. J. d'Arbaumont (Langres, 1882).

St Florent-lès-Saumur Chron   'Breve Chonicon Sancti Florentii Salmurensis', ed. P. Marchegay and E. Mabille, *Chroniques des églises d'Anjou* (Paris, 1869).

St Florent-lès-Saumur Hist   'Historia sancti Florentii Salmurensis', ed. P. Marchegay and E. Mabille, *Chroniques des églises d'Anjou* (Paris, 1869).

St Florent-lès-Saumur (Normandes)   'Chartes normandes de l'abbaye de Saint-Florent', ed. P. Marchegay, *Mémoires de la société des antiquaires de Normandie*, sér. 3, 10 (1880), 665–711.

St Florent-lès-Saumur (Saintongeaises)   'Chartes saintongeaises de Saint-Florent', ed. P. Marchegay, *Archives historiques de la Saintonge et de l'Aunis* 4 (1877), 17–93.

St Flour   *Cartulaire du prieuré de Saint-Flour*, ed. M. Boudet (Monaco, 1910).

St Georges de Rennes   *Cartulaire de l'abbaye de Saint-Georges de Rennes*, ed. P. de la Bigne Villeneuve (Rennes, 1876).

St Hilaire-le-Grand de Poitiers   'Documents pour l'histoire de Saint-Hilaire de Poitiers', ed. L. Rédet, *Mémoires de la société des antiquaires de l'Ouest* (1847), 1–362, (1852), 1–462.

St Hubert-en-Ardenne *Chartes de l'abbaye de Saint-Hubert-en-Ardenne*, ed. G. Kurth, 2 vols. (Brussels, 1903).

St Jacques de Liège J. Stiennon, *Etude sur le chartrier et le domaine de l'abbaye de Saint-Jacques de Liège* (*Bibliotheque de la Fac. de philosoph. et lettres de Liège* fasc. 124, Paris, 1951).

St Jean d'Angély *Cartulaire de Saint-Jean d'Angély*, ed. P. L. E. G. Musset, 2 vols. (*Archives historiques de la Saintonge et de l'Aunis* 30, 33, Saintes, 1901–3).

St Julien de Tours *Chartes de Saint-Julien de Tours*, ed. L. J. Denis (*Archives historiques du Maine* 12, Le Mans, 1912).

St Lambert de Liège *Cartulaire de l'église Saint-Lambert de Liège*, ed. S. Bormans and E. Schoolmeesters, 6 vols. (Brussels, 1893–1933).

St Laon de Thouars *Cartulaire de l'abbaye de Saint-Laon de Thouars*, ed. H. Imbert (*Mémoires de la société de statistique, sciences, lettres et arts du département de Deux-Sèvres*, sér. 2, 14, Niort, 1875).

St Laud d'Angers *Cartulaire du chapitre de Saint-Laud d'Angers*, ed. A. Planchenault (*Documents historiques sur l'Anjou* 4, Angers, 1903).

St Maixent Chartes *Chartes et documents pour servir à l'histoire de l'abbaye de Saint-Maixent*, ed. A. Richard, 2 vols. (*Archives historiques du Poitou* 16, 18, Poitiers, 1886).

St Maixent Chron *Chronique de Saint-Maixent*, ed. J. Verdon (Paris, 1979).

St Marcel-lès-Chalon-sur-Saône *Cartulaire du prieuré de Saint-Marcel-lès-Chalon-sur-Saône*, ed. P. Canat de Chizy (Chalon-sur-Saône, 1894).

St Martial de Limoges A. Sohn, *Der Abbatiat Ademars von Saint-Martial de Limoges (1063–1114)* (*Beiträge zur Geschichte des alten Mönchtums und des Benediktinertums* 37, Munster, 1989).

St Martin de Pontoise *Cartulaire de l'abbaye de Saint-Martin de Pontoise*, ed. J. Depoin (Pontoise, 1895–1901).

St Martin de Tournai *Chartes de l'abbaye de Saint-Martin de Tournai*, ed. A. d'Herbomez, 2 vols. (Brussels, 1898–1901).

St Martin des Champs Chartes *Recueil de chartes et documents de Saint-Martin-des-Champs, monastère parisien*, ed. J. Depoin, 5 vols. (Ligugé and Paris, 1912–21).

St Martin des Champs Liber *Liber Testamentorum Sancti Martini de Campis*, ed. J. Depoin (Paris, 1905).

St Maur-sur-Loire 'Cartularium Sancti-Mauri', ed. P. Marchegay, *Archives d'Anjou* 1 (Angers, 1843).

St Mihiel *Chroniques et chartes de l'abbaye de Saint-Mihiel*, ed. A. Lesort (*Mettensia* 6, Paris, 1909–12).

St Mont *Cartulaire du prieuré de Saint-Mont*, ed. J. de Jaurgain (*Archives historiques de Gascogne*, sér. 2, fasc. 7, Paris, 1904).

St Paul de Mausole *Cartulaire de Saint-Paul-de-Mausole à Saint-Rémy-de-Provence*, ed. E. Leroy (St Rémy-de-Provence, 1961).

St Père de Chartres *Cartulaire de l'abbaye de Saint-Père de Chartres*, ed. B. E. C. Guérard, 2 vols. (Paris, 1840).

St Philibert de Tournus (Chifflet) P. F. Chifflet, *Histoire de l'abbaye royale et de la ville de Tournus* (Dijon, 1664).

St Philibert de Tournus (Juënin) R. Juënin, *Nouvelle histoire de l'abbaïe royale et collégiale de Saint Filibert et de la ville de Tournus* 2, Preuves (Dijon, 1733).

St Pierre-au-Mont-Blandin *Liber traditionum Sancti Petri Blandiniensis*, ed. A. Fayen (*Oorkondenboeck der Stad Gent*, sér. 2, 1, Ghent, 1906).

St Pierre-de-la-Cour du Mans *Cartulaire du chapitre royal de Saint-Pierre-de-la-Cour, du Mans*, ed. S. M. d'Elbenne and L. J. Denis (*Archives historiques du Maine* 4, 10, Le Mans, 1903–7, 1910).

St Pierre de la Couture *Cartulaire des abbayes de St Pierre de la Couture et de St Pierre de Solesmes*, ed. Bénédictins de Solesmes (Le Mans, 1881).

St Pierre de la Réole 'Cartulaire du prieuré de Saint-Pierre de La Réole', ed. C. Grellet-Balguerie, *Archives historiques du département de la Gironde* 5 (1863).

St Rémy de Provence 'Saint-Remy de Provence au moyen âge', ed. M. Deloche, *Mémoires de l'Académie des Inscriptions et Belles-Lettres* 34(1) (1892), 53–143.

St Saveur-le-Vicomte L. V. Delisle, *Histoire du château et des sires de Saint-Saveur-le-Vicomte* (Valognes, 1867).

St Sépulcre de Jérusalem *Le cartulaire du chapitre de Saint-Sépulcre de Jérusalem*, ed. G. Bresc-Bautier (Paris, 1984).

St Sernin de Toulouse *Cartulaire de l'abbaye de Saint-Sernin de Toulouse 844–1200*, ed. M. J. C. Douais (Paris and Toulouse, 1887).

St Sulpice-la-Forêt '*Cartulaire de l'abbaye de Saint-Sulpice-la-Forêt*, ed. P. Anger, *Bulletin et mémoires de la société archéologique d'Ille-et-Vilaine* 34 (1905), 165–262; 35 (1906), 325–88; 37 (1907), 3-160.

St Victor de Marseille (Guérard) *Cartulaire de l'abbaye de Saint-Victor de Marseille*, ed. B. E. C. Guérard, 2 vols. (Paris, 1857).

St Victor de Marseille (Rolland) 'Chartes inédits de St Victor de Marseille', ed. H. Rolland, *Mélanges (Raoul) Busquet* (Vaison-la-Romaine, 1956).

St Vincent de Lucq *Cartulaire de Saint-Vincent-de-Lucq*, ed. L. Barrau-Dihigo and R. Poupardin (Pau, 1905).

St Vincent de Mâcon *Cartulaire de Saint-Vincent de Mâcon*, ed. M.-C. Ragut (Mâcon, 1864).

St Vincent du Mans *Cartulaire de l'abbaye de Saint-Vincent du Mans*, ed. R. Charles and S. M. d'Elbenne 1 (Mamers, 1886–1913).

Ste Croix de Quimperlé *Cartulaire de l'abbaye de Sainte-Croix de Quimperlé*, ed. L. A. Maître, 2nd edn. (*Bibliothèque Bretonne-Armoricaine* fasc. 4, Rennes, 1904).

Ste Trinité-du-Mont de Rouen 'Cartulaire de la Sainte-Trinité-du-Mont de Rouen', ed. J. A. Deville, *Collection de documents inédits sur l'histoire de France. Cartulaires* 3 (Paris, 1840).

Ste Waudru de Mons *Chartes du chapitre de Sainte-Waudru de Mons*, ed. L. Devillers, 4 vols. (Brussels, 1899–1913).

La Sauve-Majeure   Grand cartulaire de la Sauve-Majeure (Bordeaux Bibliothèque Municipale MS 769).
Sauxillanges   'Cartulaire de Sauxillanges', ed. H. Doniol, *Mémoires de l'académie des sciences, belles-lettres et arts de Clermont-Ferrand*, NS 3 (1861), 465–1199.
Savigny   *Cartulaire de l'abbaye de Savigny*, ed. A. Bernard, 2 vols. (Paris, 1853).
Savoy   S. Guichenon, *Histoire généalogique de la royale maison de Savoye*, 2 vols. (Lyons, 1660).
'Secunda pars historiae Iherosolimitanae', *RHC Oc* 3.
Sens   *Obituaires de la province de Sens*, ed. A. Molinier *et al.*, 4 vols. (Paris, 1902–23).
Sigebert of Gembloux, 'Chronica', *MGHS* 6.
Sigebert of Gembloux, 'Leodicensium epistola adversus Paschalem Papam', *MGH Libelli de Lite Imperatorum et Pontificum* 2.
'Sigeberti continuatio auctarium Aquicinense', *MGHS* 6.
'Sigeberti continuatio auctarium Ursicampinum', *MGHS* 6.
Snorri Storluson, *Heimskringla*, tr. L. M. Hollander (Austin, 1964).
Solignac   Cartulaire de Solignac (Paris Bibliothèque Nationale, MS. lat. 18363).
Solomon ben Simson, 'Chronicle', tr. S. Eidelberg, *The Jews and the Crusaders* (Madison, 1977).
Suger of St Denis, 'Epistolae', *RHGF* 15.
Suger of St Denis, *Vita Ludovici Grossi regis*, ed. and tr. H. Waquet (Paris, 1929).
Talmont   'Cartulaire de l'abbaye de Talmond', ed. L. de La Boutetière, *Mémoires de la société des antiquaires de l'Ouest* 36 (1872), 41–498.
Theodore, 'Annales Palidenses', *MGHS* 16.
Theoderic, *Libellus de locis sanctis*, ed. T. Tobler (St Gallen and Paris, 1865).
Thomas Aquinas, *Quaestiones Quodlibetales*, ed. R. Spiazzi (Turin, 1956).
Thomas Aquinas, *Summa Theologiae, Opera omnia jussu impensaque Leonis XIII edita* 4–12 (Rome, 1888–1906).
Tiron   *Cartulaire de l'abbaye de la Sainte-Trinité de Tiron*, ed. L. Merlet (Chartres, 1883).
Tours   *Cartulaire de l'archévêché de Tours*, ed. L. de Grandmaison, 2 vols. (*Mémoires de la société archéologique de Touraine* 37–8 Tours, 1892–4).
Toussaint d'Angers   F. Comte, *L'abbaye Toussaint d'Angers* (Angers, 1985).
'Tractatus de reliquiis S. Stephani Cluniacum delatis', *RHC Oc* 5.
La Trappe   *Cartulaire de l'abbaye de Notre-Dame de La Trappe*, ed. C. F. H. de Charencay (Alençon, 1889).
La Trinité de Vendôme Cart   *Cartulaire de l'abbaye cardinale de la Trinité de Vendôme*, ed. C. Metais, 5 vols. (Paris and Vendôme, 1893–1904).
La Trinité de Vendôme (Saintongeais)   *Cartulaire saintongeais de l'abbaye de la Trinité de Vendôme*, ed. C. Metais (*Archives historiques de la Saintonge et de l'Aunis* 22, Saintes, 1893).
'Triumphus Sancti Lamberti de castro Bullonio', *MGHS* 20.

Tulle   Cartulaires des abbayes de Tulle et de Roc-Amadour, ed. J.-B. Champeval (Brive, 1903).

Urban II, 'Epistolae et Privilegia', *PL* 151.

Urkunden Venedig   *Urkunden zur älteren Handels- und Staatsgeschichte der Republik Venedig*, ed. G. L. F. Tafel and G. M. Thomas, 3 vols. (Fontes rerum Austriacarum. 2 Abt. Diplomataria et acta 12-4, Vienna, 1856–7).

Die ursprüngliche Templerregel, ed. G. Schnürer (Freiburg im Breisgau, 1903).

Uzerche   *Cartulaire de l'abbaye d'Uzerche*, ed. J.-B. Champeval (Paris and Tulle, 1901).

Valenciennes   P. d'Outreman, *Histoire de la ville et comté de Valentiennes* (Douai, 1639).

'Versus de viris illustribus dioecesis Tarvanensis in sacra fuere expeditione', ed. E. Martène and U. Durand, *Veterum scriptorum . . . amplissima collectio* 5 (Paris, 1729).

Vigeois   'Cartulaire de l'abbaye de Vigeois', ed. H. Bonnhomme de Montégut, *Bulletin de la société archéologique et historique du Limousin* 39 (1890), 1-303.

Villeneuve d'Aveyron   J. Bousquet, 'La fondation de Villeneuve d'Aveyron (1053) et l'expansion de l'abbaye de Moissac en Rouergue', *Annales du Midi* 75 (1963), 538–42.

'Vita Altmanni episcopi Pataviensis', *MGHS* 12.

'Vita Chunradi archiepiscopi Salisburgensis', *MGHS* 11.

'Vita et Obitus S. Leonis Noni Pape', ed. S. Borgia, *Memorie istoriche della pontificia città di Benevento* 2 (Rome, 1764), 299–348.

Vita Meinwerci episcopi Patherbrunnensis, ed. F. Tenckhoff (*MGHS in usum scholarium* 59, Hanover, 1921).

'Vita sancti Udalrici prioris Cellensis', *MGHS* 12.

'Vita Theoderici abbatis Andaginensis', *MGHS* 12.

Walter of Thérouanne, 'Vita Karoli Comitis Flandriae', *MGHS* 12.

Wenrich of Trier, 'Epistola sub Theoderici episcopi Virdunensis nomine composita', *MGH Libelli de Lite Imperatorum et Pontificum* 1.284–99.

Whitby   *Cartularium abbatiae de Whiteby*, ed. J. C. Atkinson, 2 vols. (*Surtees Society* 69, 72, Durham, London and Edinburgh, 1879, 1881).

Wibert, 'Vita S. Leonis', *PL* 143.

William of Jumièges, *Gesta Normannorum ducum*, ed. J. Marx (*Société de l'histoire de Normandie. Publications* 43, Rouen and Paris, 1914).

WMGP   William of Malmesbury, *De gestis pontificum*, ed. N. E. S. A. Hamilton (Rolls Series 52, London, 1870).

WMGR   William of Malmesbury, *De gestis regum Anglorum*, ed. W. Stubbs, 2 vols. (Rolls Series 90, London, 1887–9).

WT   William of Tyre, *Chronicon*, ed. R. B. C. Huygens, 2 parts (*Corpus Christianorum. Continuatio medievalis* 63, 63A, Turnholt, 1986).

WT Fr   'L'Estoire de Eracles empereur et la conqueste de la terre d'Outremer', *RHC Oc* 1–2.

Zimmern 'La Chronique de Zimmern', ed. H. Hagenmeyer, 'Etude sur la Chronique de Zimmern', *AOL* 2 (1884), 17–88.
'Zur Geschichte des Investiturstreites (Englische Analekten II)', ed. W. Holtzmann, *Neues Archiv* 50 (1935), 246–319.

SECONDARY WORKS

Andressohn J. C., *The Ancestry and Life of Godfrey of Bouillon* (Indiana University Publications. Social Science Series 5, Bloomington, 1947).

Barber, M. *The New Knighthood* (Cambridge, 1994).

Barlow, F., *William Rufus* (London, 1983).

Baumel, J., *Histoire d'une seigneurie du Midi de la France – Naissance de Montpellier (985–1213)* (Montpellier, 1969).

Becker, A., *Papst Urban II*, 2 vols. (*MGH Schriften* 19, Stuttgart, 1964–88).

Blake, E. O. and C. Morris, 'A Hermit Goes to War: Peter and the Origins of the First Crusade', *Studies in Church History* 22 (1984), 79–107.

Bouchard, C. B., 'Consanguinity and Noble Marriages in the Tenth and Eleventh Centuries', *Speculum* 56 (1981), 266–87.

Sword, Miter, and Cloister (Ithaca, 1987).

Bournazel, E. *Le gouvernement capétien au XIIe siècle 1108–1180: structures sociales et mutations institutionelles* (Limoges, 1975).

Bredero, A. H., *Christendom and Christianity in the Middle Ages*, tr. R. Bruinsma (Grand Rapids, 1994).

Brundage, J. A., Adhemar of Puy: The Bishop and his Critics', *Speculum* 34 (1959), 201–12.

'An errant Crusader: Stephen of Blois', *Traditio* 16 (1960), 380–95.

'*Cruce Signari*: the Rite for Taking the Cross in England', *Traditio* 22 (1966), 289–310.

Medieval Canon Law and the Crusader (Madison, 1969).

Bull, M. G., *Knightly Piety and the Lay Response to the First Crusade* (Oxford, 1993).

'Origins', *The Oxford Illustrated History of the Crusades*, ed. J. S. C. Riley-Smith (Oxford, 1995), 13–33.

Bulst-Thiele, M.-L., *Sacrae Domus Militiae Templi Hierosolymitani Magistri* (Göttingen, 1974).

Bur, M., *La formation du comté de Champagne v.950–v.1150* (Nancy, 1977).

Cabrol, F., H. Leclercq *et al.*, *Dictionnaire d'archéologie chrétienne et de liturgie* 15 vols. (Paris, 1907–53).

Cahen, C., *La Syrie du Nord à l'époque des croisades et la principauté franque d'Antioche* (Paris, 1940).

Callahan, D. F., 'Ademar of Chabannes, Millennial Fears and the Development of Western Anti-Judaism', *Journal of Ecclesiastical History* 46 (1995), 19–35.

Cate, J. L., 'A Gay Crusader', *Byzantion* 16 (1942–3), 503–26.

Chédeville, A., *Chartres et ses campagnes (XIe–XIIIe s.)* (Paris, 1973).

Complete Peerage of England, Scotland, Ireland, Great Britain and the United Kingdom, ed. G. E. Cokayne *et al.*, 2nd edn, 13 vols. (London, 1910–40).

Constable, G., 'The Second Crusade as Seen by Contemporaries', *Traditio* 9 (1953), 213–79.

'The Financing of the Crusades in the Twelfth Century , *Outremer*, ed. B. Z. Kedar, H. E. Mayer and R. C. Smail (Jerusalem, 1982), 64–88.

'Medieval Charters as a Source for the History of the Crusades', *Crusade and Settlement*, ed. P. W. Edbury (Cardiff, 1985), 73–89.

Cook, R. F., *'Chanson d'Antioche', Chanson de Geste: le cycle de la croisade est-il epique?* (Purdue University Monographs In Romance Languages 2, Amsterdam, 1980).

Corbo, V. C., *Il Santo Sepolcro a Gerusalemme*, 3 vols. (Studium Biblicum Franciscanum. Collectio maior 29. Jerusalem, 1981–2).

Cowdrey, H. E. J., 'Pope Urban II's Preaching of the First Crusade', *History* 55 (1970), 177–88.

'The Mahdia Campaign of 1087', *English Historical Review* 92 (1977), 1–29.

'Pope Gregory VII's "Crusading" Plans of 1074', *Outremer*, ed. B. Z. Kedar, H. E. Mayer and R. C. Smail (Jerusalem, 1982), 27–40.

'Martyrdom and the First Crusade', *Crusade and Settlement*, ed. P. W. Edbury (Cardiff, 1985), 46–56.

Crozet, R., 'Le voyage d'Urbain II en France (1095–6) et son importance au point de vue archéologique', *Annales du Midi* 49 (1937), 42–69.

David, C. W., *Robert Curthose Duke of Normandy* (Harvard Historical Studies 25, Cambridge, Mass., 1920).

Devailly, G., *Le Berry du Xe siècle au milieu du XIIIe siècle* (Paris, 1973).

Douglas, D. C.,*William the Conqueror* (London, 1964).

Duby, G., *La société aux XIe et XIIe siècles dans la région maconnaise* (Paris, 1971).

The Chivalrous Society, tr. C. Postan (London, 1977).

The Knight, the Lady and the Priest, tr. B. Bray (London, 1984).

Edbury, P. W., *The Kingdom of Cyprus and the Crusades 1191–1374* (Cambridge, 1991).

Edbury P. W. and J. G. Rowe, *William of Tyre* (Cambridge, 1988).

Ellenblum, R., *Frankish Rural Settlement in Crusader Palestine* (forthcoming).

Elm, K., 'Kanoniker und Ritter vom Heiligen Grab', *Die geistlichen Ritterorden Europas*, ed. J. Fleckenstein and M. Hellmann (Sigmaringen, 1980), 141–69.

Erdmann, C., *The Origin of the Idea of Crusade*, tr. M. W. Baldwin and W. Goffart (Princeton, 1977).

Farmer, S., *Communities of Saint Martin: Legend and Ritual in Medieval Tours* (Ithaca and London, 1991).

Favreau-Lilie, M.-L., *Die Italiener im Heiligen Land* (Amsterdam, 1989).

Fletcher, R. A., 'Reconquest and Crusade in Spain c.1050–1150', *Transactions of the Royal Historical Society* 5th series, 37 (1987), 31–47.

Fliche, A., *Le règne de Philippe Ier, roi de France* (Paris, 1912).

'Urbain II et la croisade', *Revue d'histoire de l'église de France* 13 (1927), 289–306.

Flori, J., *L'Essor de la Chevalerie XIe–XIIe siècles* (Geneva, 1986).

'Guerre sainte et rétributions spirituelles dans le 2e moitié du XIe siècle', *Revue d'histoire ecclésiastique* 85 (1990), 617–49.

'Mort et martyre des guerriers vers 1100. L'exemple de la première croisade', *Cahiers de civilisation médiévale* 34 (1991), 121–39.

'Faut-il réhabiliter Pierre l'Ermite?', *Cahiers de civilisation médiévale* 38 (1995), 35–54.

Foreville, R., 'Un chef de la première croisade: Arnoul Malecouronne', *Bulletin philologique et historique du comité des travaux historiques et scientifiques* (1953–4), 377–90.

Forey, A. J., *The Military Orders* (London, 1992).

France, J., *Victory in the East* (Cambridge, 1994).

Frolow, A., *La relique de la Vraie Croix* (*Archives de l'Orient chrétien* 7, Paris, 1961).

de Gaujal, M. A. F., *Etudes historiques sur le Rouergue*, 2 vols. (Paris, 1858).

Geary, P. J., *Furta Sacra: Thefts of Relics in the Central Middle Ages* (Princeton, 1978).

Gervers, M. '*Pro defensione Terre Sancte*: The Development and Exploitation of the Hospitallers' Landed Estate in Essex', *The Military Orders*, ed. M. Barber (Aldershot, 1994), 3–20.

Gieysztor, A., 'The Genesis of the Crusades: The Encyclical of Sergius IV', *Mediaevalia et Humanistica* 5 (1948), 3–23; 6 (1950), 3–34.

Gilchrist, J., 'The Erdmann Thesis and the Canon Law, 1083–1141', *Crusade and Settlement*, ed. P. W. Edbury (Cardiff, 1985), 3 45.

Hagenmeyer, H., *Peter der Eremite* (Leipzig, 1879).

Hamilton, B., *The Latin Church in the Crusader States. The Secular Church* (London, 1980).

'The Impact of Crusader Jerusalem on Western Christendom', *Catholic Historical Review* 80 (1994), 695–713.

Hill, J. H. and L. L., 'Contemporary Accounts and the Later Reputation of Adhemar, Bishop of Puy', *Mediaevalia et Humanistica* 9 (1955), 30–8.

Raymond IV de Saint-Gilles (Toulouse, 1959).

Hodgson, M. G. S., *The Order of Assassins* (The Hague, 1955).

Hollister, C. W., 'The Anglo-Norman Succession Debate of 1126: Prelude to Stephen's Anarchy', *Journal of Medieval History* 1 (1975), 19–41.

Housley, N. J., 'Crusades against Christians: Their Origins and Early Development, c. 1000–1216', *Crusade and Settlement*, ed. P. W. Edbury (Cardiff, 1985), 17–36.

zu Isenburg, W. K., F. Freytag von Loringhoven *et al.*, *Europäische Stammtafeln*, 2nd edn, 16 vols. so far (Marburg and Berlin, 1980ff).

Jamison, E., 'Some Notes on the *Anonymi Gesta Francorum*, with Special Reference to the Norman Contingent from South Italy and Sicily in the First Crusade', *Studies in French Language and Mediaeval Literature presented to Professor Mildred K. Pope* (Manchester, 1939), 183–208.

Johnson, P. D., *Prayer, Patronage and Power: The Abbey of La Trinité, Vendôme 1032–1187* (New York, 1981).

Equal in Monastic Profession: Religious Women in Medieval France (Chicago, 1991).

Joranson, E., 'The Problem of the Spurious Letter of the Emperor Alexius to the Count of Flanders', *American Historical Review* 55 (1949–50), 811–32.

Knappen, M. M., 'Robert II of Flanders in the First Crusade', *The Crusades and Other Historical essays Presented to Dana C. Munro*, ed. L. J. Paetow (New York, 1928), 79–100.

Köhler, M. A., *Allianzen und Verträge zwischen fränkischen und islamischen Herrschern im Vorderen Orient* (Berlin and New York, 1991).

Labande, E.-R., 'Recherches sur les pèlerins dans l'Europe des XIe–XIIe siècles', *Cahiers de civilisation médiévale* I (1958), 159–69, 339–47.

Lauranson-Rosaz, C. *L'Auvergne et ses marges (Velay, Gévaudan) du VIIIe au XIe siècle* (Le Puy-en-Velay, 1987).

Lennard R., *Rural England 1086–1135* (Oxford, 1959).

Ligato, G., 'Fra Ordini Cavallereschi e crociata: "milites ad terminum" e "confraternitates" armate', *'Militia Christi' e Crociata nei secoli XI–XIII* (*Miscellanea del Centro di studi medioevali* 13, Milan, 1992), 645–97.

Maskell, A., *Ivories* (London, 1905).

Matthew, D., *The Norman Kingdom of Sicily* (Cambridge, 1992).

Mayer, H. E., 'Zur Beurteilung Adhémars von Le Puy', *Deutsches Archiv* 16 (1960), 547–52.

'Das Pontifikale von Tyrus und die Krönung der lateinischen Könige von Jerusalem', *Dumbarton Oaks Papers* 21 (1967), 143–232.

'Studies in the History of Queen Melisende of Jerusalem', *Dumbarton Oaks Papers* 26 (1972), 95–182.

Bistümer, Klöster und Stifte im Königreich Jerusalem (Stuttgart, 1977).

Mélanges sur l'histoire du royaume latin de Jérusalem (*Mémoires de l'académie des inscriptions et belles-lettres* NS 5, Paris, 1984).

'The Origins of the County of Jaffa', *Israel Exploration Journal* 35 (1985), 35–45.

'The Succession to Baldwin II of Jerusalem: English Impact on the East', *Dumbarton Oaks Papers* 39 (1985), 139–47.

The Crusades, tr. J. Gillingham, 2nd edn (Oxford, 1988).

'Angevins *versus* Normans: The New Men of King Fulk of Jerusalem', *Proceedings of the American Philosophical Society* 133 (1989), 1–25.

Metcalf, D. M., *Coinage of the Crusades and the Latin East in the Ashmolean Museum Oxford*, 2nd edn (London, 1995).

Murray, A. V. 'The Army of Godfrey of Bouillon, 1096–1099: Structure and Dynamics of a Contingent on the First Crusade', *Revue belge de philologie et d'histoire* 70 (1992), 301–29.

Nicholson, R. L., *Tancred* (Chicago, 1940).

Painter, S., 'The Lords of Lusignan in the Eleventh and Twelfth Centuries', *Speculum* 32 (1957), 27–47.

Poly, J. P., *La Provence et la société féodale (879–1166)* (Paris, 1976).

Pryor, J., *Geography, Technology and War* (Cambridge, 1988).

Reilly, B. F., *The Kingdom of Leon-Castilla under King Alfonso VI 1065–1109* (Princeton, 1988).

The Contest of Christian and Muslim Spain 1031–1159 (Cambridge, Mass. and Oxford, 1992).

Rheinheimer, M. *Das Kreuzfahrerfürstentum Galiläa* (Frankfurt-am-Main, 1990).

Riant, P., *Expéditions et pèlerinages des Scandinaves en Terre Sainte au temps des croisades* (Paris, 1865).

'Inventaire critique des lettres historiques des croisades', *AOL* 1 (1881), 9–224.

'Un dernier triomphe d'Urbain II', *Revue des questions historiques* 34 (1883), 247–55.

Richard, J., *Le comté de Tripoli sous la dynastie toulousaine (1102–1187)* (Paris, 1945).

'Départs de pèlerins et de croisés bourguignons au XIe s.: à propos d'une charte de Cluny', *Annales de Bourgogne* 60 (1988), 139–43.

Riley-Smith, J. S. C., *The Knights of St John in Jerusalem and Cyprus c. 1050–1310* (London, 1967).

The Feudal Nobility and the Kingdom of Jerusalem, 1174–1277 (London, 1973).

'Crusading as an Act of Love', *History* 65 (1980), 177–92.

'Further Thoughts on Baldwin II's *Etablissement* on the Confiscation of Fiefs', *Crusade and Settlement*, ed. P. W. Edbury (Cardiff, 1985), 176–80.

'The Venetian Crusade of 1122–1124', *I Comuni italiani nel regno crociato di Gerusalemme*, ed. G. Airaldi and B. Z. Kedar (Genoa, 1986), 339–50.

The First Crusade and the Idea of Crusading (London, 1986).

The Crusades (London, 1987).

'The Latin Clergy and the Settlement in Palestine and Syria, 1098–1100', *Catholic Historical Review* 74 (1988), 539–57.

'Family Traditions and Participation in the Second Crusade', *The Second Crusade and the Cistercians*, ed. M. Gervers (New York, 1992), 101–8.

Riley-Smith, J. S. C. (ed.), *The Atlas of the Crusades* (London, 1991).

Ritchie, R. L. G. *The Normans in Scotland* (Edinburgh University Publications. History, Philosophy and Economics 4. Edinburgh, 1954).

Robinson, I. S., 'Gregory VII and the Soldiers of Christ', *History* 58 (1973), 169–92.

Authority and Resistance in the Investiture Contest (Manchester, 1978).

Rösch, G., 'Der "Kreuzzug" Bohemunds gegen Dyrrhachion 1107–8 in der lateinischen Tradition des 12. Jahrhunderts', *Römische Historische Mitteilungen* 26 (1984), 181–90.

Round, J. H., *Studies in Peerage and Family History* (London, 1901).

Rowe, J. G., 'Paschal II, Bohemond of Antioch and the Byzantine Empire', *Bulletin of the John Rylands Library* 49 (1966), 165–202.

Runciman, S., *A History of the Crusades*, 3 vols. (Cambridge, 1951–4).

Shepard, J., 'When Greek meets Greek: Alexius Comnenus and Bohemond in 1097–8', *Byzantine and Modern Greek Studies* 12 (1988), 185–277.

Somerville, R., 'The Council of Clermont (1095) and Latin Christian Society', *Archivum Historiae Pontificiae* 12 (1974), 55–90.

'The Council of Clermont and the First Crusade', *Studia Gratiana* 20 (1976), 325–37.

Stern, S. M., 'The Succession to the Fatimid Imam al-Amir, the Claims of the Later Fatimids to the Imamate, and the Rise of Tayyibi Ismailism', *Oriens* 4 (1951), 193–255.

Sumption, J., *Pilgrimage* (London, 1975).

Tenant de la Tour, G., *L'Homme et la Terre de Charlemagne à Saint Louis* (Paris, 1943).

Tyerman, C. J., *England and the Crusades 1095–1588* (Chicago and London, 1988).

'Were There any Crusades in the Twelfth Century', *English Historical Review* 110 (1995), 553–77.

Vogel, C., 'Le pèlerinage pénitentiel', *Pellegrinaggi e culto dei santi in Europa fino alla Ia crociata (Convegni del centro di studi sulla spiritualita medievale* 4, Todi, 1963), 37–94.

Vogel C. and R. Elze, *Le pontifical romano-germanique du dixième siècle*, 3 vols. (*Studi e testi* 226–7, 269, Vatican City, 1963–72).

de Waha, M., 'La lettre d'Alexis Comnène a Robert I le Frison', *Byzantion* 47 (1977), 113–25.

Ward, B., *Miracles and the Medieval Mind* (London, 1982).

Warlop, E., *The Flemish Nobility before 1300*, 4 vols. (Kortrijk, 1975–6).

Warren, W. L., *Henry II* (London, 1973).

Wauters, A., *Table chronologique des chartes et diplômes imprimés concernant l'histoire de la Belgique*, 11 vols. (Brussels, 1866–1965).

White, S. D., *Custom, Kinship and Gifts to Saints: The Laudatio Parentum in Western France, 1050–1150* (Chapel Hill and London, 1988).

Yewdale, R. B. *Bohemond I, Prince of Antioch* (Princeton, 1924).

Index

Abbreviations

abb abbot (of); adv advocate (of); archbp archbishop (of); archd archdeacon (of); bp bishop (of); bro brother; but butler (of); cal caliph; can canon (of); cast castellan (of); chap chaplain (of); cl cleric; co-l co-lord (of); con constable (of); ct count (of); d duke (of); e emperor; k king (of); kt knight; l lord (of); m monk (of); mr master (of); n noble; patr patriarch (of); pl papal legate; pr priest (of); q queen (of); sen seneschal (of); st-b standard-bearer (of); vct viscount (of); vid vidame (of); w wife (of).

Aalst, family 96, 99
Abo of St Bonnet 197
absence from home, consequences 98, 135–9, 145–6, 155; *and see* administration of lands
Abu Ali Ahmad ibn al-Afdal, *see* Kutayfat
Achard of Born 131, 152, 226
Achard of Bully 227
Achard son of Leevin 245
Achard of Marseilles, archbp Arles 94, 97, 197, 202
Achard, cast Montmerle 63, 67, 112, 117, 197
Achard of Saintes 156
Acre 191, 193
Adalbero of Luxembourg, archd Metz 197
Adalbert, cast Metz 32
Adam I, cast Béthune, l Bethsan 227
Adam son of Michael 197
Adela of England, w Stephen of Blois 98, 110, 118, 138–9
Adela of France, w Rainald I of Nevers 101
Adelaide, mother of Garsadon of Etréchy 132
Adelaide of Burgundy, w Bertrand of St Gilles 247
Adelaide of Maurienne, w Louis VI of France 177, 247
Adelaide of Normandy, w Rainald I of Burgundy 95, 247
Adelolf 197
Adhémar of Chabannes 29
Adhémar Chatard 227
Adhémar of Felez, pr St Germain 197

Adhémar of Las Gaydias 93, 197
Adhémar II, vct Limoges 95
Adhémar III, vct Limoges 232
Adhémar IV, vct Limoges 103
Adhémar of Monteil, bp Le Puy, pl 55, 58, 87, 89, 106–8, 114, 141, 148, 197–8, 202, 211
    chaplains 87, 202
Adhémar of Roffignac 167
Adiutor of Vernon (St Adiutor of Tiron), kt 155, 158, 198
administration of lands in absence 33, 38–9, 124, 135–9, 189
Ado of Quierzy 227
Adriatic 15, 18, 36–7, 110, 141–2
advancement in career 150
al-Afdal, wazir of Egypt 180
Afflighem, abbey 154
Agnes of Beaugency, w Rainald of Nevers 99
Agnes of Courtenay, mother of Sibylla of Jerusalem 190
Agnes of Poitou-Aquitaine, empress 31, 50
Aimery 227
Aimery Andrea 239
Aimery Bernard 93, 198
Aimery Bislingueas 227
Aimery Brun, kt 67, 198
Aimery of 'Bullium' 227
Aimery, chap Chasseneuil 198
Aimery of Courron, co-l Amboise 88, 119, 156, 198

Aimery I Durnais 93, 227
Aimery II Durnais 93, 227
Aimery II Forton, ct Fézensac 95
Aimery Garaton 232
Aimery of Lusignan, con Jerusalem, k Cyprus
   and Jerusalem 190–3, 250
Aimery Michael 138
Aimery of Pont-roy 227
Aimery of St Savin 138
Aimoin Bernard 95
Ainard of La Croix 198
Airald Bardo 227
Airard 198
Alan, sen archbishop of Dol 92–3, 198
Alan III, d Brittany 40
Alan Caignart, ct Cornouaille 40, 128
Alan Fergent, d Brittany 86, 128, 198, 215
   seneschal 86, 215
Alan of Gaël 91, 94, 198
Alard of Clisson 232
Alard of 'Spiniacum' 198
Albania 9
Albara 157
Albert, kt 198
Albert, can Aachen 15, 55
Albert, ct Biandrate 198
Albert Fortis of Vitry 245
Albert, ct Parma 97, 198
Albert of St Quentin 232
Albert of Zimmern, co-l Herrenzimmern 197,
   232
Aldo, bp Piacenza 227
Aldred, bp Worcester 32, 36
Alexander II, pope 44, 49
Alexander, pr, pl, chap Stephen of Blois 87,
   148, 198
Alexandretta 158
Alexandria, Coptic patriarch 181
Alexius I Comnenus, Byzantine e 8, 12, 18,
   61, 63, 65, 79, 107, 109, 142, 154
   forged letter 79
Alfonso I, k Aragon 163
Alfonso Jordan, ct Toulouse 103
Alfonso VI, k Leon-Castile 43–4, 96
Alfonso VII, k Leon-Castile 102, 247
Alfonso I, k Portugal 102, 163
Alice of Corbeil, w Everard III of Le Puiset
   170, 249
Alice of Montlhéry, w Hugh I of Le Puiset
   248–9
Aliis of Veurne 232
Allenby, General Sir Edmund 16
Almodis of La Marche 45–6, 97, 191–2, 250
Almoravids 43
Alo Albus of L'Isle 245

Alps 141–2
Amadeus II, ct Savoy 50, 96
Amadeus III, ct Savoy 102–3
Amalfi, siege 81–2
Amand, St, relics 122–3
Amanieu III, l Albret 198
Amanieu of Loubens, kt 62, 66, 198
Amboise 7, 88, 134, 138, 156
Amiens 157
al-Amir, Fatimid cal 178, 180
Ancenis 124
Anchin, abbey 151–2
Andrew, St, apostle 13
   visions of 150–1, 154
Andrew of Baudement, sen Champagne 168
Andrew of Clermont 232
Andrew of La Haye 245
Andrew Raina 227
Anfredus, pr 227
Angerius son of Robert 232
Angers 56, 59, 76, 101, 153, 181
   archdeacon 138
   bishops 34–5, 88; *and see* individual bishops
   coinage 162
Angoulême 30, 37–8, 165
   bishop 83
Angoumois 3
Anjou 27–8, 30, 67, 88, 101–2, 124, 137, 139,
   162, 165, 182, 184–5
   counts 7, 127, 181–2; *and see* individual
   counts
Anna Comnena 55
Anonyma, leader of a sect which followed her
   goose 108, 198
Anonyma, nun of Sta Maria ad Horrea,
   Trier 107–8, 198
Anonyma of Lèves, w Ralph the Red of Pont-
   Echanfray 239, 249
Anonymous, cl 199
Anonymous, kt 199
Anonymous, armiger of Baldwin of Le
   Bourcq 198
Anonymous, d 'Bonberc'? 232
Anonymous, m Cerne 199
Anonymous Gaubert 232
Anonymous, author of the *Gesta Francorum* 199
Anonymous, father of Mainente Arcicoco 227
Anonymous of La Mote 199
Anonymous, kt, 'king of the Tafurs' 199
Anonymous, l St Thierry? 232
Anonymous, almoner of Tournemire 87, 155,
   227
Ansaldo Corso, n 242
Anse, synod 75, 77
Ansellus of Cayeux 199

Ansellus of Méry 140, 199
Ansellus of 'Valbetons' 232
Anselm of Buis, archbp Milan, pl 14, 75, 77,
    108, 199
Anselm, archbp Canterbury 77, 90
Anselm of Chantemesle 232
Anselm, bp Lucca 46, 49, 51
Anselm Parented 102, 232–3
Anselm Rascherius 199
Anselm II of Ribemont, cast Bouchain, l
    Ostrevant and Valenciennes 63–5, 74,
    122–3, 199, 221
  seneschal 122–3
Ansold (III Le Riche), l Maule 99–100
Antelme of Avignon 233
Anti-Christ 26, 29
Antioch 7, 13–14, 19–20, 30, 36, 61, 73, 78–9,
    98, 108–9, 138, 142–3, 147, 149, 151, 154,
    156–7, 166, 171
  battle 13, 144, 157
  cathedral 150
  principality 8, 158, 171, 173, 176, 178, 180
  rulers/princes 9, 23, 78, 175; *and see*
    individual rulers/ princes
  St Paul, monastery 147
  siege 13, 98, 144–5
Apt 57
Apulia 9, 18, 90, 101, 139, 172–5
Aquitaine 64, 192
  duke 42; *and see* individual dukes
Arab nationalism 16
Aragon 163
  dynasty 104–5
Archimbaud VII, l Bourbon 102–3
Archimbaud Chauderon 227
Ardouin of St Mars, kt 199
Ardouin of Vione, 'procer' of Sablé 86, 119, 199
Arles 57
Armenians 148, 170
arms and armour 14, 70, 87, 97, 110, 145
Arnald of Aigurande 76, 120, 199
Arnald the Lorrainer, vct Jericho 233
Arnald Sancho 40
Arnald Tudebode, kt 94, 199
Arni Fjöruskeiv 239
Arnold II, cast Ardres 2–3, 85, 99, 199
Arnold of Beauvais 233
Arnold II, cast Vierzon 76, 227
Arnulf, cl 199
Arnulf (Malecouronne) of Chocques, pr, pl,
    chap Robert II of Normandy, patr
    Jerusalem 87, 174, 199–200
Arnulf of Hesdin, l Chipping Norton 83,
    92–3, 200
Arnulf, bp Martirano 199

Arnulf of 'Tirs', kt 200
Arnulf son of Villicus 200
'Arqah 13
Arsuf 186
Arvedus Tudebode, kt 94, 200
Ascalon 158, 163, 172, 178–80, 182–3, 186–7
  battle 13, 20, 145
Ascelin of Grandpré 200
Ascelin, prévôt of Nivelo of Fréteval 122
Aschaffenburg 37
Asia 12, 135
  Church in 61
  trade routes 17
Asia Minor 12–15, 20, 31, 38, 50, 65, 74, 87,
    109, 142, 145, 147, 150–1, 158, 166
Aslak Hani 239
Assassins 177
Astanove II, ct Fézensac 4, 140, 227
Attropius, kt 200
Aubrey of Cagnano 200
Aubrey of Grandmesnil, kt 94, 200
Auch 129
  chapter 35, 140
Aufan of Agoult, bp Apt 200
Auger, prior of St Pierre de la Réole 124, 138
Augustine of Hippo, St 47–8
Aulnay 53
Aureil, priory 70, 121, 126, 140
Aurillac, abbey 56, 155
Austria 62, 164
authority
  of God or Christ 55–6, 61, 63–4, 73, 77,
    161–2, 164, 168
  of pope, *see* Urban II
Autran of Agoult, kt 227
Autun 29, 141
  councils 55, 89
Auvergne 30, 65
Auxerre, bishop 154
Avignon 54, 57
Aznar Exemenones of Oteiza 200

Bait Jibrin (Bethgibelin), castle 163, 183
Baldric of Bourgueil, archbp Dol 62
Baldric, sen Godfrey of Bouillon 86, 200
Baldwin, abb, chap Godfrey of Bouillon 200
Baldwin, l Ardres 103
Baldwin of Beauvais 233
Baldwin of Boulogne, ct Edessa, I k
    Jerusalem 18, 63, 70, 93, 96, 171–4, 200,
    206, 208
Baldwin, l Le Bourcq, ct Edessa, II k
    Jerusalem 8–10, 160, 162, 169–80, 182–7,
    190, 198, 200, 244–6, 248
  établissement 186

Baldwin Chauderon, kt 200
Baldwin of Ghent, adv St Pierre-au-Mont-
    Blandin, l Aalst 85, 99, 141, 200
Baldwin of Grandpré, kt 200
Baldwin I, ct Guines 93, 200
Baldwin of Hestrud 200
Baldwin of Ibelin 190
Baldwin I, k Jerusalem, *see* Baldwin of Boulogne
Baldwin II, k Jerusalem, *see* Baldwin, l Le
    Bourcq
Baldwin III, k Jerusalem 23
Baldwin IV, k Jerusalem 190–1
Baldwin V, k Jerusalem 191
Baldwin of Mons, ct Hainault 63, 99, 125,
    147, 149, 157, 201
Baldwin Tauns, kt 233
Baldwin of Vern d'Anjou 135–6, 242
Balkans 12, 20, 110, 142
Baniyas 158
banners 60, 82, 147
Barbastro 49
Bardo 51
Bardoul Le Large 81
Bari 18, 36, 141–2
Barisan the Old, con Jaffa 163, 172–3, 175,
    179, 186, 190, 241
Bar-sur-Aube 140
Bartholomew Boel, vid Chartres 47, 100, 201
Bartholomew, archbp Misis 201
Bartholomew, vct Vendôme 103
Bath, bishop 90
Bauzac 104
Bavaria 12, 30, 36
    'The Bavarian Road' 36, 142
Beatrice, countess of Tuscany 50
Beaugency 33
    church, *see* St Sépulcre de Beaugency
    family 96, 170
Beaujeu 28
Beaulieu, abbey 33
Bec, abbey 148
Bego of La Rivière 93, 201
Beirut 158
Belgrade 37, 142
Bellacosa 201
Bellay II of Montreuil-Bellay 242
Belle-Noue 120
Belval, priory, sculpture from iv, 11, 97
Bencelinus, l Brie 125, 154, 201
Benedict, St 27
Benedict, archbp Edessa 201
Berald Silvain 111, 124, 131, 201
Berengar 227
Berengar of Narbonne 201
Berengar Peter of Gignac 201

Berengar Raymond II, ct Barcelona 46, 83,
    228, 250
Berlai of Passavant-sur-Layon 201
Bernard 67, 201
Bernard Ato, vct Béziers and Carcassonne
    119, 166, 201
Bernard le Baile 201
Bernard II, ct Besalù 45, 96, 201
Bernard of Bré, family 93, 95, 102
Bernard II of Bré, co-l Bré 3, 93, 201
Bernard IV of Bré 102–3
Bernard of Clairvaux, abb Clairvaux 23, 82,
    102, 146, 162, 168
Bernard, vct Comborn 167
Bernard of Le Dognon 103
Bernard Durnais 93, 228
Bernard L'Etranger 233
Bernard Goscelm 167
Bernard V Gros of Uxelles 160, 164
Bernard of Merzé 35
Bernard Morel 116, 228
Bernard of 'Pardilum' 201
Bernard Raymond of Béziers, n 202
Bernard of St Amand 228
Bernard of St-Valéry 202, 248
Bernard (ct Scheyern) 201
Bernard of Valence, pr, chap Adhémar of
    Monteil, bp Artah, patr Antioch 87, 202
Bernard Veredun 202
Berry 76, 165
Bertha of Frisia, w Philip I of France 89
Berthold, ct (Neuffen) 202
Berthold of Sperberseck 245
Bertrada of Montfort-l'Amaury, w Fulk IV of
    Anjou, w Philip I of France 59, 89
Bertrand of Bas, pr, can Le Puy 87, 104, 148,
    202
Bertrand son of Gerard 131
Bertrand of Marseilles 94, 202
Bertrand, cast Moncontour 114, 202
Bertrand of Prévenchières, bp Lodève 233
Bertrand Porcellet, lay sacristan of the
    church of Arles 202
Bertrand II of Provence 45, 96
Bertrand of St Gilles 9, 242, 247, 250
Bertrand of St Jean, l St Jean-Poutge 103,
    129–30
Bertrand of 'Scabrica' 202, 217
Bertrand of Taillecavat 202
Besançon 140–1
Bethlehem 185
    relic of the Manger 31–2
Bèze, abbey 33, 83, 144, 149
    abbot 83
Béziers, family 96

Bira 172
blessing of crusaders on departure 82–3, 106,
    108, 141
Blois 33, 88, 123
    counts 127
    court of county 136
Bohemia 12
Bohemond of Taranto, l Taranto, ruler of
    Antioch 9, 17–18, 78–9, 81–2, 87, 99–101,
    141, 144–5, 149, 165–6, 171–2, 202, 215,
    221, 239–42
    chaplain 79
    contingent on the First Crusade 100–1
    servant 87, 215
Boleslaw III, d Poland 244
Bologna 75
Bonfilius, bp Foligno 202
Boniface, can (Le Puy?) 202
Boniface, kt 33
Bonizo, bp Sutri 46, 48
Bonneval, abbey 156
Bordeaux 57
    archbishop 57
Born, family 95
Boso of La Chèze 93, 123, 140, 202
Boso I, vct Turenne 36, 96
Bosphorus 12
Bouillon, castle 125, 128
    priory 128
Boulogne, family 96, 171
Le Bourcq of Rethel, family 171
Bourges
    archbishop 57
    viscounty 76, 117, 154
Bouzonville (Busendorf), abbey 32
Bovard 132
Bracas of Valpin 233
Le Breuil, family 93
Brienne, family 195
Brioude, college of canons regular 56
Britain 16, 165; *and see* England; Scotland
Brittany 40, 81, 91, 94, 124, 133, 141, 186
Broyes, family 171
Bruges 145–6, 154
Brunet of Treuil, can Aureil 70, 202
Bruno 202
Bruno, n, can 202
Bruno, n, can 202
Bruno of Ré 123, 228
Bruno, bp Segni, pl 78
Bulgaria 36
Burchard of Marmande, n 228
Burgundy
    French 30–1, 55, 63–4, 67, 94, 112, 154,
    159–60, 164–5

imperial 3, 72, 165
    family of counts 94–5, 97, 171, 177, 247
Busdorf, Jerusalem church 33
Byzantine empire 9, 12–13, 17–18, 30, 32,
    36–7, 50, 54–5, 60–1, 65, 79, 99, 101, 107,
    142, 147, 166

Caesarea 36–7
    lordship 193
Caffaro de Caschifelone 202
Cairo 154, 158, 178, 180–1
Calabria 142
Calahorra 33
Calixtus II, pope 8–9, 11, 78, 94, 102, 165–6,
    176–7, 242–4, 247
Cambrai 30–1
Campagna 141
canons regular 126; *and see* individual
    communities
Carcassonne 57
Carniola 142
Carolingians 64
Catalonia, Catalans 46, 61, 66–7, 71, 100
Cecilia of Le Bourcq 171, 173, 248
Centule IV, vct Béarn 96
Centule II, l Bigorre 45, 166, 202–3
Cerne, abbey 90
La Chaise-Dieu, abbey 54, 150
    tomb of St Robert 150
Chaise-le-Vicomte, priory 94, 104, 127–8, 140
Le Chalard, priory 59
Chalo VII, vct Aulnay 53–4, 57, 203
Chalo the Red of Vivonne 176, 242
Chalon-sur-Saône
    canons 125
    county 117
    family 95–6
    shrine of St Vincent in cathedral 125
Chambéry 142
Champagne 3, 54, 70, 112, 160, 165, 167
La Chanson d'Antioche 2–3, 41, 55, 144, 196
chansons 157, 196
La Chapelle-Aude, priory 120
chaplains 85–7, 99, 107; *and see* individual
    magnates
La Charité-sur-Loire, priory 147
Charles the Good, ct Flanders 159, 176, 233
Charroux of La Marche, family 192
charters as evidence 2–5, 56, 60–75, 105, 107,
    111–13, 115–17, 119, 121, 125, 129–30,
    132–4, 140, 165, 169, 173, 179–82
Chartrain 88, 118, 165
Chartres 47, 88, 100, 124, 136, 141, 156
    cathedral 79
    dean 124

Chartres (*cont.*)
   provost and canons 88
   coinage 110
   vidames 47, 88, 184; *and see* individual
      vidames
   viscounts 47, 88, 172–3; *and see* individual
      viscounts
Chastel Hernaut, castle 182
Chatard 228
Châteaudun 70
Châtillon-sur-Seine 140
Chaumont 140
Chaumont-en-Vexin, family 171
Cheminon, abbot 81
Cherfron the German 233
Les Chétifs 196
La Chèze, family 93
Chirac 54
chivalry 64
Christina of Markyate 84
Christ
   authority, *see* authority of God or Christ
   inspiration, *see* inspiration of God or Christ
   knights of 77, 161, 165
   relics 32, 150
   see also service of God in arms
churches, *see* ecclesiastical property
church lands, *see* ecclesiastical property
Cilicia 171, 233
Civitate, battle 48–9, 73
Clarembald, l Vendeuil 203
Clemency of Burgundy, w Robert II of
   Flanders 94, 98, 119, 139, 154, 247
Cleophas, St, relic 150
Clermont 54–6, 58, 81, 89, 107, 124
   council and decrees 8, 16, 19, 54–6, 58, 60,
      62–4, 66, 68, 71–3, 89, 100, 106, 146
Cluny, abbey 54–5, 74, 94–6, 107, 112, 126–7,
      130, 144, 149, 155, 175–6
   Cluniac communities 3, 95–6, 98, 122, 127,
      169–70, 175
Cluses 142
coin, bullion and precious cloth carried on
   crusade, *see* financing crusades
Cologne 28
   archbishop 112
commanders, *see* leaders of crusades
Commisago 33
commutation of vows 108
Compostela 27, 153
computing 5–6
Conan of Lamballe 203
condition of survivors 147–8
confession 28–9, 68–9, 72, 82–3
Cono, pr 203

Cono, pr, chap Robert II of Flanders 87, 141,
   203
Cono, ct Montaigu 94, 126, 148, 154, 203
Conques, abbey 27
La Conquête de Jérusalem 196
Conrad, con Emperor Henry III 203
Conrad III, k Germany 83, 103, 146, 166, 242
Conrad, ct Luxembourg 95–6
Conrad, marquis of Montferrat 191–3
Conrad, son of Taio 203
Conrad of Zimmern, co-l Herrenzimmern
   197, 233
Constance of Arles, w Robert II of France 101
Constance of Burgundy, w Alfonso VI of
   Leon-Castile 43–4
Constance of France, w Bohemond of
   Taranto 79
Constantine, e 23
Constantine son of Bernard 203
Constantinople 9, 12, 18, 36–7, 39, 59, 61, 63,
   65, 79, 101, 107–8, 141–2, 147
Constantius of Diénay 228
contrition 68, 71
conversion, inner 35, 47, 155
Corba of Thorigné, co-l Amboise 88, 156,
   203
Corbigny, abbey 137
Cormery, abbey 147
Cornouaille 40
   family 94
Coulommiers 114, 139
counter-gifts 106, 115, 118, 128, 155
Courtenay, family 171
Couvin, castle 117, 125
Crac des Chevaliers, castle 163–4, 180
Craon 138
Cremona 141
Crisenon, priory 154
Cross
   devotion to 31–2, 40, 94
   of crusaders iv, 11, 18, 29, 55, 62–3, 81–2,
      97, 106, 161
   taking the cross 7, 10–12, 14–19, 21, 46,
      55–8, 67, 74–5, 81–5, 87–9, 93–4, 96,
      100, 103, 108–9, 125, 127, 130, 144, 148,
      156, 166, 176, 183, 189, 196
   see also True Cross
Crown of Thorns, relic 32
crusades
   of 1096/1101 (First Crusade) xii–xiii, 2–4,
      7–20, 25–6, 30–1, 33–6, 39, 41, 43, 45–6,
      48, 50, 52–5, 57–80, 84–97, 99–104,
      106–16, 118–33, 136–59, 166–8, 170–1,
      174, 180, 187, 189, 191, 196–238
      aims 60–2, 68, 74

as a *furtum sacrum* 66
commentaries on 77–8
common fund 110
conditions on 86
continuation under Bertrand of St Gilles
9, 242
experiences on 14–15, 65, 78, 104, 135, 144
Frankish contribution 64–5
miraculous character 77–8
Peter the Hermit's treasury 110
regulations 106
routes of contingents 108, 141–2
size 109
visions 13, 15
of 1103 (abortive: planned by the Emperor
Henry IV) 10, 238
of 1107 (of Bohemond of Taranto-Antioch)
xiv–xv, 9, 15–16, 78–9, 81, 88, 96,
99–100, 102, 110–11, 115, 120–1, 124, 130,
136, 139, 165–7, 172, 238–42
of 1120 (of Pope Calixtus II) xiv–xv, 8–9,
15–16, 67, 78, 81, 83, 88, 102, 110–12, 115,
119, 121, 135–9, 149, 162, 165–7, 176–8,
183, 187, 238, 242–4
of 1129 (of King Baldwin II of Jerusalem)
xiv–xv, 7–10, 15–16, 100, 102, 110–11, 115,
118, 120–1, 124, 138, 140, 165–7, 179,
183–5, 187, 244–6
of 1147 (Second Crusade) 23, 73–4, 82, 87,
100–3, 130, 137, 146, 155, 160, 163, 165,
168, 190–1
of 1189 (Third Crusade) 191–4
crusading 6, 10, 34, 41, 93, 99, 101, 134,
187–8, 189–90, 195, 229
as a colonial enterprise 15–19
as a means of advancement 150
as an act of love 50, 65–6, 71, 78, 161
as an act of self-sanctification 67, 69–70, 75,
168, 189
as an alternative to or preparation for the
life of a religious 69–70, 75, 77–8, 154–5,
189
as an economic safety-valve 21, 134–5
as a penance 6, 10, 48, 66–72, 74, 78, 83
as a plundering expedition 19–21
as a war of liberation 60–2, 68, 74, 76–7
as a war-pilgrimage 15, 20, 39, 54, 62,
67–71, 74, 77–8, 113, 176
for the name of Christ 64
martyrdom 72–4
multiple 7, 148–9, 165–7
popularity of 21, 94
sources for 1–2, 64, 97–8; *and see* charters as
evidence
Cuthbert, St 27

Cyprus 20, 38, 148, 178, 193–4
kingdom 194

Daimbert, archbp Pisa, pl, patr Jerusalem 57,
108, 203, 236
Dalmatia 36–7, 141
Damascus 10, 163, 172, 177–80, 182, 185
Daniel 233
Dauphiné 33
David Four Bones, champion of Nouaillé 150
deaths 14, 146–7
Demetrius Zwonomir, k Dalmatia 51
Déols, family 76
departure on crusade 82–3, 106–9, 118–20,
125, 139–43
deserters 7, 13–14, 98, 138, 142, 147–9, 154
despoliation of churches and shrines to
finance crusaders 125–6
Diego Gelmirez, archbp Compostela 80
Dijon 140
disorder, *see* Europe
Dithmar, ct 203
doctors 87, 104
Dodo, kt 203
Dodo de Advocato 203
Dodo, l Clermont-en-Argonne 203
Dodo of Cons-la-Grandville 149, 203, 210
Dodo Donat 233
Domène, priory 3
Domenico Michiel, doge of Venice 176, 243
Donald, k Scotland 90
Donation of Constantine 64
Doon the Young of Montbéliard 233
Dorylaeum, battle 13, 20, 157
dowries 121, 123, 135
Drogo (le Frison?) 233
Drogo of Chaumont-en-Vexin, l Trie-
Château 89, 155, 228, 249
Drogo I, l Mouchy-le-Châtel 203
Drogo II, l Mouchy-le-Châtel 103
Drogo of Nesle 203
duels, judicial 92, 136, 150, 186
Dun, lordship 76
Durand Bovis 204
Durand Cheuvre 75, 228
Durazzo 9, 110
Durham 27
Durnais, family 93

Ebles, ct Roucy 45, 85, 96, 157, 232
Ebles of 'Torviars' 233
Ebro valley 43
ecclesiastical property 104, 116–19, 130–3, 137,
148, 152–3, 155
eclipse, lunar 83

Edessa 13–14, 146, 157, 174–5
  archbishop 175–6; *and see* individual
    archbishops
  county 8, 158, 169–71, 173–4, 190
Edgar Atheling 90–1, 204
  household 91
Edward the Confessor, k England 91
  staller 91
Egypt, Egyptians 13–14, 17, 20, 145, 158,
    172–3, 177–8, 180–2, 186
  galley fleet 158, 178
Eichstätt, bishop 140
Ekkehard of Aura, m Michelsberg, Bamberg
    16, 204
elderly crusaders 107, 141
Eleanor of Aquitaine, w Louis VII of France,
    w Henry II of England 103, 192, 250
Elizabeth of Montlhéry, w Joscelin I of
    Courtenay 248
Elizabeth of Montlhéry, w Philip of France
    177, 248
Elne, cathedral chapter 123
Elvira of Leon-Castile, w Raymond IV of St
    Gilles 107, 204
Emeline, w Fulcher of Bullion 107, 204
Emerias of Altejas 108, 204
Emich, ct Flonheim 157, 204
Emma of Hereford, w Ralph I of Gaël 91,
    93–4, 107, 204
Emmeline of Montlhéry, w Hugh Bardolf II
    of Broyes 248
Emprainville 114–15
endowments 4–5, 27, 35, 39, 40–1, 83, 104,
    106, 113, 118–21, 123, 125–8, 130–3,
    144–5, 147, 164, 189
  in free alms 74, 153–4, 179–80
  see also prayer
Engelelmus of St Savin 118, 124, 138, 228
Engelrand of Boves 156–7
Engelrand of Châlons-sur-Marne 204
Engelrand II, l Coucy 103
Engelrand of Coucy, bp Laon 204
Engelrand of St Pol 204
Engilbert 228
Engilbert, adv Cysoing, l Petegem, st-b
    Robert II of Flanders 99, 204
Engilbert of Tournai 204
England 3, 31, 38, 78–9, 90–2, 94, 98, 104,
    141, 153, 165, 183, 190, 194
  Norman invasion 40–1
entry gifts 35, 70, 114, 120, 123, 137
equipment 109–10, 189; *and see* arms and
    armour
Erald of Châlons-sur-Marne 204
Erard I, ct Brienne 167

Eregli, battle 13
Eremburge of Maine, w Fulk V of Anjou 139,
    183
ergotism 16
Erkenbald 233
Ermengald of Roussillon, bp Elne 94, 204
Ermengarde of Montaigu 157
Ermessens of Melgueil 46
Ermintrude of Burgundy, w Thierry II of
    Montbéliard 95, 98, 247
Essex 91
Esteial of Vern d'Anjou 135–6
Etampes 81
  abbacy 117
  viscount 146
Eu, count 194
Eudes 67, 204
Eudes Arpin, vct Bourges, m Cluny 76, 89,
    154–5, 204
Eudes the Bastard 233
Eudes (Odo), bp Bayeux 91–2, 204
Eudes of Beaugency, st-b Hugh the Great of
    Vermandois 99, 205
Eudes Betevin 70, 228
Eudes the Breton 234
Eudes I, d Burgundy 43–5, 63, 74, 89, 95–6,
    109, 120–2, 138, 141, 204–5, 247
Eudes, prior of La Chapelle-Aude 120
Eudes, l Déols 30
Eudes of Deuil, m St Denis 82
Eudes of Montfaucon 233
Eudes of Port-Mort 233
Eudes of St Mars, abb Preuilly 205
Eudes of Verneuil 205
Eudes of Vert-le-Grand 228
Eudes William, ct Burgundy 95
Eudon of St-Valéry 234, 248
Eugenius III, pope 82, 87, 102, 146
Euphrates river 172
Europe, western 6, 9, 11–12, 14, 16, 18–21, 25,
    30–2, 36–7, 65, 73, 80, 86, 91, 108, 110,
    134, 142, 145–6, 149–50, 154, 160, 162,
    168, 171, 173–6, 178, 184–5, 187–8, 195
  agricultural depression in 16, 53, 127
  disorder
    in the absence of crusaders 135, 145–6, 155
    on return 155–7
Eürvin of Creil 234
Eustace, but Robert II of Flanders 205
Eustace I Garnier, l Sidon and Caesarea 228
Eustace III, ct Boulogne 18, 91, 93, 96, 174,
    183, 205
Eustace of Boulogne 183
Everard 234
Everard I of Breteuil 249

Everard II, ct Breteuil, vct Chartres, m
    Marmoutier 47, 96, 123–4, 249
Everard III, ct Breteuil 103
Everard III of Le Puiset, vct Chartres 89,
    123–4, 170, 205, 249
Everard, pr 205
Everard Venator, huntsman 87, 205
excommunication 113, 122, 128, 131, 136, 176
Exeter, bishop 90
Exning 91
expeditio (Jherosolimitana) 67

Faith, St 27
families 41, 43–4, 46, 52, 80, 84–5, 92–105,
    129–35, 139, 156–7, 175–6, 187–90, 194–5
  and the absence of crusaders 135–9
  and crusading 8, 21–2, 93–105, 187–90, 195
  and marriage 41, 44–6; *and see* marriage
  and religious communities 124
  clusters of crusaders in 93–4, 98, 189
  extended 41, 93
  family crusades 100–2
  financing crusades 129–35; *and see* financing
    crusades
  foundations, *see* foundations
  maternal uncles 134–5
  predispositions 8, 21–2, 32, 83–4, 93–7, 99,
    104, 139, 170, 177, 187, 189, 191
  resistance to alienations of property 130–2
  solidarity 6, 21–2, 135, 139, 187–8, 194–5
  traditions of crusading 101–3, 191
  women and crusading 97–100, 102, 129–30,
    133–5
  younger sons 134
Fantin Incorrigiatus 133–4, 205
Farald of Thouars 205
Fatimid dynasty 13, 38, 158, 177–8, 180–1; *and
  see* individual caliphs
Faucon of Vierzon 234
fear on departure 118–20
Fécamp, abbey 27, 116
Fézensac, family 95
fideles beati Petri 44–7, 52, 85, 95–6
Field of Blood, battle 9, 160, 176
financing crusades 3–5, 8, 21, 34, 44, 80, 83,
    86, 88–90, 105, 109–18, 124–35, 152–4,
    187, 189, 194
  coin, bullion and precious cloth carried on
    crusade 110–11, 125
Finchale 239
Flaald 92
Flanders 30, 55, 60–1, 65, 75, 93, 96, 140, 145,
    151, 157, 159–60, 165, 175
  family 95
Fleury, abbey 27, 139

Florina of Burgundy, w Sven of Denmark 95,
    107, 205, 247
Folkmar, pr 205
foraging 110, 151
Forcalquier 57
Fortun Iniguez, l Grez 205
Fortun Sanchez 125, 130
foundations of churches and religious
    communities 104, 119–20, 127–31, 140,
    154
France 3, 12, 14–16, 20, 25, 30–1, 43–4, 54–6,
    59–61, 63, 75–6, 78–9, 82, 89, 93, 100,
    106, 108–9, 141–2, 144, 149, 155, 157,
    162–3, 169, 176, 184, 187, 190, 193
  Capetian dynasty 96
  Church in 54, 58
Franco I of Mechelen, cast Brussels 205
Frankish contribution, *see* crusades
Frederick of Bogen, adv Regensburg 205
Frederick of Châtillon 243
Frederick of Corbeil 169
Frederick I of Germany, western e 103, 191
Frederick of Montbéliard 96
Frederick II, d Upper Lorraine 96
Frederick of Zimmern, co l Herrenzimmern
    197, 228
Fréteval 112
Frumold, ministerialis of the archbishop of
    Cologne 112, 155, 205
Fulcher of Alençon 234
Fulcher of Brousse 228
Fulcher of Bullion, kt 204, 206
Fulcher of Chartres, kt 47, 206
Fulcher of Chartres, pr, chap Stephen of
    Blois and Baldwin of Boulogne 87, 140,
    206
Fulcher of 'Coversana' 234
Fulcher of Le Dognon 103
Fulcher of Faverges 228
Fulcher fitz-Gerard, can Notre-Dame de
    Chartres 47, 96
Fulcher of Melan, kt 234
Fulcher the Orphan 234
Fulk III, ct Anjou 27–36, 42, 62
Fulk IV, ct Anjou 59, 88–9, 101, 127, 156
  household 88
Fulk V, ct Anjou, k Jerusalem 7–10, 62, 88,
    119, 135, 137–9, 149, 162–3, 165–6, 176,
    181–7, 243–4, 248
  prévôts 138
Fulk of Clermont 234
Fulk Doon, l Châteaurenard 67, 69–70, 83,
    206
Fulk of Guines, l Beirut 93, 206
Fulk the Lombard, l Grasse 111, 206

Fulk I, cast Matheflon 88, 101–2, 152–3, 206
Fulk, l Le Plessis-Macé 88, 137, 243
Fulk, vicar of Pontoise 89, 228
Fulk of Solliès 94, 206
furta sacra 66, 151

G. of Las Gaydias, pr 93, 206
Gaël, family 94
Galdemar Carpenel, l Dargoire 75, 206
Galilee 19, 172–5, 179
  constables 173
Gandier 234
Gap 57, 164
Garcia Livar Castro 241
Garderade Barbotin the Old of Pons, n, kt 35
Garin of Gallardon 206
Garin son of Milson of 'Verzels' (Vercel-
  Villedieu?) 234
Garnier, ct Grez 206
Garnier Marchio 206
Garsadon of Etréchy 132, 142, 206
Garsias of Le Bignon-du-Maine 243
Garsias of Malemort 167
Gascony 40, 62
Gastinellus of Bourgueil 239
Gaston IV, vct Béarn 45, 166, 206, 234
Gaston of Béziers 234
Gaucher I, cast Châtillon-sur-Marne 3, 229
Gaucher, l Montjay-la-Tour, cast Châtillon-
  sur-Marne 103
Las Gaydias, family 93
Gaza 158
Le Genéteil, almonry 119
Genoa 9, 17, 108
Geoffrey 234
Geoffrey, chamberlain of Godfrey of
  Bouillon 229
Geoffrey, doctor 206
Geoffrey of 'Bello Mortario' 245
Geoffrey Burel, co-l Amboise 206
Geoffrey, prior of Le Chalard 58–9
Geoffrey Chotard, 'procer' of Ancenis 206
Geoffrey II, l Clervaux 88, 229
Geoffrey son of Deriadoc 207
Geoffrey II, l Donzy, ct Chalon-sur-Saône
  44, 125, 134, 207
Geoffrey son of Droon 234
Geoffrey Fulcard of Loudun 67, 243
Geoffrey son of Geoffrey of 'Perolium' 207
Geoffrey Guarin, kt 207
Geoffrey, l Issoudun 76, 139, 207
Geoffrey I Jordan, ct Vendôme 70, 114, 131,
  207
Geoffrey of Le Louet 137, 243
Geoffrey of Lusignan 192–4, 250

Geoffrey Malaterra 17
Geoffrey of 'Mali' (Mailly?) 239
Geoffrey Martel, ct Anjou 59, 181
Geoffrey of Montescaglioso 101, 207
Geoffrey of Montgin 234
Geoffrey Parented of Segré 102, 207
Geoffrey Plantagenet, ct Anjou 182–3
Geoffrey Le Râle 153, 207
Geoffrey III of Rancon 191
Geoffrey of Riveray 207
Geoffrey III, ct Roussillon 94, 100, 207
Geoffrey of St Savin 118, 124, 138, 229
Geoffrey of Signes, kt 67, 207
Geoffrey III, vct Thouars 94, 104, 191, 207
geography of recruitment 104–5
George, St
  confusion between two saints of that name
    94
  relic 151–2
Gerald 229
Gerald of Bériu, pr 229
Gerald, bp Cahors 55–6, 62
Gerald, cast Landerron 66, 124, 138, 207
Gerald Malefaide, l Noailles and St Viance
  155, 207
Gerald of Le Mont 167
Gerald Pincre 229
Gerald of 'Ponti' 234
Gerald of St Junien-la-Bregère 229
Gerald of Thouars, abb St Florent-lès-
  Saumur 37
Gerald of 'Tuda', kt 130, 207
Gerard, cl 234
Gerard, cl in household of Baldwin of
  Boulogne 208
Gerard, bp Ariano 208
Gerard of Avesnes, kt 208
Gerard Barson 207
Gerard of Buc, cast Lille 86, 151–2, 208
Gerard of Chanac 167
Gerard of Donjon 234
Gerard of Fontvannes 33
Gerard of Fréteval 113
Gerard of Gournay-en-Bray 166, 208
Gerard the Old of Meleone 208
Gerard I, l Quierzy 208
Gerard of Roucy 245
Gerard of Roussillon 94, 208
Gerard of St Gilles 234
Gerard, abb Schaffhausen 87, 207, 238
  chaplain 87, 238
Gerard, archbp York 88, 239
Gerbault of 'Castellum Winthinc' 208
Gerbault of Lille, pr 151, 208
Gerberga, w Boso I of Turenne 36

Gerento of Le Béage, l Le Béage 208
Germany 3, 14, 16, 20, 31, 44, 63, 76, 112, 142, 165
Gervase of St Cyprian, abb St Savin 208
Gesta Francorum 79, 100, 199
Gevrey-Chambertin 122
ghosts 144, 148
Gilbert of Aalst, kt 120, 208
Gilbert, abb Admont 208
Gilbert, ct Clermont 208
Gilbert of Entraigues 234
Gilbert, bp Evreux 208
Gilbert Payen of Garlande, sen King Philip I of France 88, 208
Gilbert of Rheims 235
Gilbert of Traves 208
Gilduin of Le Puiset, prior of Lurcy-le-Bourg, abb St Mary of the Valley of Jehoshaphat 169–70, 172–3, 175–6, 179, 184, 249
Girbert of Mézères 208
Girismannus 208
Gisela of Burgundy, w Humbert II of Savoy 94, 247
Godehilde of Tosny, w Baldwin of Boulogne 93, 107, 208
Godfrey Brisard 239
Godfrey of Bouillon, d Lower Lorraine, ruler of Jerusalem 18, 30, 63, 70, 84–6, 96, 111, 125, 128, 141, 146, 171, 200, 209, 222, 227, 229–32
   household 86, 230–1
   seneschal 86, 200
Godfrey Burel 209
Godfrey of Esch-sur-Sûre, n, kt 209
Godfrey Incorrigiatus 133–4, 209
Godfrey I, ct Louvain, d Lower Lorraine 242
Godfrey Parented 102, 235
Godfrey of Ribemont 243
Godric of Finchale, merchant, pirate, hermit 153, 155, 166, 209, 239
Godschalk 235
Godschalk, pr 209
Goldinellus of Curzay 239
Gomerville 132
Gontier of Aire, squire of Robert II of Flanders 235
Goths 64
Gottman of Brussels 209
Göttweig, abbey 62, 117
Gouffier, l Lastours 3, 93, 155, 209
   his lion 155
Gouffier of Bouillon 235
Gozelo of Montaigu 94, 209
Gran Conquesta de Ultramar 196–7

Grandmesnil, family 94
Great St Bernard Pass 141
Greece, Greeks, *see* Byzantine empire
Gregorianism, *see* reform movement of the eleventh century
Gregory I, pope 115
Gregory VII, pope 32–3, 39, 44–5, 47, 49–51, 66, 68
   'crusading' plans (1074) 50
Grenoble
   bishop 108; *and see* individual bishops
   cathedral 3
Grimbald, kt 149, 209
Grimoald of Maule 100, 209
grooms 109
Guarin, kt 209
Guarin of Clisson 235
Guarin Guernonatus 138, 209
Guarin of 'Petra Mora' 209
Guarin of 'Tanea' 209
Gueth-Ronan, battle 40
Guibert, abb Nogent-sous-Coucy 69–70, 108
Guigo II, ct Forcalquier 164
Guigo of 'Mara' 147, 209
Guiraut of Hirson 235
Guitard of Tulle 167
Guitier, ct Rethel 184, 248
Gunscelin, pr, can Lille 151–2, 209
Gunter, kt 235
Gunther, bp Bamberg 31, 36–9
Guy 239
Guy of Athée, dean of St Laud d'Angers 181
Guy of Biandrate, kt 209
Guy of Bré (first crusader) 93, 95, 104, 139, 209–10
Guy of Bré (second crusader) 102–3
Guy of Bujaleuf 167
Guy of Champallement 137
Guy of Château-Landon 235
Guy of Chaumont-en-Vexin 235
Guy Cornelly of Til-Châtel 159
Guy I of Dampierre-sur-l'Aube 167, 173, 184, 248
Guy Le Duc 229
Guy of Escorailles 210
Guy of Guines 93, 210
Guy of Hauteville 101, 166, 210, 239
Guy of 'Insula Bollini', kt 149, 229
Guy III, l Lastours 3, 93
Guy IV of Lastours 103, 229
Guy I of Laval 28
Guy I, vct Limoges 25, 95
Guy of Lusignan, k Jerusalem, ruler of Cyprus 190–4, 250
Guy II, ct Mâcon 95

Index

Guy, co-l Mezenc 209
Guy I, l Montlhéry 7, 169–71, 248
Guy of Morlay 235
Guy of Pers-en-Gâtinais 229
Guy Pinellus 131, 138, 229
    mother 131, 138
Guy, ct Pistoia 153–4, 210
Guy II of Ponthieu 102–3
Guy, l Possesse 3, 210
Guy of Le Puiset, l Méréville, vct Etampes
    173, 184, 249
Guy II, ct Rochefort, sen Philip I of France
    89, 145–6, 149, 170, 172, 209, 248
Guy, l Roumoulès 63, 210
Guy of Sarcé, kt 210
Guy, l Signes 67, 210
Guy of Thiers, ct Chalon-sur-Saône 111, 210
Guy Tortus of Rochefort-sur-Loire, kt 112,
    133, 243
Guy Trousseau, l Montlhéry 88, 138, 147,
    149, 210, 248
Guy IV, l Vignory 244
Guynemer of Boulogne, pirate 210

Hadvide of Chiny, w Dodo of Cons-la-
    Grandville 107, 149, 210
al-Hafiz, Fatimid cal 180, 182
Haimerad, St 29
Hakim, Fatimid cal 25, 28–9
Halldor Skaldri 241
Hamelin 235
Hamelin of Fréteval, l Montigny-le-Ganelon
    112
Hamo, abb Cerne 90, 210
Hamo of La Hune 210
Hamundr Thorvaldsson of Vatnsfjord 239
Hartmann, ct Dillingen-Kybourg 210
Hattin, battle 191
Hauteville, family 166
Helena, empress 23
Helias, l Cray 229
Helias of Didonne 35
Helias of La Flèche, ct Maine 59, 137, 210
Helias of Malemort 229
Heliodore of Blaru 235
Henry, ct 210
Henry of Alsace, bp Toul 103
Henry of Brienne 168
Henry Burgundio 102, 245
Henry I, ct Champagne 103
Henry Contarini, bp Castello 75, 210
Henry I, k England 78, 88, 90, 137, 183, 240
Henry II, k England 192, 250
Henry of Esch-sur-Sûre, cast Esch-sur-Sûre
    211

Henry of Ferrières, cast Tutbury, sheriff of
    Derbyshire 92
Henry III of Germany, western e 203
Henry IV of Germany, western e 10, 37, 51,
    96, 238
Henry of Grandpré, ct Grandpré 211
Henry of Préaux 235
Henry II, burgrave of Regensburg 62, 210
Henry I of Toul 103
Heraclius I, vct Polignac, st-b Adhémar of
    Monteil 94, 211
Herbert (leader of the Basques?) 235
Herbert of 'Campus Marini', kt 119, 211
Herbert of Chaise-Dieu, prior of Prevezac,
    chap Raymond IV of St Gilles, bp
    Tripoli 86, 150, 211
Herbert of Corbeil 169
Herbert of Sennecé 28
Herbert II, vct Thouars 82–3, 94, 104, 125,
    133, 140, 191, 211
    household 104
Herbert Vigers 229
Herbrand of Bouillon, kt 211
Herluin, pr, interpreter 211
Hermann of Canne 101, 211
Hertfordshire 91
Hervey son of Arnold 229
Hervey son of Dodeman 211
Hervey son of Durand 239
Hervey, archd Orléans 32
Hictor 33
Hildebert, ct 211
Hildegarde, w Fulk III of Anjou 34–5, 152
Hilduin of Limoges, bp Limoges 25, 95
Hilduin of Mazingarbe 211
Hodierna of Gometz 170–1, 248
Hodierna of Montlhéry, w Walter of St
    Valéry 248
Holy Fire, miracle 24–5, 31, 38
Holy Lance, relic 13, 150–1, 154
Holy Land, *see* Palestine
holy war, *see* violence
Honorius II, pope 10, 176, 185
Honour of Boulogne 91
horses and pack animals 14, 109–14, 144,
    189
    horses 38–9, 110–12
    mules 39, 111–13
Hospitallers of St John 29, 80, 159–60, 163,
    179–80, 183
    confratres 164
    constable 163
    militarization 163–4
    seneschal 164
Host of 'Castellum Ruvra' 211

households 19–20, 85–7, 109, 189; *and see* individual magnates
Hubert of Cergy 235
Huesca, bishop and canons 125
Hugh 235
Hugh, kt, m 160
Hugh of 'Almaz' 212
Hugh, l Amboise, *see* Hugh of Chaumont-sur-Loire
Hugh of Amboise, kt 212
Hugh of Apigné 212
Hugh Artmand 167
Hugh of Avranches, earl of Chester 92
Hugh Bardolf II, l Broyes 3, 211, 248
Hugh of Les Baux 235
Hugh of 'Bellafayre' 212
Hugh Bochard, cast Trivy 211
Hugh Botuns 211
Hugh of Bourbouton, Templar bro, mr Richerenches 164–5
Hugh of Bully 229
Hugh Bunel 211
Hugh I, d Burgundy 96
Hugh II, d Burgundy 73–4
Hugh of Burgundy, archbp Besançon 94, 212, 247
Hugh of 'Calniacum' 212
Hugh I, ct Chalon-sur-Saône 95
Hugh of Chaumont-sur-Loire, l Amboise 7–8, 23, 88, 119, 134, 138, 147, 156, 166, 212, 245
Hugh, abb Cluny 76, 175
Hugh of Crécy 248
Hugh Dalmace of Semur, l Dyo and Couzon? 166, 235
Hugh of Dijon 235
Hugh I Embriaco, n 242
Hugh II, ct Empurias 212
Hugh of Equevilley, kt 229
Hugh of La Ferté-Vidame, provost of Chartres cathedral 124
Hugh Lo Forsenet (or 'The Mad') 212
Hugh I, l Gallardon 88, 139, 211
Hugh Geoffrey of Marseilles 167
Hugh the Great, ct Vermandois 59–60, 88–90, 99, 108–9, 141, 148, 205, 213
Hugh Guernonatus, prévôt of Blois 88, 138, 211
Hugh of Guines 93, 212
Hugh II, l Jaffa, *see* Hugh (of Le Puiset) II, l Jaffa
Hugh III of Juillé 212
Hugh of Liège 235
Hugh V, l Lusignan 42, 45–6
Hugh VI, l Lusignan 42–3, 45–6, 96, 106, 150, 191–2, 213, 219, 250

Hugh VII, l Lusignan 42, 103, 191, 250
Hugh VIII, l Lusignan 191, 250
Hugh IX, l Lusignan 192–4, 250
Hugh of Lusignan 250
Hugh, archbp Lyons, pl 57, 75, 77, 83, 89, 211
Hugh II, l Matheflon 102, 130, 153, 246
Hugh, l Méry-sur-Seine 3, 140, 212
Hugh of 'Montbeel' 212
Hugh of Montmirail 244
Hugh of Morentin 235
Hugh of Payns, mr Templars 79, 160, 162, 165, 184–5
Hugh of Pierrefonds, bp Soissons 212
Hugh I of Le Puiset, vct Chartres 47, 248–9
Hugh II of Le Puiset, vct Chartres, l Le Puiset, (I) l Jaffa 99, 136, 172–3, 175, 239–40, 249
Hugh III of Le Puiset, vct Chartres, ct Corbeil 120, 140, 184, 245, 249
Hugh (of Le Puiset) II, l Jaffa 169, 172–3, 175, 179 80, 184–7, 249
Hugh (of Le Bourcq), ct Rethel 212, 248
Hugh of Rheims 212
Hugh of Robecq, l Hebron 236
Hugh of Rougemont 119, 229
Hugh Rufus of Champallement 137
Hugh of St Aubin-du-Désert 244
Hugh of St Hilaire 212
Hugh of St Omer, l Fauquembergues 212
Hugh II, ct St Pol 86, 212
Hugh of St Savin 138
Hugh, m St Victor 162
Hugh, cast Ste Maure-de-Touraine 83, 88, 243
Hugh, l Salagnac 236
Hugh Sansavoir of Poissy 100, 239
Hugh of Soulier 167
Hugh Tirel I, vct Poix 103
Hugh, co-l Toucy 94, 140, 148, 154, 212
Hugh I, ct Troyes 160, 163, 167
Hugh II, l Usson-en-Forez 75, 229
Hugh I, ct Vaudemont 103
Hugh Verdosius 213
Humbald, oblate 120
Humbald the White of Hubans 229
Humberge of Le Puiset, w Walo II of Chaumont-en-Vexin 107, 213, 249
Humbert III of Beaujeu 102–3
Humbert of Le Dognon 230
Humbert son of Ralph 240
Humbert II of Savoy, ct Maurienne, Savoy and Turin 45, 95, 213, 247
Humphrey son of Ralph 213
Hungary 15, 36–7, 142, 157
huntsmen, hunting 87, 152

Husechinus 213
Huy 148, 154

Ibelin, family 172
Ibn al-Qalanisi 185
Iceland 165
Ida of Boulogne, w Baldwin ct Rethel 171
Ida of Cham, w Markgraf Leopold II of
    Austria 213
Ida of Hainault, w Thomas of Marle 99, 157
Ida of Lorraine, w Eustace II of Boulogne 63,
    128
Ida of Louvain, w Baldwin of Mons 147
ideas of crusaders 56, 61–75, 168, 189
Ile-de-France 7, 42, 93, 165, 170
Ilger Bigod, con Tancred Marchisus 92, 158,
    213
Imam, Hidden 180–1
Imamis 180–1
indulgences 26, 49, 68, 71; *and see* remission of
    sins
Ingelbald 236
Ingo Flaonus 213
Ingo de Pedegola 242
Innocent II, pope 162
inspiration of God or Christ 63, 74, 81
Investiture Contest 44, 50–2
Iraq 8, 19
Isaac of Veurne, chamberlain of Flanders 243
Isabella, q Jerusalem 192–3
Ismailis 177, 180–1
Ismidon of Sassenage, bp Die 167
Isnard of La Garenne 112, 236
Isoard I, ct Die 213, 216
Isoard of Ganges, n, kt 213
Isoard of Mouzon 213
Israel 16
Italy 15, 17–18, 31, 36–7, 44, 56–7, 64, 70, 73, 78,
    96, 100, 110, 133, 141–3, 157, 165, 172–3
Itier of La Rivière 93, 230
Itier I, co-l Toucy 94, 213
Itier II, l Toucy 103
Itier of 'Tuda' 130, 213
Itier of La Vue 93, 230
Ivo, bp Chartres 48, 77, 89, 136, 155–6
Ivo of Grandmesnil, sheriff of Leicester 90,
    92, 94, 148, 214
Ivo II of Nesle, ct Soissons, con Louis VII of
    France 103

Jabal Sumaq 90
Jaffa 36, 104, 148, 157, 179, 186
    county of Jaffa and Ascalon 193
    lordship 163, 172–3, 175, 179, 186
    constables 172–3, 175

Jaligny 33
Jericho 144
Jerosolimitani 78, 119, 145, 149, 234, 237–8
Jerusalem 1, 3–4, 7–11, 13–14, 16, 18, 20,
    23–32, 35–8, 40–2, 52, 54–6, 59–63,
    65–7, 70–4, 77–81, 83, 90, 92, 94, 95,
    97–8, 102, 107–9, 111–14, 116, 119–20,
    123, 125, 130–1, 139–40, 144–50, 152–5,
    157–60, 163, 166–9, 173, 175–6, 178,
    181–2, 185–6, 189, 227, 235, 243
    Acheldamach (Hospitaller cemetery) 29
    as a female Christian name 33
    as a place in which to die 19, 29, 35, 107
    basilica of Constantine 23
    Calvary 23–5, 32
    centres of cult in the West 26–7, 32
    church of St John 24
    church of St Stephen 159
    Column of Flagellation, stone from as relic
        32
    contamination of 62
    Garden of Gethsemane 47
    Golgotha 23
    'heavenly Jerusalem' 120, 158
    Holy Sepulchre 9, 14, 23–5, 26, 28–9, 31–3,
        38, 50, 61, 63, 66–7, 69, 78–80, 85, 95,
        149–50, 154, 167, 169, 185
        canons 80, 154, 163
        church of 23–5, 159
        gifts to 32–3
        proprietary churches of 32–3
    kingdom 8, 165, 170, 173–4, 176–9, 182–4,
        187, 190–4
        arrière ban 179
        constable 190, 193
        money fiefs 194
        parlement 174
    Mount of Olives 7, 23, 150
    patriarchs (Greek and Latin) 8, 25, 32–3,
        56–7, 139, 154, 160, 182, 184, 186; *and see*
        individual patriarchs
    relics from 31–2
    St Mary of the Latins, abbey 80
    St Mary of the Valley of Jehoshaphat,
        abbey 8, 80, 169, 175, 179–80
    siege 13–14, 19, 86, 156–7, 171
    Temple 24–5, 159–60
Jews 25–6
    persecutions of 12, 20, 25–6, 41–2, 60, 90,
        157
John the Baptist, St, relic 150
John XIX, pope 40
John 236
John, pr 230
John, chamberlain 214

John of 'Alis' 236
John of Bréval 236
John of Capistrano OFM 76
John of Draché 230
John, l Joinville 81
John of Mantua 46–8, 51
John Michiel 214
John of Nijmegen 214
Jordan, river 38
Jordan of Le Breuil 93, 214
Josbert 236
Josbert Alboin 124, 167, 241
Josbert Cabrun 230
Josbert of Malemort 95
Josbert of Les Murs 93, 214
Josbert of St Hilaire 214
Joscelin, cl 236
Joscelin, provost of Chartres cathedral 230
Joscelin I of Courtenay 248
Joscelin of Courtenay, l Galilee, ct Edessa
    169–72, 174–5, 190, 214, 248
Joscelin of Lèves 131, 240, 249
Josceran of Vitrolles 214
Josceran of Vitry 240
Joseph of Arimathea, St 78
Judaean hills 182
Judith, w Adalbert of Metz 32
Juhel of Mayenne 87
Jumièges, abbey 35
Just, St, relic of 53

'Koprisianos' 240
Kutayfat, wazir and ruler of Egypt 180–2,
    186–7

Lagman, k Man 83, 214
Lambert 214
Lambert 214
Lambert, doctor 214
Lambert Ghezo 214
Lambert Magus 214
Lambert of Montaigu 94, 148, 154, 214
Lambert the Poor 214
Lampert, m Hersfeld 36–7
Lancelin, cast Beaugency 33, 96, 114
Lancelin, m Noyers 118, 124
Landécourt, priory 154
Landolt, kt 140, 244
Lanfranc Drubesci or Roza 214
Langeais, priory 33
Languedoc 31–2, 45, 62, 112, 160, 165
Lantelmus, gonfalonier (adv) of Piacenza
    cathedral 230
Laon 157
Laron 140

Lassicourt, priory 140
Lastours, family 93
Latakia 19, 36–8, 104
Lateran Council, First 11, 136
Latin East xvi, 1–2, 17, 174, 177, 184, 187,
    191
  service in as a religious duty 19
  settlement in 1, 5, 7–10, 18–19, 111, 149,
    157–9, 171–3, 176, 182–3, 187–8, 190
laudatio parentum 130–1
lay condition as a vocation 27
lay patrons 123, 181–2
lay people and the financing of crusades
    129–35
leaders of crusades 17–18, 20–1, 30, 55–6, 62,
    64, 78, 106–7, 141, 151, 196
Lebanon 9, 13–14, 86
Leger 214
Leicester, sheriffdom 90
Leo IX, pope 48–9, 73
Leodegar, can Chartres 230
Leofranc Donat 236
Leomer Musart 236
Leon 43–4
Leopold II, markgraf of Austria 213
leprosy 159, 191
Lérins, abbey 69, 111
  abbot 66–7, 69–70, 83
Leteric, l Châtillon 76, 230
Lethold of Tournai, kt 214–15
letters from crusaders 138–9, 142
Levant 25, 148, 157–8; *and see* Latin East
Lézat, abbey 96, 119
  abbot 119
Liège, diocese 125–6
Lietbert, bp Cambrai 33, 36, 38
Lietgard of Aalst 120
Ligonnat, family 167, 244
Lille 140, 151–2
  castellans 85; *and see* individual castellans
Limoges 25, 29–30, 56–9, 63
  bishop 57; *and see* individual bishops
  cathedral of St Etienne 58
  canons 155
  family 95
Limousin 3–4, 31, 57, 67, 70, 84, 93, 95, 102,
    104, 121, 126, 155, 165, 167
Lisbon, siege 73
Lisiard of Flanders 215
Lisois of Amboise 156
Lithard of Cambrai, vct Jaffa 236
Le livre au roi 194
Lobbes, abbey 126
Loire river 58
Lombardy 14, 77, 108, 142

Longpont-sous-Montlhéry, priory 96, 119, 126–8, 131, 140, 148, 170
lordship 80, 83–93, 104–5, 112–13, 131, 136, 187–9
  subjects forced to crusade or forbidden to do so 84–5
Lorraine 3, 11, 30, 56, 71, 86, 97, 118, 141, 146, 154, 157, 165, 171
Lothian 91
Louis VI, k France 157, 170, 172, 177, 247
Louis VII, k France 23, 82, 102–3, 190
Louis IX, k France 97
Louis, ct Mousson 95, 215, 247
Louis, archd Toul 215
love, *see* crusading; violence
Lucca 141, 143
  coinage 110
Lurcy-le-Bourg, priory 169
Lusignan, family 42, 190–5
Luxembourg 31
  family 95
Lydda 179
  bishop, *see* Ramle
  tomb of St George 151
Lyonnais 31
Lyons 54

Ma'arrat-an-Nu'man 157
Mabel of Bellême, w Roger II of Montgomery 92
Mabel of Hauteville, w William of Grandmesnil 101
Mabel of Roucy, w Hugh II of Le Puiset 96, 99, 172–3, 175, 240, 249
Mâcon 54
Maguelonne 57
Mahaut of Angoulême, w Hugh IX of Lusignan 192
Mahdia 51
Mahuis of Clermont 236
Maillezais, abbey 35
Mainard 236
Maine 30, 137, 165
Mainfinit, sen Alan Fergent of Brittany 86, 215
Mainfred of Magdeburg 36
Mainz 12, 31
  archbishop 31; *and see* individual archbishops
Mala-Corona, servant of Bohemond of Taranto 87, 215
malaria 147
Malemort, family 95
Malikis 181
Malta 159

management of lands in absence, *see* administration of lands in absence
Manasses, bp Barcelona 215
Manasses of Clermont 215
Manasses, archbp Rheims 73–4
Manasses Robert of Guines 93, 215
Le Mans 54, 56, 59, 76, 81, 89
  coinage 110, 153
La Marche, 32, 192–4
  counts 192
Marcigny, priory 116, 147
Margaret, q Scotland 90
Marmoutier, abbey 7, 47, 70, 85, 88, 118–19, 122–8, 132, 140
  abbot 123–5, 132
  prior 132
marriage 41, 44–6, 84, 137, 139, 152, 156, 171–2, 176, 183; *and see* families
Marseilles 167
  family 94, 97
Martin, ct 236
martyrdom 37
  in military orders 162
  in war 15, 48, 50, 72
  on crusade 72–4
Mary, Blessed Virgin
  assumption 169
  relic 150
  tomb 169
Mass 26–7, 37, 73, 119–20
material gain from crusading 8, 15–21, 106, 134–5, 149–53
Matheflon, castle 152
Mathilda of Boulogne, w Stephen of Blois, k England 183
Mathilda of Le Bourcq 184, 248
Mathilda of England 183
Mathilda, daughter of Hugh the Great of Vermandois 99
Mathilda, countess of Tuscany 46–51, 96
  Mathildine scholars 46–9, 51
Matthew, sen Jerusalem 230
Matthew, kt 215
Matthew of Edessa 170
Matthew Giraud 120, 123, 246
Maule 99–100
Maur, St 35
Maurice Bourdin, bp Coimbra 240
Maurice of Glons 155
Mauro de Platea Longa 215
Mediterranean Sea 18, 148, 158
  commerce 17
Meinwerk, bp Paderborn 33
Melgueil, coinage 110

Melisende, q Jerusalem 8–10, 165, 176, 182–4, 186, 248
Melisende of Montlhéry, w Hugh I of Rethel 248
Melun, viscount 88; *and see* individual viscounts
Mer son of Garin 236
mercenaries 158, 163, 171
merchants 17, 36
Merhem, nunnery 120
merit in fighting 48–50, 71, 74, 155; *and see* indulgences; penances; penitential warfare; remission of sins
Méry-sur-Seine 140
Metz 30
    family 94
Mezenc 112–13
Miles 236
Miles of Bray, cast Bray, vct Troyes 3, 70, 119, 138, 140, 148–9, 215, 248
Miles of Clermont, kt 230
Miles Louez, kt 215
Miles of Vignory 4
military orders 5, 103, 158, 160–5; *and see* Hospitallers of St John; Templars
milites ad terminum, see para-crusaders
Millau 54
millenarianism 26, 29–30
miracles 27
Moissac, abbey 32, 57
Molesme 122
    abbey 119–20, 126
monastic profession 84, 147, 155
monks, nuns and religious 106–8, 116, 118–20, 122–6, 131, 137, 140, 145–8, 150–3, 155–6, 160–2, 164, 167; *and see* monastic profession; religious communities
Mont Cenis Pass 142
Mont St Michel, abbey 153
Monte Cassino, abbey
    abbot 65
    chronicle 66, 69
Montferrat, family 191
Montfort-l'Amaury, family 170
Montierneuf de Poitiers, abbey 96
Montlhéry, family 7–8, 18, 42, 96, 101, 145, 169–77, 179–80, 184–7, 190–1, 193–5, 248–9
    Montlhéry sisters 99, 123, 171, 248
Montmoreau 130
Montpellier 57
Morellus, cl 236
Morigny, abbey 128, 132, 145
    abbot 145
    chronicle 146

Mortagne, family 96
motivation 15–22
Mozac 89
mules, *see* horses and pack animals
Münster 31
Les Murs, family 93
Muslims 13, 23–5, 37–8, 42–3, 49, 61–2, 66–7, 69, 71, 73, 78, 80, 87, 107, 148, 151, 176, 178–82, 186, 191
    Shii 177, 181
    Sunni 177
musters 125, 140–1, 179

Nablus council 160, 173, 176
Nantes 104
Navarre 31
neighbours on campaign 104
Nérac 57
Neumoustier, abbey 56, 148, 154
Nevers 31
    family 99
new knighthood 161
Newmarket 91
Nicaea 12, 14, 20, 156–7
Nicene creed 51
Nicholas, St 94
    miracula 148
    relics 141, 150
Nicholas of Normandy, abb St Ouen de Rouen 95
Nîmes 54, 57
    council 58, 89, 108
Nivelles 16
Nivelo, cast Fréteval 62, 71–2, 88, 112–15, 122, 138, 215
    prévôt 122
Nogent-le-Rotrou, abbey 96, 128, 144
Norfolk, earldom 91
Norgeot, bp Autun 215
Norgeot of Cruz 103
Norgeot I, co-l Toucy 94, 139–40, 166, 215
Norman of Morvilliers 215
Normandy 4, 28, 30–1, 35–6, 39, 90–1, 94, 104, 112, 117, 125, 137, 141, 148, 165–6, 184–5, 194
    family 95
Normans in southern Italy 17, 36–7, 48, 73, 99–100
North Africa 43, 51
Northumberland 90
Norway 165
Norwich 91
Notre-Dame de la Ferté-Avrain, priory 32
Notre-Dame de la Règle de Limoges, abbey 58

Notre-Dame de Saintes, abbey 53
Nouaillé, abbey 150
Noyers, abbey 83, 118, 126
  abbot 118
nuns, *see* monks, nuns and religious

Oberalteich, abbey 140
Obert, bp Liège 125–6, 128
Oberto Usu de Mar 242
obits 35, 120
oblates 35, 84, 120, 137
Odard, kt 35
Odeline of Maule, w Walter II of Poissy 100
Odeline of Le Puiset, w Joscelin of Lèves 249
Odilus of Morlhon 35
Odo, *see* Eudes
Olgerius, kt 144
Oliver of Jussey, kt 215
Oliver of Lastours 139
Oliver of Venise 236
Omne datum optimum 162
Onulf, sen Robert II of Flanders 141, 215
Opizo Mussus 215
Ordelafo Falier, doge of Venice 242
Orderic Vitalis, m St Evroul 9, 185–6
oriflamme 82
Orléannais 76
Orléans 25–6, 30–1
Osbert Bassus de Insula 216
Osbert son of Lambert de Marino 216
Osmund of Boudeville 40–1
Otto, cl 216
Otto Altaspata 216
Otto, bp Freising 103
Otto, abb Ilsenburg 230
Otto, bp Strasbourg 216

pack animals, *see* horses and pack animals
Paderborn 30, 33
Pagano of Volta 216
Palestine 7–11, 14–17, 19–20, 26, 34, 36–9,
  79–80, 87, 102, 110, 116, 127, 135, 151,
  155, 157–61, 163, 165–6, 169, 172, 175–7,
  179–80, 183–4, 187–8, 190–4
palm fronds 144–5
papacy 10, 21, 44, 46–8, 50–2, 55, 57, 59, 64,
  72, 78, 80, 83, 94–6, 98, 136, 164, 176–7,
  185, 194
  golden rose 59
  papal tiara 58–9
  see also individual popes
papal legates 55, 57, 75, 78, 83, 89, 106, 108,
  160, 185; *and see* individual legates
para-crusaders 158–60, 165
Paris 30, 88–9, 99, 108, 124, 146, 170

diocese 137
parish churches 120, 123, 152
Paschal II, pope 42, 45, 52, 75, 77–8, 83, 111,
  136, 154–5
Paschale Noscentius Astor 216
patrimony 123, 130–1, 133–4
Payen, ct (Kontopaganos) 240
Payen, sergeant 216
Payen of Beauvais 216
Payen of 'Camelli' 237
Payen of Chevré 237
Payen of Mondoubleau 88, 230
Payen Peverel, st-b Robert II of Normandy
  90, 216
peace decrees 146
Pechenegs 37
penances 28–9, 34, 42, 48–52, 53, 106, 108,
  113, 123, 139, 155–6, 161, 172, 189
  and armsbearing 39, 69, 156
  see also crusading; merit; penitential
  warfare; pilgrims
penitential warfare 48–52, 55, 63–4, 66–72,
  74, 77, 160–2, 189
Périgord 3, 38
Périgueux, diocese 63, 137
Peter, St 47–8, 51
  service to, *see fideles beati Petri*
Peter Abon, Hospitaller bro 164
Peter III Aimery of Bré 102–3
Peter Airoveir, l Trouillas 216
Peter of Alifa, kt, l Plastencia 101, 217
Peter, bp Anagni 230
Peter I, k Aragon 166, 216
Peter Badoaro, patr Grado 75
Peter Bartholomew, servant of William Peyre
  of Cunlhat 13, 87, 150–1, 154, 216
Peter Bastard, kt, co-l Mezenc 216
Peter Carbonel 33
Peter, vct Castillon 217
Peter of Chevanville 130–1
Peter of Coudes, cl 230
Peter of Courtigny 237
Peter, l Dampierre-le-Château, ct Astenois 217
Peter Desiderius, pr, chap Isoard I of Die 216
Peter Fasin 216
Peter of Fay, co-l Fay-le-Froid 65, 94, 217
Peter Fortis 216
Peter of Friac 217
Peter of La Garnache 217
Peter Gaubert 230
Peter son of Gisla 217
Peter, bp Glandèves 216
Peter Guernonatus 138
Peter the Hermit, cl 55–6, 76–7, 89, 100, 107,
  110, 142, 148, 154, 217

Peter Jordan, l Châtillon 66, 147, 154, 217
Peter, bp Limoges 63, 137
Peter Lombard, kt 217
Peter Loup, Hospitaller bro 163
Peter, abb Maillezais 76, 216
Peter (I Le Riche), l Maule 99
Peter II, ct Melgueil 45, 96
Peter of Mercœur, pr 217
Peter of Narbonne, pr, bp al-Barah 217
Peter, l Noailles 167
Peter of 'Picca', pr, chap Bertrand of
     'Scabrica' 217
Peter II, cast Pierre-Buffière 3, 104, 216
Peter Postels 237
Peter Raymond, l Hautpoul 217
Peter Raynouard 217
Peter of Roaix 217
Peter Robert of Champagne 230
Peter Rostagn of 'Poncianum' 241
Peter of 'Tuda' 130
Peter Tudebode, pr 94, 217
Peter of Vallières, l La Narce 217
Peter of Vic 35
Peter of Vihiers 237
Peter of La Vue 93, 121, 140, 230
  his bed 121
Philip of Bouillon 237
Philip of Briouze 231
Philip I, k France 43, 59, 76, 79, 88–91, 108,
     124, 154, 170, 177, 208–9, 224
  constable 88, 224
  seneschal 88, 170, 208–9
Philip II, k France 191, 193
Philip of France 177
Philip of Gloucester 103
Philip the Grammarian of Montgomery, pr
     91–2, 217
Philip of Montoro 240
Philippa of Toulouse, w William IX of
     Aquitaine 46, 250
Piacenza, council 55
Pibo, bp Toul 32
pilgrimages, pilgrims 1, 3–5, 10–11, 24–39, 47,
     49, 52–4, 56, 66–9, 80–3, 85, 92, 95–7,
     107, 120, 125, 130, 139, 141, 144–5, 147,
     153–4, 160, 163, 166–8, 172, 174, 181, 184,
     189
  as penances 28–9, 34, 39, 69, 82, 189
  ceremonial homecomings 38–9, 145
  financing 33–4, 39
  peregrinationes religiosae 29, 39, 69, 189
  pilgrims and the bearing of arms 39
  roads to Jerusalem 36–8, 141–2
  symbols (purse and staff) iv, 4, 69, 81–3,
     97, 140

reception 82–3
  vows 29, 82
Pisa 17, 51, 108
Pisellus 217
Pistoia, canons 153
planning crusades 55, 106–12, 124
pledges 3–4, 27, 33–4, 39, 90, 92, 106, 111–13,
     115–17, 122–3, 124–6, 128–34, 137, 149
  terms 33–4, 116–17, 125, 133; *and see vifgages*
  to religious communities 125–6, 128
plunder 19–21, 43, 68, 106–7, 110, 134
Poissy, family 93, 100
Poitiers 57–8, 78, 140, 150, 176
  bishops 42, 57, 82, 139–40
  church of St Hilaire-le-Grand 176
  tomb of St Hilary 176
  coinage 110
  council 75
  prévôté 150
  The Royal Meadow 140
Poitou 29, 31, 42–3, 94, 104, 114, 137, 139–40,
     149, 165, 191, 193
Poitou-Aquitaine, family 96
Polignac, family 94
Pons 231
Pons of 'Balazun' (Balazuc?), n 218
Pons of Cuiseaux 35
Pons II of Fay, co-l Fay-le-Froid 65, 94, 218
Pons of Grillon, chap Raymond Decan
     218–19
Pons, co-l Mezenc 218
Pons Palatinus 244
Pons Raynouard, kt 218
Pons the Red, kt 147, 218
Pons, ct Toulouse 45–6
Pons, ct Tripoli 250
Pontarlier 141
Pont-Echanfray, family 171
Pontia of La Marche, w Wulgrin II Taillefer
     of Angoulême 192
Pontlevoy, abbey 119
  battle 119
poor on crusade 12–13, 16–17, 141–2
prayer, desire for 27, 35, 39, 74, 85, 105,
     118–20, 127–8, 140, 154, 189
preaching crusades 10, 14, 21, 54–80, 81–2,
     89, 100, 102–3, 107–9, 123–4, 165
precious cloth carried by crusaders 111, 125
preparations for crusades 8, 105–40, 187, 189
Primo Embriaco 218
protection of crusaders properties and
     families 106–7, 136; *and see* security
Provence, Provençaux 13, 54, 63–4, 67, 69,
     160, 164, 167, 196
Prussia 159

Le Puiset 140
  family 42, 47, 96, 99, 123–4, 170–2, 184, 249
  priory 47
purgatory 26–7
Le Puy 54–5, 58, 104, 112
  cathedral 119
  coinage 110
  cult of Blessed Virgin Mary 119
Pyrenees 43

Quino son of Dodo 4, 71, 118, 218

R. Gabard 137, 244
Raimbert of Chevanville 131, 231
Raimbert, bp Verdun 37
Raimbold of Commercy 237
Raimbold Croton, kt 155–6, 218
Raimbold II, ct Orange 218
Raimondino son of Donnucci 153–4, 218
Rainald 218
Rainald 237
Rainald, sen Hugh VI of Lusignan 213, 219
Rainald I of Bailleul 164
Rainald I, ct Bar-le-Duc and Monçon 102–3,
  166, 245, 247
Rainald of Beauvais, kt 218
Rainald of Broyes, kt 218, 248
Rainald Burgundio, l Craon 101, 132, 138
Rainald I, ct Burgundy 247
Rainald II, ct Burgundy and Mâcon 94, 158,
  218, 247
Rainald III, l Château-Gontier and Segré 88,
  101–2, 107, 109, 138, 149, 218
Rainald of La Chèze 93, 140, 218
Rainald of Martigné, bp Angers 88, 119,
  137–8, 243
Rainald I, ct Nevers 101
Rainald of Nivelles 237
Rainald Porchet, n, kt 73, 219
Rainald of the Principate 101, 218
Rainald Superbus 231
Rainald of Thiviers, bp Périgueux 57, 63, 137,
  218
Rainald, ct Tonnerre 103
Rainaldo de Rudolpho 219
Rainer 237
Rainer, cl, chap Robert II of Flanders 87,
  219
Rainer III, marquis of Montferrat 247
Ralph 237
Ralph of Aalst 19, 219
Ralph, ct Beaugency 33, 88, 99, 114, 145, 219
  household 145
Ralph of Beaugency, burgess in Jerusalem
  166

Ralph of Caen, kt 240
Ralph Dolis 219
Ralph of Escorailles 219
Ralph of Fontaines, kt 219
Ralph I, l Gaël 91, 94, 107, 204, 219
Ralph Glaber, m 29
Ralph 'Licei' 240
Ralph of Lusignan 194
Ralph I of Montpinçon, steward of England
  92
Ralph of Montpinçon, kt 92, 158, 166, 231
Ralph of 'Monzon', kt 231
Ralph Rabaste 240
Ralph the Red of Pont-Echanfray 101, 166,
  219, 239–40, 249
Ralph of 'Scegonges', n 219
Ralph of Simas 237
Ralph of Tosny 36
Ramle 36, 179
  battle 154
  bishop (of Ramle-Lydda) 151, 185, 221
Ramnulf Silvain, archpriest, m St Jean
  d'Angély 124
Ramnulf of 'Tuinac' 117, 231
ransoms 149
Raymond 231
Raymond of Aguilers, pr, chap Raymond IV
  of St Gilles 63, 154, 219
Raymond of Les Baux 219
Raymond Berengar I, ct Barcelona 45–6
Raymond Berengar III, ct Barcelona 163
Raymond Bertrand of L'Isle-Jourdain 219
Raymond of Burgundy 44, 247
Raymond of 'Castellum' 219
Raymond the Chamberlain 220
Raymond of Curemonte, kt 4, 219
Raymond Decan, lay dean of the church of
  Arles, l Posquières 218–19
Raymond Ebo, bp Lectoure 28
Raymond Eic, cl 119–20, 231
Raymond of Gensac 231
Raymond Pilet, l Alès 220
Raymond of Le Puy, mr Hospitallers 163–4
Raymond IV of St Gilles, ct Toulouse 9, 19,
  43, 45–6, 50, 55–6, 59, 62–4, 86, 96, 104,
  106–7, 112, 119, 138, 141, 150, 191–2, 204,
  219, 222, 250
  chaplains 150, 219, 222
Raymond Trencavel, vct Béziers and
  Carcassonne 103
Raymond II, ct Tripoli 250
Raymond III, ct Tripoli 191–2, 250
Raymond, vct Turenne 3–4, 104, 219–20
Raymond William 237
recruitment to crusades 76, 80, 83–105, 185

reform movement of the eleventh century 34, 44, 46–7, 50, 52, 54–5, 75, 77, 89, 94–100, 126, 133, 189
Regensburg 31
reinforcements 108–9, 142, 158
Reinhard of Hamersbach, kt 220
Reinhard III, ct Toul 220
Reinhard of Verdun 237
Reinhold, n 220
Reinhold, vct 'Firmamentum' 220
relics 13, 23–5, 27, 30–2, 40, 53, 73, 122, 144, 146, 150–2, 154, 182, 185
  humiliation of 122–3
religious communities 5, 27, 34–6, 40, 52, 83, 90, 100, 104–5, 113, 115–16, 118, 123–33, 160, 162, 164, 189
  and finance 125–33
  and recruitment 76, 105
  monastic reform 98, 127, 164
  see also families; foundations; monks, nuns and religious
remission of sins 51, 66, 72, 106, 119
  and crusading 49, 68–72, 74–5, 168
Renier Brun 240
renunciations of rights 28, 34, 39, 40, 70–1, 83, 85, 104, 113, 115, 118–19, 121–4, 139, 167
  for cash 34, 112–15, 133
repayment of debts 152–3
returning from crusades 20, 77, 144–57, 166
  ceremonial homecomings 144–5
Rheims 54, 85, 89, 96, 141, 157
  archbishop 89; *and see* individual archbishops
Rhineland 12, 90, 157
Rhodes 159
Rhône river 54
Richard (of Caiazzo and Alife) son of Count Ranulf 101, 220
Richard I, prince of Capua 50
Richard 'Carus Asini', kt 220
Richard of Chaumont-en-Vexin 231, 240, 249
Richard I, k England 191–4, 250
Richard son of Fulk the elder of Aunou, kt 148, 155, 220
Richard of Harcourt 237
Richard of Mâcon 237
Richard II, d Normandy 29–30, 32, 95
Richard of Pavia 237
Richard the Pilgrim 3, 220
Richard of the Principate, ct Salerno 101, 220, 240
Richard (of Le Puiset) 240
Richard, abb St Vanne de Verdun 29–32, 36–7

Richard, abb St Victor de Marseille, cardinal 231
Richard of 'Valpin' 237
Richard of Verdun 237
Le Riche of Maule, family 99–100
Richer, bp Verdun 125
Richerenches, Templar commandery 165
riches brought back to Europe 149
Rigaud IV, l Tournemire 87, 231
Rillé 119
Riou of Lohéac 220
La Rivière, family 93
Robert, vicar 231
Robert of Anzi 221
Robert of Arbrissel 76
Robert II, ct Auvergne, Hospitaller bro 164
Robert, l Boves, ct Amiens 103
Robert (of Buonalbergo) son of Gerard, con and st-b Bohemond of Taranto 101, 221
Robert I Burgundio, l Sablé-sur-Sarthe 85–6, 88, 99, 101–2, 107, 109, 119, 124–5, 132, 138–40, 220
  chaplain 85
Robert Burgundio, kt, mr Templars 102, 159–60, 246
Robert Burgundio, son of Robert I Burgundio 132, 138
Robert of Burgundy, bp Langres 44
Robert of Buzançais 245
Robert Dalmace, l Collanges 130, 240
Robert I, ct Dreux 102–3
Robert of 'Durenzan' 237
Robert I, ct Flanders 31, 79, 95–6
Robert II, ct Flanders 3, 45, 52, 56, 61–4, 71, 85–7, 94, 99, 113, 119, 122, 139–42, 145, 149, 151–2, 154, 159, 203–5, 215, 219–20, 222, 235, 247
  chaplains 85, 87, 152, 203, 219, 222
  household 85–6
  seneschal 85–6, 206
Robert II, k France 101
Robert son of Godwin, kt 91, 221
Robert III of Grandmesnil 92
Robert Guiscard, d Apulia 18, 45, 96, 99, 101, 166, 173
Robert of Lagarde-Enval 167
Robert Marchisus 101, 221
Robert of Matheflon 102, 242
Robert of Maule 100, 240
Robert Michael 112, 138, 221
Robert, abb Molesme 122
Robert (of Molise) son of Tristan, l Limosano 100, 221
Robert of Montfort-sur-Risle, con King Henry I of England 240

Robert of Mowbray 90, 92
Robert of Nevers 99, 221
Robert I, d Normandy 27–8, 36, 39, 95
Robert II, d Normandy 4, 76, 87, 90–2, 104,
    141–2, 144, 153, 183, 200, 216, 221, 241
  chaplains 87, 174, 200
Robert of Paris 93, 221
Robert of Rheims, prior of Senuc 62
Robert of Roches-Corbon 134, 156
Robert of Roffignac 167
Robert of Rouen, pr, bp Ramle-Lydda 87,
    221
Robert of Sourdeval, l Torosse? 100, 221
Robert of Vipont 241
Rodez, bishop 57
Rodulf 244
Roger, abb, chap Anselm II of Ribemont 221
Roger, d Apulia 142
Roger of Barneville 101, 221
Roger of Bétheniville 221
Roger I of Béziers 103
Roger Bigod, sheriff of Norfolk 92
Roger of Bouesse 244
Roger, l Choiseul 242
Roger of Courson 167
Roger the Emperor 237
Roger, earl of Hereford 91
Roger, cast Lille 141, 222
Roger Mandeville 74
Roger, l Mirepoix 222
Roger II of Montgomery, earl of Shrewsbury
    40, 92
Roger, l Mowbray 103
Roger of Rozoy, cast Jaffa 222
Roger of Salerno, prince-regent of Antioch
    171, 173
Roger I, ct Sicily 17
Roger II, k Sicily 164
Roger, archbp Tarsus 221
Roger son of Turold 40
Roman empire 64
Romans 54
Rome 27, 36–7, 40, 83, 141
  council 108
  St Peter's Basilica 141
Ronan, St 40
Le Ronceray d'Angers, abbey 137, 152–3
  abbess 153
Rossello 123, 222
Rostagn Dalmace 231
Rothold, kt 222
Rotrou, ct Perche and Mortagne 104–5, 136,
    144–5, 155, 166, 222
Roucy, family 173
Rouen 81, 141

  archbishop 81
Rouergue 3, 30, 32
Roussillon, family 94
Rual de Vern d'Anjou 135–6
Rudolf, ct (of Sarrewerden?) 222
Ruthard, in household of Godfrey of
    Bouillon 85
Ruthard son of Godfrey 222

Sablé 56, 124, 132, 139–40
Sagrajas, battle 43, 46
St Amand, abbey 122–3
St Arnoult-en-Iveline 145
St Aubin d'Angers, abbey 125
St Bénigne de Dijon, abbey 121, 159
St Benoît-sur-Loire, *see* Fleury
St Catherine on Mt Sinai, monastery 30
St Chaffre du Monastier, abbey 113–14, 126
  abbot 114
St Cybard d'Angoulême, abbey 38
St Dagobert de Stenay, priory 128
St Denis, abbey 82
St Etienne de Vignory, priory 5
  prior 5
St Florent-lès-Saumur, abbey 125, 140
  abbot 140
St Flour, abbey 56
St Gilles 54, 58, 141, 163
St Guilhem du Désert, abbey 119
St Hilaire-le-Grand de Poitiers, *see* Poitiers
St Hubert-en-Ardenne, abbey 125–8, 146,
    149
  abbot 128
St Jacques de Liège, abbey 155
St Jean d'Angély, abbey 53, 57, 111, 117, 124,
    126–7, 130–1, 152
  abbot 111, 131
St Jean-en-Vallée de Chartres, abbey 184
St Julien, priory 53–4
  prioress 53–4
St Julien de Tours, abbey 147
St Laud d'Angers, college of canons regular
    128, 181–2, 186–7
St Léonard-de-Noblat, college of canons
    regular 78
  miracula 78
St Loup, abbey 35
St Maixent, abbey 42, 45, 57
St Marcel-lès-Chalon-sur-Saône, priory 96
St Martial de Limoges, abbey 38, 58, 95
St Martin de Pons, priory 35
St Martin des Champs de Paris, priory 96
St Maur-sur-Loire, abbey 34–5
St Michel de Cons, priory 128
St Mihiel, abbey 71

St Nicolas d'Angers, abbey 59, 130, 133
 abbot 119
St Paul de Lyon, church 147
St Père de Chartres, abbey 114, 124, 131
St Philibert de Tournus, abbey 35, 43–4
St Pierre de Lille, college of canons regular
 119
St Pierre de la Réole, priory 124, 126
St Saveur de Lohéac, priory 128
St Sépulcre de Beaugency, priory 33, 96, 145
St Serge d'Angers, abbey 152
St Thierry-lèz-Reims, abbey 85, 119, 141
St Valéry, family 171
St Victor de Marseille, abbey 117, 126
St Vincent du Mans, abbey 126–7
Ste Croix de Quimperlé, abbey 40, 128
Ste Maure-de-Touraine, church 83
Ste Trinité-du-Mont de Rouen, abbey 40–1
SS Marie et Perpétue de Dinant, church
 126
Saintes 57
 bishops 42, 57
Saintonge 31, 33, 38
Saladin, ruler of Egypt and Syria 191
Salerno 101
 Salernitan medicine 87
sales 4, 89, 106, 112–13, 115–18, 124–6,
 128–34, 154
 to religious communities 125–6, 128
 see also counter-gifts
Salisbury, bishop 90
Salzburg, master 97
San Benigno di Fruttuaria, abbey 33
Sancho Iniguez of Cinnito 222
Sancho IV Ramirez, k Aragon 50, 96
Sannardus, pr, chap Robert II of Flanders 87,
 222
Sansareux, church 128
Santiago de Compostela, *see* Compostela
'Sarakenos' 241
Saswalo of Phalempin 222
Saure, mother of Bertrand of St Jean 130
La Sauve-Majeure, abbey 35
Sauxillanges, priory 56, 96, 127
Savanès 129–30
Savary of Vergy 44, 125, 134
Save river 142
Scandinavia 9, 91
Scotland 79, 90–1
sea transport 15–16, 36, 38, 104, 110, 142,
 147–8, 152, 154, 158; *and see* shipping
security of lands and families 135–9
Segré 102
Seguin of Mauléon 237
Seguin of Nevers 238

Seiches-sur-le-Loir 152–3
Seine river 140
Seljuk Turks 38; *and see* Turks
Senlis, bishop 89
Sergius, St, relic 150
servants 87, 109, 150
service of God in arms 63–4, 70, 158–60
Shafis 181
shipping 20, 91, 104, 108–9, 142, 147–8, 152,
 158, 178
Sibyl of Burgundy, w Eudes I of Burgundy
 95, 247
Sibylla of Anjou, w Thierry I of Flanders 103
Sibylla, q Jerusalem 190–2, 250
Sichard, kt 222
Sicily 30, 42, 91, 100–1, 193
sickness, *see* condition of survivors
Siegfried, archbp Mainz 28
Sigebert, m Gembloux 48, 50–1, 77
Sigemar of Mechelen 222
Siger, abb St Pierre au Mont-Blandin 241
Sigurd I Jorsalafara, k Norway 9, 241
Simon 140, 222
Simon, chap? Raymond IV of St Gilles 222
Simon of Anet 241
Simon son of Herbert, con? Jerusalem 231
Simon of Ludron 222
Simon of Nouâtre 241
Simon of Poissy 93, 148, 222
Simon of Vermandois, bp Noyon 103
simony 118, 152
sinfulness, obsession with 26–8, 69–72, 83
Sorde, abbey 40
Spain 19, 43–4, 46, 49, 66, 80, 85, 160, 196
 Reconquest (including the crusade) 42–4,
 49, 79–80, 105, 106, 108, 164, 166
 taifa kings 43
squires 109
Stabelo, chamberlain of Godfrey of Bouillon
 84–5, 222
Stephana of Bré 139
Stephanie, w William Tête-Hardi of
 Burgundy 177
Stephen, St, relic 175–6
Stephen 132
Stephen Adrachapel 231
Stephen, ct Aumale 92, 223
Stephen of Bar-le-Duc, bp Metz 102–3
Stephen of Blois, ct Blois and Chartres 14, 64,
 87–9, 98, 107, 109–10, 118, 127–8, 138–9,
 141–2, 148, 183, 206, 223
 chaplains 87, 206
Stephen of Blois, ct Boulogne, k England
 183–4
Stephen Bonin, l Ars 222

Stephen I, ct Burgundy and Mâcon 94, 222, 247
Stephen of Chartres, abb St Jean-en-Vallée de Chartres, patr Jerusalem 184
Stephen Gasteuil 238
Stephen of Lioriac 223
Stephen Mandeville 74
Stephen I, cast Neublans 72, 113, 166, 223, 244
Stephen son of Richilda 223
Stephen of Valence, pr 223
Stephen of Vitry-sur-Seine, kt 148, 231
Stephen Walter 231
Stewart, family 92
subsidies to crusaders 3–4, 86, 88, 112, 133, 187
Suger, abb St Denis 42, 78
Suwaidiyah 108
Sven II, k Denmark 96
Sven of Denmark 95, 205, 223, 247
Swabia 31, 157
Symeon 238
Symeon of Trier, m, hermit 30
Syria 9, 11, 13, 17, 19–20, 23, 36, 56, 62–4, 73–4, 86, 90–1, 95, 104, 110, 114, 143, 150–1, 158, 169, 176–7, 188, 191

Tancred Marchisus, l Galilee, regent of Antioch 70, 101, 133, 213, 223
Taranto 18
Tarascon 54
Tarragona 66–7, 71
Tartus (Tortosa) 148
tau, ivory 181–2
Telin?, ct 238
Templars 80, 102, 159–65, 183–4, 194
  confratres 162–3
  critics 162
  Rule 160
Teutonic Knights 159
Thibald of Payns, abb St Colombe de Sens 103
Thibald of Ploasme 133, 223
Thibaut I, ct Blois 96
Thibaut of Dampierre-sur-l'Aube 248
Thiemo, archbp Salzburg 223
Thierry of Chièvres 245
Thierry I, ct Flanders 103, 166
Thierry of Mathonville, abb St Evroul 36
Thierry II, ct Montbéliard 45, 247
Thierry, abb St Hubert-en-Ardenne 37
Thierry, ct Trier 28
Thomas Aquinas OP 74, 160–1
Thomas, l Marle and La Fère 99, 156–7, 223
Thouars 140

family 94
Tiberias 179
Tilbashir (Turbessel) 171
Tiron, abbey 120
tithes, *see* ecclesiastical property
Toledo 43
Toucy, family 94
Toul 31
Toulouse 46, 57
Touraine 130
Tournai, bishops 64, 154
Tours 29, 57–9, 76, 81, 88, 101, 127, 140, 156
  basilica of St Martin 59
  church of St Maurice 59
  council 58
Transjordan, lord 186
La Trappe, abbey 166
Treasury of Merits 71
Trier 30, 107
  archbishop 28
La Trinité de Vendôme, abbey 114, 131, 145
  abbot 114, 145
Tripoli 36, 86
  counts 175; *and see* individual counts
  county 8, 158, 163, 180
Troyes 140
  council 160
True Cross, relic 23–5, 31–2, 40, 146, 150–1, 182, 185
Tudebode family 94
Tudela 43–4
Tulle, abbey 36, 167
Turenne, family 96
Turks 8, 12–14, 16, 31, 38, 50, 78, 108, 145, 170, 185; *and see* Seljuk Turks
Turonicus of St Martin, kt 223
typhoid 147
Tyre 9, 177–80, 191
  archbishop 185; *and see* individual archbishops

Udelard of Wissant, n, kt 223
Ulric Bucel, kt 70, 223
Ulric, bp Orléans 31
Ulrich, m Breisgau 38
Ulrich, bp Passau 223
Ultreia, ultreia 77
unsuitable crusaders 106–8
Urban II, pope 6–8, 10–12, 14, 16–18, 52, 54–78, 81, 83, 88–9, 97, 101, 106–8, 112, 123–4, 126–7, 129, 136, 141, 146, 189
  authority for crusade 56, 68–9
  preaching journey 54–61, 75–8, 81, 89, 126–7
Urraca, q Leon-Castile 44, 247

usury 116
Utrecht, bishop 31
Uzerche, abbey 56, 126
  abbot 167

Valence 54
  coinage 110
  council 75
Vallombrosa, abbey 60–1
vassalage 86, 109, 113, 139
Vassalis of Roaix 238
Velay 31, 104
vendettas 41–2
Vendôme 56, 89
Venice 17, 75, 110, 146, 165, 176, 178
La Venjance Nostre Seigneur 41
Verdun 29–30, 81
  bishop 30; *and see* individual bishops
vexillum sancti Petri 60
Vézelay 82
via Egnatia 36, 141
Victor II, pope 46
vifgages 33–4, 116–17, 125, 133
Vigeois, abbey 95, 127
  abbot 124, 167
Villeneuve d'Aveyron, priory 32, 35
violence
  and churchmen 42, 44–52, 72–3, 77
  and laity 38–52, 161–2
  and piety 40 52, 189
  and saints 41
  as an expression of love 49–50, 65–6, 161
  theories of 42–4, 46–52, 55, 77; *and see* ideas
    of crusaders
  see also martyrdom; merit in fighting;
    penitential warfare; Urban II
visions and dreams 13, 15, 56, 73, 84–5, 150–1,
    154, 176
vocations 119, 147, 154–5
vows 7, 10–12, 14–19, 21, 29, 46, 55–8, 67,
    74–5, 81–5, 87–9, 93–4, 96, 100, 103,
    108–9, 125, 127, 130, 144, 148, 156, 166,
    176, 183, 189, 196
La Vue, family 93

Walbert, cast Laon 223
Walbricus, kt 223
Walchelin II of Pont-Echanfray 241
Waleran of Bavaria 238
Waleran I, ct Breteuil 47, 249
Waleran II, ct Breteuil 249
Waleran, ct Meulan 103
Waleran of Le Puiset, l Bira 169, 172, 175,
    249
Walker of Chappes, l? Chappes 3, 223–4

Walo II of Chaumont-en-Vexin, con Philip I
    of France 88, 213, 224, 249
Walo of Lille 224
Walter 238
Walter 238
Walter 238
Walter, cl 231–2
Walter, kt 238
Walter, m 241
Walter of Berga 224
Walter of Breteuil 224, 249
Walter II of Brienne 167–8
Walter of Condat 167
Walter of Couches, bp Chalon-sur-Saône 224
Walter of Mayenne 88, 243
Walter of Montsoreau 139, 166, 241
  wife 139
Walter II of Poissy, l Boissy-sans-Avoir 88,
    93, 100, 224
Walter, adv St Valéry-sur-Somme, vct
    Domart-en-Ponthieu 224, 248
Walter Sansavoir of Poissy, kt 89, 93, 100,
    142, 224
Walter Tirel III, cast Pontoise, vct Poix 245
Walter of Tours, kt 35
Walter of 'Verra', kt 224
Walter of Verveis 224
Walter son of Walter 126, 224
Welf, kt 224
Welf IV, d Bavaria 45, 96, 99, 224
Welf VI of Bavaria, d Spoleto 103
Wenrich of Trier 51
Wezelin, n 51
Wibert of Ravenna, anti-pope 97, 141
Wicher the German, ministerialis of Fulda
    224
widows 147
William 238
William Aiguillon II of Trie, l Trie-Château
    103
William Amanieu II, vct Bezaume and
    Bezanne, l Albret 224
William of Apremont 225
William Arnold of Nerpoy, l Luppé 232
William VIII, d Aquitaine 46, 50, 96
William IX, d Aquitaine 45, 96, 125, 140, 150,
    166, 225
William X, d Aquitaine 250
William VI, ct Auvergne, Clermont and
    Velay 75, 226
William VII, ct Auvergne 103
William of Baffie, bp Clermont 225
William of Bayeux 225
William of Beauvais 238
William of 'Bernella' or 'Archis', kt 225

William (of Bohemia) 225
William Bonofilius, kt 224
William de Bono Seniore 225
W(illiam) Boterat of Flée 225
William Botinus, kt 225
William of Bréteau, l Dangeul 238
William of Le Breuil 93, 226
William of Bures-sur-Yvette, l Galilee 169,
　172, 174–5, 184, 248
William Calvus 244
William of the Camera, prévôt of Poitiers
　150, 226
William Caputmalei, consul of Genoa 225
William the Carpenter, vct Melun 43, 226
William of Chanac 167
William Claret 241
William Clito 183
William, l Courtenay 103
William Dandozille, archbp Auch 162
William I Embriaco, l Jubail 225, 242
William II, k England 4, 83, 90–2, 125, 137
William Ermingareus 225
William Eudes of Bré 102–3
William of Ferrières 92, 225
William of La Ferté-Vidame 118, 124, 245
William III, ct Forez and Lyons 75, 225
William of Forz 232
William Fredelann, l Blaye 35
William Hugh, l Les Baux 167
William Hugh of Monteil, l? Crac des
　Chevaliers 86, 225
William of Ghent 241
William of Grandmesnil 94, 101, 226
William Jordan, ct Cerdagne 225
William IV, ct Mâcon 102–3
William Malfara 40
William Maluspuer, kt 225
William Marchisus 101, 225
William, co-l Mezenc 225
William Miscemalum 131, 232
William of Montfort-l'Amaury, bp Paris 89,
　137, 226
William V, ct Montpellier 158, 166, 226
William VI, ct Montpellier 45
William, l Les Moulières 3, 232
William of Les Murs 93, 226
William II, ct Nevers 99, 122, 141, 225
William III, ct Nevers 103
William of 'Nonanta', st-b William II of
　Nevers 226

William I, d Normandy, k England 40, 90–1
William of Normandy, illegitimate son of
　Robert II of Normandy 241
William the Old, marquis of Montferrat
　102–3
William of Orange, bp Orange 108, 226
William, bp Pavia 224
William of Percy, l Topcliffe and Spofforth
　90, 232
William Peter 232
William II Peverel 103
William Peverel of Dover, kt 103
William Peyre, l Cunhlat 86–7, 216, 226
　servant 87, 216
William Pichard, n, kt 226
William of Ploasme 133
William of Poissy 93, 148, 226
William, ct Ponthieu 102–3
William son of Richard 226
William I, l Sabran 225
William of Senlis 238
William IV Taillefer, ct Angoulême 30,
　36–8
William Tête-Hardi, ct Burgundy 44–5, 50,
　94–6, 102, 247
William IV, ct Toulouse 46, 250
William, archbp Tyre, chancellor of
　Jerusalem 1–2, 171, 176, 184, 186, 190,
　192
　chronicle 192
William Venator, huntsman 87, 243
William of Le Vast 116, 226
William III of Warenne, earl of Surrey
　102–3
wills 3, 34–6, 39, 117, 120–1, 123, 128, 130–3,
　140, 146, 148–9, 163
　on campaign 104, 146
Winrich of Flanders, butler of Jerusalem 232
Winther, Hospitaller bro 164
wives 97–100, 102–3, 107, 138–40, 149
Wolfker of Kuffern, n 62, 112, 226
women and crusading 97–100, 102, 106–8,
　138–40, 149
Worcester, bishop 90
Würzburg, bishop 10
Wyno, abb Helmarshausen 33

Zaizolfus, chap Gerard of Schaffhausen 87,
　238
Zimmern, chronicle 197

CPSIA information can be obtained
at www.ICGtesting.com
Printed in the USA
LVHW011551170821
695509LV00004B/204

9 780521 646031